THE ARAB AND JEWISH QUESTIONS

RELIGION, CULTURE, AND PUBLIC LIFE

RELIGION, CULTURE, AND PUBLIC LIFE

Series Editor: Matthew Engelke

The Religion, Culture, and Public Life series is devoted to the study of religion in relation to social, cultural, and political dynamics, both contemporary and historical. It features work by scholars from a variety of disciplinary and methodological perspectives, including religious studies, anthropology, history, philosophy, political science, and sociology. The series is committed to deepening our critical understandings of the empirical and conceptual dimensions of religious thought and practice, as well as such related topics as secularism, pluralism, and political theology. The Religion, Culture, and Public Life series is sponsored by Columbia University's Institute for Religion, Culture, and Public Life.

For a complete list of titles, see pages 305–306.

The Arab and Jewish Questions

GEOGRAPHIES OF ENGAGEMENT
IN PALESTINE AND BEYOND

EDITED BY

Bashir Bashir
and Leila Farsakh

Columbia University Press
New York

Publication of this book was made possible in part
by funding from the Institute for Religion, Culture,
and Public Life at Columbia University.

Columbia University Press
Publishers Since 1893
New York   Chichester, West Sussex
cup.columbia.edu

Library of Congress Cataloging-in-Publication Data
Names: Bashir, Bashir, 1976– editor. | Farsakh, Leila, editor.
Title: The Arab and Jewish questions : geographies of engagement in Palestine and beyond /
edited by Bashir Bashir and Leila Farsakh.
Other titles: Religion, culture, and public life.
Description: New York : Columbia University Press, [2020] | Series: Religion, culture, and public
life | Includes bibliographical references and index.
Identifiers: LCCN 2020017701 (print) | LCCN 2020017702 (ebook) | ISBN 9780231199209
(hardback) | ISBN 9780231199216 (paperback) | ISBN 9780231552998 (ebook)
Subjects: LCSH: Jewish-Arab relations. | Arab-Israeli conflict. | Palestinian Arabs—Politics and
government. | Jews—Politics and government. | Palestinian Arabs—Legal status, laws, etc. |
Jews—Legal status, laws, etc. | Political rights—Palestine. | Nationalism—Palestine.
Classification: LCC DS119.7 .A67164 2020 (print) | LCC DS119.7 (ebook) | DDC 956.94—dc23
LC record available at https://lccn.loc.gov/2020017701
LC ebook record available at https://lccn.loc.gov/2020017702

Columbia University Press books are printed on permanent and durable acid-free paper.
Printed in the United States of America

Cover design: Lisa Hamm
Cover image: Adobe Stock

*To Gertraud Auer-Borea d'Olmo, who paved the way
for these engagements and much more,
with love and admiration*

CONTENTS

ACKNOWLEDGMENTS

We are indebted to the Bruno Kreisky Forum for International Dialogue in Vienna for hosting a series of workshops and to the Forum's team for their generous and warm hospitality. The workshops that served as the basis of this volume were convened at the Bruno Kreisky Forum under the themes "Arab Engagements with the Jewish Question" and "Jewish Engagements with the Arab Question." We thank all the participants of the workshop series for enriching and provocative intellectual exchanges that shaped this volume. In addition, we are grateful for the rigorous and encouraging comments of two anonymous reviewers on the manuscript of this volume. Finally, we thank Rachel Busbridge, Azar Dakwar, Amos Goldberg, Nadim Khoury, Dirk Moses, Lena Salaymeh, and all the contributors of this volume for their comments on various versions of the introduction.

THE ARAB AND JEWISH QUESTIONS

THREE QUESTIONS THAT MAKE ONE

BASHIR BASHIR AND LEILA FARSAKH

Over the past two decades, Middle Eastern and European politics have been impacted by three critical developments that call into question dominant understandings of nationalism, citizenship, and decolonization. First, "the question of Palestine" has not yet been answered. The aggressive and ongoing colonization of Palestine created irreversible realities that cast serious doubts on the feasibility of partition and the "two-state solution." At the same time, Palestine's colonization deepened the entwinements between Israeli and Palestinian lives, rendering inseparable the question of present and future rights of Arabs and Jews. Second, the Arab uprisings that erupted in a number of Middle Eastern and North African countries in 2011 signaled the demise of grand assimilationist ideologies like Arabism, Ba'athism, and Islamism, calling thereby into question the overarching "we" that cements the citizenry together. Those who rebelled against their authoritarian regimes also brought to the fore the diverse ethnic and cultural realities of their societies, a diversity they are reclaiming but which their authoritarian regimes denied by repressing, or oppressing, many minorities, such as Kurds, Yazidis, Arab Jews, Chaldeans or Berbers. Third, Islam and Muslims have become the new internal signifiers of otherness, particularly in the West, posing serious challenges to existing conceptions of citizenship and democracy in the West. The rise of Eurocentric and Islamophobic notions of citizenship are connected to the

suppressed memories of Europe's colonial "past" as well as to the globaliza-
tion of the neo-liberal political economy and the associated decline of the
welfare state. They reflect, though, an intimate conceptual and historical
link between Judeophobia and Islamophobia in Europe that has not always
been well explored.[1]

Many scholars have studied the causes underlying these developments.
Gilbert Achcar, for example, argues that deep roots of the Arab uprisings are located mainly in the specific economic features that characterize
these societies rather than in simplistic political or cultural explanations.[2]
Sholto Byrnes maintains that Islamophobia in Europe is being normalized by intellectuals who depict Islam and Muslims as aliens and external to Europe.[3] Virginia Tilley, meanwhile, opposes territorial partition as
the best way for meeting the demands of rival ethno-national projects for
self-determination, and calls instead for decolonized political unification
models of sovereignty premised on individual rights.[4] These perspectives
provide a much-needed critical analysis that goes beyond the dominant
discourses on Arab uprisings, European Islamophobia, and Israeli-Palestinian conflict. However, they overlook the underlying links between these
supposedly disconnected developments that are taking place in three different geographical sites.

No study has explored the intersections between the rise of Islamophobia in the West, the failure to resolve the Arab-Israeli conflict, and the political meanings of the Arab uprisings. Neither have many scholars examined
how these developments are tied to three seemingly unrelated questions,
namely the question of Israel-Palestine, the Arab-Muslim question, and the
Jewish question. These questions, this book argues, are not only entangled,
but also belong to the same history—one that continues to foment tensions
in the Middle East, Europe, and the United States. The book seeks to shed
new light on this history by offering a new, critical investigation of the Arab
and Jewish "questions." More specifically, it aspires to revisit contemporary
Arab engagements with the question of Jewish political rights (as individuals, religious communities, and/or a national collective) under the light of
European anti-Semitism and Zionism. It also explores Jewish engagements
with the Arab question, namely how Zionism and non-Zionist Jewish voices
dealt with the Palestinian presence and political rights in historic Palestine.
These two key political questions have been historically debated, but not
juxtaposed, despite the fact that they have become inextricably intertwined.

THE JEWISH QUESTION AND ARAB ENGAGEMENT
WITH THE "OTHER"

The "Jewish question" was concerned with defining the political rights of people who were considered a minority in countries that embarked on exclusionary nation-building projects, even while sometimes resorting to political ideologies that promised universal emancipation and equality to all citizens. More precisely, the Jewish presence in Europe turned into a "question" as a result of the centrality of Christianity as a defining characteristic of the social, cultural, and political makeup of Europe, and of nationalism as a defining modern political identity. Both forces of nationalism and Christianity viewed Jews-as-an-organized-community as the ultimate "other" and thus to be treated with suspicion and alienation. For Christians, Jews needed to convert, while for national republicans they had to confine their religiosity to the private sphere and resemble other citizens in public. Ironically, the success of Jewish emancipation in the second half of the nineteenth century in following these imperatives led to a new modality of anti-Semitism, as Jews were blamed for modernity's consequences—like industrial society and urbanization—and for political treachery during and after the First World War in Central Europe in particular.[5] For anti-Semites, Jews remained an Oriental people.[6] The radicalization of anti-Semitism and anti-Bolshevism in the far right led ultimately to ethnic cleansing and extermination (the Holocaust) during the Second World War.[7] It is partly in light of the failure of European nationalism to accommodate the Jewish presence in its midst, coupled with its colonial interests in the Ottoman Empire in the Levant, that the Jewish question "migrated" to the Middle East, and to Palestine in particular.[8]

Early Arab engagements with the "Jewish question" were mediated mainly through European colonialism and the Zionist aim to colonize historic Palestine. Since their early encounters with the Zionist movement, the Arabs and the Palestinians viewed Zionism as an alien and colonial movement that sought to de-Arabize Palestine.[9] As Yuval Evri and Hillel Cohen explain in chapter 6, prominent Palestinian figures during the 1920s, such as Musa Kazim al-Husseini (Musá Kāẓim al-Ḥusaynī), the president of the Palestinian Arab Congress, and Jamal al-Husseini, the secretary to the executive committee of the Palestinian Arab Congress, viewed local/ native Jews (not Zionist foreign Jews) as Palestinians and as an integral part of the Palestinian people and homeland. As Michelle Campos demonstrates, this idea of equal citizenship in a shared homeland in which local Jews, not Zionist immigrants, are an integral part was also dominant in Arab-Palestinian discourse during the late Ottoman era.[10] The distinction between Palestinian local Jews, who were viewed as integral to the Palestinian people and the country's political rights and aspirations, and Zionist European Jews, who were regarded as colonizers, continued to inform Arab and Palestinian intellectual and political discourse after the 1948 war until the late 1970s. The program that Fatah and the PLO (Palestine Liberation Organization) advocated in the early 1970s calling for the establishment of a democratic non-sectarian state for Muslims, Christians, and Jews in Palestine defined Palestinian identity as including Palestinian Jews.[11] It was only with the PLO's adoption of the Ten Points Program in 1974 that Palestinian Jews became de-Palestinized and de-Arabized. This shift away from the one-state platform to the de facto acceptance of partition as a solution to the Israeli-Palestinian conflict signified a drift from an inclusive, largely civic, Palestinian nationalism to an ethicized Palestinian nationalism.[12] This ethicized nationalist discourse that squeezed out the Palestinian Jews paradoxically ended up reproducing a Zionist discourse that insisted on eliminating the distinction between Jews and Zionists.[13] Meanwhile, Arab and Palestinian intellectuals, with the exception of a few like Edward Said, have hardly engaged with the complexity of the "Jewish question," anti-Semitism, and the Holocaust and their centrality to contemporary Jewish identity and political discourse.[14]

To be sure, a number of Palestinian and other Arab intellectuals have sought to examine the implications of the Holocaust in any discussion of Jewish rights in Palestine.[15] In his landmark book *The Arabs and the Holocaust*, Gilbert Achcar maps out the various Arab responses and attitudes toward Nazism, the Holocaust, and Jews, exploring the historical and ideological/intellectual contexts of these responses as well as their diversity. Omar Kamil examines the response of Arab intellectuals to the views of European intellectuals—such as Arnold Toynbee, Jean-Paul Sartre,[16] and Maxime Rodinson—held on the question of Jewish rights in Palestine and its implications for the Israeli-Arab conflict. According to Kamil, Arab intellectuals favored or disfavored the works of these European intellectuals based on whether or not the latter supported the Palestinians. Examining the writings of these Arab intellectuals, he demonstrates how their focus on

French and British colonialism as well as on Zionism and Israel, marginalized, and even displaced, any serious Arab discussion of the Holocaust.[17] At the same time, Palestinian and Arab writers have found in literature a productive space to unpack the implications of the Holocaust for Palestinian, and Jewish, political rights in Palestine (e.g., Ghassan Kanafani, Elias Khoury, Susan Abulhawa, Rabai al-Madhoun, and Akram Musallam).[18] In his novella *Returning to Haifa* (1969), Ghassan Kanafani—one of the most prominent Palestinian intellectuals of his time and a member of the Popular Front for the Liberation of Palestine—brings together in a tragic interlocking of destinies a family of Holocaust survivors and a family of Palestinian refugees. Although the novella ends in an impasse and a reaffirmation of war, it gives a human voice to the colonizer and colonized while showing how their lives were intertwined. Finally, in a number of his works, especially *The Question of Palestine* (1980) and *Freud and the Non-European* (2003), Edward Said explored the tragic entanglement of the Jewish question and the Holocaust with the question of Palestine and the Nakba.[19]

ARAB NATIONALISM AND THE ARAB JEW

The political turmoil unleashed by the Arab uprisings in 2011 generated renewed interest in the question of how individual and collective political rights can be protected in an egalitarian and inclusive democratic polity in the twenty-first century. It also provided a unique opportunity to revisit the Jewish question, especially by a young generation of writers and thinkers who have questioned the assimilationist creed of Arab nationalism. These writers have shown a renewed interest in the role of the "Arab Jews" in Arab culture. Whereas Arab Jews in the past featured as characters only in novels written by Arab Jews living in Israel (like Sami Michael and others), more recently Arab Jews are appearing in mainstream and major Arab cultural productions, particularly in novels and films.[20] These works, produced mainly after 2003, show a growing interest in the history of the Arab-Jewish communities in various Arab countries.[21] They highlight how Jews were an integral part of the political, cultural, and socioeconomic fabric in Iraq, Yemen, Morocco, Syria, Egypt, Algeria, Libya, and Tunisia.[22] While each of these Jewish communities had their own particularities and specific histories within their respective contexts, the overwhelming majority left or were displaced from the Arab world during the 1950s. Since then, and until the late 1990s, this integral and deeply rooted component of Arab society was excluded, marginalized, and sometimes even erased from the formal and dominant historiography, memory, and national narrative of many Arab countries. Novels by Ali Bader (Iraq), Ali Muqri (Yemen), and Kamal Ruhayyim (Egypt), among others, seek to redress this erasure by representing Arab-Jewish characters and communities as an organic part of the social and cultural fabric of Arab history.

This uncoordinated revived literary interest in the character of the Arab Jew is a product of introspective reflection on the meaning of national identity after the Iraq War and the Cold War.[23] Several Iraqi intellectuals, for example, reconsidered the state-sanctioned national and historiographic discourse that dominated Ba'athist Iraq for decades, which mixed patriotism and seemingly socialist ideas with pan-Arab identity, but that proved hollow after the collapse of the national order in 2003. Literary efforts were thus devoted to moving away from the assimilationist Ba'athist discourse of a transcendent homogenous identity by drawing attention to Iraq's diversity and complexity. According to Ronen Zeidel, the figure of the Jew in post-2003 Iraqi novels helps highlight the pluralistic composition of Iraqi society in the past, and thereby inform and inspire a process of remaking Iraqi identity in the present. It offers a liberal version of Iraqi nationalism, one in which cultural and religious diversity is celebrated and is proposed as an alternative to the chauvinistic and homogenizing Ba'athi nationalism.[24]

The concept of the Arab Jew is of course not new.[25] The pioneering and influential work of Ella Shohat since the 1980s stands out because she was the first contemporary Jewish voice to reaffirm the centrality of Arab identity to Jewish identity. Moreover, she demonstrates the entanglements between the question of Palestine and the question of the Arab Jew.[26] She critically explores the historical developments (colonial modernity and its discursive correlatives in the forms of Orientalist fantasies and Eurocentric epistemologies) that split the "Arab" and the "Jew," rendering them as mutually exclusive categories. This Orientalist splitting became more intensified and explicit with the emergence of Zionism and the unfolding translation of its idea into political reality in Palestine, which involved the dispossession and dispersal of the Palestinians to Arab countries and the concomitant dislocation of Arab Jews mainly to Israel. According to this

Orientalist splitting and separation, the "Arab Jew," a post-partition figure, became 'an ontological oxymoron and an epistemological subversion'
that undermines and interrogates segregationist narratives and identities
while opening up new horizons and potentialities.[27] Following a similar
line of analysis, Yehouda Shenhav also deployed the "Arab Jew" in order
to challenge the dichotomous opposition between the Arabs and Jews in
the Zionist discourse and perspective.[28] Meanwhile, the work of Moshe
Behar and Zvi Ben-Dor Benite, has been important in shedding new light
on the intellectual legacy of Arabic-speaking Jews in the Arab world, who
have often been marginalized in the Jewish modern canon dominated by
European-Jewish intellectual writings. These works also highlight the complexity, and at times unequivocal positions, that many of these Arab Jews
have taken toward Zionism and its implications for their understanding of
their identity and political rights.[29]

Indeed, sociologically and demographically Arab Jews barely exist today
in the Arab world. However, the makeup of the majority of Arab societies continues to be culturally and ethnically diverse, as Kurds, Armenians,
Yazidis, and Amazighs, among other groups, are intrinsic to the region.
This diversity has been posing serious challenges to rigid and exclusionary
forms of Arab nationalism. Thus, while the Arab Jew serves as an important component in the task of addressing the question of cultural and ethnic diversity, our analysis does not claim or seek to turn the Arab Jew into
the ultimate and only symbol of human rights and inclusive citizenship in
the Arab world. Other marginalized groups in these Arab societies continue to form significant components of the composition of the Arab states,
but their rights and political participation are silenced, if not under assault.
Resurrecting the concept of the Arab Jew thus can also serve as a means
to unearth buried histories and push the conversations about equality and
political rights beyond the discourse of nationalism and minority politics.

ZIONISM AND ITS ENGAGEMENT WITH THE ARAB QUESTION

Contemporary Jewish engagements with the Arab question have also been
rare, as well as conceptually problematic. "The bride is beautiful, but she
is married to another man," allegedly stated the two Viennese rabbis who
were sent in 1897 to explore the possibility of establishing "a Jewish state" in
Palestine.[30] Overlooking the presence of "that man," namely the Palestinian

Arabs, Theodor Herzl and other leading Zionists promoted Jewish colonization of Palestine. They thus created what came to be known as the "Arab
question," namely what to do with the existence and resistance of the indigenous Arab population in Palestine to the Zionist project. Some scholars
defined the "Arab question" as "the relations between Jews and Arabs in
the country."[31] For others[32], the "Arab question" stemmed from the fact that
the Arab population of Muslims and Christians, who had inhabited and
constituted the majority in Palestine for hundreds of years, did not welcome the new Zionist settlers who claimed they were returning to their
ancestor's homeland. The mainstream Zionist approach has been to either
ignore the native Arab presence, underestimate its attachment to the land
and intensity of its resistance to their colonial endeavor, or maintain that
the economic development Zionism was going to bring will benefit the
native population.

According to Neil Caplan, although the "Arab question" meant different things to different parties, one can identify three major attitudes that
existed during the period 1917–1925.[33] First, an active minority saw it as a
major problem that posed a serious challenge to the very moral foundation of Zionism; they thus sought to accommodate Arab opposition and
advocated seeking peace and compromise with them. Second, a larger
segment of the Zionist Yishuv did not assign much significance to it and
viewed it as a challenging obstacle that needed to be handled carefully.
Third, the largest segment viewed it as a serious challenge that required
designing and developing effective countermeasures to respond to the
Arab demographic, political, and psychical threats. The dominant Zionist
moral discourse, however, remained mainly introspective, meaning that it
hardly engaged ethically with the Arab as a "significant other," one whom
many regarded as beyond "the range of normative persuasion."[34] As Caplan
argued, if Zionist figures—including Menachem Ussishkin, Leo Motzkin,
Theodor Herzl (in *Altneuland*, published in 1902), Max Nordau, and Ber
Borochov—mentioned the presence of Arabs in Palestine in their writings
or speeches, it was often to point out the great benefits Arabs would gain
from the modernization Zionists would bring to Palestine.[35]

Some critics[36] have argued that the general trend among influential
Zionists was to adhere to the widely published statement of Golda Meir
that "there were no such thing as Palestinians."[37] This view has remained
one of Zionism's mantras, adopted by mainstream Zionist leaders from

David Ben-Gurion to Yitzhak Shamir, Chaim Weizmann to Naftali Ben-nett. Their main concern was not the reality in Palestine but how to use the historic Jewish affiliation with the land to establish a Jewish state that would solve Europe's Jewish problem. While Herzl knew that Palestine was populated by Arabs, he viewed these native Arabs as primitive and back-ward. He maintained that Zionism would bring the Arabs—as individuals, not as a collective—prosperity and modernity. Yitzhak Epstein, by con-trast, referred to the lack of Zionist engagement with the existence of the Arabs of Palestine as "a hidden question" that he considered deeper than any other question. He viewed the Arab presence in Palestine, as well as their culture and national identity, as a serious challenge to Zionist aspira-tions, one that requires serious engagement and requires reaching a histori-cal compromise with the native Arab population.[38] He never doubted the validity of Zionist historical claims in Palestine but insisted that the success of Zionism in Palestine depends on winning the consent of the Arabs and sharing the land with them, rather than ignoring their collective national rights. Like other Zionists, however, he believed that Zionists were bearers of Western civilization and that Arabs would welcome the benefits of the modernization Zionists would bring to Palestine. While he did not advo-cate for a binational state, he called for a Zionist integrative state in which a strengthened Arab community live and thrive together with, rather as separate from, Zionists.[39]

Revisionist Zionists, most notably Ze'ev Jabotinsky, on the other hand, insisted that attempts by mostly labor or socialist Zionists to address the Arab question were either naïve (buying Arab consent and loyalty through money) or suicidal. Jabotinsky expected that the native Arabs, like every indigenous people, would resist colonial settlers as long as they could. He thus concluded that a more appropriate way to deal with the Arabs would be to erect an "iron wall" of Zionist military force that is capable of break-ing Arab resistance.[40] Others rejected this approach, arguing as Simon Rawidowicz and Yizhar Simlansky did, that "the Palestinian question isn't an Arab question but entirely a Jewish question."[41] They maintained that Jewish claims cannot be separated from Palestinian rights and aspirations. Brit Shalom and Ihud, Zionist organizations that were established in the 1920s and early 1940s, pushed further for reaching an agreement with Arab leaders based on a binational solution in Palestine.[42] These integrative approaches, though, were the concern of minority intellectuals. They were shelved with the creation of Israel in 1948 and the predominance of the Iron Wall mentality in Israeli politics ever since.

After the creation of Israel, especially between 1948 and 1967, Zionism sought to eliminate the Arab question by various means, including negation, denial, marginalization, and colonial oppression. After the 1967 war and the rise of the PLO, Israeli politics became focused on expanding its colonial grip on Palestinian land while making the question of Palestine an Arab refugee problem to be resolved with neighboring Arab states, not with the Palestinians, within the framework of United Nations Security Council Resolution 242. The First Intifada proved the limits of this approach. It paved the ways for the Oslo peace process, which provided the first official Israeli recognition of the Palestinians and their political demands. During this period, Israel engaged with Palestinians through managing the conflict with them rather than attempting to reach a historical reconciliation. Concurrently, Israeli revisionist historians and sociologists in the late 1980s and early 1990s unraveled critical assessment of the Zionist and Israeli engagements with the Arab question. Based on newly available Israeli archival sources in the late 1980s, the "new historians" in Israel challenged the dominant and celebrated Israeli historiography by indicating, among other things, the active and major role Israel played in the expulsion of the Palestinians in 1948.[43] While this revisionist works received public and academic recognition, it remained marginal in its impact on Israeli politics. Indeed, in the past two decades mainstream and Zionist political strands have shifted further to the right, reinvoking and reinforcing traditional Israeli historiography. According to the coordinates of this historiography, the Palestinians are largely invisible and their political rights contested.[44]

EUROPE AND THE QUESTION OF THE JEWISH AND MUSLIM "OTHER"

The complicated processes of splitting Arabs and Jews and delinking the Jewish and Arab/Muslim questions are deeply entrenched in contemporary mainstream Western political thought. Perhaps one clear illustration of these delinking processes can be found in the deployment of the term "Judeo-Christian civilization." This post-World War II term is not only deployed to assume Europe's political, cultural, and epistemic superiority but also to suppress or recast its colonial past internally (i.e., the

Holocaust) and externally (imperialism) while legitimizing its fight against Islam. Stated differently, "Judeo-Christian civilization" is often affiliated with progress, freedom, democracy, and liberal Western values; it presents the intellectual history of the West and affirms its civilizational superiority compared to other civilizations, particularly Islam.[45] However, invoking this discursive ideological construct underestimates the post-Holocaust process of recasting the Jews as Europeans, after having depicted them as Semites deserving exclusion or annihilation.[46]

Furthermore, "Judeo-Christian civilization" ignores the place and role of Islamic civilization that existed and flourished in the Iberian Peninsula, the Arab world, Persia, and the Ottoman Empire from the ninth until the nineteenth centuries. It is the Christian conquest of Spain and Portugal that led to forced conversions and expulsion of Jews and Muslims; tens of thousands of Jews were given refuge in Muslim North Africa and the Ottoman Empire.[47] It was not until the First World War, and more precisely the Balfour Declaration, that the relationships between Arab Muslims and Christians and Arab Jews were seriously damaged and constructed as ones of enmity. Through his profoundly critical archeological reading of classical and canonical Western texts, Gil Anidjar traces the intimate, though concealed, intersections between the Jewish question and the Arab-Muslim question, revealing them as one question belonging to one complex history.[48] Anidjar offers a wider philosophical perspective for understanding and linking the Christian West's constructed, yet invisible, enmity between Jews and Arabs , Judeophobia and Islamophobia.[49] These splits and enmity have also penetrated and dominated mainstream Jewish and Arab political thought and history.

Against this complex background, this volume explores the possible productive relationships between the Arab and Jewish questions. These questions continue to inform, feed, and kindle conflicts in Europe, the Middle East, and the United States. Revisiting the Jewish and Arab questions is also a timely necessity in view of the crisis that Palestinian, Jewish, Arab, and European nationalisms are facing today. The fragmentation of the Palestinian community among those who are citizens of Israel, refugees disbursed in the Middle East and abroad, Palestinians under siege in Gaza, and the few others living with limited political rights in the West Bank has undermined the value of the Palestinian national state project. It is forcing a rethinking of the ways in which political rights can be protected outside the framework of territorial partition, ethnic sovereignty, and exclusive nation-states.[50] The announcement of President Trump's Middle East peace plan has made such rethinking all the more necessary.[51] The intensification of a chauvinist racist discourse in Israel is, moreover, jeopardizing the notion of Zionism as a legitimate democratic project, even in the eyes of some of its followers.[52] The intensification of Israel's aggressive colonial expansion has also kept the Palestine question alive, both within Arab and Islamic societies as well as internationally, despite Zionist efforts to dilute and fragment it.

The persistence of the Arab question today, meanwhile, has not diminished the weight of the Jewish question and the need to engage with it. For Zionism, while remaining a settler colonial project, has also created a vibrant Israeli cultural and political community in Palestine that provides meaning and political rights for over six million Jews and many Jews globally.[53] This is a reality that both Palestinian and Arab nationalism need to contend with, if only to find an answer to the notion of the rights of Jews, whether within the boundaries of their national identities or outside them. Moreover, the violence and sectarianism unleashed over the past two decades in several Middle Eastern countries have unraveled the necessity of defining the rights of the "other" within, be they Christian, Jewish, Kurdish, Chaldean, or Berber. Addressing the history of the Arab Jews, thus, becomes an important means of delving into this debate. The rise of Islamophobia and Judeophobia brings back Europe's colonial past and highlights the need to decolonize the present, if Europe is to genuinely create inclusive and egalitarian democracies.

This volume draws on multiple disciplines, ranging from political thought, cultural studies, history to anthropology. It seeks to fill a lacuna in the literature on European colonialism, Jewish and Arab nationalisms, and Israel/Palestine by examining the inseparability of the Arab and Jewish struggle for self-determination and political equality. This volume includes new and original contributions from leading Arab, Jewish, and (other) international scholars who interrogate essentialist national identities and question the opposition and enmity between the "Arab" and the "Jew." The contributors draw links between otherwise segregated struggles, histories, and possibilities. They address the question of diversity and inclusive citizenship by investigating the conceptualization of territorial separation in the twenty-first century, and by considering possible venues of decolonization and historical reconciliation within the stubborn existing reality of various forms of heterogeneities in the Middle East. Such a critical approach to the intertwined Arab and Jewish questions also allows us to go beyond the boundaries of Israel/Palestine and Zionism/Palestinian nationalism and reach out to Europe and the Arab, Jewish, and Muslim worlds.

The volume is divided into three sections. Part I examines the Arab and Jewish questions by highlighting them as constitutive of Europe's history (e.g., anti-Semitism) and present (e.g., Islamophobia). Gil Anidjar's chapter insightfully asks this question: Was there—is there—an Arab-Jewish dialogue? This question, he claims, has insistently accompanied, perhaps silently governed, whether overtly or covertly, the so-called German-Jewish dialogue. He goes on to argue that the Arab-Jewish dialogue, whether real or not, is the unavoidable correlate of the German-Jewish dialogue. One might even argue that, if there has been dialogue, it could only have been conducted *between* these two sets of dialogue. This connection is so for reasons that have to do with the history of Christian political theology and the structural associations it created between the Jew and the Arab. These associations should continue to remind us that it was not only "the Jewish question" that was exported to the Middle East, but the Arab (and Muslim) question as well. More proximately, the two dialogues merge with the rise of that "providential couple," Aryans and Semites, and its particular, albeit not unique, history in Germany.

Widely published pictures in the press showed Benjamin Netanyahu, Israel's prime minister, enthusiastically and warmly being greeted at the Elysée Palace in Paris by France's President Emmanuel Macron during an official visit on July 16, 2017. Brian Klug offers a critical reading of these pictures, arguing that they are emblematic of what "the Jewish state" (represented by Netanyahu) means to "New Europe" (personified by Macron) and vice versa. His analysis applies not just to a summer's day in Paris and not merely in terms of mutual political interests, but rather to the context of a complex relationship between Europe and the Jews that extends over centuries. By unpacking these pictures, he argues, a third party comes into this reading by virtue of being absent: the Palestinian people. Their presence-absence spoils the party. It complicates the celebration encapsulated by the image of the two intertwined leaders: the (ostensible) healing of wounds between Europe and the Jews. The Palestinians constitute a problem because they exist—not per se but as Palestinians. Klug's main aim is to make *Europe*, rather than Palestinians or Jews, the "problem."

Amal Ghazal's chapter provides a counterargument to the European debate on Jews, Muslims, and Palestinians by examining how North Africans defined their identity in the face of European colonialism. It looks at how the question of Palestine, namely the Palestinian struggle against the Zionist usurpation of their land, shaped Algerians' understanding of pan-Arabism and pan-Islamism in the interwar period, between 1920 and 1939. Ghazal focuses on a group associated with the religious reformist movement led by the Association of Algerian Muslim Ulama to explore how they interpreted developments in Palestine while challenging French colonialism on their soil. She argues that the question of Palestine was originally regarded as one of a number of equally important questions in the Arab world, until 1936, when the Palestinian revolt shifted the focus to its regional implication. The revolt, Ghazal shows, further sharpened a pan-Arab and pan-Islamic identity that was associated with anti-colonialism. At the same time, the way reformist newspapers in Algeria reported on events in Palestine and associated with them further highlight the fluid borders between pan-Islamism and pan-Arabism.

Part II discusses the construction of the dichotomous opposition between Arabs and Jews. By revisiting the narrative of the splitting of the Oriental/Semite figure into Arab and Jew, Ella Shohat's chapter explores the place of the Arab Jew, or the Jewish Arab, within this ruptured Orientalized unit. During the *longue durée* of Orientalism, Arab and Middle Eastern Jews, she suggests, were located firmly—indeed as firmly as any Arab or Middle Eastern community in terms of claims to indigenous belonging—within the territories of the actual "Orient." Exploring instances taking place both before and after the bifurcation, she traces moments in which the Jew-in-the-Orient began "his" terminological journey of shifting from "the Arab" to "the Jewish" side of the equation. In what ways did the imperial rescue of minorities impact such ruptures, recoding co-regional affiliations and engendering ambivalent indigeneity? And in what ways did the civilizing mission, in tandem with the arrival of the already de-Orientalized European Jew in the Orient, undermine the millennial syncretism of Judeo-Islamic culture? Within the skewed version of a colonizing Enlightenment, Jews "in the Orient," she argues, experienced a double colonization, with its corollaries of assimilation and dispossession. One colonization generally targeted "the natives," while the other was specifically programmed for the Jewish natives. The bifurcated Semite narrative, then, must account for the "travel" of an Orientalist discourse to the Orient where it encountered Arab-Jewish hybridity in the flesh. Thus, her chapter reconsiders the bifurcation in light of a significant assimilationist de-Orientalization (and later an explicit de-Arabization) project directed at Jews within the imperialized Orient, producing what Shohat regards as "the split-within-the-split."

Hakem Al-Rustom's chapter probes the principal parameters of the Jewish and the Arab questions in order to question European Fascism and colonial violence. More precisely, the exclusion of Arab Jews from the Arab-Jewish engagement, he argues, propagates Eurocentric and Zionist readings of history, thus limiting the possibilities of an integral engagement that is fully realized within the simultaneous critique of European Fascism and colonialism. With the aim of further supporting and substantiating his argument, Al-Rustom resorts to Walter Benjamin's account of history in order to analyze the case study of two Cairo synagogues (Shaar Hashamayim and Ben Ezra).

Yuval Evri and Hillel Cohen's chapter, meanwhile, offers a renewed reading into the reception of the Balfour Declaration by Sephardi Jews in Palestine. Contrary to the tendency in the literature to focus on the Zionist-British angle, the authors trace the reactions and interpretations of natives of Palestine (non-Jews and Jews) to the declaration and explore the tensions between different identity worlds. They point to alliances that were proposed and rejected and examine a series of loyalties and partnerships that supported the idea of a shared homeland and preceded the false binary division between "Jews and Arabs." Derek Penslar's chapter examines the development of the academic fields known as "Israel Studies" and "Palestine Studies." He discusses to what extent they are or should be independent entities, as well as if they reflect expressly political debates about Israel/Palestine, within the university and beyond. Penslar concludes that a combinatory field of Israel/Palestine Studies is a necessity. However, it will remain an impossibility unless scholars in both Israel and Palestine studies, as they are currently constituted, can get out of ironclad frameworks and challenge their perspectives.

Part III explores stubborn realities and alternative visions for Palestine/Israel. Focusing on the striking and systematic invisibility of the Palestinians in Zionism and Israel, Jacqueline Rose's chapter views it as an ethical demand to begin to explore the question of Jewish engagement with the Arabs by looking inward, inside the thought of Zionism itself, to try to grasp what this constitutive blindness might consist of. She starts her chapter by asking what might be the motives, often unconscious, that—on the side of Israel—obstruct the path to understanding of the other, a blockage in what she risks calling "the national mind." Then she asks what role literature might have to play in creating an alternative path to understanding, a topic she has extensively pursued.[54] Rose concludes that Israel today is locked in what seems to be a spiral of destruction toward the Palestinian people and toward itself, not least because it fails to see the link between the two—the utter interdependency of the two peoples on each other.

Moshe Behar's chapter revisits important developments in the framing of the question of Palestine as an anti-colonial struggle in Arab, Palestinian (Marxist-Leninist PFLP), and Israeli-Jewish-Marxist (Matzpen) political thought from 1917–1967 in order to offer critical insights on the one-state solution debate in Israel/Palestine in the twenty-first century. Until 1967, the frame of reference for the struggle was 1917 and anti-colonial struggle vis-à-vis pre-1948 Euro-Zionism, and post-1948 Israel, it was articulated mainly along the lines of the Algerian/Vietnamese struggles. For a rainbow of reasons, in 1967 the struggle's frame of reference changed to 1948. The question essentially became how to normalize in the territory the existence of some 2.3 million Israeli Jews without insisting on their return to their countries of origin as standard anti-colonialism demands. Critically assessing the views of the Marxist-Leninist PFLP and the post-1962 Israeli-Jewish-Marxist Matzpen on this question sheds an interesting light on the current one-state debates in Israel/Palestine.

Focusing on Palestinian and Israeli-Jewish national identities, Maram Masarwi's chapter examines questions about how we define and redefine an identity as it undergoes continual disassembly and reconstruction, considering potential benefits presented by this process of change and redefinition. Masarwi explores the dialectic between these two national identities in terms of the national model and the binational model. She argues that under certain conditions, a binational model and its various components could challenge the national model by opening up fresh new horizons for analysis, highlighting important values in a new way, and prompting the evolution of an alternative, or even subversive, dialectic of identities.

It is our belief that, read together, these ten chapters provide a promising venue to link seemingly separate questions, and thereby pave the way for a deeper understanding of the conflicts that continue to inform, shape, and kindle the histories, cultures, and politics of the Middle East, Europe, and beyond. We hope that this book will encourage others to further map the entangled geographies of engagements we have provisionally outlined in this introduction, unravel untold histories, project unimagined futures, and help us move beyond the limits of nationalist discourses and segregated histories.

NOTES

1. There are few attempts to explain the similarities and differences between anti-Jewish and anti-Muslim racisms. See, for example, James Renton, "Does Europe's Far Right Hate Muslims the Same Way They Hate Jews?," *Haaretz*, December 1, 2017, available at https://www.haaretz.com/world-news/europe/does-the-far-right-hate-muslims-the-same-way-they-hate-jews-1.5627029; *Antisemitism and Islamophobia in Europe: A Shared Story?*, ed. James Renton and Ben Gidley (London: Palgrave Macmillan, 2017); *Racialization and Religion: Race, Culture and Difference in the Study of Antisemitism and Islamophobia*, ed. Nasar Meer (London: Routledge, 2016); Lena Salaymeh and Shai Lavi, "Secularism," in *Key Concepts in the Study of Antisemitism*, ed. Sol Goldberg, Jonathan Judaken, Adam Teller, Scott Ury, and Kalman Weiser (forthcoming).
2. Gilbert Achcar, *The People Want: A Radical Exploration of the Arab Uprising* (Berkeley: University of California Press, 2013).
3. Sholto Byrnes, "The Rise of Islamophobia in Europe Is Being Normalized by Intellectuals—But They Are Pushing at an Already Open Door," *The National*, June 4, 2018.
4. Virginia Tilley, "After Oslo, a Paradigm Shift? Redefining 'Peoples,' Sovereignty and Justice in Israel-Palestine," *Conflict, Security and Development* 15, no. 5 (2015), 425–453. Through closely examining works of contemporary Arab and Jewish literature, Gil Z. Hochberg demonstrates the inseparability of the signifiers "Jew" and "Arab" and the ties that bind the Arabs and Jews despite their present animosity. See Gil Z. Hochberg, *In Spite of Partition: Jews, Arabs, and the Limits of Separatist Imagination* (Princeton, N.J.: Princeton University Press, 2007). See also Lital Levy, *Poetic Trespass: Writing Between Hebrew and Arabic in Israel/Palestine* (Princeton, N.J.: Princeton University Press, 2014).
5. Walter Laqueur, *A History of Zionism: From the French Revolution to the Establishment of the State of Israel* (New York: Random House, 2003).
6. Ivan Kalmar and Derek Penslar argue that Jews have always been constitutive of the Western image of the East and Muslim Orient. *Orientalism and the Jews*, ed. Ivan Davidson Kalmar and Derek J. Penslar (Waltham, Mass.: Brandeis University Press, 2005). See also Ella Shohat's contribution in this book, and A. Dirk Moses, "The Contradictory Legacies of German Jewry," *Leo Baeck Institute Yearbook* 54 (2009), 36–43.
7. Paul Hanebrink, *A Specter Haunting Europe: The Myth of Judeo-Bolshevism* (Cambridge, Mass.: Harvard University Press, 2018).

8. Laura Robson traces the emergence of ethnic separatism in the modern Middle East. This ethnic separatism was, she argues, the result of the convergence of European strategic moves with late Ottoman political practice and a newly emboldened Zionist movement to create an unprecedented push to physically divide ethnic and religious minorities (Armenian, Assyrian, and Jewish) from Arab Muslim majorities. Laura Robson, *States of Separation: Transfer, Partition, and the Making of the Modern Middle East* (Berkeley: University of California Press, 2017). Also, it is worth mentioning that the Jewish Question was part of several other questions that characterized the nineteenth century and beyond as discussed in Holly Case, *The Age of Questions: Or, A First Attempt at an Aggregate History of the Eastern, Social, Women, American, Jewish, Polish, Bullion, Tuberculosis, and Many Other Questions in the Nineteenth Century, and Beyond* (Princeton, N.J.: Princeton University Press, 2018). Focusing on Hindu-Muslim conflict in India, Aamir Mufti examines the inscription of the "Jewish question" in a non-Western society undergoing modernization under colonial rule: Aamir Mufti, *Enlightenment in the Colony: The Jewish Question and the Crisis of Postcolonial Culture* (Princeton, N.J.: Princeton University Press, 2007).

9. See, for example, Fayez Sayegh, *Zionist Colonialism in Palestine* (Beirut: Research Centre, Palestine Liberation Organization, 1965); Jamil Hilal, "Imperialism and Settler Colonialism in West Asia: Israel and the Arab Palestinian Struggle," *Utafi* 1, no. 1 (1976), 51–70.

10. Michelle Campos, *Ottoman Brotherhood: Muslims, Christians, and Jews in Early Twentieth-Century Palestine* (Palo Alto, Calif.: Stanford University Press, 2011). For more on how the Arabs and Zionists understood each other during the late Ottoman era, see Jonathan Marc Gribetz, *Defining Neighbors: Religion, Race, and the Early Zionist-Arab Encounter* (Princeton, N.J.: Princeton University Press, 2015).

11. For more on these programs, see Bashir Bashir, "The Strengths and Weaknesses of Integrative Solutions for the Israeli-Palestinian Conflict," *Middle East Journal* 70, no. 4 (2016), 560–578; Leila Farsakh, "A Common State in Israel-Palestine: Historical Origins and Lingering Challenges," *Ethnopolitics* 15, no. 4 (2016), 380–392.

12. Bashir, "The Strengths and Weaknesses of Integrative Solutions."

13. In her work, Ella Shohat offers a critique on how various Arab nationalist discourses gradually ended up reproducing a Zionist discourse by failing to clarify and act on the distinction between Jews and Zionists, partly leading to the dislocation of Arab Jews: Ella Shohat, "Sephardim in Israel: Zionism From the Standpoint of Its Jewish Victims," *Social Text* 19/20 (Autumn 1988), 1–35; Ella Shohat, "Rupture and Return: Zionist Discourse and the Study of Arab-Jews," in *Taboo Memories, Diasporic Voices* (Durham, N.C.: Duke University Press, 2006), 330–358.

14. The literature on Arab nationalism is predominantly concerned with the beginnings of Arab nationalism. See, for example, *The Origins of Arab Nationalism*, ed. Rashid Khalidi, Lisa Anderson, Muhammad Muslih, and Reev S. Simon (New York: Columbia University Press, 1991) and Mahmoud Haddad, "The Rise of Arab Nationalism Reconsidered," *International Journal of Middle East Studies* 26, no. 2 (1994), 201–222; for the methodological and epistemological problems in the literature on Arab nationalism, see Khalidi et al., *The Origins of Arab Nationalism*; for the debates around the rise, failure, and revival of Arab nationalism, see Adeed Dawisha, *Arab Nationalism in the Twentieth Century: From Triumph to Despair* (Princeton, N.J.: Princeton University Press, 2003) and Martin Kramer, "Arab Nationalism: Mistaken

Identity," *Daedalus* (Summer 1993), 171–206; and for the issue of sectarianism, see Azmi Bishara et al., *The Sectarian Question and the Manufacturing of Minorities in the Arab World* (Beirut: Centre for Research and Policy Studies, 2017 [in Arabic]).

15. See, for example, Azmi Bishara, "The Arabs and the Holocaust: An Analysis of the Problematical Nexus" [in Hebrew], *Zmanim* 13, no. 53 (1995), 54–71; Bashir Bashir and Amos Goldberg, "Deliberating the Holocaust and the Nakba: Disruptive Empathy and Binationalism in Israel/Palestine," *Journal of Genocide Research* 16, no. 1 (2014), 77–99; *The Holocaust and the Nakba: A New Grammar of Trauma and History*, ed. Bashir Bashir and Amos Goldberg (New York: Columbia University Press, 2018).

16. For the reception of the ideas of Jean-Paul Sartre among Arab intellectuals, see Yoav Di-Capua, *No Exit: Arab Existentialism, Jean-Paul Sartre, and Decolonization* (Chicago: Chicago University Press, 2018).

17. Omar Kamil, *Der Holocaust im arabischen Gedächtnis. Eine Diskursgeschichte 1945–1967* (Göttingen, Germany: Vandenhoeck und Ruprecht Verlag, 2012).

18. Ghassan Kanafani, *Returning to Haifa*, in *Palestine's Children: Returning to Haifa and Other Stories*, trans. Barbara Harlow and Karen E. Riley (London: Heinemann, 1984); Elias Khoury, *Gate of the Sun*, trans. Humphrey Davies (London: Vintage, 2006) and *Children of the Ghetto: My Name Is Adam* [*Awlad el-ghetto: Esmi Adam*] (Beirut: Dar Al-Adab, 2016); Susan Abulhwa, *Mornings in Jenin: A Novel* (New York: Bloomsbury, 2010); Rabai Al-Madhoun, *Destinies: Concerto of the Holocaust and the Nakba* (Beirut: Arab Studies Institute; Haifa: Kul-Shee Library, 2015); Akram Musallam, *A Girl from Shatila* [*Bent Min Shatila*] (Amman, Jordan: Al-Dar Al-Ahlia for Publishing and Distribution, 2019).

19. Edward Said, *The Question of Palestine* (New York: Vintage, 1980) and *Freud and the Non-European* (London: Verso, 2003). For an interesting and provocative account that links the persistence of the Question of Palestine with the persistence of the Jewish Question, see Joseph Massad, "The Persistence of the Palestinian Question," *Cultural Critique* 59 (Winter 2005), 1–23.

20. Marcia Lynx Qualey, "True Histories: Renaissance of Arab Jews in Arabic Novels," *The Guardian*, October 29, 2014, available at https://www.theguardian.com/books/booksblog/2014/oct/29/renaissance-arab-jews-arabic-novels-ali-bader-mohammad-al-ahmed.

21. The novels include Iraqi novelist Ali Bader's *The Tobacco Keeper* (2008), Syrian novelist Ibrahim al-Jubain's *Diary of a Damascus Jew* (2007), Egyptian novelist Mutaz Fatiha's *The Last Jews of Alexandria* (2008), Yemeni Ali al-Muqri's *The Handsome Jew* (2009), and Algerian Amin Zaoui's *The Last Jew of Tamentit* (2012), written in French; and Egyptian Kamal Ruhayyim's trilogy: *Diary of a Jewish Muslim; Days of Diaspora; and Minorahs and Minarets*. The films include *Salata Baladi* (2007) by the Egyptian director Nadia Kamel; *Tinghir-Jerusalem: Echoes of the Mellah* (2013) by the French-Moroccan producer Kamal Hachkar; *Forget Baghdad* (2003) by the Iraqi-born, Zurich-based director Samir; *Homage by Assassination* (1991) by the Palestinian director Elia Suleiman, and *El Hara* (2017) about the Jewish quarter of Tunis co-directed by Margaux Fitoussi and Mo Scarpelli.

22. Najat Abdulhaq focuses on the role the Jewish and Greek minorities played in the economy of pre-Nasser Egypt: Najat Abdulhaq, *Jewish and Greek Communities in Egypt: Entrepreneurship and Business before Nasser* (London: I.B. Tauris, 2016).

23. It was also partly the outcome of the decline in the centrality of the question of Palestine in the Arab world as a result of the Oslo "peace process."

24. Ronen Zeidel, "On the Last Jews in Iraq and Iraqi National Identity: A Look at Two Recent Iraqi Novels," *Journal of Modern Jewish Studies* 17, no. 2 (2018), 207–222.

25. For more on the debates around the Arab-Jew, see Lital Levy, "The Arab Jew Debates: Media, Culture, Politics, History," *Journal of Levantine Studies*, 17, no. 1 (Summer 2017), 79–103.

26. The dispossession of the Arab-Jews from Arab countries has been often used by Israelis for diplomatic campaigns. These campaigns, among other things, problematically equate between the dispossession of the Jews from Arab countries and the expulsion of the Palestinians during the Nakba. For more on this, see Shohat, "Sephardim in Israel: Zionism From the Standpoint of Its Jewish Victims," *Social Text* 19/20 (Autumn 1988), 13; Richard Irvine, "Israel's Cynical Campaign to Pit Arab Jews Against Palestinian Refugees," *The Electronic Intifada*, July 1, 2012, available at https://electronicintifada.net /content/israels-cynical-campaign-pit-arab-jews-against-palestinian-refugees/11395.

27. Ella Shohat, *On the Arab-Jew, Palestine, and Other Displacements* (London: Pluto Press, 2017), 2–4. See also Ella Shohat, *Israeli Cinema: East/West and the Politics of Representation* (Austin: University of Texas Press, 1989) and Shohat, "Sephardim in Israel."

28. Yehouda Shenhav, *The Arab Jews: A Postcolonial Reading of Nationalism, Religion and Ethnicity* (Stanford, Calif.: Stanford University Press, 2006). For more on the Arab-Jew, see Orit Bashkin, *New Babylonians: A History of Jews in Iraq* (Palo Alto, Calif.: Stanford University Press, 2012) and Sarah Stein, *Saharan Jews and the Fate of French Algeria* (Chicago: Chicago University Press, 2014).

29. *Modern Middle Eastern Jewish Thought: Writings on Identity, Politics, and Culture*, ed. Moshe Behar and Zvi Ben-Dor Benite (Waltham, Mass.: Brandeis University Press, 2013).

30. Though the origin of the statement is uncertain, it does, nevertheless, represent a dominant view among Zionist quarters starting from the late nineteenth century. See also Ghada Karmi, *Married to Another Man—Israel's Dilemma in Palestine* (London: Pluto Press, 2007).

31. See, for example, Abigail Jacobson, "Sephardim, Ashkenazim and the 'Arab Question' in pre-First World War Palestine: A Reading of Three Zionist Newspapers," *Middle Eastern Studies* 39, no. 2 (2003), 105–130; Martin Buber, "The Bi-National Approach to Zionism," in *Toward Union in Palestine: Essays on Zionism and Jewish-Arab Cooperation*, ed. M. Buber, J. L. Magnes, and E. Simon (Jerusalem: Ihud [Union] Association, 1947).

32. Neil Caplan, *Palestine Jewry and the Arab Question, 1917–1925* (New York: Frank Cass, 1978).

33. Caplan, *Palestine Jewry*, 3. See also Laqueur, *A History of Zionism*.

34. Uriel Abulof, "National Ethics in Ethnic Conflicts: The Zionist 'Iron Wall' and the 'Arab Question,' " *Ethnic and Racial Studies* 37, no. 14 (2014), 2653–2669; Farsakh, "A Common State in Israel-Palestine," 380–392.

35. Caplan, *Palestine Jewry*.

36. See Simha Flapan, *Zionism and the Palestinians* (London: Croom Helm, 1979).

37. Israeli prime minister Golda Meir made this statement in an interview published on June 15, 1969, in London's *Sunday Times*.

38. Yitzhak Epstein, 'The Hidden Question,' Lecture Delivered at the Seventh Zionist Congress in Basel, 1905. Available at http://www.balfourproject.org/wp-content/uploads/2014/05/Yitzhak-Epstein.pdf.

39. For more on this point, see Alan Dowty, "'A Question that Outweighs All Others': Yitzhak Epstein and Zionist Recognition of the Arab Issue," *Israeli Studies* 6, no. 1 (Spring 2001), 34–54.

40. Vladimir Jabotinsky, "The Iron Wall," *Jewish Herald*, November 26, 1937 ["Razsviet," November 4, 1923]. On the centrality and persistence of the Iron Wall strategy in shaping Zionism's engagements with the Arabs, see Avi Shlaim, *The Iron Wall: Israel and the Arab World* (New York: Norton, 2000); Ian Lustick, "Abandoning the Iron Wall: Israel and 'the Middle Eastern Muck,'" *Middle East Policy* 15, no. 3 (September 2008), 30–56; Abulof, "National Ethics in Ethnic Conflicts," 2653–2669.

41. For more on the views of Simon Rawidowicz, see David Myers, *Between Jew and Arab: The Lost Voice of Simon Rawidowicz* (Waltham, Mass.: Brandeis University Press, 2009); http://www.wrmea.org/2009-december/israel-and-judaism-even-some-zionists-foresaw-corruption-of-jewish-values-by-blind-support-for-israel.html.

42. For interesting discussions on these thinkers, see Jacqueline Rose, *The Question of Zion* (Princeton, N.J.: Princeton University Press, 2005); Judith Butler, *Parting Ways: Jewishness and the Critique of Zionism* (New York: Columbia University Press, 2012); and Paul Mendes-Flohr, *Martin Buber: A Life of Faith and Dissent* (New Haven, Conn.: Yale University Press, 2019).

43. For more on these revisionist historians and sociologist in Israel, see Benny Morris, *1948: A History of the First Arab-Israeli War* (New Haven, Conn.: Yale University Press, 2008); Ilan Pappé, *The Ethnic Cleansing of Palestine* (Oxford: One World, 2007); Avi Shlaim, *The Iron Wall. Israel and the Arab World* (New York: Penguin, 2014) and "The War of Israeli Historians," *Annales* 59, no. 1 (January–February 2004), 161–167.

44. Beshara Doumani, "Palestine Versus the Palestinians? The Iron Laws and the Ironies of a People Denied," *Journal of Palestine Studies* 36, no. 4 (Summer 2007), 49–64; Rashid Khalidi, *The Hundred Years' War on Palestine: A History of Settler Colonialism and Resistance, 1917–2017* (New York: Metropolitan Books, 2020).

45. Anya Topolski, "The Dangerous Discourse of the 'Judaeo-Christian' Myth: Masking the Race-Religion Constellation in Europe," *Patterns of Prejudice* (April 29, 2020) https://doi.org/10.1080/0031322X.2019.1696049; *Is There a Judeo-Christian Tradition? A European Perspective*, ed. Emmanuel Nathan and Anya Topolski (Berlin: De Gruyter Mouton, 2016). The attempt here is not to deny the common Judeo-Christian ideas and practices, which indeed are deep since both traditions rely on the same scripture and emerged in the same socio-historical space. Rather, the attempt is to situate them in their historical and political contexts. For more details on the polemical relationship between Judaism and Christianity, see Israel Jacob Yuval, *Two Nations in Your Womb: Perceptions of Jews and Christians in Late Antiquity and the Middle Ages* (Berkeley: University of California Press, 2006).

46. Anya Topolski, "Breaking the Post-Shoah Silence About Race in Europe: Whiteness, Antisemitism and Islamophobia," *Critical Philosophy of Race* 6, no. 2 (2018), 280–286.

47. See, for example, Amnon Raz-Krakotzkin, "Secularism, the Christian Ambivalence Towards the Jews and the Notion of Exile," in *Secularism in Question: Jews and Judaism in Modern Times*, ed. Ari Joskowicz and Ethan B. Katz (Philadelphia: University of Pennsylvania Press, 2015), 276–298; Shohat, *On the Arab-Jew*, 79, 408. According

to Shohat, the Christian imaginary in Iberia that demonized both Jews and Muslims stands in contrast to the contemporary version of Orientalism that has separated "the Jew" from "the Muslim" within the public sphere and especially in contrast to their separation in Zionist and Arab nationalist discourses. See Ella Shohat, *Taboo Memories, Diasporic Voices* (Durham, N.C.: Duke University Press, 2006).

48. See also Ammiel Alcalay, *After Jews and Arabs: Remaking Levantine Culture* (Minneapolis: University of Minnesota Press, 1993).

49. Gil Anidjar, *The Jew, the Arab: A History of the Enemy* (Stanford, Calif.: Stanford University Press, 2003) and *Semites: Race, Religion, Literature* (Stanford, Calif.: Stanford University Press, 2007).

50. See Nadim Rouhana, "The Palestinian National Project: Towards Restoring the Settler Colonial Paradigm," *Majjalaṭ al-Dirasat al-Filistiniyah* (*Journal of Palestine Studies*) 19 (2014), 18–36 (in Arabic); Leila Farsakh, "The 'Right to Have Rights': Partition and Palestinian Self-Determination," *Journal of Palestine Studies* 47, no. 1 (2017), 56–68; Bashir Bashir and Rachel Busbridge, "The Politics of Decolonization and Binationalism in Israel/Palestine," *Political Studies* 67, no. 2 (May 2019), 338–405. See also "Equal Rights for All: A New Path for Israel-Palestine?" (proceeding of a two-day conference held at Birkbeck College, University of London), March 14–16, 2015. https://www.kreisky-forum.org/wp-content/uploads/2019/04/Equal-Rights-for-All-Conference-Proceedings.pdf.

51. Marawn Bishara, "Trump's 'Peace Plan': The Farce, the Fraud, and the Fury," *Aljazeera*, January 29, 2020, https://www.aljazeera.com/indepth/opinion/trump-peace-plan-farce-fraud-fury-200128164004266.html.

52. Zeev Sternhell, "Here Is the Proof That Zionism Can Achieve Its Goals Within the Green Line," *Haaretz*, October 3, 2015, https://www.haaretz.com/.premium-time-to-draw-the-lines-1.5404721; Avraham Burg, "The End of Zionism," *The Guardian*, September 15, 2003, https://www.theguardian.com/world/2003/sep/15/comment; Peter Beinart, *The Crisis of Zionism* (New York: Picador Paper, 2013); Philip Weiss, "Jewish Ethno-nationalism Is a 'Poison'—Crabapple and Goldman Clobber Zionism in Intellectual Journals," *Mondoweiss*, November 20, 2018, https://mondoweiss.net/2018/11/nationalism-crabapple-intellectual/.

53. Rashid Khalidi, *The Hundred Years' War on Palestine*; Raef Zreik, "When Does a Settler Become a Native? (With Apologies to Mamdani)," *Constellations* 23, no. 3 (September 2016), 351–364; Leila Farsakh "The Right to Have Rights: Partition and Palestinian Self-Determination," *Journal of Palestine Studies* 47, no. 1 (Autumn 2017), 56–68.

54. For more on this, see Jacqueline Rose, *The Last Resistance* (London: Verso, 2007) and *Proust Among the Nations: From Dreyfus to the Middle East* (Chicago: University of Chicago Press, 2012).

PART I

Interrogating Europe

Anti-Semitism, Islamophobia, and Colonialism

Chapter One

JACKALS AND ARABS

Once More on the German-Jewish Dialogue

GIL ANIDJAR

1

"How rare dialogue is," laments Maurice Blanchot, who knew something of dialogues and conversations, even infinite conversations.[1] I write
"laments," but this is perhaps not the right word, for Blanchot hardly offers
his untimely thoughts on dialogue under the bright heading of pleasure
or happiness. Instead, he describes dialogue—that rare thing—as painful, as that which provokes surprise, yes, but "an unusual event, almost
more painful than remarkable." Blanchot is writing of literary, novelistic
dialogue, but there are broader implications at play that are inscribed quite
recognizably on the surface of his remarks. Keeping in mind at all times
that my own concerns remain with *the form of dialogue, dialogue as a form*,
it is to those broader implications that I shall devote myself here in order
to reflect on what might be called "the Arab-Jewish dialogue."[2] The phrase
is obviously meant to resonate with the German-Jewish dialogue of old, as
both dialogues "might well have seemed doomed to literary existence at
best," while remaining sites of searing pain.[3] We will have occasion to see, at
any rate, that the Arab-Jewish dialogue overdetermines, resonating *in and
throughout*, the German-Jewish dialogue.[4]

Blanchot identifies, in any case, three "great directions" or forms, which
he says are represented and practiced by André Malraux, Henry James, and

Franz Kafka. Having borrowed my own title from Kafka, I shall soon turn to him as well, and not only to him, but before doing so I want to linger with Blanchot and with dialogue, with "the pain of dialogue"; what it suggests (promises and threatens) with regard to the dialogue—if it was or is one (or two)—that shall occupy me here.

The first form Blanchot calls "the stance of discussion." Its hero is Socrates, of course, "a man who is sure that it is enough to talk to reach agreement: he believes in the efficacy of speech. . . . Speech must necessarily get the better of violence," for violence cannot interrupt "reasonable language." In Malraux's novels, it is not Socrates who speaks, but rather, through the characters, "the voices of the great thoughts of history . . . forces battling in some grave conflict of our time." Here, the characters (violent men or historical forces) "discuss, for they want to be right, and this rightness is served by the ardent vivacity of words, which still remain in contact with a thought common to all, the preserved communality of which each one respects." Agreement may remain a distant goal, while violence unavoidably and cyclically returns, but dialogue does continue, and violence itself is transformed, "because it could not break the discourse or this respect for the communal speech that persists in each of these violent men."

In the second form, neither togetherness nor truth constitute the goal of the conversation. Truth is rather a hidden, structuring, and mediating core. James's protagonists "wonderfully understand each other by the intermediary of this hidden truth they know they do not have the right to hear, communicating actually around the incommunicable." What James uniquely manages to do, Blanchot explains, is "to make *the third party* . . . that obscure element that is the center and the state of his books and to make it not only the cause of misunderstandings but the reason for anxious and profound understandings." That third party, "the unknown, the unexpressed," brings about a community or communality nonetheless; it "brings words together."

In Kafka, however, "there is a scission, impassable distance, between the two sides of discourse." Yet the division does not only occur between the interlocutors or within the rules of discourse. No doubt, "the rigor of logic, the stronger need to be right and to speak without losing any of the prerogatives of reasonable discourse" are at play. "Kafka's characters discuss and refute." On each side, there is "the obstinacy of the will to live, the confidence that life cannot be wrong." There is also, within each side, "the force of the enemy . . . that is always right." The conflict operates according to different lines and trajectories, as it divides between two "laws" as well, one answerable to logic (to which the characters remain implacably bound, and to which they happily—or unhappily—subject themselves and agree, even in defeat), the other "foreign to the rules and in particular to the rule of noncontradiction." The authority of logic is such that, even in his defeat, the vanquished wishes to continue arguing according to its rule. He "wants to raise more objections, to argue and refute, that is to say, to appeal to logic one last time." In that very appeal to logic, he cannot but challenge it, too: "He challenges it and, already beneath the knife, invokes against it the will to live, which is pure violence: doing so makes him an enemy of reason and thus with reason condemned." Unflinching in the face of this painful dialogue, Blanchot insists that there remains a kind of unity in it, although such unity is not discursive; it is not the *result* of dialogue. Thus, "the distance that separates the speakers is never impassable; it becomes so only for one who persists in crossing it with the aid of discourse." It is there, within "the chill oscillating space, inserted by Kafka between the words in conversation," in discourse and dialogue, that "duality reigns and where it engenders always more duplicity and those false intermediaries that are its doubles." There is a lesson there, an imperative for further study since, "far from being negative, the impossibility of relation-ships becomes the basis for a new form of communication in Kafka—that is what we must study." And yet, before undertaking this study (something he arguably did in *The Infinite Conversation*), Blanchot preemptively diverts, as if innocuously, the vector of his own query.[5] He breaks off the dialogue, after having squarely, and uniquely, located its form at the center of any discerning reading of Kafka. A dialogue *sans* dialogue, one might say after Blanchot's own manner. What "remains clear," Blanchot says, in any case, is that Kafka's "conversations are at no time dialogues."

The characters are not interlocutors; words cannot be exchanged and, though com-munal in meaning, never have the same range or the same reality: some are words on top of words, words of a judge, words of commandment, of authority or temp-tation; others, words of deception, of evasion, of lies, which would be enough to prevent them from ever being reciprocal.

Here is not the place to endorse or dispute the significance of Blanchot's thoughts on dialogue. Suffice it to say that, as he pursues the distinction he makes here between conversation and dialogue, he continues to invoke Kafka ("Kafka, of course, suspects dialogue is impossible, but for this reason we must engage in it") and the form of dialogue, dialogue as a form ("It is clear . . . that the stops that punctuate, measure, and articulate dialogue are not always of the same kind: some block conversation. Kafka wondered at what moment and how many times, when eight people are seated within the horizon of a conversation, it is appropriate to speak if one does not wish to be considered silent. But such silence, even if disapproving, constitutes the part that moves discourse").[6] Blanchot is, I have said, very clear that he writes about literature, indeed, about novels. Yet from these last remarks and from other references to history and to violence, to "forces battling in some grave conflict of our time," indeed, from the powerful commentary Kafka has been understood to provide with regard to modernity, the Jewish question, Palestine, colonialism, and binationalism, little doubt remains as to the general significance of these reflections on dialogue.[7] At this fortuitous juncture, I shall move one step closer to Kafka by recalling an earlier reader of his, one whose own assertions on dialogue, the German-Jewish dialogue, have touched multifariously upon some of the grave and painful events of our time.

2

Invited to contribute to a volume honoring the poet and writer Margarete Susman, Gerschom Scholem (from whom I borrow my subtitle) responded with embarrassment, dismay, and incomprehension, and with an open letter to the editor of the volume. Which is to say that Scholem *responded* to the invitation *not* by accepting it but, moved to speak to the question of dialogue it raised, by construing both (the invitation and the dialogue) otherwise. His letter was, it might be noted, published in the volume— a failed dialogue in the form of dialogue. Perhaps a felicitous one as well. "For as ready as I find myself to pay homage to the venerable phenomenon that is Margarete Susman with whom I have deeper ties than opinions on which we may agree or differ [*mit der mich Tieferes verbindet als Meinungen, in denen wir übereinstimmen oder auseinandergehen*], as decisively must I decline an invitation to provide nourishment to that illusion, unintelligible to me [*mir unfaßbaren*], of 'a German-Jewish dialogue, the core of which is indestructible,' which this volume . . . is intended to serve."[8] Scholem was intent on giving reason or reasons, he wanted to argue and refute, he wished to insist that "it takes two to have a dialogue, who listen to each other, who are prepared to perceive the other as what he is and represents, and to respond to him." Or to her, as it happened.

It should at any rate be apparent that, with Blanchot, we have been treading at once very close and very far from the numerous debates Scholem initiated and shaped on the "German-Jewish dialogue."[9] But what this ambiguous, even dubious, proximity should make manifest is—or so I want to propose—a different truth, the content of which is growing, I think, increasingly evident. Uncertain of its dialogic dimension, I shall articulate this truth in the form of three initial assertions.

First, the form of dialogue, dialogue as a form, has remained at "the unknown, the unexpressed" center of the debates on the German-Jewish dialogue. It is indeed remarkable ("almost more painful than remarkable," as Blanchot phrases it) that few have attended to dialogue as a form, as a representation and a form of representation—rhetorical, philosophical, literary, epistolary—in the German-Jewish dialogue.[10] Does it matter, for instance, that Gottfried Ephraim Lessing's initial contribution, and opening salvo, was put down in dramatic form? That Moses Mendelssohn wrote on sentiments in "the form of an epistolary philosophical dialogue"?[11] That Heinrich Heine cannily turned to Edom, turning the entire history of disputation on its head?[12] Or that another towering figure of the German-Jewish dialogue was Martin Buber, a philosopher of dialogue if there ever was one?[13] And what about Davos (Martin Heidegger, Ernst Cassirer) or that "hidden dialogue" that took place between Carl Schmitt and Leo Strauss?[14] What about the significance of numerous other correspondences, the masses of letters exchanged across the nineteenth and twentieth centuries, beginning, no doubt, with Kant and Herz and all the way to Scholem and Walter Benjamin ("one of the major intellectual dialogues of this century," as Alexander Gelley aptly puts it), or indeed to Scholem and Hannah Arendt and beyond?[15] After all, if Arendt was lacking in "the love of Israel," was she not the German for his Jew?[16] "I regard you wholly as belonging to our people and as nothing else [*durchaus als Angehoerige dieses Volkes und als nichts anderes*]," famously wrote Scholem, as if to confirm that one might think otherwise, that one might be both German *and* Jew, after all. Had he not found in Arendt, "as in so many intellectuals who came from the German left . . . little trace" of that very "love of the Jewish people"?[17] In his concern with "dialogue in any genuine sense whatsoever, i.e., *as a historical phenomenon*," at any rate, Scholem himself seems to have considered (and engaged in) more than one dialogue—such as the "model example of a dialogue without an object [*ein gegenstandsloses Gespräch*], in which the participants are talking about different things [*von verschiedenen Dingen reden*]." Scholem also affirmed, over the course of this dialogue, which was not one, and with little hint of hesitation, that "there were relations and discussions [*Beziehungen und Auseinandersetzungen*] between Jews and Germans," that "historical relations of a passionate and vehement kind [*historische Beziehungen leidenschaftlicher und vehementer Art*] existed between the Germans and the Jews, even though in a wholly different manner from both sides," and that "no one, of course, would think of disputing [*wird natürlich niemandem zu bestreiten einfallen*]" such states of affairs. Scholem did immediately go on to dispute and contest, if not to dialogue with, "the introduction of sublime and solemn-sounding terms like *dialogue* in order to designate wholly trivial states of affairs like the one that historically determined relations and discussions [*Beziehungen und Auseinandersetzungen*] between two groups." But to argue over the word, to fail to recognize that Scholem had "clearly and distinctly differentiated between a dialogue and discussions of this general kind [*zwischen einem Gespräch und Auseinandersetzungen dieser allgemeinen Art*]"; to employ it in any other way than "in that heightened and tolerably precise sense . . . in which the philosophers of the 'dialogue' introduced it for certain spiritual-intellectual discussions [*für bestimmte geistige Auseinandersetzungen*]"; to contradict [*zu widersprechen*] Scholem himself "by talking of something completely different [*von etwas ganz anderem redet*] is as easy as it is unfruitful for a discussion [*wie für eine Discussion unfruchtbar*]. We are talking past each other [*Wir reden aneinander vorbei*]." Who could talk back or respond, and who would contradict? And would this be a dialogue? A conversation? A spiritual-intellectual discussion? Could that be said to exist? To have existed? Between who and whom?

Second, among all the authors who might be invoked under the heading of "the German-Jewish dialogue," Kafka is arguably the only one who has plausibly offered, as Blanchot strikingly discerns, "a new form of communication." Strangely, that very form, the dialogic form, has attracted surprisingly little attention on the part of Kafka's readers, Blanchot's contribution notwithstanding.[18] On the other hand, what else could Scholem have been saying when he described Kafka's *Trial* as attaining anew "the linguistic world of expression of the Book of Job"—unless the *dialogue* between God and Job is said (as it surely could be) never to have occurred? Still, attending to "In the Cathedral" and to "the parable which describes the guardian of the law" ("a kind of summary of Jewish theology," says Scholem), "many readers have certainly already listened to the voices which burst forth from this chapter, from these few pages."[19] Many readers have, indeed. And few among them, no doubt, would dispute the singular insistence of the dialogic form throughout Kafka's prose.[20] Does not the doorkeeper himself repeatedly conduct, in that most famous of parables, "little interviews" with the man from the country, extending his odd benevolence to the point of *shouting* into the latter's enfeebled ears? And is not the man from the country "asking time and again to be admitted," cursing, grumbling, asking the fleas, and asking again about the remarkable fact that he alone attempted to gain an audience with the law? From "The Judgment" to *The Trial*, from "An Imperial Message" to "Letter to the Father," from "Description of a Struggle" to "A Report to an Academy" and "The Burrow," from *The Man Who Disappeared* to *The Castle* and beyond, Kafka plunges us again and again in direct and indirect speech, a vortex of rumors and reports, investigations and dispatches, dialogues and conversations—infinite and infinitely interrupted conversations.[21] Surely, Kafka's narrators and characters appear and disappear under a broad variety of shapes and roles ("a rainbow of colors" is the way Scholem phrases it), but none as frequent as speaker and listener (reader, writer, and eavesdropper, too). They may or may not be interlocutors, as Blanchot has it, but they are effusive conversationalists and storytellers, compulsive orators, reticent rhetors, garrulous administrators, desperately gushing artists and talking animals—all extending and receiving (sometimes withholding or withdrawing) greetings and announcements, words and letters, missives and accusations, reproaches and imperious directions, innocuous remarks or ominous advice, queries left unanswered and uncertain noises, fraught intimations or senseless repartees and countless *non sequiturs*, pathetic cries or contrived appeals, contorted gestures and pregnant body language. And then there is silence, that of the Sirens, of course, which Ulysses did not hear, and "the silence which rises up around me as the ultimate answer." One after the other, with and against the other(s), no less often *as* the other, Kafka's creatures singularly and collectively call up or pipe up ("Piping is our people's daily speech, only many a one pipes his whole life long and does not know it"), ambiguously interpellating a reader ("The emperor, so a parable runs, has sent a message to you . . . to you alone"), a viewer or auditor ("The great Theatre of Oklahoma is calling you! . . . We are the theatre that has a place for everyone, everyone in his place!"), an entire town, the landscape or even a burrow ("It is for your sake, ye passages and rooms, and you, Castle Keep, above all, that I have come back . . . What do I care for danger now that I am with you? You belong to me, I to you, we are united; what can harm us?"), or else "dogs like you and me," other animals and great, anonymous audiences ("especially when danger is most imminent").[22] "A pack of nobodies." Like the hunger artist and like Gregor Samsa himself, they also speak, or scream, to themselves—as to another ("to hear only my own scream which met no answer nor anything that could draw its force away, so that it rose up without check and could not stop even when it ceased being audible"). A master of prosopopoeia and of prolepsis, Kafka tirelessly gives voice ("and when I explained to myself: 'that is my hunger,' it was really my hunger that was speaking and having its joke at my expense'") and takes it away ("At that point I asked myself: How is it that she is not amazed at herself, that she keeps her lips closed and makes no such remark?"). He stages conversation ahead of conversation: where conversation has already failed ("Dearest Father, You asked me recently why I maintain that I am afraid of you. As usual, I was unable to think of any answer to your question"), where it has yet to succeed ("'It is the aim of this pamphlet'—so I ended up all too melodramatically, but it corresponded with my feelings at that time—'to help in giving the schoolmaster's book the wide publicity it deserves. If I succeed in that, then may my name, which I regard as only transiently and indirectly associated with this question, be blotted from it at once.'"), where it is useless ("The assistant doesn't actually plead in words, for he is afraid of Blumfeld, who is ostensibly doing his accounts; moreover, ordinary speech is useless, since the servant can be made to hear only by excessive shouting"), and where it is simply false ("the universal interpretation of this dialogue seemed to me entirely and completely false"). Kafka juxtaposes understanding and non-understanding, "a whole world of non-understanding" at once ("He interrupted me: 'I'm glad I haven't understood a word you've been saying'. Irritated, I said quickly, 'Your being glad about it proves that you have understood it.'"), agreement and disagreement ("'Are you dead?' 'Yes,' said the Hunter . . . 'But you are alive too,' said the

Burgomaster. 'In a certain sense,' said the Hunter, 'in a certain sense I am alive too'"), as well as the ever present possibility of conversation occurring in order to annul its very occurrence ("Strange as it may seem to you, and sitting here it surprises even me, it's a fact that you are not the talk of the town, however many subjects may be discussed you are not among them"). And one could adduce as many illustrations, that is, dialogues and conversations, as there are stories, parables, and chapters in his novels. Did not Odradek—even Odradek—partake of a dialogue ("'Well, what's your name?' you ask him. 'Odradek,' he says. 'And where do you live?' 'No fixed abode,' he says and laughs; but it is only the kind of laughter that has no lungs behind it. It sounds rather like the rustling of fallen leaves. And that is usually the end of the conversation")? And then there is the correspondence, Kafka's massive exchange of letters, and of course his conversations (with Max Brod, with Gustav Janouch, and with others).

As well—and this is my third and final assertion—Kafka has made eminently clear that the German-Jewish dialogue was always also the Arab-Jewish dialogue. At the origins of binational thought, it would be easy to invoke Kafka's Prague to substantiate this claim. But one could just as easily begin earlier than Kafka, perhaps with Kant's famous reference to those "Palestinians among us," and onward to everything we know about Oriental Jews (*Ostjuden, mizrachim*), and of course about Aryans and Semites. The demonstration would have to include the inevitable returns of (and to) Buber and Arendt, Scholem and Benjamin, Freud, Theodor Adorno and, again, Kafka, all of whom appear unavoidable today when considering that other desperate—or inexistent—dialogical site we call Israel-Palestine.

3

Was there—is there—an Arab-Jewish dialogue? As I have suggested above, this question has insistently accompanied, perhaps silently governed, whether overtly or covertly, the so-called German-Jewish dialogue. For reasons I have attended to elsewhere, which have to do with the structural associations between the Jew and the Arab through the history of Christian political theology, we might remember that it was not only "the Jewish Question" that was exported to the Middle East, but the Arab (and Muslim) Question as well.[23] More proximately, the two dialogues merge with the rise of that "providential couple," Aryans and Semites, and its particular, albeit not unique, history in Germany.[24] The Arab-Jewish dialogue, whether or not it was ever real ("What is it that makes you all behave as though you were real?" asks Kafka in "Description of a Struggle"), is the unavoidable correlate of the German-Jewish dialogue. One might even argue that, if there has been dialogue, it could only be conducted *between* these two sets of dialogue. And it continues to be.[25] Closer still to Kafka, Dimitry Shumsky puts the matter most concisely when he writes about how "Jackals and Arabs" "incorporates a dual reference to the relations between Jews and non-Jews in both Bohemia and Palestine."[26]

At the center of "Jackals and Arabs" is a conversation, a development that, true to the arguments I have been making, takes the form of a dialogue.[27] This could not be more obvious, bordering on banal, just as it seems to appear to the protagonist (and narrator) of the story, whose surprise is restricted to his being the addressee of the jackal's speech and to the content of it, rather than a response to the fact that he is engaged with an animal in conversation. "'That is surprising,' said I, forgetting to kindle the pile of firewood which lay ready to smoke away jackals, 'that is very surprising for me to hear.'" And yet, no less central is the missing dialogue that structures the story in equally decisive a manner. For "jackals and Arabs" do not, for their part, speak with each other. However we identify them (and we cannot avoid that which has been recognized, with varying degrees of good faith, by numerous critics, namely that the story puts into play a "web of relations of power, fear, need, tradition, and circumstance . . . an elastic structure that sustains varied projections—flexible identifications possible from the position of an author poised between identities"),[28] we cannot fail to recognize that dialogue is at once present and absent between them—an impossible dialogue. In contrast to the narrator, with whom they both converse, the two collectives named in the title appear multifariously as instances of "forces battling in some grave conflict of our time" (as Blanchot had put it), forces and voices that do "discuss, for they want to be right," but do so only there, where "violence once again asserts itself." Telescoping Blanchot's distinctions, it is as if these "protagonists wonderfully [understood] each other by the intermediary of the hidden truth they know they do not have the right to hear," communicating—or not—with another other. It is, at any rate, "around what escapes direct communication that their community restructures itself." More precisely perhaps, there is for both sides, "on one hand, the obstinacy of the will to live, the confidence that life cannot be wrong. But on the other hand, it is already the force of the enemy in them that is always right." It is then exactly as Blanchot says: "The distance that separates the speakers is never impassable; it becomes only so for one who persists in crossing it with the aid of discourse, where duality reigns and where it engenders always more duplicity and those false intermediaries that are its doubles . . . The characters are not interlocutors."[29]

The dialogue that does take place, which seems nevertheless to mark its participants as interlocutors, confirms in any case that there is, indeed, a grave conflict ("it seems to me a very old quarrel; I suppose it's in the blood, and perhaps will only end with it"). As the narrator reports, there is also a deep, perhaps even deeper, agreement ("what you have just said agrees with our old tradition"). Distance, both spatial and temporal, is covered swiftly and "what had been so far away was all at once quite near." The pack confronts the narrator, their "lithe bodies moving nimbly and rhythmically, as if at the crack of a whip." There is need ("we want you to end this quarrel that divides the world"), the longing for peace ("no more bleating of sheep knifed by an Arab"), and there is a (false) stance of equality ("one jackal came before me, nudging right under my arm, pressing against me, as if he needed my warmth, and then stood before me and spoke to me almost eye to eye"). There is also the shared sense of exile, as the narrator, awaited for generations, has himself traveled "from the far North." The jackals, for their part, have been "exiled" among the Arabs ("Is it not misfortune enough for us to be exiled among such creatures?"). There is a meeting of intelligence—also out of place—a meeting of collective minds, a plural address: "You Northerners have the kind of intelligence that is not to be found among Arabs." The narrator may be alone at the moment, but he is hardly one of a kind. He himself mentions sleeping, traveling companions ("die Gefährten"). Whether he is here the only Northerner is less relevant than the collective, geographical identification that marks him. "'You misunderstand us,' said [the jackal], 'a human failing which persists apparently even in the far North.'" The Arab later confirms this when he avers that "every European" is approached in the same manner by the jackals ("Every European is offered it for the great work; every European is just the man that Fate has chosen for them"). Finally, there are questions and answers, the reiteration of a genuine, albeit ambivalent query ("What do you jackals want, then?" "What are you proposing to do?" "Well, what do you want?"), compassionate worries and secular concerns ("How can you bear to live in such a world, O noble heart and kindly bowels?").

There is also violence of course, the display of weapons: a foreshadowed whip and an actual whip, muskets ("they'll shoot you down in dozens with their muskets"), teeth—or "bite," *das Gebiß* ("we have nothing but our teeth; whatever we want to do, good or bad, we can tackle it only with our teeth"), knives ("knifed by an Arab"), all-powerful hands, and "a small pair of sewing scissors, covered with ancient rust, dangling from an eyetooth."[30] And there is, of course, blood. And through it all, everything is nonetheless as if a deeper agreement was at work, a covenant and an understanding of sorts. Fear—that powerful engine of violence—is there to be explicitly denied ("never in the history of the world has any jackal been afraid of an Arab. Why should we fear them?"). There is a strange kind of truce, a state of separation filled with contempt, to be sure, and the hateful desire for non-contamination ("We're not proposing to kill them. All the water in the Nile couldn't cleanse us of that. Why, the mere sight of their living flesh makes us turn tail and flee into cleaner air, into the desert, which for that very reason is our home"), the profundity of disgust ("Filth is their white; filth is their black; their beards are a horror; the very sight of their eye sockets makes one want to spit; and when they lift an arm, the murk of hell yawns in the armpit"), the longing for cleanliness ("Cleanliness, nothing but cleanliness is what we want"). It is impossible to deny "the logic of elimination" here at work,[31] and yet it would still be "a mistake to think that the chill, oscillating space, inserted by Kafka between the words in conversation, only destroys communication."[32] There is, as I have said, no direct dialogue between jackals and Arabs, but is there no conversation? Is there not the form of a dialogue, dialogue as a form? Here is Blanchot again:

The definition of conversation (that is, the most simple description of the most simple conversation) might be the following: when two people speak together, they speak not together, but each in turn: one says something, then stops, the other something else (or the same thing), then stops. The coherent discourse they carry on is composed of sequences that are interrupted when the conversation moves from partner to partner, even if adjustments are made so that they correspond to one another. The fact that speech needs to pass from one interlocutor to another in order to be confirmed, contradicted, or developed shows the necessity of interval. The power of speaking interrupts itself, and this interruption plays a role that appears to be minor—precisely the role of a subordinated alternation. This role, nonetheless, is so enigmatic that it can be interpreted as bearing the very enigma of language: pause between sentences, pause from one interlocutor to another, and pause of attention, the hearing that doubles the force of locution.[33]

How to understand, comprehend, or simply read the simultaneous distance and even the complicity between jackals and Arabs, the sequence of interruptions and pauses that registers in the narrator's place, role, and function? These pauses and interruptions are not merely filled with silence but rather with the reiterated sound of voices, the distant howls, "the natural plaintiveness" of the jackals' voice, the (barely) recognizable musicality ("all the jackals howled together; very remotely it seemed to resemble a melody"), the repeated laments ("they were all lamenting and sobbing"), the renewed lifting of voice ("the jackals lifted up their voices"), ecstasy ("they lifted their head; half swooning in ecstasy"). Is there, or is there not, a dialogue, the form of dialogue (what Blanchot calls "conversation"), between them? It is not merely that hate is a powerful bond, a "wounded attachment," if there ever was one.[34] It is rather the obsessiveness of their strange cohabitation, the controlled distance—temporal and spatial—that binds and separates them: "Well, here's the scissors at least, and high time to stop!" The jackals flee in haste, but they stop "at some little distance rallied in a close huddle, all the brutes so tightly packed and rigid that they looked as if penned in a small fold girt by flickering will-o'-the-wisps." Indeed, they are treated as domestic animals, a spectacle ("Well, you've seen them"), part of the Arabs' entertainment ("'So you've been treated to this entertainment too, sir,' said the Arab, laughing as gaily as the reserve of his race permitted"). There is a common knowledge of a historical—and spatial—bond, a shared existential, and exilic, fate ("it's common knowledge; so long as Arabs exist, that pair of scissors goes wandering through the desert and will wander with us to the end of our days"). There is spite, yes ("They have the most lunatic hopes, these beasts; they're just fools, utter fools"), but there is a shared futurity (hope, the end of our days), there is affection and admiration ("we like them; they are our dogs; finer dogs than any of yours"). There are invisible bonds ("as if irresistibly drawn by cords each of them began to waver forward"), and the power of forgetting ("They had forgotten the Arabs, forgotten their hatred"), there is "as much determination as hopefulness to extinguish some raging fire"), the rallying of energies ("every muscle in his body twitched and labored at the task"), and "laboring in common." There is more admiration at the very strength of an affective bond ("Marvelous creatures, aren't they? And how they hate us!").

Commentators have been quick to identify the numerous stereotypical discourses that are mobilized throughout the story. The jackals (and the Arabs, too) "are saturated with the common stereotypes."[35] They "represent the Western fantasy of the Jews as always haunting the edges of 'culture,' unable to truly alter their instincts . . . The jackals have all the Jewish markers of difference."[36] And yet, we know by now the perils of allegorical treatments of Kafka, of "de-metaphorization" and secure identifications.[37] In other words, we know that his stories—and "Jackals and Arabs" among them, as Kafka himself told Buber—are not easily translated "parables." We have begun to recognize that we are confronted, in this text and others, with a "web of relations of power, fear, need, tradition, and circumstance . . . an elastic structure that sustains varied projections—flexible identifications possible from the position of an author poised between identities."[38] Critics have thus remarked that even the Northern traveler "could be identified as an acculturated 'German-speaking Prague Jew'" or as the Messiah himself.[39] And indeed, Kafka stages a striking fluidity (a magnetic circulation?) between the jackals and the narrator. As he describes the overpowering disgust seizing the jackals at the evocation of the Arabs' "living flesh," the narrator speculates that they are perhaps "trying to conceal" that disgust. It is their disgust, of course, yet it is "a disgust so overpowering *that I felt like leaping over their heads to get away* [es war, als wollten sie einen Widerwillen verbergen, der so schrecklich war, *daß ich am liebsten mit einem hohen Sprung aus ihrem Kreis entflohen wäre*]" (my emphasis). But it is of course what is shared—that is, as Blanchot has it, the nonreciprocal distance, as well as the fact that "the aim is still unity. The distance . . . is never impassable," even there, where their "conversations are at no time dialogues." We have seen how much this is the case already, but I want to bring this conversation to a close by underscoring another "stereotypical" (that is, Orientalist) association that further complicates the assurance with which critics have read the jackals as Jews and, with equal (if understandable) assurance, the Arabs as Arabs.[40] For the jackals also have, after all, all the Arab markers of difference, markers that are signified quite explicitly in the text. They share the Oriental desert as well as their wandering nomadism along with elaborate ritual practices ("The irony is that Jewish and Islamic ritual practices are certainly closer to each other than to European ideas of ritual slaughter," writes Sander Gilman).[41] Most importantly, the devouring of a camel so vividly described bears all the marker of the totem meal about which Freud, and Kafka too, learned in the writing of William Robertson Smith in *Religion of the Semites*. As Freud recounts, the victim of the sacrifice is, in fact, a camel, around which a band of Bedouins come together and descend, following the cue of their leader,

and when the leader of the band has thrice led the worshippers round the altar in a solemn procession accompanied with chants, he inflicts the first wound . . . and in all haste drinks of the blood that gushes forth. Forthwith the whole company fall on the victim with their swords, hacking off pieces of the quivering flesh and devouring them raw with such wild haste, that in the short interval between the rise of the day star . . . and the disappearance of its rays before the rising sun, the entire camel, body and bones, skin, blood and entrails, is wholly devoured.[42]

Freud goes on to add that "this barbaric ritual, which bears every sign of extreme antiquity, was no isolated instance but was everywhere the original form taken by totemic sacrifice." The similarity with the scene described by Kafka hardly merits commentary, but it leaves us with some questions, the same questions—or perhaps others—with which this "strange dialogue" originated: "Are we Greeks? Are we Jews? But who, we?"[43] But I digress. Are Arabs white? ("The tall, white figure of an Arab passed by") Are Jews? Are the jackals Arabs? Or are the jackals Jews? Are the Arabs Jews or the Jews Arabs? And what about the Germans, the German-Jews? Is there, can there be, and has there ever been, an Arab-Jewish dialogue? In Europe or in Palestine? On Earth or in a poem?

4

It was another reader of Kafka, another patient and generous interlocutor of his, who, recapitulating and expanding Blanchot's insights, concisely demonstrated that if dialogue is possible, merely possible, what is there to discuss? Mahmoud Darwish did not quite conclude the discussion, leaving the next (if not the last) word, the uptake, to another poet. "The enemy and I," Darwish wrote as if commenting on "Jackals and Arabs," are stuck in a hole, "partners in one trap."[44] We who are in that trap can, in short order, have a conversation made exclusively of sequences, whether of speech ("I, a selfish optimist, will whisper to myself without wondering what my enemy whispers to himself") or of interruptions ("and he'd say: me first and I'd say: me first"). We can also wait in awkward togetherness, unified in its aim for survival and separation, expecting "the rescue rope so we can part ways by the edge of the hole—the chasm, and go to what remains for us of life and war . . . if we are able to survive." There will be no dialogue ("He and I are frightened and don't exchange any words about fear, or other than fear since we are foes . . ."), yet we might still "partner up," awaiting luck or rescuers ("we wait for luck, the rescuers might find us here and toss a safety rope our way"), or a snake we will kill ("We will partner up in killing the snake to survive together or alone . . ."). We might or might not "share a phrase of gratitude and congratulations on what we have accomplished together," but we shall not engage in dialogue; "we did not converse: I remembered the law of communication [*fiqh al-hiwārāt*] over mutual frivolity when he once told me: What has become mine is mine and what is yours is yours and mine . . ." There might come a time when "boredom and silence broke what's between us," a time for talking, a time for dialogue perhaps. A time for change. Or metamorphosis. There will be forgetting and there will be remembering. There will be memory for forgetfulness.

HE SAID: Where will hope come from?
I SAID: From the air
HE SAID: Did you forget I buried you in a hole like this?
I SAID: I almost did, because an alluring worn out
       tomorrow pulled me by the hand . . .
HE SAID: Will you negotiate with me [*tufāwaḍni*] now?
I SAID: Over what now in this hole, this grave?
HE SAID: Over your share and mine
       of our void and our mutual grave
I SAID: What's the use? Time has run away
       from us, and destiny doesn't follow the rule,
       the murdered and his murderer sleep in this hole,
       and another poet must see this script through
       to its end!

Dear Houria,

*It has been a long time I should have written to you, and I apologize for
the delay. I feel (or perhaps I would merely like to think) that we have been
conducting a conversation, a dialogue even, and that for quite some time
(we have, but then I should also tell you about Vienna). Which is of course
no excuse for having failed to give voice to what I can only hope is a kind of
attentive listening, a careful reading. Since your book came out, at any rate,
it is very clear to me that I owe you a response—a responsible response, as
Derrida used to say—and that I must first of all thank you for the gesture you
yourself have made in that stunning open letter of a book.*[45] *You apostrophized,
you called out to us all. You revived a dialogue—or is it a conversation? You
did so, at any rate, as an adult, not as fashion has it still in Paris, where one
smugly turns to children, to one's own offspring, not-yet mature and silent
addressees who populate French letters. As if everything—everything—had
to be explained, as if everything could be explained, but only to the youngest
among us, only to those deprived of a right to respond, or indeed to question.
You have high expectations. I mean that in many ways. And surely, I am not
unlike Kafka's Abraham here ("True faith is not lacking to him, he has this
faith; he would make the sacrifice in the right spirit if only he could believe
he was the one meant"). I mean by this that I cannot be certain that I am the
one to answer your high expectations—or your lower ones. How would I know
whom you meant? As what, and as whom, do I answer you? Am I white? Jew?
Arab? The decision, as you know, is not entirely mine. But I feel addressed
nonetheless. I shall let you decide which one, among your chapters, I am most
qualified to answer. But if there is a lesson here, it is that there are pauses
and interruptions to any conversation (there is violence too, and one may be
called upon to speak and answer, with and without laughter, to murderers).
And in these pauses and interruptions, in and through their uptake, I am—we
are—changed. Speaking of toleration and tolerance: will we accept the change?
Will we show ourselves capable of what you, with your high expectations, are
asking us to do? Are we capable of pause, of interruption—interrupting you or
ourselves—and of transformation? Into Arabs, or Jews? Or both? Or more?*

Gil

New York, May 2017

NOTES

I am grateful to Joelle Marelli, without whom none of this would have been written. Thanks are also due to Mayanthi Fernando and Mana Kia, for the conversations and the careful reading; to Bashir Bashir and Leila Farsakh for their kind insistence; and to the AJQ-JAQ group, at the Bruno Kreisky Forum, from beginning to end. I presented a version of this essay at the University of California, Santa Barbara. I thank Elisabeth Weber and Elliot Wolfson for the invitation, and the audience for the engaged conversation.

1. Maurice Blanchot, "The Pain of Dialogue," trans. Charlotte Mandell, in Maurice Blanchot, *The Book to Come* (Stanford, Calif.: Stanford University Press, 2003), 150–158; my commentary is restricted to pages 151–155, from which all quotes are drawn.

2. On form, "the dialogic form," and its "transformative possibilities," see Mana Kia, "Indian Friends, Iranian Selves, Persianate Modern," *Comparative Studies of South Asia, Africa and the Middle East* 36, no. 3 (2016), 401, 409, 413.

3. I quote Jonathan Boyarin, who here and elsewhere pertinently testifies to proximate dialogues. In the quote above, Boyarin is describing the French-Jewish community circa 1968, omitting, as he writes, the demographic change that community had undergone with decolonization. Memory for forgetfulness (see Boyarin, *Storm from Paradise: The Politics of Jewish Memory* [Minneapolis: University of Minnesota Press, 1992], 10).

4. See, e.g., Jacques Derrida, "Interpretations at War: Kant, the Jew, the German," trans. Moshe Ron, in Derrida, *Acts of Religion*, ed. Gil Anidjar (New York: Routledge, 2002), 163; and see, in a different perspective, the survey of complex and changing, and not always reciprocal, engagements provided by Bashir and Farsakh in their introduction to this volume.

5. Maurice Blanchot, *The Infinite Conversation*, trans. Susan Hanson (Minneapolis: University of Minnesota Press, 1993).

6. Blanchot, *The Infinite Conversation*, 76, 182.

7. See, e.g., Seloua Luste Boulbina, *Le singe de Kafka et autres propos sur la colonie* (Lyon, France: Sens Public, 2008); Jens Hanssen, "Kafka and Arabs," *Critical Inquiry* 39 (Autumn 2012), 167–197; Dimitry Shumsky, "Czechs, Germans, Arabs, Jews: Franz Kafka's 'Jackals and Arabs' Between Bohemia and Palestine," *AJS Review* 33, no. 1 (2009), 71–100; Omri Ben-Yehuda, "Kafka's Muslim: The Politics of Semitism," *Tel Aviver Jahrbuch für deutsche Geschichte* 45 (2017), 211–233.

8. Gershom Scholem, "Against the Myth of the German-Jewish Dialogue," trans. Werner J. Dannhauser in Scholem, *On Jews and Judaism in Crisis: Selected Essays*, ed. W. J. Dannhauser (New York: Schocken Books, 1976), 61–64; and see Abraham Rubin, "The 'German-Jewish Dialogue' and Its Literary Refractions: The Case of Margarete Susman and Gershom Scholem," *Modern Judaism* 35, no. 1 (February 2015), 1–17.

9. But see *The German-Jewish Dialogue Reconsidered: A Symposium in Honor of George L. Mosse*, ed. Klaus L. Berghahn (New York: Peter Lang, 1996).

10. In a rich commentary on Friedrich Schlegel's dialogue (that is, polemical dispute) with Lessing, Jeffrey Librett explicates Schlegel's treatment of dialogue as a form (admittedly, "a form that is almost no form at all") (J. S. Librett, *The Rhetoric of*

Cultural Dialogue: Jews and Germans from Moses Mendelssohn to Richard Wagner and Beyond [Stanford, Calif.: Stanford University Press, 2000], 207–216).

11. Librett, *The Rhetoric of Cultural Dialogue*, 43.

12. Heinrich Heine's *An Edom* closes Amos Funkenstein's essay on "The Dialectics of Assimilation," *Jewish Social Studies* NS 1, no. 2 (Winter 1995), 1–14; elsewhere Funkenstein traced the changes in the Jewish-Christian disputation (the form of dialogue), and Amnon Raz-Krakotzkin pointed to the end of the disputation, often thought of as the beginning of the Jewish-Christian dialogue, one that answers more precisely to the description offered by Heine (see Amos Funkenstein, *Perceptions of Jewish History* [Berkeley: University of California Press, 1993]; Amnon Raz-Krakotzkin, *The Censor, the Editor, and the Text: The Catholic Church and the Shaping of the Jewish Canon in the Sixteenth Century*, trans. Jackie Feldman [Philadelphia: University of Pennsylvania Press, 2007]).

13. See Martin Buber, *Ich und Du* (Heidelberg, Germany: Lambert Schneider, 1983), and for two concise and pertinent treatments, Paul Mendes-Flohr, "Ambivalent Dialogue: Jewish-Christian Theological Encounter in the Weimar Republic," in Mendes-Flohr, *Divided Passions: Jewish Intellectuals and the Experience of Modernity* (Detroit, Mich.: Wayne State University Press, 1991), 133–167, and Mendes-Flohr, "Martin Buber and Martin Heidegger in Dialogue," *Journal of Religion* 94, no. 1 (January 2014), 2–25.

14. On Davos, see Peter E. Gordon, *Continental Divide: Heidegger, Cassirer, Davos* (Cambridge, Mass.: Harvard University Press, 2010); and see as well *Heidegger's Jewish Followers: Essays on Hannah Arendt, Leo Strauss, Hans Jonas, and Emmanuel Levinas*, ed. Samuel Fleischacker (Pittsburgh, Pa.: Duquesne University Press, 2008); on Schmitt and Strauss, see Heinrich Meier, *Carl Schmitt and Leo Strauss: The Hidden Dialogue*, trans. J. Harvey Lomax (Chicago: University of Chicago Press, 1995); one might consider other vectors of awkward reciprocity connecting Schmitt to Benjamin and to Jacob Taubes.

15. See Robert Leventhal's essay, "The Jewish Physician as Respondent, Confidant, and Proxy: The Case of Marcus Herz and Immanuel Kant," in *On the Word of a Jew: Religion, Reliability, and the Dynamics of Trust*, ed. Nina Caputo and Mitchell Hart (Bloomington: Indiana University Press, 2018), 222–244. On Scholem and Benjamin, see A. Gelley, "On the 'Myth of the German-Jewish Dialogue': Scholem and Benjamin," available at https://english.chass.ncsu.edu/jouvert/v3i12/gelley.htm (accessed May 17, 2017). I have written about the fraught dialogue between Scholem and Benjamin in my *"Our Place in al-Andalus": Kabbalah, Philosophy, Literature in Arab Jewish Letters* (Stanford, Calif.: Stanford University Press, 2002), 102–165; Vivian Liska also attends to "diachronic and synchronic dialogues and conversations," the exchanges between Arendt and Scholem, Benjamin and Scholem, and Celan and Ingeborg Bachmann in *German-Jewish Thought and Its Afterlife: A Tenuous Legacy* (Bloomington: Indiana University Press, 2017), as does Todd S. Presner in *Mobile Modernity: Germans, Jews, Trains* (New York: Columbia University Press, 2007), and see as well Abraham Rubin, "Reading Kafka, Debating Revelation: Gershom Scholem's Shadow Dialogue with Hans-Joachim Schoeps," *Literature & Theology* (2016), 1–21.

16. On Scholem and Arendt and the question of dialogue (under the heading of binationalism), see, among his many pertinent writings, Amnon Raz-Krakotzkin, "Binationalism and Jewish Identity: Hannah Arendt and the Question of Palestine," in *Hannah Arendt in Jerusalem*, ed. Steven E. Aschheim (Berkeley: University of

California Press, 2001), 165–180; "Jewish Peoplehood, 'Jewish Politics,' and Political Responsibility: Arendt on Zionism and Partitions," *College Literature* 38, no. 1 (Winter 2011), 57–74; "Exile and Binationalism: From Gershom Scholem and Hannah Arendt to Edward Said and Mahmoud Darwish" (Carl Heinrich Becker Lecture of the Fritz Thyssen Stiftung 2011) (Berlin: Wissenschaftskolleg zu Berlin, 2012); and see also Idith Zertal, *Israel's Holocaust and the Politics of Nationhood*, trans. Chaya Galai (Cambridge: Cambridge University Press, 2005), 128–163.

17. Scholem, "On Eichmann," in *On Jews and Judaism*, 302, trans. modified.

18. Having noted that "no one has made a thorough investigation of dialogue in his fiction," Anthony Droste Northey left unpublished his own remarkable contribution to that missing conversation (Northey, "Dialogue in the Works of Franz Kafka" [Montreal, Quebec: McGill University, 1974], 4); and see for another brief and punctual treatment, R. Lane Kauffmann, "The Other in Question: Dialogical Experiments in Montaigne, Kafka, and Cortázar," in *The Interpretation of Dialogue*, ed. Tullio Maranhão (Chicago: University of Chicago Press, 1990), 157–194; attentive to Kafka's "dialogical style," Mark Blum proposes a more expansive "social discourse" as Kafka's concern and method, acknowledging that "every page of Kafka is a complex conversation with himself, fellow-writers, writers who have lived and died before him and a reading public . . . Kafka conducts this conversation in virtually every sentence" (Blum, *Kafka's Social Discourse: An Aesthetic Search for Community* [Bethlehem, Pa.: Lehigh University Press, 2011], 7).

19. Gershom Scholem, "On Kafka's *The Trial* (1926)," trans. Jonathan Chipman, in Scholem, *On the Possibility of Jewish Mysticism in Our Time and Other Essays*, ed. Avraham Shapira (Philadelphia: The Jewish Publication Society, 1997), 193; it is also to the dialogue in the Cathedral that Omri Ben Yehuda turns in order to argue that "Jewish literature's formalism is what enables its vital dialogism" (Omri Ben Yehuda, "'In Quest of *Du*': Dialogue in Kafka and Agnon," *Prooftexts* 37 [2019], 554, repeated on 571); preoccupied with the dialectics of Jewish identity, Ben Yehuda insists that *The Trial* is exceptional, that an "emphasis on verbal exchange is rather unusual" in Kafka (556, but see 572n10). Later he approvingly recalls Werner Kraft, who "meticulously summarized Kafka's prose as a rhythmic exchange of word and answer (*Wort und Antwort*)" (570).

20. All references are to Kafka, *The Complete Stories*, ed. Nahum N. Glatzer (New York: Schocken, 1971).

21. Ritchie Robertson briefly mentions that Kafka's earliest narrative fragments are written in "dialogue form," announcing the literary—and dialogic—breakthrough that is "The Judgment" (Robertson, *Kafka: Judaism, Politics, and Literature* [Oxford: Clarendon Press, 1985], 28). Robertson goes on to assert that "the most striking qualities" of that story "are dramatic." And the same can be said about "The Metamorphosis," the "three main episodes" of which "resembles the three acts of a play" (34). Importantly, Robertson is among the few who explicitly identifies Kafka as a significant participant in the German-Jewish dialogue, including "Jackals and Arabs" in his edited collection, *The German-Jewish Dialogue: An Anthology of Literature Texts 1749–1993* (Oxford: Oxford University Press, 1999).

22. On animals in Kafka, and the pertinence of another binary, see Naama Harel, *Kafka's Zoopoetics: Beyond the Human-Animal Barrier* (Ann Arbor: University of Michigan Press, 2020).

23. See Gil Anidjar, *The Jew, the Arab: A History of the Enemy* (Stanford, Calif.: Stanford University Press, 2003) and *Semites: Religion, Race, Literature* (Stanford, Calif.: Stanford University Press, 2008).

24. Maurice Olender, *The Languages of Paradise: Aryans and Semites, a Match Made in Heaven*, trans. Arthur Goldhammer (New York: Other Press, 2003).

25. See, centered on Kafka's reception in German and in Arabic, Atef Botros, *Kafka: Ein jüdischer Schriftsteller aus arabischer Sicht* (Wiesbaden, Germany: Reichert Verlag, 2009).

26. Shumsky, "Czechs, Germans, Arabs, Jews," 77.

27. Kafka, "Jackals and Arabs," trans. Willa and Edwin Muir, in Kafka, *Complete Stories*, 407–411; the story is also available online at www.kafka.org/index.php?id =162,165,0,0,1,0 (accessed May 29, 2017).

28. Scott Spector, *Prague Territories: National Conflict and Cultural Innovation in Franz Kafka's Fin de Siècle* (Berkeley: University of California Press, 2000), 192; Atef Botros distinguishes between the "non-Jewish," Western context (the German reception) and the colonized, Arab East (the Arab reception) (Botros, *Kafka*, 183–226).

29. Just as earlier, I am here quoting from Blanchot, "The Pain of Dialogue," 151–155.

30. For more on Kafka and weapons, see my "The Dignity of Weapons," *Law, Culture and the Humanities* (2015), 1–11.

31. Patrick Wolfe, *Settler Colonialism and the Transformation of Anthropology: The Politics and Poetics of an Ethnographic Event* (New York: Cassel, 1999), 27; as Blanchot writes in another, yet relevant, context, "there is in Kafka's image something that brings to light a disquieting violence. It is a matter of exterminating, of doing away with; and speech would be what brings death to the inhuman, that which is in possession of nothingness and destruction" (Blanchot, *The Infinite Conversation*, 182).

32. Blanchot, "The Pain of Dialogue," 154.

33. Blanchot, *The Infinite Conversation*, 75.

34. Wendy Brown, *States of Injury: Power and Freedom in Late Modernity* (Princeton. N.J.: Princeton University Press, 1995), 52–76; according to Heselhaus, hate, and more specifically hate speech, is at the core of the story (see Herrad Heselhaus, "Resignifying Hate Speech: Doing and Undoing the Performative in Franz Kafka's 'Schakale und Araber'" *Studies in Language and Literature (Literature Bulletin)* 64 [2013], 85–116.).

35. Iris Bruce, *Kafka and Cultural Zionism: Dates in Palestine* (Madison: University of Wisconsin Press, 2007), 156.

36. Sander Gilman, *Franz Kafka: The Jewish Patient* (New York: Routledge, 1995), 150; Gilman mentions "the *foetor judaïcus*," the odor attributed to Jews; they are also "*mauschel*," speaking plaintively, "but it is the eating habits of the jackals that most set them apart from their neighbors in the desert, the Arabs" (150). Gilman goes on to identify accusations of "ritual murder" (152); Iris Bruce elaborates on these themes, on the pertinence of the Zionist context, and she underscores as well that the story is "a satire of Diaspora existence" (Bruce, *Kafka and Cultural Zionism*, 154). Robertson endorses the view of previous scholars who showed that "the jackal was an accepted image for the Diaspora Jew, who was seen as incapable of manual labour and confined to a parasitic existence at the expense of his host society" (Robertson, *Kafka*, 164).

37. See Heselhaus, "Resignifying Hate Speech," 85–116.

38. Spector, *Prague Territories*, 192.

39. Bruce, *Kafka and Cultural Zionism*, 154; in her concise but powerful reading, Selloua Boulbina unhesitatingly identifies "Jackals and Arabs" as "un dialogue entre le narrateur, le 'Seigneur,' un voyageur juif, et le chef d'une bande de chacals" (Boulbina, *Le singe de Kafka*, 54); on the narrator as Messiah, see William C. Rubinstein, "Kafka's 'Jackals and Arabs,'" *Monatshefte* 59, no. 1 (Spring 1967), 13–18.

40. Consider, once again, the deep and stable agreement that subtends the two interpretive traditions Atef Botros meticulously compares: either the Arabs represent the surrounding, non-Jewish world of the "Jewish question" (the German reception), or, upholding "the Arab question," they are the native victims of colonialism and of Zionist settler colonialism (the Arab reception). The identity of the jackals as Jews, and of the narrator as European, allows here for no deviation from some opaque literality (Botros, *Kafka*, 182–183).

41. Gilman, *Kafka*, 151; to which Heselhaus adds that "surprisingly the argument against the brutality of Jewish ritual slaughter is expressed by the jackals themselves denouncing the slaughter by the Arabs" (Heselhaus, "Resignifying Hate Speech," 112).

42. Sigmund Freud, *Totem and Taboo: Some Points of Agreement Between the Mental Lives of Savages and Neurotics* (New York: Routledge, 2004), 161, quoting Robertson Smith, *Religion of the Semites* (New York: Routledge, 2017).

43. Jacques Derrida, "Violence and Metaphysics," trans. Alan Bass, in Derrida, *Writing and Difference* (Chicago: University of Chicago Press, 1978), 192; the expression "strange dialogue" is also Derrida's.

44. Mahmoud Darwish, "A Ready Script," trans. Fady Joudah, *American Poetry Review* 37, no. 6 (November/December 2008), 11.

45. Houria Bouteldja, *Whites, Jews, and Us: Toward a Politics of Revolutionary Love*, trans. Rachel Valinsky (South Pasadena, Calif.: Semiotext(e), 2017).

Chapter Two

AN EMBLEMATIC EMBRACE

New Europe, the Jewish State, and the Palestinian Question

BRIAN KLUG

AN EMBRACE IN PARIS

On July 16, 2017, France's President Emmanuel Macron greeted Benjamin Netanyahu, Israel's prime minister, at the Elysée Palace in Paris. Press photographs show the two men embracing warmly. In one picture, their noses seem to brush. In another, they are cheek to cheek, arms wrapped around each other. In a third, each looks deeply into the other's eyes, Macron's left hand resting upon Netanyahu's right shoulder. Had this been London, such a demonstrative welcome by the head of state might have raised eyebrows. But this was Paris, where it is probably normal for the president to clasp a visiting foreign dignitary to his bosom. Nonetheless, seen from a certain angle, the intimacy of this particular embrace takes on a meaning that transcends diplomacy. When I saw these pictures it struck me that they are emblematic, signifying what "the Jewish state" (represented by Netanyahu) means to "New Europe" (personified by Macron) and vice versa—not just on a summer's day in Paris and not merely in terms of mutual political interests, but in the context of a complex relationship between Europe and the Jews that extends over centuries.[1] This chapter gives a reading of this embrace, detaching it from its factual context and seeing it from the angle I have just described. It is an attempt to unpack what, in a flash, the image seemed to me to capture.[2]

A third party comes into this reading by virtue of being absent: the Palestinian people. The absence of the Palestinians is conspicuous as they are not *merely* absent: they are excluded, which makes them present. Their presence-absence spoils the party. It complicates the celebration encapsulated by the image of the two intertwined leaders: the (ostensible) healing of wounds between Europe and the Jews. The Palestinians constitute a problem because they exist—not per se but as Palestinians. Ironically, the "problem" that their identity poses is reminiscent of the "problem" the Jews posed for Europe down the centuries. In the European script, the Jews *as* Jews fundamentally did not belong. One way of putting this is to say that if only they had not been Jewish there would have been no "Jewish question." It is similar with the Palestinians and Israel but with a twist: if only they *were* Jewish then there would be no "Palestinian question." And were it not for this question, the Palestinian people would not, by virtue of their absence, be present in the intimate embrace in Paris.

In the triangle formed by Europe, Palestinians, and Jews, Europe looms largest by far. Its influence on the interface between Jews and Palestinians has been devastating. Whether this situation is decisive for the future is, in a way, the fundamental question confronting Arabs and Jews today in their engagement with each other, for nothing dominates that engagement more than the confrontation between Jews and Arabs in Israel-Palestine. This question is constantly in my mind as I write this chapter. In a sense, the whole point of the chapter is to put this question center stage—to make *Europe* the "problem" rather than the Palestinians or the Jews.

As the chapter develops, I try to bring the symbolic meaning of the Paris embrace—what it signifies for each of the three parties—into focus. Given its salience, I devote more space and pay more attention to Europe than to the two other parties, beginning with the way New Europe defines itself. I then turn to the crucial role the Holocaust plays as a "foundational myth" both for New Europe and for the Jewish state. This leads into a discussion of Jewish otherness, which, through its vicissitudes, has a lethal knock-on effect for the Palestinians. I conclude with a brief, whimsical peek at a possible future.

This chapter is an essay on the structure of the present, not an exercise in political science; it is more art than science, more speculative than conclusive. I am offering a bird's-eye view of a wide terrain, which means failing to see the trees for the wood; in other words, neglecting detail for the sake of an overall prospect. While I draw on a variety of sources, I use them not so much to *prove* a point as to *articulate* one. In the end, what I am seeking to offer is a synopsis.

In short, the essay is a take on what the editors say in their introduction when they refer to "three questions that make one": the Jewish question, the Arab-Muslim question, and the question of the future for Jews and Palestinians in their single land with its double name: Palestine-Israel.

DEFINING NEW EUROPE

If the phoenix of Greek mythology arose from the ashes of its predecessor, then the phoenix of New Europe originates in the ashes of Auschwitz, the cinders (so to speak) of Old Europe. In a keynote address given at a seminar in Brussels in February 2004, Romano Prodi said, "The first thing I did after my investiture as president of the European Commission was to visit Auschwitz."[3] The *first* thing he did, as if it were an act of piety; as if he were ritually putting Old Europe to rest again; as if the graves of the people murdered at Auschwitz were the tomb of the European past.

Another set of graves are included in this myth of the death and rebirth of Europe: the graves of the victims of the war that engulfed the world but broke out between European states on European soil. In his speech, Prodi alludes to both sets of graves, identifying them as formative influences for New Europe: "The horror of the Shoah and the terrible loss of life caused by the Second World War deeply marked Europe's founding fathers . . ."[4] (That is to say, the "founding fathers" of *New* Europe.) Two kinds of political carnage, or two different ways of meting out death, characterize Old Europe: war and mass murder: violence *between* states and violence *within* a state where the state turns on a group on account of the group's identity, on account of its "difference." It is clear from his speech that Prodi had both kinds of carnage in mind when he visited Auschwitz. Thus, though its primary significance is the Holocaust, Auschwitz comes to stand for the ruin of the old order as a whole.[5]

If New Europe arose from the ashes of Auschwitz, it did so by an act of negation: it defines itself as precisely *not* the Old.[6] Not that it emerged from the Second World War like Athena springing from the head of Zeus: fully formed. It is more accurate to say that, with the cessation of hostilities and the liberation of the camps, the incremental process of coming into existence—a process which is ongoing to this very day—began. Essentially, New Europe is a concept or idea. "The European idea," said Prodi, "was based on the firm determination to make sure the Europe of the future would be different—a Europe of peace, tolerance, and respect for human rights."[7] In other words, the new Europe would be marked by both the absence of war *between* states and the rejection of racism *within* a state: a "Union of diversity where differences are accepted and perceived as enriching the whole." This is the liberal Europe for which Macron is a standard-bearer. It is embodied today in the European Union (EU), although the *idea* is larger than any single organization or institution. The Council of Europe, along with the European Convention on Human Rights (and the European Court of Human Rights that supervises its enforcement), is animated by the same idea. Thus, New Europe is a work in progress, a living project. The project takes a variety of forms and is expressed through numerous international bodies, inspired by an open-ended set of liberal principles, and self-defined as a radical rupture with the past.[8]

Europe, however, is more than the sum of its principles. It is the product of its history, which, like Aristotle's substratum, persists through time, underlying the events that occur at the surface, carrying the past inexorably forward into the present. In other words, the past cannot be simply defined away, and the new Europe is not quite as discontinuous from the old as its proponents might like to think. The new Europe that Macron represents in the Paris embrace might be *new* but it is still *Europe*. In my reading of that embrace, the old Europe lies coiled in the new like an incubus, inflecting the very project that repudiates it. In short, while the new Europe defines itself as "not the old," it is better defined as *defining* itself as "not the old." This revised definition allows for the possibility that New Europe is not quite what it thinks it is; that it does not altogether know its own mind; that it knows only that part of its mind that consists of principles but not (or not wholly) the part that is shaped by the past.

"The Europe of today," Prodi said toward the end of his Brussels speech, "is not the Europe of the 1930s and 1940s." He added, "We must never forget what happened then, because remembering the past is a way of ensuring that such terrible events never recur."[9] This is well said, as far as it goes. But what if the past is remembered in a way that occludes the present? Or if memory is partial or selective? What if *some* "terrible events" are never forgotten while *others* are glossed over or swept under the carpet of history? What story does New Europe *not* tell when telling the story of its beginnings?

Indirectly, the historian Charles Maier raises this question in his essay "Consigning the Twentieth Century to History: Alternative Narratives for the Modern Era." Maier points out that there are "at least two divisions of the dominant narratives of moral atrocity."[10] One, "the Holocaust narrative," focuses on the Nazi Holocaust "as the culminating historical experience of the century."[11] The other, "the imperialist narrative," fastens onto "the domination of the West" in the form of imperial rule and colonization. However, we don't necessarily have to choose between these two narratives; indeed, if they turn out to be intimately connected, we *cannot* choose between them without distorting history. As Maier observes, "Recent interpretations of the Holocaust stress its continuity with genocidal practices in the colonies . . . as much as with specific anti-Semitism."[12] This works in both directions. So, on the one hand, "students of American slavery or South African apartheid have found the experience of German and European Jews extremely relevant for insisting on the moral horror of the experiences they are committed to studying."[13] On the other hand, Hannah Arendt, Aimé Césaire and others have argued that Hitler was not altogether innovative: the methods he employed and the atrocities he committed were forged in the European colonies. In the words of Césaire, Hitler "applied to Europe colonialist procedures which until then had been reserved exclusively for the Arabs of Algeria, the 'coolies' of India, and the 'niggers' of Africa."[14] In a similar vein, David Theo Goldberg writes, "The death of Middle Passage [was] a formative step on the path to the camps."[15] Certainly, there is room for argument about how far such claims can be pressed—about the precise ways in which the two narratives, one centered on the Holocaust and one centered on imperialism, are connected. But this much is certain: they are joined at the European hip.

Nonetheless, says Maier, there is a split over which narrative is emphasized by whom. Whereas, for the West, the key narrative is focused on the Holocaust, for "many observers outside the Atlantic world . . . the domination of the West over the massive societies of what once could be called the Third World established the preeminent historical scaffolding of the century."[16] In this difference lies the answer to the question I asked earlier: What story does New Europe *not* tell when telling the story of its beginnings? It does not narrate its colonial past.

"The Shoah," said Prodi, "was the most horrendous crime ever committed on European soil."[17] Although it is difficult to measure degrees of horrendousness, it would not occur to me to dispute this statement. It is, in a way, a wonderful thing that the Holocaust or Shoah is "a foundational myth" (to borrow a phrase from Helmut Dubiel) for New Europe.[18] However, horrendous crimes were perpetrated by Europe on *non*-European soil, too. The soil might not have been European, but the perpetrators were just as European as the Nazi perpetrators of the Shoah. These crimes belong to the *other* story, the story that New Europe does *not* tell when it narrates its beginnings. But both sets of crimes lie at the heart of the darkness of Old Europe.

To acknowledge this is not to diminish one iota the horrendousness of the Holocaust; it is only to expand the scope of Prodi's "We must never forget" to include other "terrible events."[19] Auschwitz, writes Goldberg, "exceeds comprehension . . . no matter how much we know about its details."[20] Yet he believes there is a cost to pay for the "contemporary focus on the unspeakable horrors of the Holocaust and the prickliness about anti-Semitism."[21] The cost of remembering is exacted in the form of forgetfulness. The "stress on the Holocaust," in his view, accounts for "what Stuart Hall . . . has characterized as historical amnesia, the now deafening silence in Europe concerning its colonial legacy."[22] Be that as it may, New Europe will never succeed in negating the Old if it glosses over the darkness of its "offshore" crimes, sweeping them under the rug, oblivious of their legacy for Europe today and for the world beyond Europe. In the end, both sets of crimes—home and abroad—emanate from the same European self.

Furthermore, the sundering of these two narratives is divisive. It sets up an unhealthy tension between Jews and other racialized minorities, whose experience of otherness is rooted in "horrendous crimes" that are part of Europe's colonial past. More to the point, emphasizing the Holocaust narrative at the expense of the imperialist narrative comes between Palestinian and Jew, which is the consequence that concerns me most in this essay.

THE HOLOCAUST AS FOUNDATIONAL MYTH

As a "foundational myth," the Holocaust or Shoah places Jews collectively at the heart of the New European idea. This point needs clarification.

The phrase "the Holocaust or Shoah" seems to suggest that the two terms are interchangeable. Actually, sometimes they are and sometimes they are not. "Shoah" (Hebrew for "destruction") specifically names the genocide against the Jews (just as "Nakba" specifically names the Palestinian catastrophe).[23] But "Holocaust" is often used to refer generally to a variety of kinds of mass murder carried out by the Nazis, including extermination of *all* groups—not only the Jews—to which the Nazi doctrine of *Lebensunwertes Leben* ("life unworthy of living") applied. The Roma (or Gypsy) population of Europe, perhaps a quarter of whom were murdered, fell into this category. So did people regarded as "unfit" either on medical grounds, such as the disabled, or on "moral" grounds, such as gay men. The Nazis also slew en masse political opponents, Jehovah's Witnesses, ethnic Poles, Soviet prisoners of war, and others; and it is not always clear which of these groups are encompassed by the word "Holocaust" and which are not. There is no sharply defined boundary around the word nor does there need to be. But if it is hard to determine its outer limits, it is clear that in its narrowest sense it names the annihilation of the Jews. Used *this* way, it is interchangeable with "Shoah." However, even when it is *not* used this way, the Jews are the group that immediately spring to mind. Possibly this is because of proportions: the (approximately) six million deaths amounted to two-thirds of the Jewish population of Europe and about one-third of the Jewish people globally. Or perhaps it is because anti-Semitism was such a fundamental axiom of Nazi ideology, and the so-called Final Solution of the so-called Jewish problem was a priority on the Nazi agenda. Whatever the reasons, the point is this: the word "Holocaust," like "Shoah," picks out the Jews, even if and when they function as a synecdoche for the victims of Nazism as a whole. Hence, whether we say "Shoah" or "Holocaust," Jews, as Jews, are written into the New European script with a distinctive significance— just as formerly they had been distinctively written *out*.

Let us now return to the big hug in Paris and see how the script plays out in the speech that Macron gave on the day. Netanyahu was in Paris at Macron's invitation in order to speak alongside him at a ceremony held at the site where the Vel d'Hiv (Winter Stadium) used to stand, in the 15th arrondissement, close to the Eiffel Tower. The ceremony, an annual event, commemorated the 75th anniversary of an infamous wartime episode in Vichy, France: the roundup by French police on July 16, 1942, of thousands of Jews, carried out in compliance with the wishes of the occupying

Nazi authorities. The roundup continued the following day, the number of
Jews detained in the indoor stadium (in atrocious conditions) swelling to
13,152.[24] All the detainees were soon deported to Nazi camps, eventually
perishing (apart from a handful of survivors) at Auschwitz or other extermination camps.

No one reading Macron's speech—nor, I imagine, anyone who was there
that day and heard him—could fail to be affected by the way he recalls
and narrates the terrible events they were commemorating. In one passage he dwells on the children—over four thousand aged between two and
sixteen—who were included in the roundup and then dispatched in "sealed
waggons [sic] for an apocalyptic journey."[25] He remarks movingly, "This
suffering—their suffering—beggars belief and cannot be put into words."
(Saying this, he comes as close as anyone can get to doing the thing he says
cannot be done.) I respect the eloquence and the compassion with which
he speaks of the fate of these children. My focus, however, is on the overall
thrust of his speech and its bearing on the question of how to interpret his
embrace with Netanyahu.

Macron opens with a mea culpa on behalf of the French state, owning
the actions of the collaborationist regime of Marshal Philippe Pétain. He
recalls the address given by Jacques Chirac in 1995 at the equivalent ceremony when a French president publicly recognized, for the first time, that
France was responsible. "So, yes, I will say this here," declares Macron: "It
is France that organized the roundup" as well as the "subsequent deportation." True, it was *wartime* France. But Macron hastens to make it clear that
Vichy was a continuation of prewar France in more than just name: "Vichy
and its doctrine unleashed the vices that were already a stain on the Third
Republic: racism and anti-Semitism." Moreover, if "Vichy was not the starting point for anything," it "was not the end of anything either." He explains,
"In today's France, the corruption of minds and moral and intellectual
weakness that racism and anti-Semitism represent are still present." What
has changed, however, is French resolve. "By acknowledging its faults," says
Macron, "France has opened the way to repairing them." He adds, "That is
to its honour. That is the sign of a strong nation that can face its past." The
overall thrust, then, is a variation on the idea of New Europe as a noble idea
but a work in progress. Vichy, in this speech, corresponds to Auschwitz in
Prodi's speech. And Macron's determination to face the past for the sake of
the future recalls Prodi's "We must never forget."

Again, this is well said, as far as it goes. But how far does it go? Which past does the new France face? Macron observes that the Third Republic was "the France where anti-Semitism metastasized in the elite and in society." But he does not point out how it was also the France that incubated anti-Arab racism when it developed a colonial empire in (among other places) North Africa. He remarks that neither racism nor anti-Semitism has disappeared. But he glosses over the first. Moreover, in the list he gives of victims of anti-Semitic attacks, the perpetrator in every case is Muslim and speaks Arabic. No mention of anti-Semitic acts carried out by the French far right. Nor any allusion to the discriminatory colonial policies on the part of the French state, which lie in the background of current tensions between Arabs and Jews of Maghrebi extraction.[26] In short, he chooses (to recall Maier's distinction) "the Holocaust narrative" over "the imperialist narrative," maintaining (in Goldberg's phrase) a "deafening silence" about France's colonial legacy. Is this a nation acknowledging its faults? Or is it a case of selective memory, where certain crimes are hidden behind the memory of others?

"But," someone might say, "given the occasion, is it not understandable that Macron dwelt on France's role in the Holocaust more than on its colonial empire?" Yes, except for three considerations. First, it is not just a question of this particular speech. It is clear from the whole way in which the state approaches the problems of the *banlieues* and issues raised by the Muslim identity of much of the "immigrant" population that France precisely does not face its colonial past.[27] Second, Macron himself brings up the persistence of racism alongside anti-Semitism. Yet, while he acknowledges the faults in France that account for the latter, he says nothing—not *less* but *nothing*—about France's responsibility for the former. It is one thing to place the emphasis on the Holocaust narrative—to dwell "more" on it— and another to pass over the imperialist narrative in total silence. As I said earlier, the sundering of these narratives is divisive. In this case, it tends to reinforce tensions between Jews and Arabs in France, thus *reproducing* the past rather than *transcending* it. This speaks to the general issue that lies in the background of this essay: engagement between Arabs and Jews today. But the topic on which I want to focus is the bearing Macron's speech has on the conflict in Israel-Palestine. Passing over the imperialist narrative in silence, Macron says nothing about the repercussions of the Holocaust for the Palestinians. Which is the third consideration.

I shall approach his silence via a spin that he puts on the theme of the two "vices" that Vichy "unleashed": racism and anti-Semitism. "In today's France," he says, "the corruption of minds and moral and intellectual weakness that racism and anti-Semitism represent . . . take new shapes, new faces and choose more surreptitious wording." He continues: "You only need to stop for a moment . . . to see, behind the new façade, the racism of old, the entrenched vein of anti-Semitism." This is a bit opaque. But later, when he says that the "vile monster is coming out of the shadows," the context makes it clear: he means specifically anti-Semitism. We are in suspense: What is he hinting at? What is the new shape or face of the monster? What "more surreptitious wording" does it go by? Near the end of his speech he gives the monster a name: anti-Zionism: "So yes, we will cede no ground to messages of hate, we will cede no ground to anti-Zionism, for it is a mere reinvention of anti-Semitism."[28] The sharp edge of his speech, then, is this: anti-Zionism is the new anti-Semitism.[29]

The sharp edge is blunted slightly by the fact that Macron defines neither Zionism nor anti-Zionism in his speech at the Vel d'Hiv ceremony. Later that day he delivered a speech at the Elysée in which, echoing the official policy of the EU, he indicated his opposition to the expansion of Jewish settlements on the West Bank and expressed his support for "a two-state solution," with Jerusalem as the capital of both states.[30] From that we can infer that he does not endorse any kind of Zionism that fails to meet these criteria. However, the question of what kind of Zionism Macron does or does not endorse is, in the end, beside the point. When he folds anti-Zionism, *whatever Zionism is taken to mean*, into anti-Semitism, he collapses a crucial distinction. He takes something that is always debatable—opposition to a form of nationalism—and turns it into something that is never acceptable: a species of racism.[31]

Which is exactly what occurs in the national discourse of the State of Israel. For, if the Holocaust or Shoah, seen through the lens of anti-Semitism, is a foundational myth for New Europe, unquestionably it plays the same role for Israel. And if, in the one myth, the phoenix of New Europe arises from the ashes of Auschwitz, so, in the other myth, does the Jewish state—a parallel Netanyahu was keen to emphasize in the speech *he* gave at the Vel d'Hiv ceremony. The first point to note is that he presented himself as speaking "on behalf of the State of Israel, on behalf of the Jewish people," thus conflating the two.[32] He then observed, "After the horrific world war,

France built itself anew . . ." Then came the parallel: "So did the Jewish people."[33] He continued, "Out of the ash [sic] of destruction, we established the
Jewish State," adding at once, "And it is the strength of Israel that is the one
certain guarantee that the Jewish people will never undergo a Holocaust
again." (He repeated it: "Never again," and a third time: "We will never let
it happen again.") The "we" that rose from the ashes after the war, the "we"
that established the Jewish state, the "we" that will never let the Holocaust
happen again, and the "we" for which Netanyahu, as prime minister of
Israel, assumed he is entitled to speak, is the collective "we" of the entire
Jewish people. The corollary is that any view that diminishes "the strength
of Israel" is a threat to the survival of the Jewish people, a step in the direction of another Auschwitz. Or, as Netanyahu put it at a news conference
in Budapest two days after his visit to Paris, "There is a new anti-Semitism
expressed in anti-Zionism."[34] It could have been Macron speaking.

Thus, the clinch in Paris was not purely a physical affair. Just as the two
men wrapped their arms around each other, so their words were interwo-
ven. Certainly, there are differences in the fine print, and their domestic
and foreign policies diverge in significant respects. But, fundamentally,
what each of them represents is a similar story of collective rebirth from
the same ash heap of the old Europe. The double phoenix—the Jewish state
and the new Europe arising from Auschwitz—is, in a way, the meaning
of the embrace in Paris between Macron and Netanyahu. New European
meets new Jew.[35]

Paris is an apt location for a romantic tango, and when I contemplate the
pas de deux between Netanyahu and Macron, a George Robey song from
the First World War comes to mind: "If you were the only girl in the world
and I were the only boy . . ." But they are not the only boy and the only
girl, which evidently is what they forget as they commemorate the same
truly "terrible events" together, the same tragic past that is their common
point of origin as New Europe and the Jewish state. Even as they remember,
they forget. They forget that their shared foundational myth of rebirth is
the starting point of catastrophe for a third party, the Palestinian people,
and their continuing dispossession. They forget that the Shoah led to the
Nakba. Either they forget it or they do not notice it, but I think it is neither
the one nor the other. It is more like repression of an inconvenient truth,
for the Nakba disrupts the sanguine reunion between a repentant Europe
and its age-old internal Other: the Jew.

THE VICISSITUDES OF JEWISH OTHERNESS

In *The End of Jewish Modernity*, Enzo Traverso observes, "The rejection of anti-Semitism and the political integration of Jews into the Western world did not lead to a dissolution of their alterity but, paradoxically, to its valorization."[36] This is a crucial insight. It means that the transition from Old Europe to New did not involve normalization of Jewish status but the recalibration of Jewish otherness, its transposition into another key: admired model rather than despised foil. This is how Prodi presents "the Jews of Europe" in the 2004 keynote address from which I quoted earlier. Referring to them as "the first, the oldest Europeans" and as "Europe's archetypal minority," he points to the Jews as a group that everyone should emulate: "We, the new Europeans, are just starting to learn the complex art of living with multiple allegiances," whereas the Jews "have been forced to master this art since antiquity."[37] Moreover, despite being persecuted, "they have made an immense contribution to European culture," not only as individuals "but also as a community." Thus, the Jews, collectively, are twice over a model. "The values that have guided them through the centuries," says Prodi, have provided a reference for us." Given the centuries of denigration and vilification, there is something wondrous about this testimonial to "the Jews of Europe." But it is also somehow unsettling; it certainly makes me, as a European Jew, uncomfortable. Once again, Jews as a group are being singled out. If at one time lower than the rats, as in the poem by T S Eliot ("The rats are underneath the piles/The Jew is underneath the lot"), now we are placed on a pedestal.[38] Setting out to right a wrong, Prodi reproduces the very essence of that wrong: setting the Jews apart as a group with a set of traits that they possess collectively by virtue of being Jewish. Whatever this is, it is not normalization. It is, as Traverso recognizes, another variation on the theme of Jewish otherness; and inevitably, if subliminally, it leads to the Palestinians being cast as the negative to the Jewish positive. The Palestinians have suffered twice over from Europe's othering of the Jew: first, under the dominion of the old Europe, then in the dispensation of the new. Let me try to bring this into sharper focus.

If New Europe defines itself by what it says it is not, so did Old Europe, which, from the beginning, defined itself as *not Jewish*. *Ab initio*, the Church announced to the world that it was precisely *not* the Synagogue, and the die was cast. What began in antiquity became an inveterate habit written into

Europe's cultural DNA. Esther Romeyn describes two of the forms that this habit took in modernity. Speaking first of the eighteenth century, she writes, "For the Enlightenment, with its investment in universalism and civilization, the Jew was a symbol of particularism, a backward-looking, pre-modern tribal culture of outmoded customs and religious tutelage."[39] In other words, Jewish is precisely what Enlightened Europe saw itself as *not*.[40] In the following century, the figure of the Jew was inverted: "For a nationalism based on roots, the distinctiveness of cultures, and allegiance to a shared past, the Jew was an uprooted nomad or a suspect 'cosmopolitan' aligned with 'abstract reason rather than roots and tradition.'"[41] Either way, the "not" tied Europe to the Jews.

It is "nationalism based on roots"—ethnic nationalism—that the new Europe primarily has in its sights when it repudiates the old. Take, for example, Germany, whose prewar ethnic logic of its national identity, in which "the Jew" was a foil to "the German," was replicated (more or less) by other ethnic nationalisms in Europe. Germany, in this sense, is a model of "nationalism based on roots." Moreover, it is where modern anti-Semitism begins. It begins with Wilhelm Marr, the journalist who coined the word *Antisemit* ("anti-Semite") and in 1879 founded the *Antisemiten-Liga* ("League of Anti-Semites").[42] If you were a German in the nineteenth century, you did not need to be an Anti-Semite (with a capital A) to be an anti-Semite (with a small a). Marr's anti-Semitic ideology struck a chord with the Germany of his day and, as it were, the next day and the day after that—all the way through to the rise of German ethnic nationalism in its most extreme form in the 1930s: the Nazi state. That is to say, anti-Semitism was not a mere fringe movement on the far right of German politics. It was, in effect, a nationalist technique. Indirectly, it was a method of inclusion: defining the true German by the false, the in by the out, the "is" by the "is not."

In a sense, *anti*-anti-Semitism—negating the negation of the Jew—has taken the place of anti-Semitism in postwar Germany,[43] which is not to say that anti-anti-Semitism is a *nationalist* technique exactly. Nonetheless, it is a technique for defining the state. Look at it this way. The redefined Germany is precisely *not* the nationalist Germany that culminated in the Third Reich, the *völkisch* Germany based on exclusion of the Other. The Jew was the archetypal stigmatized Other, excluded ultimately from life itself: the Final Solution to the Jewish question." Postwar Germany, defining itself as the polar opposite to Nazi Germany, sees itself as precisely *not* exclusionary. Which means that there is room for the Other—especially for Jews since Jews were especially excluded. What this means, in effect, is that the Jew becomes the archetypal *valorized* Other.[44] It is in *this* mode that Jews are included. They have not lost their Otherness, but they *have* lost their stigma. Moreover, they have acquired a certain status: they are the living proof that the new Germany is precisely not the old. To borrow a phrase from Michal Bodemann, this is the "ideological labour" that, as a minority, they perform for the majority society: it is the useful service they provide without having to lift a finger.[45] All they have to do is be Jewish. Jews are, so to speak, the Them *inside* today's German Us. They are an integral element in this Us—but precisely as Them.[46] Such are the vicissitudes of Jewish Otherness.

In and of itself, the rejection of anti-Semitism in the postwar German state is certainly something to be welcomed, even something to marvel at. But, seen in the light of the "shift from the stigmatization of Jewishness to its valorization" (Traverso), it is not quite what it seems.[47] For, insofar as the State of Israel is seen as the global Jewish collective ("the nation-state of the Jews"), the valorization of Jewish otherness leads to the valorization of Israel. As a result, rejecting anti-Semitism, which in itself is a worthy cause, is liable to elide into a different cause altogether: combating anti-Zionism.

Political anthropologist Esra Özyürek has uncovered exactly that in her research into "anti-Semitism-prevention training courses" in Berlin. Basing her conclusions on firsthand observation and a review of the material used on these courses, she writes, "Training programs designed for Arabs and especially for Palestinians work to show them that they are not victims in the Middle East conflict but rather equal partners in it."[48] If these programs are successful, Özyürek explains, "Palestinian students will see that there is no need to perceive themselves as victims and feel hostile toward Israel."[49] As an educational goal, this objective might be at home in a curriculum designed by the Israeli Ministry of Education for use in Palestinian schools in Israel. But what is it doing in a course taught to young Palestinians in Berlin in the name of countering anti-Semitism? A cynic will assume that these courses are merely a mode of *hasbara* (propaganda on behalf of the State of Israel). But I am not writing as a cynic. My skepticism goes deeper. It is based, partly, on my own encounter with the attitudes and the sympathies of Germans when I have visited Berlin to lecture on anti-Semitism and Zionism. Courses like these are symptoms of a society that is still entangled in its Jewish question—and for the same underlying reason as in the bad old days: angsting over its own identity as German. For which reason, the *Jewish* question is, and always was, the *German* question.

As it is with Germany, so it is with Europe as a whole. The Jewish question is, and always was, the European question: Europe's preoccupation with its own identity. In the old Europe, Jews paid the ultimate price for this question with the Shoah. As the Shoah led to the Nakba, the cost was transferred to the Palestinians. Now, the Palestinians are paying the price again. They pay twice over: once for Jews being the *stigmatized* Other and a second time for Jews being the *valorized* Other. First they pay the price for the anti-Semitic *exclusion* of Jews in Europe. Then they pay for their anti-anti-Semitic *inclusion*. Heads they lose, tails they lose. It is a double whammy, where both whammies are the consequence of Europe's immersion in its own question.

When I contemplate Macron embracing Netanyahu in Paris, what I see is a Europe that remains immersed in its own question. As for the Jewish state, it is immersed in (what could be called) its European complex. It would take another chapter—or rather a massive tome—to explore the ambiguities and nuances of what Europe means for the Zionist idea of Israel as the nation-state of the Jews. On the one hand, there is escape from Europe, the place where Jews were the internal Other, which prevented them from thriving. There is also the narrative of return to a distant homeland beyond the bounds of Europe. On the other hand, the stamp of Europe was impressed deeply on the way that political Zionism redefined Jewish identity and conceived of the Jewish state.

This ambiguity is present in the pages of Herzl's pioneering pamphlet *Der Judenstaat*. Was the state that Herzl envisaged a place where people who could not be Jewish in Europe could be Jewish, or was it a place where people who could not be European in Europe could be European? The wobble could not be clearer than in the section where he discusses the question of which territory to "choose" for the Jewish state: Palestine or Argentina? (Think about the chutzpah of that word "choose"—though it is not *Jewish* chutzpah but *European* chutzpah: it is the chutzpah of a Europe that regards the rest of planet Earth as its oyster.) Argentina, muses Herzl, has some material benefits to recommend it. But Palestine "is our ever-memorable historic home."[50] Here "our" clearly refers to "us" *as Jews*. In the same breath, he says, "We should there form a portion of the rampart of

Europe against Asia, an outpost of civilization as opposed to barbarism."[51] Here "we" means "us" *as Europeans*. In a similar vein (but more explicit and more pronounced), Max Nordau, speaking at an early Zionist Congress, said this: "We will endeavor to do in the Near East what the English did in India. It is our intention to come to Palestine as the representatives of culture and to take the moral borders of Europe to the Euphrates River."[52]

It is true that neither Herzl nor Nordau had the last word on Zionism, only the first; the modern State of Israel is not Herzl's *Altneuland*; demographically its population is not what he envisaged; a variety of distinctly Jewish forms of life thrive there; and so on. The world has changed. But it also stayed the same. Israel's geopolitical stance would not come as a surprise to Herzl. Like his theoretical *Judenstaat*, the actual Jewish state sees itself as an extension of Europe. It represents itself this way, it behaves this way. It even *thinks* this way in its view of "the Arabs."[53] It behaves (to adapt a phrase of Ehud Barak) as if it were the Western villa in the Eastern jungle. Which is just how Netanyahu portrayed Israel in his Vel d'Hiv speech. He described a world in which "militant Shiites" and "militant Sunnis" [jungle] are seeking to "eliminate European civilization." He added, "Israel [villa] is merely the first Western nation that stands in their way."[54] He followed this up three days later with this emphatic declaration: "We are a part of the European culture. Europe ends in Israel. East of Israel, there is no more Europe."[55] It could almost have been the voice of Nordau speaking from beyond the grave.

As I contemplate the Paris embrace in my mind's eye, it occurs to me that this is not a real embrace at all. What I see are two *self*-embraces, where each of the two parties is caught up in its own concerns. There is Europe (personified by Macron) embracing its newness via the valorized Jew, and there is the Jewish state (represented by Netanyahu) wrapping itself in Europeanness, happy to discard the cloak of the despised Other—which has settled firmly on the shoulders of the Palestinian in its midst, like a hand-me-down. The Jewish pariah of Europe has metamorphosed into the Palestinian pariah of Israel. Such are the vicissitudes of Jewish otherness.

AN EMBRACE IN JERUSALEM?

Bearing in mind the baleful role Europe has played, it is painful to contemplate the image of "the Jewish state" *embracing* Europe, new or old, while spurning (to put it much too mildly) the other people in its midst: the Palestinians. As an antidote, I want to close with an image of a different pair of partners, based on an article by Bashir Bashir and Amos Goldberg, in which the authors propose "a binational approach to the question of Israel-Palestine *vis-à-vis* the memories of the Holocaust and the Nakba."[56] As they make abundantly clear, they do not necessarily mean a binational *state*.[57] They are talking about an *approach* to the question of the future, the *spirit* in which the political debate is engaged. There is a variety of possible constitutional arrangements that might be consistent with the way of thinking that they have in mind. And that is the point: it is a way of thinking: thinking of the future for Palestinians and Jews together; seeing the two identities side by side rather than pitted against each other in a head-to-head conflict. In short, going from *binary* thinking to thinking *binationally*.[58]

With this thought in mind, imagine an embrace happening not in Paris but in Jerusalem—an embrace of the future shared by two parties, neither of which is Europe: two parties with one land between them. Though it might seem faint and farfetched at the moment, the image hovers tantalizingly in my mind's eye. I see it as emblematic.

NOTES

1. For what I mean by "New Europe," see the "Defining New Europe" section of the chapter. "The Jewish state" is how the State of Israel, seeing itself as the nation-state of the Jewish people, officially describes itself. For more than one reason the description is problematic. Consequently, the scare quotes should always be understood even when they do not appear in the text. For a thorough exploration of the idea of Israel as "the Jewish state," see Yaacov Yadgar, *Israel's Jewish Identity Crisis: State and Politics in the Middle East* (Cambridge: Cambridge University Press, 2020) and *Sovereign Jews: Israel, Zionism, and Judaism* (New York: SUNY Press, 2017).
2. The chapter began as a talk given at an "Arab-Jewish Engagement" meeting held at the Bruno Kreisky Forum for International Dialogue, Vienna, June 2016.
3. "Romano Prodi, President of the European Commission: A Union of Minorities Seminar on Europe—Against Anti-Semitism, for a Union of Diversity," Brussels, February 19, 2004, European Commission, http://europa.eu/rapid/press-release_SPEECH -04-85_en.htm. The event was jointly organized by the European Commission, the European Jewish Congress, and the Congress of European Rabbis.
4. Prodi, "A Union of Minorities."
5. It is significant that Prodi's first port of call was Auschwitz and not any of the bombed cities nor the site of any major battle in the war.
6. The distinction between "old" and "new" Europe as I am drawing it does not altogether coincide with the way Tony Judt draws it in *Postwar: A History of Europe Since*

1945 (New York: Penguin Press, 2005). Judt observes, however, that it was in the period immediately following the Second World War that "a new Europe was being born" (237). Moreover, by the end of the twentieth century, "Holocaust recognition" had become the "contemporary European entry ticket" (803, see also 820).

7. Prodi, "A Union of Minorities."

8. This is not to say that every head of every European state—even within the EU— necessarily subscribes (or subscribes without reservations) to all the liberal principles of "the new Europe," nor that there is consensus about how to interpret or apply these principles. The resurgence of the radical right in several European states prompts the thought that Europe today is becoming less "new" by the minute.

9. Prodi, "A Union of Minorities."

10. Charles S. Maier, "Consigning the Twentieth Century to History: Alternative Narratives for the Modern Era," *American Historical Review* 105, no. 3 (2000), 827. Although I am discussing narratives of New Europe rather than narratives of "moral atrocity," there is an underlying connection between the two topics, such that I am able to adapt Maier's argument to mine.

11. I have simplified Maier's thesis for the purposes of this chapter. The first of the two "divisions" he mentions includes not only the narrative that is focused on the Holocaust but also the narrative that is focused on the Gulag and the political killings under Stalin. However, as a *Soviet* agency, the Gulag falls outside the Europe that is under discussion here.

12. Maier, "Consigning the Twentieth Century to History," 827.

13. Maier, "Consigning the Twentieth Century to History," 827.

14. Aimé Césaire, *Discourse on Colonialism* (New York: Monthly Review Press, 2000), 36. The primary source for Arendt is *The Origins of Totalitarianism* (New York: Schocken, 1951).

15. David Theo Goldberg, "Racial Europeanization," *Ethnic and Racial Studies* 29, no. 2 (2006), 341. See also 336–337.

16. Maier, "Consigning the Twentieth Century to History," 826. More precisely, on Maier's account the key narrative for the West is either the Holocaust narrative on its own or together with the narrative focused on the Gulag or just the latter: "The Western narrative, retold by historians and philosophers, museum curators, film producers, and legal experts, focuses on the Holocaust and/or Stalinist Communist political killing as the culminating historical experience of the century . . ." (826). See note 11 above.

17. Prodi, "A Union of Minorities."

18. Helmut Dubiel, "The Remembrance of the Holocaust as a Catalyst for a Transnational Ethic?," *New German Critique* 90 (2003), 68. Needless to say, Dubiel does not use the word "myth" in the sense of fiction rather than fact (which would make him a Holocaust denier). He uses it in the sense of a narrative that is constitutive of the European Union's concept of itself. Throughout this chapter I use the word "myth" in the same general way: to denote the role or function of a narrative and not its truth status. "The Holocaust or Shoah": on the semantics of these terms, see "The Holocaust as Foundational Myth" section.

19. Compare Michael Rothberg, who refers to "a thinking of the human that is simultaneously post-Holocaust and postcolonial": *Multidirectional Memory: Remembering the Holocaust in the Age of Decolonization* (Stanford, Calif.: Stanford University Press 2009), 102.

20. Goldberg, "Racial Europeanization," 337.

21. Goldberg, "Racial Europeanization," 341.

22. Goldberg, "Racial Europeanization," 337.

23. The comparison here is between "Shoah" and "Nakba" as names, not between the events they name. That said, Bashir Bashir and Amos Goldberg point out (without making comparisons in terms of the scale of violence and murder) that, for Palestinians and Jews respectively, the Nakba and the Shoah are both "foundational catastrophes": see *The Holocaust and the Nakba: A New Grammar of Trauma and History*, ed. Bashir Bashir and Amos Goldberg (New York: Columbia University Press, 2019), 2.

24. "16/07/1942: The Vel d'Hiv Roundup," Holocaust Memorial Day Trust, http://hmd .org.uk/content/16071942-vel-d%E2%80%99hiv-round.

25. "Speech by the President of the French Republic at the Vel d'Hiv Commemoration," Consulate General of France in New York, July 16, 2017, https://newyork.con-sulfrance.org/Speech-by-the-President-of-the-French-Republic-at-the-Vel-d-Hiv -Commemoration. All subsequent quotes from Macron's speech are from this source.

26. See, for example, Maud S. Mandel, *Muslims and Jews in France: History of a Conflict* (Princeton, N.J.: Princeton University Press, 2014); Ethan B. Katz, *The Burdens of Brotherhood: Jews and Muslims from North Africa to France* (Cambridge, Mass: Harvard University Press, 2015); Paul A. Silverstein, *Postcolonial France: Race, Islam and the Future of the Republic* (London: Pluto, 2018); Paul A. Silverstein, "The Context of Antisemitism and Islamophobia in France," *Patterns of Prejudice* 42, no. 1 (2008).

27. See previous footnote for some of the references in a massive literature on this subject.

28. The original French text for the speech reads: "l'antisionisisme . . . est la forme réinventée de l'antisémitisme": see "Macron au Vel d'hiv: l'antisionisisme est la forme réinventée de l'antisémitisme', *L'Express*, July 16, 2017, https://www.lexpress .fr/actualite/politique/macron-au-vel-d-hiv-c-est-bien-la-france-qui-a-organise-la -rafle_1927737.html. "Mere" has been inserted in the official translation into English. This adds a certain emphasis but does not affect the basic sense of the statement. If anything, the definite article in "*la* forme" (not "*une* forme") strengthens the claim Macron is making. Literally: anti-Zionism "is the reinvented form of anti-Semitism."

29. Macron here adds his voice to the choir of voices that, especially since the turn of the millennium, have discerned a "new anti-Semitism" based on hostility to Israel. I have critiqued the "new anti-Semitism" thesis in several articles, including the following: Brian Klug, "The Collective Jew: Israel and the New Antisemitism," *Patterns of Prejudice* 37, no. 2 (2003), "The Myth of the New Anti-Semitism," *The Nation* 278, no. 4 (2004), and "Interrogating 'New Anti-Semitism,'" in *Racialization and Religion: Race, Culture and Difference in the Study of Antisemitism and Islamophobia*, ed. N. Meer (London: Routledge, 2014). For an illuminating account of the politics associated with the "new anti-Semitism" thesis, see Antony Lerman, "Antisemitism Redefined: Israel's Imagined National Narrative of Endless External Threat," in *On Antisemitism: Solidarity and the Struggle for Justice*, ed. Jewish Voice for Peace (Chicago: Haymarket Books, 2017), 7–20.

30. "Joint Statement by the President of the Republic and the Israeli Prime Minister," Elyseé Palace, July 16, 2017, http://www.elysee.fr/declarations/article/declaration -conjointe/. EU poicy is set out in the document "Middle East Process," EU, June 15, 2016, https://eeas.europa.eu/headquarters/headquarters-homepage/337/middle-east -process_en.

31. Which is not to say that anti-Semitism cannot be expressed as anti-Zionism. See references in note 29.

32. "PM Netanyahu's Remarks at Ceremony Commemorating the Deportation of French Jews," Israel Ministry of Foreign Affairs, July 16 2017, http://mfa.gov.il/MFA /PressRoom/2017/Pages/PM-Netanyahu-remarks-at-French-Holocaust-commemoration -ceremony-.aspx. All subsequent quotes are from this source. The conflation of the Jewish people and the state of Israel is the minimum definition of Zionism as a political ideology.

33. Netanyahu also says, "So did the Jews of France," though I am inclined to see this as an empty diplomatic gesture in the presence of his host, especially after his track record, calling for French Jews to emigrate to Israel following the Charlie Hebdo and Hypercacher shootings in January 2015. See his tweet from January 10, 2015: Benjamin Netanyahu (@netanhayu), "To all the Jews of France, all the Jews of Europe, Israel is not just the place in whose direction you pray, the state of Israel is your home," Twitter, January 10, 2015, 5:00 P.M., https://twitter.com/netanyahu/status/554035156474793984. I discuss this topic in "To Flee or Not to Flee: Is That the Question?," *International Journal of Public Theology*, 10 (2016).

34. Marton Dunai, "Hungary's Orban Welcomes Netanyahu, Vows to Fight Anti-Semitism," Reuters, July 18, 2017, http://www.reuters.com/article/us-hungary-israel-idUSKBN1A312O. Compare with "the spreading twin diseases of anti-Semitism and anti-Zionism" are "one and the same": see "Prime Minister Benjamin Netanyahu's address on the occasion of International Holocaust Remembrance Day, today at Yad Vashem in Jerusalem," Facebook page of the prime minister of Israel, January 27, 2015, https://www .facebook.com/IsraeliPM/posts/1022197521128326.

35. The "new Jew," in Zionist thought, is the opposite of the old, supposedly passive, Jew of the diaspora. This jaundiced view of Jewish life in the world down the centuries is known as "the negation of the diaspora." Israel, like new Europe, defines itself by negating the old.

36. Enzo Traverso, *The End of Jewish Modernity* (London: Pluto, 2016), 56.

37. Prodi, "A Union of Minorities."

38. "Burbank with a Baedeker: Bleistein with a Cigar," in T. S. Eliot, *Selected Poems* (London: Faber & Faber, 1954), 25. The poem was written in 1920.

39. Esther Romeyn, "Anti-Semitism and Islamophobia: Spectropolitics and Immigration," *Theory, Culture and Society* 31, no. 6 (2014), 92. The quotes within the quote are from Sarah Hammerschlag, *The Figural Jew: Politics and Identity in Postwar French Thought* (Chicago: University of Chicago Press, 2010), 7, 20. I have benefitted also from reading Romeyn's "Liberal Tolerance and Its Hauntings: Moral Compasses, Anti-Semitism and Islamophobia," *European Journal of Cultural Studies* 20, no. 2 (2017).

40. This is an oversimplification. The historian Adam Sutcliffe points out that there were "shifts and ambiguities" in the way Judaism was thought about in the Enlightenment; see Adam Sutcliffe, *Judaism and Enlightenment* (Cambridge: Cambridge University Press, 2003), 6. Nonetheless, predominantly it was seen as alien: "In much Enlightenment thought, the vital conceptual space of that which is most deeply antithetical to reason—Enlightenment's defining 'Other'—was occupied above all by the Jews" (5).

41. Romeyn, "Anti-Semitism and Islamophobia," 92.

42. Editors' notes in *The Jew in the Modern World: A Documentary History*, ed. Paul Mendes-Flohr and Jehuda Reinharz (Oxford: Oxford University Press, 1995), 332.

43. Not that this happened overnight, as Judt emphasizes: see Tony Judt, "From the House of the Dead: An Essay on Modern European Memory," the epilogue in his *Postwar: A History of Europe Since 1945* (London: Vintage, 2010). Moreover, I am not suggesting that the old anti-Jewish hostility has disappeared nor that it could not increase. I am speaking of the *idea* of Germany and Germany as a site of the New European project: *New* Germany, as it were.

44. Valorized is certainly the opposite of stigmatized, but I am not speaking here of philo-Semitism: the love of Jews and all things Jewish. The change I mean is a change in status, not a change in the place of the nation's affections. As valorized, the Jew becomes a symbol placed on a pedestal—not an object of love. I am grateful to Gertraud Auer Borea d'Olmo for a remark that alerted me to the need to make this distinction.

45. Michal Bodemann, "Ideological Labour: Theses on Jewish and Non-Jewish Theatres of Memory in Germany," in *Desintegration: A Congress of Contemporary Jewish Positions*, ed. Max Czollek and Sasha Marianne Salzmann (Berlin: Kerber Verlag, 2017), 37. I do not mean to imply that Bodemann would endorse either the use to which I am putting his concept or the overall argument of this chapter.

46. I am not suggesting that the old anti-Jewish hostility has disappeared from Germany nor that it could not intensify. What I am describing is Germany's official view of itself.

47. Traverso, *The End of Jewish Modernity*, 130.

48. Esra Özyürek, "Export-Import Theory and the Racialization of Anti-Semitism: Turkish-and Arab-Only Prevention Programs in Germany," *Comparative Studies in Society and History* 58, no. 1 (2016), 58.

49. Özyürek, "Export-Import Theory," 59. The irony here is that programs of this nature—programs designed to indoctrinate young Palestinians not to feel victimized by Israel—are themselves a form of victimization, even if the motive of the people designing these courses is benign.

50. Theodor Herzl, *The Jewish State: An Attempt at a Modern Solution of the Jewish Question* (London: Henry Pordes, [1896]1993), 30.

51. Herzl, *The Jewish State*, 30.

52. Quoted in Tom Segev, *One Palestine Complete: Jews and Arabs Under The British Mandate* (New York: Henry Holt, 2000), 150.

53. Including Arab Jews. See, for example, Ella Shohat, *On the Arab-Jew, Palestine, and Other Displacements* (London: Pluto, 2017).

54. Netanyahu, "PM Netanyahu's Remarks at Ceremony."

55. Barak Ravid, "Netanyahu Launches Blistering Attack on EU: 'Their Behavior Toward Israel Is Crazy,'" *Haaretz*, July 19, 2017, http://www.haaretz.com/israel-news/1.802143.

56. Bashir Bashir and Amos Goldberg, "Deliberating the Holocaust and the Nakba: Disruptive Empathy and Binationalism in Israel/Palestine," *Journal of Genocide Research* 16, no. 1 (2014), 79.

57. Bashir and Goldberg, "Deliberating the Holocaust and the Nakba," 93.

58. Bashir and Goldberg, "Deliberating the Holocaust and the Nakba," 79.

Chapter Three

PALESTINE IN ALGERIA

The Emergence of an Arab-Islamic Question in the Interwar Period

AMAL GHAZAL

There is no question about the centrality of the Palestinian question in shaping pan-Arabism and pan-Islamism in the twentieth-century Arab world. Though taken for granted, this particular topic remains underresearched and in need of further elaboration to explore the ways through which the question of Palestine came to define nationalist and pan-nationalist ideologies and intersected with regional anti-colonial movements.[1] The literature available on the topic focuses on the Mashriq (Arab East) and mostly on the years after 1967. In contrast, there is a lack of focus on the Maghrib (North Africa) and the interwar period. This chapter sheds light on how Muslim reformers in the interwar period responded to developments in Palestine and how those further solidified an Arab-Muslim identity as it was emerging in colonial Algeria. While the literature has mostly discussed the Messalist views on Zionism in the interwar period,[2] this study focuses on a group associated with the religious reformist movement, represented by the Association of Algerian Muslim Ulama. It analyzes content in the Association's newspaper *al-Shihab* and newspapers of Ibadi reformers associated with Abdelhamid bin Badis. It argues that the question of Palestine was originally regarded as one of a number of equally important questions in the Arab world, until 1936–1939, when the Palestinian revolt shifted the question of Palestine to the centre of attention. With that shift, the question of Palestine further sharpened a pan-Arab-Islamic identity in Algeria that was associated with anti-colonialism, be it against Zionist, British, or French colonialism. The way reformist newspapers in Algeria reported on events in Palestine and associated with them further highlights the fluid borders between pan-Islamism and pan-Arabism in the interwar period. Embedded in this identity was a rising tension with "the Jew," a tension defined by colonial practices in both Algeria and Palestine. Situating the Palestinian question at the intersection of British, French, and Zionist colonialism and anti-colonial nationalism is a testament to the entanglement of the Palestinian question, the Arab-Muslim question, the Jewish question, and Europe, as articulated in the introduction.

ALGERIA-PALESTINE IN ARAB HISTORIOGRAPHY

In her work on Palestine in post-colonial Maghreb, Olivia Harrison shows how Palestine became the figure par excellence of the colonial in the purportedly postcolonial present.[3] This strong presence for Palestine in the Maghribi political landscape goes back to the 1930s, when the 1936 strike in Palestine, followed by the revolt, increased public awareness of the Palestinian question and solidified it as the focal point of a regional discussion of colonialism and anti-colonial struggle. Thus, "Palestine as a metaphor" for the colonial, as Harrison describes it, predates the 1960s.

One of the first Algerians to voice concerns over the nature of the colonial project in Palestine was the Algerian writer and artist Omar Rasim (1884–1959). He wrote in 1914 condemning Rashid Rida's proposal to either conclude an agreement with the Zionists and accommodate the interests of both parties or devote all energy to fight Zionism. "This is a grave mistake by the owner of *al-Manar*," Rasim commented, "because he wants to please the intruders by asking the indigenous to concede and accept equality." Rasim categorically rejected Rida's proposal to reach an agreement with Zionists. That was not an option "because it acknowledges the leadership of the Jews and accepts these foreigners; [it acknowledges] sharing a land bought by [the Palestinians]' fathers' blood. No one but an Arab can own the land and no banner can fly but that of Islam . . ."[4]

Experiencing settler colonialism in Algeria, Rasim was perhaps more aware than Rida of the implications of a project that would empower European settlers at the expense of the indigenous population. The resemblance between the two colonial projects, one in Algeria and another in Palestine, did not escape Rasim's attention. If his comments indicate anything, it is that Algerians could better foresee the implications of the Zionist project in Palestine than some Mashriqis and thus should reject all forms of accommodation that meant concession.

Rida's position at the time, leaving the door open to several possibilities in dealing with the Palestinian question, was common among Arab intellectuals in the interwar period. Mapping the different reactions and propositions to the Palestinian question in the interwar period awaits further research. What is evident is that public attention at the regional level to the Palestinian question was sporadic before the 1930s; the Palestinian question was not yet perceived as more important than other questions, such as the question of the Caliphate or the Yemeni-Saudi feud.[5] Commenting on the Islamic Congress convening in Jerusalem, Basheer Nafi observed, "In 1931, the Palestinian question was not yet regarded as a problem of international dimensions. For most Arabs and Muslims, a proper understanding of the situation was still lacking, let alone a clear assessment of the ominous dangers to the very existence of the Palestinian people."[6]

The Palestinian revolt (1936–1939) changed that and made Palestine the centre of attention and a focal point for anti-colonial movements. The revolt did not only lead to a flurry of political actions in the Arab world but also to a dramatic increase in reporting on events in Palestine. This coincided with the proliferation of the press in the Maghrib, in Algeria in this case, and cross-border circulation of Arabic newspapers in the 1930s. Awareness of the regional and international dimensions of the Palestinian question increased due to the press and broader circulation of the news.

The revolt, Nafi also argues, led not only to increased awareness of developments in Palestine but also to the Arabization of the Palestinian question. His analysis, however, echoes the earlier historiography of nationalism that missed the strong connections between Arabism and Islam in the Mashriq and focused on versions of Arab nationalism that were devoid of religious overtones. Moreover, he does not pay much attention to the Maghrib, where the Arabization of the Palestinian question occurred in tandem with the crystallization of national identities, and often in different forms than in the Mashriq. To the opposite, the Palestinian question remained an important element of pan-Islamism in the Maghrib (and within certain circles in the Mashriq as well) following the revolt. This is not surprising given that both Arabism and Islam weighed equally in defining national identities and

ideologies in the interwar Maghrib, as they also did in the case of Palestinian nationalism at the time.[7] The case of nationalism in Algeria is illustra-
tive of this trend.[8]

Thus, this chapter looks at the engagement with the Palestinian question
through newspapers run by Muslim reformers who saw Palestine through
the prism of both Islam and Arabism, and of both the "Muslim world"
and the "Arab world" as new political concepts. It takes samples from four
reformist newspapers, the first three in Algeria: *al-Shihab* (1925–1939) of
Abdelhamid bin Badis, *Wadi Mizab* (1926–1929), and *al-Umma* (1934–1938)
of Ibrahim Abu al-Yaqzan; the fourth was in Cairo: *al-Minhaj* (1925–1931)
of Ibrahim Atfiyyash. While much is known about bin Badis, as a leading
religious reformer in Algeria and the founder of the Association of Algerian
Muslim Ulama, less is known about Ibrahim Abu al-Yaqzan and Ibrahim
Atfiyyash, who were religious reformers associated with bin Badis but
belonged to the minority Ibadi community and not the majority Maliki
one. Abu al-Yaqzan (1888–1973) was born in Guerrara in the Mzab Valley
of Algeria. He went to study in Tunisia in 1914, where he co-supervised the
Mzabi student mission. He became a member of the Tunisian Dustur Party in
1917, returning to Algeria in 1925. His experience in Tunisia writing for the local
press and getting involved in politics had a profound impact on him. Upon
his return to Algeria, he founded eight newspapers between 1926 and 1938:
Wadi Mizab, *Mizab*, *al-Maghrib*, *al-Nur*, *al-Bustan*, *al-Nibras*, *al-Umma*,
and *al-Furqan*. Each emerged after French colonial authorities closed down
its predecessor for criticizing French policies in Algeria and colonialism
in the Arab world. Abu al-Yaqzan established his own printing press in
Algiers, *al-Matba'a al-Arabiyya*, in 1931 with the help of friends such as
the Syrian religious reformer Muhibb al-Din al-Khatib, who resided in
Cairo.[9] A prominent religious reformer, al-Khatib founded and edited two
journals, *al-Zahraa* and *al-Fath*, the latter enjoying a status similar to that
of Rashid Rida's *al-Manar*. *Al-Fath* became a main source of information
on Palestine reaching the Maghrib in the 1930s. Al-Khatib had become
interested in the journalistic ventures of Abu al-Yaqzan through another
Mzabi, Ibrahim Atfiyyash (1886–1965), who also went to Tunis to super-
vise the student missions but was exiled in 1923 by the French authorities
for his political activism with the Tunisian Dustur Party. He lived in exile
in Cairo, where al-Khatib sponsored him and provided him with a press
license he owned. Atfiyyash used that license to found and edit the journal

al-Minhaj.[10] Both Abu al-Yaqzan and Atfiyyash considered al-Khatib a partner in the mission of Islamic reform and Arab and Muslim unity. The former cited *al-Fath* as being unique in the contributions it made toward those ends. Thus, like bin Badis, Abu al-Yaqzan and Atfiyyash were embedded in religious reformist networks encompassing both the Maghrib and the Mashriq, and to whom both Islam and Arabism were equally important as markers of identity and politics. Toward that goal, Abu al-Yaqzan, too, was a founder of the Association of Algerian Muslim Ulama. He invested in the press due to his belief that there was much need for the Arabic press in Algeria as a platform to criticize colonialism, defend Arabism and Islam, and promote the religious reformist project, and that need was associated with his politicization through regional affairs. For example, Abu al-Yaqzan mentioned the war in Tripolitania between Italy and the Ottoman Empire in 1911–1912 as the spark that ignited his passion for news and convinced him of the need for an Arabic press in Algeria. It was through the Arabic press—mainly from Tunis and the Mashriq—circulating in the Mzab that he was informed about the war in Tripolitania and other regional developments.

His itinerary thus sheds light on the importance of the press in forging regional networks of Muslim reformers and in exposing readers to regional developments, including those in Palestine. It is primarily through the Arabic press in the interwar period that the Palestinian question was introduced, explained and collectively discussed. As shown below, reports on Palestine were transmitted from one newspaper to another, with increased interest in the details as the Arab revolt was unfolding. It is how and how often Palestine was reported that shaped the regional association with it. As the interwar period witnessed the proliferation of national and pan-national ideologies, Palestine was bound to play a key role in shaping them. As it emerged as an "Arab" or a "Muslim" question, and given its religious symbolism as well, it became part of the Arab and Muslim political map, its cause associated with colonialism that those movements, reformist or otherwise, were fighting. This idea was best captured in Abu al-Yaqzan's description of *al-Umma* as "the echo of the East and of Islam in the Arab Maghrib, having the roar of Palestine, the rise of Syria, the awakening of Egypt, the life of the Hijaz, the ambition of Iraq, the wailing of Tripoli, the cry of Tunisia, and the pleas of Morocco."[11]

REPORTING PALESTINE: THE WESTERN WALL REVOLT

Both the Italian invasion of Tripolitania and the First World War galvanized North African activists to reach out to their counterparts in the
Mashriq. One of their major goals was to assist the Ottoman Empire in
its war efforts against European powers—Italy in the first instance, and
particularly France and Britain in the second. They hoped that an Ottoman victory would ultimately put an end to colonialism, especially French
colonialism in Algeria and Tunisia.[12] Those connections between Mashriqi
and Maghribi activists did not dissipate in the interwar period or with the
collapse of the Ottoman order. Different networks of connection emerged
in the interwar period, with Muslim reformism being the most prominent, enabled by the reformist press. While preoccupied with reviving the
Caliphate in the 1920s, Muslim reformers were also engaged in defining
the different versions of nationalism that emerged in the wake of both the
collapse of the Ottoman Caliphate and of European colonialism. In Algeria
in particular, Muslim reformers played a defining role in shaping Algerian nationalism to rest on the two pillars of Islam and Arabism. Algeria
became defined as both Arab and Muslim, and not one or the other, as
was the case with some versions of nationalism in the Mashriq. Bin Badis
played a key role in defining that version of Algeria nationalism with which
most Algerians identified, as did the postindependence nation-state.[13] Abu
al-Yaqzan played a role as well in the articulation of an Algerian identity
that was both Arab and Muslim.[14] Although ethnically Amazigh, Abu al-
Yaqzan and Atfiyyash endorsed Arabism as an anti-colonial identity and as
a pillar of Algerian nationalism echoing a larger trend whereby Arabism
and Islam were pillars of national identities developed in an anti-colonial
context. Parallel to Arabism and Islam there developed also the concepts
of an "Arab world" and an "Islamic world" that demarcated and embodied
Arabism and Islam. The local plight against colonialism was seen through
a regional prism, defined either as Arab or as Muslim-Islamic. In the late
1920s and increasingly in the 1930s, Palestine was becoming part of that
regional plight, and reporting and commenting on Palestine had become a
collective anti-colonial exercise. In the meantime, the Palestinian question
was increasingly defining both pan-Arabism and pan-Islamism.[15]

Writing from Cairo in January–February 1926, Atfiyyash's *al-Minhaj*
reported on "the States of Affairs in Palestine" under the headline "The

Islamic World," a news section reporting on different topics related to Muslims from around the world. He warned that Zionism was a threat to the East, and in particular to Islamic movements (of anti-colonialism and religious reform), as well as a British tool to establish colonial projects in the region, especially in the Arabian Peninsula. *Al-Minhaj* commented on the disparity in the living conditions between Zionists and Palestinians and dismissed the claim of Zionists that they were the indigenous population of Palestine. It published excerpts from the report of the Executive Committee of the 7th Arab Palestinian conference, outlining the privileges extended to Zionists by the British at the expense of the Palestinians.[16]

In another volume, under the headline, "Palestine's Calamities," *al-Minhaj* asserted that Palestine was a Muslim country with a leading role in early Muslim conquests, and the site of Bayt al-Maqdis, whose surroundings have been blessed. For those reasons, Muslims should pay attention to it and what is being plotted against its inhabitants. It warned against plans to turn it into another Andalusia, thus raising alarms regarding not just the possible loss of Palestine but also the loss of its Arab-Islamic identity and heritage. The British government, *al-Minhaj* stated, was not only enabling the Zionist project but also favoring Christians over Muslims. It cautioned that developments in Palestine might lead to a big explosion that would reverberate in the Muslim world.[17]

While *al-Minhaj* was raising alarms about the Zionist threats and British plans in the region, reporting on Palestine remained sporadic, until 1928–1929, when news spread about the Western Wall events. As Avraham Sela stated, the 1929 crisis had far reaching implications than previously assessed, both locally and regionally. At the regional level, it turned the Palestinian question "from an inter-communal to a regional one, and heralded a reassessment of Britain's Zionist policy."[18]

Wadi-Mizab published an article on May 18, 1928, submitted by the leading reformer and former statesman Sulayman al-Baruni (1872/3–1940), reflecting on the Western Wall events. Al-Baruni, and Ibadi from the Nafusa Mountains in modern day Libya, and a close friend of Mzabi reformers, was a towering political figure whose career also included serving on the Ottoman Parliament and leading Ottoman war efforts against the Italian invasion of Tripolitania in 1911–1912. His anti-colonialism cost him a life in exile, as the British, the French and the Italians prohibited him from staying in territories they controlled. The sultan of Oman, Sa`id bin Taymur, secured British permission for al-Baruni to reside in Oman, where he stayed until his death in 1940. Al-Baruni was kept informed on regional affairs through the press, which he received while in exile and where he often weighed in on major developments, publishing them in various newspapers, including Mzabi ones.[19]

Under the headline "The Descent of Jesus," al-Baruni, mixing eschatology and politics, explained the Zionist project as a step toward reviving the Caliphate in Istanbul, which would precede the descent of Jesus. This was his explanation of a prophetic hadith linking the prosperity of Bayt al-Maqdis to the destruction of Yathrib (Medina), and the destruction of the latter to Armageddon, which would lead to the conquest of Constantinople, the consequent appearance of the anti-Christ, and the eventual return of Christ. Listing additional hadiths with similar content, al-Baruni concluded that the construction around Bayt al-Maqdis sponsored by the Jews and the British, the destruction of Medina (presumably by the Wahhabis), the wars in Damascus, and the erasure of the Islamic heritage from Constantinople by "the atheists of Ankara" validated the above cited hadiths. Upon Christ's return, his supporters will be Muslims and faithful Christians (excluding British colonials) and his enemies will be Jews and atheist Turks. By bringing Jews to Palestine, the British will make them victims as they will not be able to defeat the united Christian and Muslim patriots. The Muslim conqueror of Constantinople will rid it of atheist and materialist Turks, with the help of faithful Turks and others. While it has been common to understand Zionism in eschatological terms, al-Baruni's comments reflect a primary political concern at the time that revolved around reviving the Caliphate.[20] Palestine, in his opinion, was the road leading to fulfilling that objective.

In December 1928, Abu al-Yaqzan commented on Jewish attempts to take over Bayt al-Maqdis, seeing it as a step to establish their own national country. He thanked Muslims in Palestine, Syria, and Transjordan for defending the sacred places of Islam on behalf of the Muslim world. He stated that news on Palestine had been scarce and brief, preventing him from discussing those matters in detail. Now that the details had become available, there was no excuse to remain silent. He provided the readers with information copied from *al-Manar*, putting the Zionist project in the context of British policies to divide Arabs and control their lands.[21] Britain's ultimate goal, however, was to divide and conquer the Arab world, using

Zionists against Arabs, and the Sharif family against al-Saud. Since the Balfour Declaration, he added, the British goal had been to separate the Arabs of Egypt from those of Syria and Iraq.[22]

In September 1929, *al-Shihab* reported on the Western Wall events, describing Palestine as one of the wretched Islamic countries that had not witnessed, since the Crusades, anything like it was now witnessing. *Al-Shihab* was surprised with what was transpiring between Muslims and Jews but reminded the readers that the culprits were extreme Zionists who were arrogant and belligerent, trying to humiliate Muslims in their own land. Wise Jews, however, it continued, had warned against this Zionist project since the Balfour Declaration. The only road to peace, it added, was to announce the failure of the project of "the Jewish homeland in Palestine," and for Jews to live in peace with Muslims as "Ahl al-Dhimma" (non-Muslims granted legal protection under Muslim rule). "That is there," *al-Shihab* added, but here "we live in harmony and peace with our Jewish neighbors.[23] *Al-Shihab*'s commentary reveals how the "internationalization" of the Palestinian question was also impacting Muslim-Jewish relations in the broader region. As commentators pondered how Muslim-Jewish relations were unfolding within the context of the Zionist project, they compared and contrasted such relations within their own local contexts. As we will see below, awareness of the Palestinian question was shaping Muslim-Jewish relations within the Algerian context.

Al-Shihab published in the next issue a condemnation in the name of Muslim Algerians of the horrors in Palestine, and called upon the French government to condemn developments in Palestine that hurt the feelings of its subjects, whose sacred religious sites were being violated. Their protest, it explained, was against "Zionists and not all Jews, and it extended to France of all countries."[24] Commenting further on developments surrounding the Western Wall events, *al-Shihab* described Palestine as a martyr country subject to colonial Zionist greed that was causing bloodshed, death, and destruction. It would only be when Arabs started defending their honor against Zionists that the world would start to recognize their cause and acknowledge their rights. The culprit was Britain, it continued, which was tied to the Balfour Declaration and to their need for gold "owned by Jews."[25]

Although alarms about the dangers of the Zionist project on Palestine were raised early on in Algeria, it is only after 1928–1929, David Cohen explains, that North Africans started to identify with the struggle of Arabs in Palestine and against the British mandate and the Jewish colonizers. They became more aware, and even more suspicious, of the Zionist activities in their own countries.[26] Thus, the events in Palestine, while raising awareness of the implications of the Zionist project in Palestine, were starting to inform Jewish-Muslim relations in the Algerian context and beyond. Connecting Zionism to broader colonial projects was also becoming more systematically articulated. At that moment the Palestinian question was seen or was at least reported as being part of the larger question of colonial designs in the region. The scale and severity of developments in Palestine became a mirror of the larger problem facing the former Arab provinces of the Ottoman state in terms of the loss of a political anchor and political umbrella against European powers. Thus, lamenting Palestine's fate under the British and the Zionists was part of a larger trend of lamenting the state of Muslims and Arabs in the interwar period. As Cemil Aydin notes, the interwar politics boosted pan-Islamic politics and revived "the illusion of the Muslim World."[27] The World Islamic Congress of Jerusalem was one embodiment of the idea of the "Muslim World," and symbolized Muslim solidarity over the question of Palestine. The Congress also featured an unprecedented Maghribi presence. To start with, the idea of an Islamic Congress in Jerusalem was the Tunisian Abd al-Aziz al-Thaalibi's, a pillar of the religious reformist movement in the interwar period. Among the attendees was also Ibrahim Atfiyyash, a close friend of al-Thaalibi since the former's days in Tunis. Reporting on the conference in 1937, the French considered it to be a considerable effort of organization by Muslims not only against Zionism but also against the "Western world"[28] and remarked that the Magribis at the Congress were among those who condemned European colonialism most vehemently.[29] Thus, events such as the World Islamic Congress of Jerusalem put on a display not only of solidarity with Palestine and attempts to discuss strategies but also ways in which different layers of colonialism, nationalism, and anti-colonialism intersected with the question of Palestine.

CENTERING PALESTINE: THE 1936-1939 ARAB REVOLT

This revolt in Palestine further galvanized anti-colonial movements and brought the Palestinian question to the center of attention on a larger scale than earlier events. The revolt coincided with increased activities of national and pan-national movements across the Mashriq and the Maghrib, for whom the struggle for Palestine was part of a longer geneal-ogy of anti-colonial struggle.[30] It also coincided with a proliferation of the Arabic press, including the religious reformist press that provided extensive and systematic reporting on the revolt. Throughout 1936–1938, al-Umma published its own editorials on Palestine, communiques from the Arab High Commission in Cairo, eyewitness accounts printed in various Arabic newspapers, and poems lamenting the state of affairs in Palestine or extol-ling the bravery and determination of Palestinian rebels, and al-Shihab provided regular updates and analysis.

For example, on November 3, 1936, al-Umma published an eyewitness account under the title "The Certain News on Palestine: The First Letter of an Eyewitness Who Visited Palestine. A Tour in the Martyred Country—Painful Scenes—Killing and Brutality—Burning and Destruction—Persecution and Assassination—Exile and Devastation," penned in Cairo by "the sad Arab." The reporter cut his vacation in Lebanon short and went to Palestine to closely observe what was taking place following the news about the escalation in Palestine. The passengers accompanying him from Beirut were all talking about the Palestinian question, he commented. One was listing "the horrors at the hands of the British, another recounting the assassination and abuse of Muslims by Jews, and another counting the big number of dead, the martyred, the injured and the devastated among Muslims and Christian Arabs at the hands of the British and Jews." Upon crossing the borders, they saw the devastation of the Zib village, a devasta-tion he described as being so painful to witness they could not stay longer. They proceeded to Acre and entered it after 171 days of a general strike and a revolt, "which is a Jihad carried out by Palestine with no precedent in history . . . since to hold a strike and a revolt simultaneously and for six months is miraculous."[31]

On the same page, al-Umma included news on Egypt, Syria, Lebanon, and Palestine under the headline "The Muslim World." This was followed by two reports on Palestine on the next page of the same volume. One was titled "Palestine Moves from One Jihad to Another," copied from al-Khatib's al-Fath, and the other "A Statement from the Arab Palestinian Committee in Cairo on Some Brutalities in Martyred Palestine."[32]

In August 1937, al-Umma criticized the partition plan as a solution based on British power rather than on justice, thus exacerbating the conflict in

Palestine and leaving a scar on the British legacy. It asserted that Palestine was the homeland of the indigenous Palestinian population and not of the Jewish immigrants, whose right to it existed only through the Balfour Declaration.[33]

As for *al-Shihab*, it included a report on Palestine, under the headline "the Political Month in the Worlds of the East and the West," commenting on how the Palestinian question had turned into a general Arab question, and not just one between the British and the Arab executive committee.[34] In the next volume, and under the same headline as above, it published a report with the title "The Calamities of Islam in Palestine," speculating when Zionist colonialism would end and for how long Palestine's struggle and its destruction would continue. It commented that Palestinians were not drawing sympathy from the world because they were Arabs and Muslims.[35] In the next volume, *al-Shihab* asked Arabs and Muslims all over the world to realize what the British and Zionist projects were in Palestine, and to remember those who sacrificed their money and their lives "under the wall of Arabism and Islam . . . to guard that sacred heritage which, if neglected by Muslims and Arabs today, it will certainly get lost.. and Palestine will be Jewish . . . Would the Muslim world and the Arab world be silent over the tragedy of their brothers in Palestine until complete destruction befalls them?"[36]

While *al-Umma* usually reported on the Palestinian revolt on the first page, *al-Shihab* did so after first reporting on Algerian affairs, followed by a report on North African ones. On the one hand, the Association of Algerian Muslim Ulama was one of several movements trying to shape Algerian politics, and thus asserting its role through analysis and news reports of local affairs was an utmost priority. However, the positioning of the news on Palestine at the time after those of Algeria and North Africa reflected not so much the list of priorities but the layers of identity of the Association. It was Algerian, North African, and Arab-Muslim. Palestine fell within that larger circle of belonging.

Projecting the impact of the events in Palestine on the Algerian scene, *a-Umma* reported on the People's Party's decision at its general meeting on August 4 to officially work for the Arab-Palestinian cause and "to fulfill its duty as an Arab-Muslim party in an Arab-Muslim country to defend the violated honor of Arabism and Islam in Palestine through the wicked cancer of British colonialism." As a result, it established the "Committee for the Defense of Arab Palestine," and held meetings in six different cities, attended by sixty thousand people, during which Msali al-Hajj and other Party leaders delivered speeches condemning "savage Zionist and British acts in a piece of sacred Arab land kneaded by the bones of the honorable Companions." A decision was subsequently taken to collect donations for the fighters in Palestine. *Al-Umma* followed this by another statement issued by the People's Party indicating that on August 14, 1937, while party volunteers were collecting donations "for Arab Palestine in cafes and shops, as foreigners did for Spain and Jews for Zionists," police forces forcibly and brutally arrested, beat, and imprisoned the volunteers and confiscated their papers and donations. The statement denounced those attacks and mockingly wondered if they were part of the freedom that France had promised Algerians a long time ago. In an infuriated tone, the Committee for the Defense of Palestine stated, "We are free, first and foremost. Our freedom should be respected and our honor protected, and we cannot remain patient for longer over the disrespect of our religion, freedom, feelings and honor."[37]

As such, the Palestinian revolt was another impetus for Muslim Algerians to contest French colonial policies and ascertain their rights to freedom of political action, similar to other groups who enjoyed such rights (hence the reference to foreigners and Jews). In that sense, the struggle for Palestine was an extension of the struggle for Algeria.

On October 26, 1937, Abu al-Yaqzan apologized for being distracted by local concerns and not giving Palestinian news the attention needed: "We have been distracted from shedding a warm tear for our sister Palestine, that the British colonialism subjects in this age of civilization and enlightenment to what Spanish colonialism did to the lost paradise of Islam 'al-Andalus' in the dark ages." Listing recent developments, he warned that British brutality and violence in Palestine would fail as they did in Egypt and Iraq, and that Palestinians would govern Arab and Muslim Palestine the same way Iraqis and Egyptians defied the British and led their governments.[38]

In addition to reporting on Palestine from a variety of Egyptian and Syrian newspapers, *al-Umma* published a poem with the title "Oh Arabism, Where Is Your Honor?" lamenting the state of affairs in Palestine by an Omani as an indication of "the impact of the Palestinian *nakba* (catastrophe) on isolated places." "We send our condolences to colonialism for awakening through its injustice every sleeping individual in the Eastern world," it added.[39]

The trope of Palestine as another Andalusia appeared again in the title of an article published on March 1, 1938. Most likely authored by Abu al-Yaqzan, it described the agony and suffering of Muslims all over the world due to colonialism. However, this was a preface to declare that no calamities equalled those of Palestine, which was "defending its Arabism and Islam." For twenty years, Palestine had been defiantly fighting colonialism and Zionism, and protecting the sacred sites of Islam, but it was being pushed to the abyss where its Arabism, Islam, and past glories would be wiped out. *Al-Umma* called upon Muslims to be offended by British policies of imprisoning and exiling Palestinian leaders and Ulama.[40] According to Abu al-Yaqzan's biographer, Muhammad Nasir, the French colonial authorities revoked *al-Umma*'s license after two reports published in March 1938, in which it criticized colonial policies in general and warned Muslims from putting their trust in foreigners, since they posed "a grave threat to Muslim unity," referring to British policies in Palestine and French ones in Algeria.[41]

As for *al-Shihab*, it reported on "Palestine the Martyr," with bin Badis reminding Jews how they had lived peacefully and freely in Palestine and how the marriage between British colonialism and Zionism had made a large number of them greedy and forgetful of that past. "They have turned Palestine into a hell," he elaborated, "and wounded the heart of Islam and Arabs." Bin Badis commended anti-Zionist Jews and reminded his readers that the situation in Palestine reflected enmity between Zionism and British colonialism on the one hand and Islam and Arabs on the other, making it clear that the enmity was not between all Jews and all Arabs in Palestine, or between Jews and Muslims. Zionism, he asserted, was rather a tool in the hands of British colonialism to divide the Arab body and defame Jerusalem. Only the Arab world and the Muslim world, he lamented, were raising their voices against developments in Palestine because "we—Muslims—are enemies of injustice, even if it occurred to those unjust to us." As an example, he recounted a conversation with a shop owner who was saddened by the German persecution of Jews while being aware of what Jews were doing to Palestinians. Bin Badis's commentary further revealed the degree to which the local context intersected with the regional and European ones. He concluded by reminding Muslims of their duty to defend Palestine, and that both Zionism and British colonialisms would realize that they faced "both the Muslim world and the Arab world, not only Palestine."[42]

Both the tone and the frequency of reports on Palestine during the revolt differed from previous years. There was more anger, frustration, and above all, stronger awareness of the colonial depth and breadth of the

Palestinian question. There were also stronger connections between local plights and regional ones. There is also the local Algerian context of the 1930s that witnessed an escalation between Jews and Muslims. There is no doubt that the events in Palestine further raised tensions between Muslims and Jews in Algeria and in the Maghrib in general. In Algeria in particular, what is known as the Constantine riots between Jews and Muslims took place in August 1934, two years before the Palestinian revolt. As Joshua Cole explains, "Jewish citizens and Muslim colonial subjects found that the terms of their inclusion in the political process drove them into different alliances with the colonial state and its local representatives, exacerbating tensions between Muslims and Jews in the city."[43] The Palestinian question, in the eyes of Algerian Muslims, validated their position toward Algerian Jews and thus added to those tensions. This was best articulated by Abu al-Yaqzan in 1934, a few weeks after launching *al-Umma*, in the wake of the Constantine events. Commenting on the events, he began by quoting a report from a newspaper from the Arab East in which the author described Jews' actions in Palestine as a turning point in their history, as they pivoted from being flexible, peaceful, and diplomatic to being rigid and confrontational, warning that those actions in Palestine had had repercussions all over the Muslim world. Abu al-Yaqzan saw similar changes among Jews in Algeria. They, too, he commented, deviated from their old practices and became hostile toward Muslims in Algeria. He warned that while Muslims could be lenient when it came to their national rights, they were not so when it came to their religious dignity. The riots in Constantine and the attacks on Jews were thus, he added, acts of defense against the sacredness of Muslims' religious sites. As such, Abu al-Yaqzan drew parallels between Jews in Palestine and those in Algeria, between the actions of Jews in both Palestine and Algeria, and those of Muslims in both places, concluding that the former were aggressors, the latter victims.

CONCLUSION

In his study on Palestine and Arab nationalism, Anis Sayegh noted that the "Arabs of North Africa have been guided by the events of the East since Algeria rose for the first time in this century, in the wake of the 1933–1934 incidents in Palestine . . . In 1937–1938, after the Palestine Revolt had broken out, the spark of revolt was transmitted to Tunisia and Morocco. The revolt developed into an all North African Arab nationalist movement uniting nearly everybody against the two common enemies, France and Zionism."[44] It is common in the historiography to portray North Africa as being at the receiving end of Arab politics, rather than being part of regional connections that can go in different directions. The revolts in Tunisia and Morocco in the 1930s were rather related to their own local genealogy of revolt and anti-colonialism rather than being a direct result of the Palestinian revolt. The latter came at a crucial time in the Maghrib, when nationalist movements had become more organized and more articulate about their anti-colonialism. The Palestinian revolt came to shape the regional dimensions of the anti-colonial struggle and to solidify cross-border connections sharing anti-colonial platforms. It also gradually centralized Palestine in national and pan-national identities, as they were articulated in the context of anti-colonialism and within the concepts of the "Muslim World" and the "Arab world." In the case of Algeria, the two worlds overlapped and intersected, with Palestine moving gradually to occupy a central space in both. That space was the platform through which Algerians criticized colonial projects in the region and created an association with the broader anti-colonial movements. It was also the platform through which they directly and indirectly contested French colonial rule by creating regional associations based on both Islam and Muslim unity and Arabism and Arab unity, tools and ideologies with which Algerians resisted French colonialism. Between Algeria and Palestine, colonial projects intersected and informed dynamics within anti-colonial movements, whether they articulated an Arab or Muslim identity of the colonized or the definition of Muslim-Jewish relations within the national framework.

NOTES

1. The major work in English on the role of the Palestinian question in the rise of pan-Arabism and pan-Islamism remains that of Basheer Nafi, *Arabism and Islamism and the Palestine Question, 1908–1941: A Political History* (Reading, UK: Ithaca, 1998). Abdel-Razzaq Takriti, *Monsoon Revolution: Republicans, Sultans and Empires in Oman, 1965–1976* (Oxford: Oxford University Press, 2013) is a valuable contribution to the importance of the Palestinian question in shaping leftist movements in the 1960s and 1970s.

2. Nedjib Sidi Moussa, "A Contingent Nationhood: The Jewish Question and the Palestinian Cause Within the Algerian Independence Movement," *Hamsa: Journal of Judaic and Islamic Studies* 4 (March 2018), 105–118. However, there is more focus in Arabic sources on the place of the Palestinian question on the political platform of

religious reform movements, including the Association of Algerian Muslim Ulama. See Bushra Ali Khayr Bek, *Mawqif al-Harakat al-Wataniyya fi Aqtar al-Maghrib al-ʿArabi (Tunis-al-Jazaʾir-al-Maghrib) min Qadiyyat Filastin bay al-ʿAmayn 1917–1939* (Damascus: Manshurat al-Hayʾa al-ʿAmma li al-Kitab, 2015).

3. Olivia C. Harrison, *Transcolonial Maghreb: Imagining Palestine in the Era of Decolonization* (Stanford, Calif.: Stanford University Press, 2015).

4. Muhammad Nasir, *al-Maqala al-Sahafiyya al-Jazaʾiriyya: nashʾatuha, tatawwuruha, aʿlamuha* 1, 403 (Algiers: al-Sharika al-Wataniyya li al-Nashr wa al-Tawziʿ, 1978).

5. This is evident in Nafiʾs *Islamism and Arabism and the Palestine Question*. It is also observed by reading Arabic newspapers in the 1920s.

6. Nafi, *Islamism and Arabism and the Palestine Question*, 123.

7. See Musa Budeiri, "The Palestinians: Tensions Between Nationalist and Religious Identities," in *Rethinking Nationalism in the Arab Middle East*, ed. James Jankowski and Israel Gershoni (New York: Columbia University Press, 1997), 191–206.

8. See James McDougall, *History and the Culture of Nationalism in Algeria* (Cambridge: Cambridge University Press, 2008).

9. Muhammad Nasir, *Abu al-Yadhan wa Jihad al-Kalima* (n.p., 1979).

10. Muhammad Nasir, *Al-Shaykh Ibrahim Atfiyyash fi Jihadihi al-Islami* (Muscat, Oman: Maktabat al-Damiri, 1992).

11. Muhammad Nasir, *Abu al-Yaqzan* (n.d.), 273.

12. Amal Ghazal, "Counter-currents: Mzabi Independence, Pan-Ottomanism and WWI in the Maghrib," *First World War Studies* 7, no. 1 (2016), 81–96.

13. McDougall, *History and the Culture of Nationalism in Algeria*.

14. Amal N. Ghazal, "Tensions of Nationalism: The Mzabi Student Missions in Tunis and the Politics of Anti-Colonialism," *International Journal of Middle East Studies* 47 (2015), 47–63.

15. This was even the case among Omanis in Zanzibar whose reporting on Palestine between 1936 and 1939 occurred in the context of defining Zanzibar as both Arab and Muslim, and part of the Arab-Muslim nation. See *Al-Falaq*, 1936–1939.

16. *Al-Minhaj* 1, no. 7 (January–February, 1926), 385.

17. *Al-Minhaj* 3, no. 1–2 (July 1927), 88–92.

18. Avraham Sela, "The Wailing Wall Riots (1929) as a Watershed in the Palestine Conflict," *The Muslim World* 84, no. 1–2 (1994), 60.

19. See Amal Ghazal, "An Ottoman Pasha and the End of Empire: Sulayman al-Baruni and the Networks of Islamic Reform," in *Global Muslims in the Age of Steam ad Print*, ed. James L. Gelvin and Nile Green (Berkeley: University of California Press, 2013), 40–58.

20. *Wadi Mizab*, vol. 83 (May 18, 1928), 1.

21. *Wadi Mizab*, vol. 112 (December 14, 1928), 3.

22. *Wadi Mizab*, vol. 112 (December 14, 1928), 3.

23. *Al-Shihab* 8, no. 5 (September 1929), 31–32.

24. *Al-Shihab*, 9, no. 5 (October 1929), 39.

25. *Al-Shihab* 10, no. 5 (November 1929), 44.

26. David Cohen, "Les Nationalistes Nordafricains face au Sionisme (1929–1939)," *Revue francaise d'histoire d' outre-mer*, 76–87 (1989/1990–2000), 6.

27. Cemil Aydin, *The Muslim World: A Global Intellectual History* (Cambridge, Mass.: Harvard University Press, 2017), 136.

28. Archives d'Outre-Mers, 10APOM/713, "Le Congrés Musulman de Jerusalem de 1931," June 18, 1937, p.1, Aix-en-Provence, France.

29. "Le Congrés Musulman de Jerusalem de 1931," 7.

30. Michael Provence, "Ottoman Modernity, Colonialism, and Insurgency in the Inter-war Arab East," *International Journal of Middle East Studies* 43 (2011), 205–225.

31. *Al-Umma* 97 (November 3, 1936), 2.

32. *Al-Umma* 97 (November 3, 1936), p. 3.

33. *Al-Umma* 134 (August 17,1937), 2.

34. *Al-Shihab* 8, no. 12 (November 1936), 384–385.

35. *Al-Shihab* 8, no. 12 (November 1936), 384–385.

36. *Al-Shihab* 12, no. 7 (October 1936), 346.

37. *Al-Umma* 135, no. 1 (August 24, 1937), 2.

38. *Al-Shihab* 141 (October 26, 1937), 1–3.

39. *Al-Shihab* 141 (October 26, 1937), 3.

40. *Al-Shihab* 156 (March 1, 1938), 2.

41. Nasir, *Abu al-Yadhan wa Jihad al-Kalima*, 283–4. Nasir is here referring to *al-Umma* 157 (March 8, 1938).

42. *Al-Shihab* 14, no. 6 (August 1938), 307–311.

43. Joshua Cole, "Constantine Before the Riots of August 1934: Civil Status, Anti-Semitism, and the Politics of Assimilation in Interwar French Algeria," *Journal of North African Studies* 17, no. 5 (2012), 839. See also Sophie B. Roberts, *Citizenship and Anti-Semitism in French Colonial Algeria, 1870–1962* (Cambridge: Cambridge University Press, 2017).

44. Anis Sayegh, *Palestine and Arab Nationalism* (Beirut: Palestine Liberation Organiza-tion Centre, 1970), 63–64.

ARCHIVES

Archives d'Outre-Mers, 10APOM/713, "Le Congrès Musulman de Jerusalem de 1931," June 18, 1937, p.1, Aix-en-Provence, France.

NEWSPAPERS

Al-Minhaj (Cairo)
Al-Shihab (Algiers)
Al-Umma (Algiers)

PART II

Beyond the Binary Division Between "Jews" and "Arabs"

Revisiting National Constructs

Chapter Four

ON ORIENTALIST GENEALOGIES

The Split Arab/Jew Figure Revisited

ELLA SHOHAT

Commonplace sentiments such as "Jews and Muslims have hated each other for millennia" and "Arabs and Jews have always been at each other's throats" have come to form taken-for-granted doxa within the global political landscape. At least since the partition of Palestine, such claims, widely disseminated in everyday conversation and in the media, and supported by a gallery of neo-Orientalist experts, continue to advance the trope of perennial enemies locked in perpetual conflict. Terrorist events in France—such as the "Charlie Hebdo" attack that also targeted the Hypercacher minimarket, which largely victimized North African Jews—have sparked countless comments of this type, enlisting yet another piece of visual evidence to buttress a seemingly unshakable historical truth. This idea of an eternal and intractable enmity, however, is in fact a relatively recent invention. In geopolitical terms, Jews and Muslims, at least up to the twentieth century, were often allied, having in common the enmity of (European) Christians. During their passionate march to the Holy Land, the Crusaders assailed the Jews as well as the Muslims within the territories that fell under their dominion. Not coincidentally, the (European) Christians regarded those sometimes called the "Jews of Islam" as welcoming or joining forces with the Arab/Muslim conquest, especially during the Moorish expansion into Iberia. As such, Jews epitomized the proverbial Trojan horse facilitating the infiltration of those variously called Ishmaelites, Saracens, Persians, Arabs,

Moors, Mohammedans, Ottomans, Berbers, Kabyls, Turks, Moslems, or simply Orientals. Christian theologians diabolized Jews and Muslims as a twinned allegorical unit, a kind of Janus-faced figure of "the enemy." Conceived together, the Jewish and the Muslim infidels became the joint objects of Christian fears and phobias, dwelling side by side within the Christian imaginary.

With the nineteenth century, as Western empires were expanding territorially and lording it over much of the globe, North Africa/the Middle East gained special significance. The 1798–1801 Napoleonic invasion of Egypt and Greater Syria orchestrated a political procession of a triumphant West trampling on a supine East, or, within a revised geographical relationality of North over South. At the same time, these imperial interventions unmasked, as it were, a religious unconscious whose antecedents could be traced back to the various Crusades and to the centuries-long wrestle between the European-Christians and the Arabs/Moors/Ottomans/ Muslims. Yet, within imperial modernity, religious formations were also increasingly converted into racial principles. Within this transformed grammar, the Hebrew/Arab, the Sephardi/Moor, and the Jew/Muslim were resignified within a new colonial order, performing initially jointly, but increasingly separately, in a still overwhelmingly Eurocentric arena.

THE BIFURCATED ORIENTAL RECONSIDERED

Beginning with eighteenth-century philological genealogies and proceeding to nineteenth-century racialized geographies, Eurocentric discourse produced a parallel series of otherized groups, most notably the (American) Indian, the Black/African, as well as the Asian/Oriental, which included the Semite—all positioned in contradistinction to the White/Aryan.[1] With the emergence of nineteenth-century biological sciences, and especially with the rank-and-measure racist theories that organized the "people of the world" within an ossified hierarchy, Hebrews/Jews, and Arabs/Muslims were classified together under the broad rubric of "the Oriental," and more particularly, as "the Semite." Eighteenth-century linguistic families transmuted into nineteenth-century biological kinships, engendering fixed maps of civilizational origins and ethnological archetypes, at once physiological and cultural.[2] This perceived kinship took many forms, found, for example: in Voltaire's Enlightenment account of the ancient Hebrews and

Arabs as vagabonds "infected with leprosy"[3] characterized by "the same thirst for plunder, the same division of the spoils,"[4] lacking in the requisite manners and spirit of nations; or in Ernest Renan's deterministic demarcation between the superior Indo-European and the inferior Semite, viewed as an "incomplete" race that failed to contribute "to this organic and living whole which is called civilization," and thus owed "neither political life, art, poetry, philosophy, nor science," and thus "nothing at all;"[5] or in Georg Wilhelm Friedrich Hegel's progressive philosophical synthesis that classified inferior civilizations, including the Semitic, as living "outside of History," and delineated world history as traveling unidirectionally "from East to West, for Europe is absolutely the end of History."[6]

Although the critique of Orientalism currently tends to be associated primarily with the objectification of Islam and Muslims, Judaism and Jews were Orientalized within the very same Eurocentric thesis or "negative dialectics." Jews and Muslims came to occupy the denigrated side of the Orientalist East-versus-West binary, at best embodying civilizational primitivity going back to "the beginning of time." Through a manifest hostility toward degenerate peoples, or sometimes even through an affectionate embrace of exotic others, the Hebrew/Jew and the Arab/Muslim were Orientalized conjointly. In Edward Said's rendering of this aspect of Orientalism's "Semite," he also pointed to the occurrence of a significant split between the negative and the positive poles of this archetype. Through "a concatenation of events and circumstances," Said writes, "the Semitic myth bifurcated in the Zionism movement; one Semite went the way of Orientalism, the other, the Arab, was forced to go the way of the Oriental."[7] At the same time, even prior to Zionism, with the Enlightenment, assimilationist emancipation, and the Hebrew *haskala*, it could be argued that the (European) Jew, who had gradually emerged as part of modernity, was sanitized of its tainted (presumed) Eastern extraction. This process was later further consecrated with Zionism's aim of redeeming the "Diaspora Jew" (the *ostjuden*, literally Eastern Jews) through affiliation with the West. Hence, the Zionist project paradoxically involved a de-Semitization of the Jew (as evidenced in the visual Aryanization of the Sabra phenotype and in the linguistic modernization of Hebrew designed to undo its Semitic syntax and pronunciation) even while simultaneously claiming an originary Semitic lineage. As the nationalist project became more palpable, Zionist discourse completely severed "the Jew" from "the Arab," abandoning those earlier variations of romanticizing the Bedouin and the local Arab shepherd as incarnating the Hebrew ancestors.[8] The de-Orientalization, in the sense of the whitening of "the Jew," increasingly took on more exclusivist characteristics manifest in the teleological readings of excavated archeological layers and, more recently, of the tracing of genetic roots in the East.[9]

In my earlier engagement with Said's genealogical critique of Orientalism, I was concerned with situating the Sephardi/Oriental/Arab-Jew vis-à-vis this bifurcation thesis. Invariably, for Orientalist discourse "the Jew" in question was assumed to be internal, located *in* Europe even if with fixed Semitic origins traced back to the East, while the conjured-up Arab was external, located *outside* of Europe. Within Orientalism, the Oriental Jew, I suggested, also went, like the *locus classicus* colonized native, the way of the Oriental (the Arab), rather than the way of the Orientalist (the Jew).[10] Already prior to Zionism, the Middle East/North Africa was subjected to the civilizing mission that was also demonstrably aimed at the indigenous Jews. But with the Zionist project, Jews in Muslim spaces, in order to be subsumed into a Eurocentrically defined homogenous nation, had to be systematically shorn of their Orientalness, violently cleansed of Arabness. The omission of the figure of the Arab-Jew has often reflected a broader ambivalence about the national affiliation of indigenous Jews in the post-partition casting of belonging. In my work, I tried to position the Arab-Jew within a relational mapping of complexly plural Arab/Muslim spaces, one which transcended the Eurocentric narratives of both "Jewish History" and the "Arab-versus-Jew" divide. Evoking the hyphenated Arab-Jew (or for that matter Jewish-Arab) has offered, it seems to me, a way to: (a) complicate the neat Orientalist division between the Hebrew/Jew and the Arab/Muslim, whether before or after the bifurcation into negative and positive poles; (b) rearticulate the nuanced spectrum between "the Arab" and "the Jew," especially given the historically vibrant presence of indigenous Jews of the Middle East/North Africa; and (c) reframe the perennial enmity narrative to stress a thoroughly syncretic Judeo-Muslim culture. The Arab-Jew, both as an empirical category and as a critical trope, has embodied not merely a mutually constitutive cultural past but also an imaginative future potentiality.

Although today "the Arab-Jew" has gained some visibility in critical discourse, the widespread notion of "the Jew" continues to be tacitly assumed to be European (Ashkenazi), whether or not (depending on one's position within the controversy over Jewish origins and indigeneity in Palestine or *Eretz Israel*) defined as "truly" of "Semitic descent." Thus, implicit in the question of the Arab-Jew is the elusive issue of who is this imagined Jew and who is this imagined Arab?—this pair that was once conceived together, only to be split later. Here I would like to examine the specific bifurcation that began prior to the Eurocentric formulation of Jewish nationalism, and focus on the place of the Arab-Jew within the imperial vision of the Orient. This chapter attempts to account for the ruptures generated in the colony even prior to the spread of Zionism and the massive dislocation of Middle Eastern/North African Jews in the post-partition era, a historical process that I termed elsewhere the "ruptures-before-the-Rupture."[11] The location of the Jew "in" the actual Arab geography raises a question about the Orientalist classification of Arab Jews: did they inhabit "the Arab" or "the Jewish" side of this tale of ancestral lineage? Today, given partition, diasporization, and competing nationalist imaginaries, the Arab-Jew can be said to silently occupy an ambivalent position within the bifurcation. Its ambiguous presence has much to do with persistent ideological realignments around Israel and Palestine. Probing representations in the era prior to the advent of Zionism and the emergence of Arab nationalism, meanwhile, allows us to ask: where would the indigenous Jew of "the Orient," and more specifically the Arab-Jew, conceptually fit within the split?[12]

Revisiting the narrative of the splitting into the two Semites, I am interested here in continuing to explore the place of the Arab-Jew, or the Jewish-Arab, within this ruptured Orientalized unit. During the *longue durée* of Orientalism, Arab/Middle Eastern Jews, I suggest, were located firmly— indeed as firmly as any Arab/Middle Eastern community in terms of claims to indigenous belonging—within the territories of the actual "Orient." The epidemic of scientifically formulated racial ideas that traveled from Europe to the colony did not pass over the Orient's Jews. Exploring instances taking place both before and after the bifurcation, I trace moments in which the Jew-in-the-Orient began "his" terminological journey of shifting from "the Arab" to "the Jewish" side of the equation. In what ways did the imperial rescue-of-minorities interventions impact such ruptures, recoding co-regional affiliations and engendering ambivalent indigeneity? And in what ways did the civilizing mission, in tandem with the arrival of the already de-Orientalized European Jew in the Orient, undermine the millennial syncretisms of Judeo-Muslim culture? Within the skewed version of a colonizing Enlightenment, Jews "in the Orient," I argue, experienced a double colonization, with its corollaries of assimilation and dispossession. One colonization targeted "the natives" in general, while the other was programmed specifically for the Jewish natives. The bifurcated Semite narrative, then, must account for the "travel" of an Orientalist discourse to the Orient where it encountered Jewish-Arab hybridity in the flesh. Thus, this chapter will reconsider the bifurcation in light of a significant assimilationist de-Orientalization (and later an explicit de-Arabization) project directed at Jews within the imperialized Orient, producing what could be regarded as the-split-within-the-split.

THE JEW-IN-THE-ORIENT: THE ANTINOMIES OF A CLASSIFICATION

In some instances, Orientalist discourse proper specifically thematized the indigenous Jew-in-the-Orient, transforming "the Jew" of the (still unified) Oriental figure into a particular Semite, at once Arab and Jew. More generally, the Orientalist representation of indigenous Jews within Muslim spaces rarely revolved around their Jewishness per se. From the nineteenth century, and at times on through the middle half of the twentieth century, Jewishness as a religious or racial category was subsumed under broader organizing principles premised on geographical location—region and country. Firm classificatory distinctions between Arab and Jew, as we have come to know them, began to take shape largely with the emergence of a Jewish nationalist vision whose traveling gaze zoomed in on the "exotic" Jews, sorting them out of their ambient materiality. Yet cracks and fissures had already been surfacing within Orientalist discourse with regards to the Jew-in-the-Orient. Here, I will address some specific moments in the formation of such fissures, prior to the grand rupture brought on with the emergence of Zionism and the partition of Palestine—i.e., those moments when colonial regimes first infiltrated Arab/Muslim spaces. Drawing largely on examples from Orientalist visual culture, the remainder of this chapter analyzes the Arab-Jew figure through a poly-perspectival grid in terms of the orchestration of desires and fears in relation to the diverse religious, national, and ethnic constituencies which formed the subjects/objects (and at times the audiences) of such drawings, paintings, and photographs. With the imperial expansion into North Africa and the Middle East, a rift began

to take shape in the iconography of the usually hitherto intertwined classifications of the Hebrew and the Arab, or the Sephardi and the Moor, or the
Jew and the Muslim. Some pictorial representations inadvertently capture
this shift, a transformation that dramatically impacted the perception and
conceptualization of Jewish belonging within Muslim spaces, resulting in
an ambivalent indigeneity.

Returning time and again to the scene of "the East," Orientalist discourse
took the form of varied subgenres that included: realistic accounts of the
contemporaneous East; historical narratives based on ancient and modern
events; present-day tales incorporating the ancient past as backdrop for
adventure, mystery, and romance; and fantastic tales adapted from mythology, the Bible, and travel literature. Sharing the homogenizing fixity characteristic of Orientalism, these subgenres, to varying degrees, portrayed a
colorful "peoples of the world" assortment, often including representations
of indigenous Jews to spice up the ethnological documentation with additional outlandish curiosities. Colonial visual culture "revealed" Jewish lives
in both the city and countryside within the contemporaneous Arab/Mus-
lim lands. Since the beginning of the nineteenth century, French depictions
of the Orient's *indigène* encompassed local Kabyl/Arab Jews, rendered, like
their non-Jewish neighbors, as a "natural" facet of the regional "scenes"
and "types." British representations of Iraq, similarly, recorded "authentic"
pictures of city and countryside "Natives," also including local Arab and
Kurdish Jews. Photographic albums arranged around regions and themes
had as their organizing principle a set of classifications that amalgamated
Jews with their Muslim neighbors, even when the caption indicated their
Jewish affiliation. An examination of this visual archive may shed light on
the place of the Arab-Jew within the Oriental/Orientalist split in the post-
Enlightenment era, a time when Europe's emancipated Jew was being whitened and de-Orientalized, just as the Arab was becoming darkened and
imperialized.

The photographs in the postcard series *Atlas Marocain* or *Moorish Atlas*
(c. 1912–1915), for example, documented Jews in exterior settings, in identical fashion to the representations of Muslim inhabitants, seen in *Group
de Juives à Tin-Mel* (*A Group of Jewish Women at Tin-Mel*, and in Arabic,
Isra'iliyat min jabal al-Atlas). And the series of Tunisian interiors featured
not only Muslim but also Jewish women as reclining odalisques, as is evident in *6207 scénes et types.—Femme Juive Tunisienne* (*6207 Scenes and*

Types.—Jewish Tunisian Woman) and *Femme juive* (*Jewish Woman*), dating back to the first quarter of the twentieth century. Other visual portrayals displayed city dwellers in their colorful traditional garb, as in Théodore Chassériau's *Juives d'Alger au balcon* (*Jewesses of Algiers on the Balcony*, 1849) and in his depiction of Constantine's Jewish quarter, such as *Scène dans le quartier juif de Constantine* (*Scene in the Jewish Quarter of Constantine*, 1851). The penetrating gaze into the inner sanctum of Jewish homes combined domesticity with erotica in a manner reminiscent of the Orientalist trope of the harem. Still other images focused on exterior scenes of busy souks and narrow alleyways, often featuring a synagogue or a feast, as in Eugene Delacroix's *Noce juive au Maroc* (*Jewish Wedding in Morocco*, c. 1839). In their ensemble these images now offer us a veritable Judeo-Arab colonial archive.

In travel literature, paintings, and photographs, the representation of the Orient tended to figure the local Jew as an integral part of the regional ethnic/racial landscape. In this sense, the Arabs were assumed by implication to be a multi-faith "race," with the Jewish-Arab implicitly forming a sub-category of "the Arab," alongside the Muslim-Arab and the Christian-Arab. Even while recognizing religious difference, Orientalist discourse rarely engaged the Jews-in-the-Orient as essentially distinct; they were conceived as part and parcel of Muslim spaces, alongside other ethnic and religious communities. The racialist view with which the Oriental/Arab was theorized in this sense included the native Jew. In fact, due to their religious affinity with the European imperial powers, Christian Arabs were in some ways more likely than Jewish Arabs to be split off from Muslim Arabs, as the cases of the colonial courting of Assyrians in Iraq and Maronites in Lebanon suggest. Both in content and form, Maghrebi and Mashreqi Jews were thus often exoticized in a similar manner to Muslims, regarded as just as indigenous to the region as their non-Jewish neighbors.

FROM JUDEO-MUSLIM SYNCRETISM TO AMBIVALENT INDIGENEITY

Although still uncommon in nineteenth century Orientalist representations, depictions of Muslim violence toward Jews began to surface, even if only sporadically. Alfred Dehodencq's painting *L'exécution de la Juive* (*The Execution of the Jewess*,[13] original 1860, surviving reproduction by the artist,

1861[14]) dramatically visualized the execution of a Jewish woman, imaged at the moment just prior to her beheading in the Fez public square. The painting was prompted by the 1834 case of Solica Hatchouel (or Zoulikha Hachuel), commonly known as Sol, a young Jewish woman from Tangier accused of apostasy (in Arabic *riddah*/*irtidād*), although, as the Jewish-Moroccan tradition relates, she insisted that she never took the *shahada* ("testimony" of joining Islam) in the first place. Sol, as recounted a century later by the Jerusalem-born journalist of Moroccan descent, Abraham Elmaleh, was falsely accused after refusing the romantic advances of a Muslim neighbor, and subsequently imprisoned and transferred to Fez, where the prince, the son of the Sultan Mulai Abd al-Rahman ibn Hisham (or in other versions the Sultan himself), also pursued the beautiful Jewess, promising to raise her to the throne.[15] During the three years of the case, the authorities offered her the opportunity to become Muslim in accordance with *shari'a* law. Some versions recount that the *qadis* (Muslim judges) even sent the *hakhams* (rabbis) to influence her, pleading with her to convert to Islam to save her life (an option permitted by Maimonides[16]). But Sol insisted that she had never abandoned her Jewish faith in the first place, and thus never renounced Islam. Her refusal to recant, despite imprisonment, torture, and seductive marriage offers, turned her into a folkloric heroine known as *"Sol ha-tzadika"* ("The Righteous Soul" in Hebrew). For the traumatized Jewish community, she became a symbol of piety and martyrdom, eulogized in written and oral form. Liturgical poems (*piyyutim* in Hebrew) and vernacular stories (*qiṣṣot*, from the Arabic word *qiṣṣa* for story, but in the Hebrew-based feminine plural suffix) were dedicated to the popular heroine, persisting within contemporary literature, for example, in the poetry of the Algerian/Moroccan-Israeli Erez Bitton.[17]

The story underwent significant permutations in function of distinct perspectives on the event. In one version, the Sultan became paralyzed immediately after the execution. Upon understanding the gravity of his crime, he visited her grave to plead for forgiveness, and Sol answered the Sultan's prayers and healed him. In gratitude, the Sultan, every day for the rest of his life, sent olive oil and candles to be lit for her soul in line with the Jewish tradition (*'ilui neshama*). Sol's grave became a site for *hiloula* celebrations, a pilgrimage for miracle seekers, especially for parents mourning the loss of a child, for infertile women desperate to conceive, and for the families of newborn baby girls asking for protection from misfortune.

FIGURE 4.1 Alfred Dehodencq, *L'exécution de la Juive* (1860).
© RMN—Grand Palais/Art Resource, NY.

Sol also became a figment of a transposed European imaginary, often portrayed as a Jewish Jeanne d'Arc. European narrators, especially French and
Spanish, highlighted the efforts made by their diplomatic services to save
Sol.[18] The Muslim Moroccan narrative, meanwhile, highlighted Sol's taking
of the *shahada*, and thus her apostasy, and even, in some versions, her blasphemy against the Prophet. Within twentieth-century anti-colonial discourse, meanwhile, the suspicious regard sometimes cast toward religious
or ethnic minorities reflected a wariness about their possible collaboration
with the colonial power. Whether or not such collaboration systematically
occurred, and whether for justifiable or unjustifiable reasons, the fact of
the colonial is crucial for narrating the ruptures within which such events
unfolded.

Today, nearly two centuries after the execution, and over half a century since the establishment of Israel and the concomitant dislocation of
the majority of Maghrebi Jews, Muslim Moroccans commonly have shown
their respect for the pilgrimages to Sol's gravesite, located adjacent to the
Jewish quarter, the *mlah*, in Fez. Leading visitors to the cemetery, some
guides make a point of confessing their own Jewish ancestry.[19] Apart
from a possible investment in promoting fables for touristic consumption, the very act of their enunciation suggests the absence of an anxiety
about Jewish ancestry, in contrast to the phobia historically associated with
the state/church-sponsored "*limpieza de sangre*," but which transmuted
into nineteenth-century racialist theories, including the Aryanist thesis
of tainted blood. Such touristic narratives give expression to the fluidity between Jewishness and Muslimness, understood as both biological/
familial and religious/cultural. While it is not unusual for revered Jewish
figures to become holy also for Muslims,[20] given the charges against Sol
it is unusual that she, too, according to some versions, became a holy figure, known as "Lalla Sulica" ("Lady Sulica").[21] In some popular versions of
Muslim-Moroccan rituals, Sol is also venerated as possessing healing powers, and her grave attracts not only Jews but also Muslims.[22]

Painted three decades after the execution, at the zenith of colonial rule
in Algeria and the ongoing French attempt to fully expand into North
Africa (and to generally seize lands from the declining Ottoman Empire),
L'exécution de la Juive can hardly be reduced, as it often is today, to a visual
demonstration or proof, a mimetic record, as it were, of the miserable conditions of Jews under brutal Muslim oppressors. The image, however, could

be viewed as a document of the fissures within the intertwined imaginaries of the Jew and the Muslim that were beginning to form within the post-Enlightenment colonial West, and which have had long-lasting ramifications for the perception—and the self-perception—of Jews within Muslim spaces. In this modern version of visualizing a violent history, the Orient is represented in an implicitly diacritical opposition to the Enlightened Occident, in this case to France's historic Emancipation of the Jews (1791). It also absorbs Jews-within-Islam into the pictorial template of Christians martyred by Muslims, not merely in relation to the Crusades' history but also in relation to contemporaneous Christians-within-Islam. In the painterly history of the three monotheistic religions, Orientalist canvases tended to spotlight the Muslim shedding of Christian blood. Delacroix's painting *Scène des massacres de Scio* (*The Massacre at Chios*, 1824), which was triggered by the events of the 1821 Greco-Turkish war that devastated the island, for example, depicted a horrific illustration of Greeks massacred by Turks. The emergence of images of Jews massacred by Muslims, meanwhile, instantiates a historically novel visual chasm between the two racialized religious groups in the Orient.

At the same time, however, even in the instances of depicting a conflict between native Muslims and Jews, the spectacle of horror is nonetheless anchored in the otherization of both, albeit within a subtly revised hierarchy which now places the Jew over the Muslim. In Dehodencq's title, *L'exécution de la Juive*, the Jewish woman remains nameless, devoid of historical specificity, although Sol's family ancestry at least partially traces back to the Sephardim who settled largely in Muslim-dominated regions when the *Reconquista*, the Inquisition, and the Edict of Expulsion drove the Jews out of Iberia. As commonly passed on in Moroccan-Jewish folklore, Sol uttered in Español/Spanish: "*Hebrea nací, y Hebrea quiero morir*" ("Hebrew I was born, and Hebrew I wish to die").[23] With its stress on "the Jewess," the painting's title, in contrast, transports the Sephardi/Maghrebi into the realm of the generic other, represented with the same objectifying gaze as the rest of "the Natives." Her Jewishness itself, furthermore, constitutes a rather ambiguous designation. Vis-à-vis the imperially desired geography of North Africa, the Jewess was rendered as a sacrificial symbol of Islamic fanaticism. Yet, vis-à-vis the France of the *lumière*, the traditional Jewess was anathema to modernity, to the Emancipation of the Jew. Within a homogenizing nation-state project, France's assimilation of "the other" was carried out according to the ideal of the (presumed) universal-over-the-particular. Although within the victim/victimizer duality *"la Juive"* is distinguished from *"les musulmans,"* she is also a premodern figure implicitly in need of the light of reason. The Jewess, like her people, has thus to be saved not simply from Muslim intolerance but also from the all-embracing backwardness of the Orient, simultaneously Muslim and Jewish.

As a metonym for her land, the Jewess becomes a gendered colonial trope par excellence of the kind of rescue phantasies propagated by penetrating European powers. Despite the modern split introduced into the coupled imaginary of the Jew and the Arab within Orientalism, in other words, the indigenous Maghrebi Jew remained, like the Muslim, in need of the universal civilizing mission. It would take almost two centuries and an epic-scale reconceptualization of belonging to redefine Jews as fully separate from their ambient Muslim culture, resulting in the contemporary reclassification of Jews as "naturally" and even "essentially" different from Arabs, and, for that matter, from their Berber, Persian, and Kurdish neighbors. The Orientalist polarizing of the Arab-Jew as distinct from the generic "Arab," and the dissolving of the Judeo-Muslim hyphen in favor of the Judeo-Christian hyphen, would take more than a century to become axiomatic. In the 2012 exhibition of the Paris Musée d'art et d'Histoire du Judaïsme entitled *Les Juifs dans l'orientalisme* (*The Jews in Orientalism*),[24] that distinction was indeed axiomatic. The Dehodencq painting is exhibited as a signal moment of "Jewish History," conceived as unified and unique, but this time under Islam. In the present-day reception of such imagery, the Jewish quarter is framed as a document of ghetto-like conditions, while the Muslim sword metonomizes brutal persecution—all within the trace-the-dots narrative that moves inexorably from pogrom to pogrom. The contemporary fixation on the Muslim sword-waving hand aiming at the Jewess's throat has produced it as an iconic emblem, incorporating it into a modern visual archive of supposed perennial maltreatment. (Dehodencq's graphic painting was perhaps not coincidentally selected for the cover of *The Legacy of Islamic Anti-Semitism*.[25]) Rather than merely an instance of what could be called "the pogromization" of the history of Jews-in-Arab-lands, *L'exécution de la Juive* reflects the formation of cracks between the indigenous co-regionists traversing the imperial seismic shift.

SCAPE-GHOSTS: ISLAM AS NEGATIVE EXCEPTIONALISM

The Dehodencq painting ironically cannot escape the particularity of its own civilizational heritage in both content and form. In content, it frames Muslims as essentially bloodthirsty, epitomized by the sword-holding hand and the threatening men hovering over the kneeling Jewish woman, as the assembled mob around the stage cheeringly watches, while one set of hands, presumably Jewish, pleads from the crowd. Betraying a certain air of *mauvaise foi*, this kind of French depiction of the-Muslim-versus-the-Jew has the effect of disavowing Christianity's own history of intolerance. In the tragic case of Sol, the *qadis* did not actively initiate forced conversion but implemented the *shariʿa* law concerning apostasy and blasphemy against the Prophet. The purpose of this comparison here is hardly to justify execution or to sidestep events of forced conversions within Muslim history but rather to suggest that the sudden sympathetic European investment in the plight of Jews-under-Islam was conspicuous in its lack of a lucid autocritique of its own Christian past. Within the post-Enlightenment moment, modern Europe now projected this unsavory history of violence and forced exodus onto a medieval alter ego—Islam. The image of the Muslim-as-killer-of-the-Jew submerged a history of the Christian-as-killer-of-the Jew during a period of over a millennium of religious wars. To an extent, the Muslim figure became a scapegoat for Christian culpability toward the Jew. The "fanatic Muslim" also masked anti-Semitism—or Judeophobia—within post-Enlightenment spaces, which manifested racial ambivalence toward the Jew as a foreign Oriental element on Western soil. Thus, the Jew-in-the-Orient got caught up in the narcissistic dualism of "tolerant West" and "intolerant East." The Oriental/Orientalist bifurcation shaping post-Enlightenment Europe, furthermore, was now being shipped to the colony,[26] splitting the indigenous "Semite" into the Jew and the Arab, or in a slightly different parlance, the "Oriental" into the Sephardi and the Moor.

Symptomatically, Sol became the subject of diverse passionate portrayals that took on a life of their own long after her death, from the account by the Spanish Eugenio Maria Romero's *El martirio de la joven hachuel, ó la heroina hebrea* (*The Martyrdom of the Young Hachuel, or The Hebrew Heroine*, 1837) to Bernard de Lisle and Dr. Mace's *Sol Hatchuel, The Maid of Tangier: A Moorish Opera in Three Acts* (1906). Focusing on the contemporaneous incident, Romero's text produced a dramatic chronicle that contrasted the joy of the fanatic Moors witnessing the horrid scene with the deep sorrow of the helpless Jews who were unable to avert Sol's fate.[27] Such liberal narratives emerged particularly after Napoleon's 1808 invasion of Spain when Enlightenment ideas were arriving in Iberia, and when the Inquisition, which had been officially inaugurated in 1478, was formally abolished in 1834.[28] It was the beginning of the decline of official *Reconquista* policies, which were only formally rescinded over a century later with the overturning of the 1492 Alhambra Decree in 1968.[29] Francisco José de Goya y Lucientes' critical gaze at the Inquisition in *Por linage de ebros* (*For Being of Jewish Ancestry*, circa 1814–1824) and *Escena de Inquisición* (*The Inquisition Scene*, 1812–1819) was also infused with this novel humanist spirit. In *Por linage de ebros*, the Jew occupies the visual paradigm of the traditional Christ's portrayal, now with the Church as the crucifier, offering in this sense a historical auto-critique. In Romero's text, in contrast, "the Moor" is rendered as the contemporary crucifier. At the same time, despite their different emphasis—one on self-indictment and the other on the indictment of the Muslim—both Goya's and Romero's descriptions of intolerance were imbued with Enlightenment ideals.[30] And yet, despite their critique of the church, such figural representations also relied, paradoxically, on a Catholic visual model for depicting martyrs.

In a historical irony, the liberal Spanish discourse avoids explicitly recognizing that the Jewish martyr from Tangier descended from Jewish martyrs from Spain.[31] Such texts do not express either a conscious mea culpa or a possible comparative historical reflection on the place of Jews within Christianity and Islam.[32] But this liberal document of Moorish barbarism did ultimately blur the traces of European intolerance. Alarmed by Muslim zeal, these texts give the impression of settling a long-repressed score with the ghost of the Moor, now traded over the Jew's body. The Iberian past is projected onto the Orient, ultimately cleansing Christian Europe of its history of spectacular religious killing. Although liberal texts may be read as employing Islam only as an allegorical example of a broader religious intolerance, nonetheless it is Islam that is singled out, in a kind of negative exceptionalism, as characterized by a pronounced propensity for fanaticism. At a time when the Inquisition policy was being abolished, precisely in the same year as Sol's execution (1834), such texts implicitly positioned Spain within modernity and rendered the Maghreb as "allochronically" medieval. In fact, however, the very representation of the martyrdom event was already entangled within the broader seminal event of its time, namely colonialism. As a haunting figure, the Muslim historically constituted the emblematic invader threatening Christian Europe. With the advent of imperialism, the unyielding *indigène* posed an additional new threat. Scapegoating the Muslim for religious intolerance also had the function of displacing colonial violence, especially that of France and Spain vis-à-vis Morocco. The historical ghost of the Muslim lingered on in the form of a modern scapegoat, becoming what could be termed a "scape-ghost."

The Muslim/Jewish divide was fully imbricated in the imperial "translation" of the Enlightenment modernity project. The vision of "*Liberté, égalité, fraternité*," with few exceptions, did not extend to the colonized and the enslaved. In Europe, the Enlightenment did not put an end to virulent anti-Semitism or Judeophobia. While in Europe even the assimilated Jew was subjected to post-Enlightenment racialization, in the Orient, the indigenous Jew was beginning to undergo a certain symbolic "whitening" but only vis-à-vis the Muslim natives. Not coincidentally, Sol, within a colonial-racial chromatic hierarchy, is visualized as lighter skinned than the darker Moors/Arabs/Muslims. The literal and metaphoric whitening of the Maghrebi Jew, in conjunction with the darkening of the Maghrebi Muslim, began to craft an Orientalist illusion of a de-indigenized not-quite-white Jew in the heart of the Orient; racial tropes were now divisively superimposed on local religious identities.

Reflecting this moment of de-Orientalization, *L'exécution de la Juive*, perhaps not coincidentally, shows a Jewish woman willing to die in the name of God visualized without the traditional head covering—a gendered practice of concealment in the public space shared with Muslim women. Indeed, in her novel *Road to Fez* (2001), Ruth Knafo Setton describes Sol as arriving at the execution site with "a long veil" over "her face and body," which the executioner forcefully "slashed . . . from her face."[33] Dehodencq's painting, in contrast, displays Sol's long, curly, dark hair devoid of any head covering even on the execution ground to hint that it might have been dropped. Her neck and upper chest, along with her shoulders, are also bare, with a certain ambiguity as to whether their uncovering was due to a violent act. In his portrait of Sol (c. 1860–1863) Dehodencq, similarly, paints the upper torso with a low neckline, just slightly above the breast, and displays Gypsy-like flowing dark hair—a style replicating his 1851 *A Gypsy Dance in the Gardens of the Alcázar, in Front of Charles V Pavilion*. Yet generally in his

sketches and paintings of Jewish-Moroccan women, Dehodencq did visual-
ize their colorful veils or head coverings, for example in *Mariée juive* (*Jewish Bride*, c. 1856–1863) and *Mariée juive au Maroc* (*Jewish Bride in Morocco*,
also known as *Juive et négresse, Jewess and Negress*, c. 1870). Rather than a
case of inconsistency, this comparison may illuminate a moment of relative de-Orientalization of the native Jew discernible even in the work of
the same painter. The décolletage, which is fashioned more in line with the
taste of the modern French viewer, furthermore, would have facilitated a
sympathetic reception of a traditional Jew. By shaping a Jewish figure who
is visually un-Jewish, the faithful Jewish-Oriental woman could embody an
imaginatively more assimilable figure in the West.[34]

Against the backdrop of the shared exoticization of Jews and Muslims, which involved colorful attire and a wide array of female coverings,
Dehodencq's semi-unveiling signifies a kind of termination of the Sephardi and the Moor as a Janus-faced figure.[35] The literal and metaphoric
unveiling of the Jewish woman reinforced the broader project of cultural
de-Orientalization. If the positioning of the Jew-within-Islam that dupli-
cated the massacred Christian-within-Islam detached the Jew from the
Muslim, the association of the Jew with a presumably higher civilizational stage furthered the conceptual de-indigenization of the Jew. Yet, the
very act of splitting paradoxically underscored the interconnectedness of
Muslim and Jew—i.e., it suggested that a racial and cultural process of de-
indigenization would be required to turn Jews, in contrast with Muslims,
into outsiders, foreigners, not truly indigenous. Today, in postcolonial
spaces, Maghrebi Jews, not coincidentally, have come to be conflated with
pied noirs, although the term initially referred to the white French colonial-
settlers in Algeria. But due to the rupture between indigenous Jews and
Muslims, the term has come to be applied retroactively to Maghrebi Jews.
Such designations and redesignations have come to underscore the ambiguous affiliation of the Arab-Jew, which began to unfold with the arrival of
the Oriental/Orientalist bifurcation in imperialized spaces. In the wake of
traveling modernity and colonizing Enlightenment, on the one hand, and
of the emergence of anti-colonialist nationalism on the other, the Orientalist de-Orientalization—i.e., of separating the Jew from the Muslim—had
further interjected an ambiguous indigeneity for the Arab-Jew, producing
an anxious positioning within the post-independence nation-state. A long
temporal "distance," nevertheless, would have to be traveled between the

not-yet-fully-colonized nineteenth-century North Africa/Middle East and postcolonial France/Britain before the Jew and the Muslim would be projected onto opposite ends of the civilizational clash generated by modernity.

THE-SPLIT-WITHIN-THE-SPLIT: A DOUBLY
COLONIZING ENLIGHTENMENT

Although French expansionism in Africa is clearly not the theme of *L'exécution de la Juive*, Dehodencq's painting reverberates with echoes from the colonial machine. Sol's execution itself took place in 1834, at a time when the Maghreb was defending its territories against French troops. After the seizure of Algiers in 1830, Morocco mobilized to fight the French, only to withdraw its troops in 1832, while also continuing to support the ongoing Algerian anti-colonial struggle. That intervention led to the Franco-Moroccan war in 1844, and resulted in the Treaty of Tangier, often regarded as a capitulation to the French. Against this backdrop, the stress on the 1861 representation of blood-thirsty Muslims in *L'exécution de la Juive* was embedded not simply in three decades of Algeria's colonization but also in the ongoing French/Maghrebi conflict. The painting appeared during the era of France's imperial project of fuller domination in the region, formally installed with the French Protectorates in Tunisia in 1881 and in Morocco in 1912.[36]

Taking place during this highly charged moment of colonial drama between the north and south shores of the Mediterranean, the 1834 Sol event itself prompted interest far beyond the Maghreb.[37] In the public outcry, the Muslim-killing-of-the-Jew came to be interpolated into a newly gendered narrative of minorities-rescue in the imperial outposts. Despite its horror, however, the event cannot be viewed simply through a binarist tolerance/intolerance lens. At a moment when imperial eyes were watching from across the Mediterranean and within freshly-occupied Algeria, the deeming of Sol Hachuel as a Jewish Jeanne d'Arc was historically overdetermined and replete with imperial overtones. Rather than an act of Catholic-Jewish solidarity, the "elevation" of Sol into a Christian iconic figure was embroiled in the effort to enlist Maghrebi-Jewish sympathies toward the French infiltration. France courted the Berbers/Amazighs in a similar way, highlighting their historic battles against the Arab invaders, at times arguing for their European ancestry, while also introducing legal regimes that subjected Muslims to differentiated systems of jurisdiction, for example the *shari'a* for Arabs and the *jama'a* for Berbers (as was the case of the 1930 *al-Dhahir al-Barbari*, or "Berber Decree").[38] Campaigning on behalf of minorities in a context of recently initiated colonial turmoil generated considerable pressure on both the Muslim authorities and the Jewish community, far beyond any intra-indigenous theological clash among the *ahl al-kitab* ("people of the book").

The sudden spotlight on "minorities" on one level meant potential benefits and support from an empire more powerful than the local regime. In its desperation, Sol's family, for example, is said to have received help from the Spanish consulate in Tangier—in yet another ironic historical twist for the descendants of the exiled Sephardim. On another level, the effort to modify the verdict outside of the local system signaled the danger of opening the gates to the invading colonizers. In their attempt to undermine a syncretic local political culture, imperial powers enlisted relatively disempowered groups to assist in the domination of the region. The Jewish/Muslim intercommunal decorum of negotiating cross-religious interactions, especially conflicts, as a result, was increasingly enunciated and performed on an imperial stage. In this shifting context, such negotiations were beginning to be framed and resignified within an imperial schema. The majority/minority dynamic within Muslim spaces came under colonial legal regimes, which spoke on behalf of the Universal while simultaneously mobilizing the dark undercurrents of the Enlightenment. The iconography of the sword approaching the throat—a vivid literalization of the "always-at-each-other's-throat" topos—masked the imperial gestures that were molding the Jewish/Muslim rupture.

Narrated within clashing religious and national desires, Sol's body has continued to be an object of contestation. Her name has been mobilized within a wide array of both universalist and particularist narratives. On one level, it was enlisted as evidence for: the pitfalls of religious intolerance; the dangers of Muslim fanaticism; *shari'a* oppression of non-Muslims; the perennial victimization of Jews everywhere; the specific oppression of Jews in Arab lands; and Muslim male power to possess Jewish women. On another, it gave evidence for: the role of minorities in the Arab world as a fifth column; the stereotyping of Muslims; the Orientalist caricature of Islam; and the tragedies engendered by colonialist meddling in the Maghreb and the Arab world more generally. Echoed in the contemporary era, including the unofficial realm of social media, violent acts have been explained within an Arab-nationalist perspective as encapsulating France's divide-and-conquer attempt to breed conflict between Jews and Muslims who had long lived together peacefully. Within a synthesizing multivocal approach, Saïd Sayagh's 2009 historical novel, *L'autre juive: Lalla Soulika, la tsadika* (*The Other Jewish Woman*; in Arabic, *Al-Yahudiyya al-ukhra*), meanwhile, reclaims Sol as Moroccan, implicitly at once Jewish and Muslim. The novel captures the calamitous moment prior to Sol's death, when "Jews, Muslims and the whole country" realize that "[t]he French have entered Algeria!"[39] The omniscient narrator compares the "stupor and a panic" (62) experienced by Tangier's residents—both Jewish and Muslim—to the anxieties triggered by the exodus from Al-Andalus. The reverberations of the shared Muslim/Jewish *Reconquista* trauma in the imperial present are rendered through a gendered privileging of the terror felt both by Jewish and Muslim women, described as "screaming" and "praying to as many saints as they could" (62). *L'autre juive* suggests that French colonial incursions led to an increasingly destabilized climate. Fearing that Jews were defying "the *Dhimma* pact which forbids alliances with the enemies of Islam" (64), Muslims came to distrust Jews. Sol's brother informs her that arbitrary Muslim violence against Jews had begun to occur with greater frequency (66). It is against this colonial backdrop that Sol's trial is said to have taken place. Later in the novel, in another calamitous moment during the French bombardment of Tangier, Sol's brother recalls her death, wistfully reflecting "if only . . . she had pronounced the shahada" (156–157)—regretting that Sol did not respond to the pleas to convert (or feign conversion) and thus ensure her own survival.

Though the novel describes the political disparities between the Muslim majority and Jewish *dhimmi*, it also ruminates on deeply shared Moroccan cultural heritages and familial bonds. In the following passages, the novel describes a world without borders, whether geographical, biological, racial, or linguistic. For the narrator, Sol's father Haim saw the North African past as one of not-infrequent changes of religious allegiance: "Over time, Haim had acquired the conviction that the person now called Abdallah actually descended from Alberto [i.e., Christian] or Benjamin [i.e., Jewish]. And this mixed past heritage was true of all the others" (74). Observing the mixed crowd in Tangier's marketplace, Haim celebrates the spectrum of physical traits: "[T]here was no fixed frontier separating the faces. Moroccan features crossed with Spanish and Saharan traits and complemented one another. Every whitish tint was touched with brown and every darker taint was touched by a white wave" (73). The languages overheard were equally mixed: "Berber words slipped into Arabic expressions with a djebel accent which geminates sounds and twists syntax and prosody and adds in words from Castile and Lusitania" (73). And for Haim, it was not a question of Babel-like cacophony, since "everyone understood everyone" (73). Here the trope of blood loses its connotations of religious purity (*limpieza de sangre*) or of class and racial superiority (*sangre azul*). The Jewish father, who believes that the "same blood flows within all veins," expresses his love for "all" (73). Through the depiction of this multi-faceted "mélange" (73), the novel transcends Jewish and Muslim religious differences to emphasize their deep and longstanding familial and cultural connections. The father even casts doubt on the aquatic border between the north and south shores of Gibraltar. Analogizing Tangier to an "open vulva" (73) to the Strait, watered by Spain, the Rif, and the southern lands, the father affirms that the Strait can never "separate" (73) Spain from Morocco. The novel, in this sense, invokes Al-Andalus/Sefarad not only as a trope of trauma but also of nostalgia for *convivencia*. Tangier serves as a microcosm of Moroccan hybridity—a *métissage* blessed by the Jewish father figure. As a historical prototype, the righteous daughter of Tangier, thus, comes to symbolize not only courageous sacrificial readiness to give one's life for one's ideals, but also the very fluidity of Moroccan Jewish/Muslim culture. *L'autre juive* interprets the Sol event as part of the predicament engendered by a French domination that shredded the Maghreb's social fabric. But, as encapsulated in the subtitle's epithets, meaningfully expressed in Amazigh, Arabic as well as in Hebrew—"*lalla*" and "*tsadika*"—this revisionist text "returns" the disappeared Jew back into indigenous Maghrebi history, allegorically reuniting the split Oriental figure.

RUPTURES-BEFORE-THE-RUPTURE: THE SUB-COLONIAL ENCOUNTER

Since the advent of Zionism, such violent episodes have been invoked for affirming a rather anomalous colonial/national project. The suffering of "Jews in Arab lands" has furnished an explanation for their departure to "the Jewish homeland," mobilized to justify Palestinian dispossession. In the French postcolonial context, the emancipatory metanarrative, meanwhile, has facilitated the admission of the ex-colonized into the presumably universal history of acceptable (subliminally Christian) modes of *laïcité* within the Hexagon republic. Yet, already in the pre-Zionist era, the emergence of imperialism's "minorities" discourse, and more specifically, the gendered narrative of saving-Jews-from-their-Muslim-captors, prepared the ideological ground for the post-partition severing of Jews from Arab spaces. The imposition of a colonialist Arab-versus-Jew narrative undermined the legitimacy of Muslim civilizational norms and axioms, and, with it, the place of Jews in the larger convivium of multiple communities. In these various imperial configurations, the indigenous Jew was conceptually torn from the past religious intersecting frameworks of both Islam and Judaism, a rift that would have long-term consequences for potential Jewish participation in decolonized forms of any future indigeneity.

Testifying to the formation of a fresh paradigm, this ambiguously colonial "minorities" discourse also manifested the cunning of imperialism's hypocritical reason. Within the realm of imperial prestige, the portrayal of the Jew in the colony as closer to the West than to the Muslim clearly conveyed a message of aligning the indigenous Jews with Europe. Emerging republican Enlightenment ideals were now enlisted in the service of imperialism, producing colonized peoples as at once *"frères"* and *"sujets."* Republican values, as we know, were "translated" in perverse ways in the colonies—hence French slavery continued because it was justified, as Montesquieu suggested, in certain climates[40]—a subject passionately debated by Haitian revolutionaries such as Toussaint L'Ouverture.[41] The contradictions of the Enlightenment became especially manifest throughout the Americas, but they were also visible in the Middle East/North Africa: first in the very entitled act of colonization, and then in the discriminatory practices of colonial rule. A shrewdly calculated policy of empowerment and disempowerment produced new colonized subjects who gained certain privileges over the majority, evident most visibly in the Algerian case, but with structurally similar tendencies elsewhere in the region. Thus, the point is not that there reigned an idyllic harmony between indigenous Jews, Christians, and Muslims (and, for that matter, between Arabs and various other regional communities such as Berbers/Amazighs, Kurds, and Turkmen), but rather that the production of the oppressed-minorities discourse and its translation into policies capitalized on some existing tensions and conflicts. At the same time, the novel imperial setting actively initiated and produced new real conflicts and symbolic rivalries, devastating a millennial fabric of relationality and engendering new material rifts whose ghosts still haunt us today.

Narrating the multifaceted cultural imbrication between Jews and Muslims in the *longue durée* is especially germane given the historical shift in the meaning of the very terms "Arab," "Jew," and "Arab-Jew." The shift transpired, then, even prior to the emergence of Zionism, in the wake of colonial modernity, with its discursive correlatives in the form of racialized tropes, Orientalist fantasies, and Eurocentric epistemologies. Against this backdrop, the conceptual schism between "the Arab" and "the Jew," or alternatively between "the Muslim" and "the Jew," can be traced back to the imperialized Middle East and North Africa. With the Enlightenment and its corollary, the Euro-Jewish *Haskala*, and later with Zionism, the Orientalist schema "whitened" the (Western) Jew, as the old schema began to be projected exclusively toward "the other" Semitic figure—"the Arab." The Arab-Jew, I have suggested, came to occupy an ambivalent position within the Orientalist splitting of the Semitic figure. Divide-and-rule imperial policies, furthermore, enunciated a new racialized grammar for a dynamic Muslim/Jewish religious-cultural matrix that had existed for over a millennium. In colonized Algeria, for example, the 1870 *Décret Crémieux* granted French citizenship to indigenous Jews but denied it to their Muslim neighbors, assigning the latter an inferior status pronounced in the 1877 *Code de l'indigénat*. Although an expression of the ideal of protecting-minorities, the decree engendered a significant parting that was forming long before the century-later partition in yet another colonial space, British-Mandate Palestine. The Arab-Jew, it can be said, came to possess an ambivalent indigeneity, "of" the Maghreb or Mashreq but "in excess" of the Arab/Muslim geography. Thus, the protecting-minorities paradigm was tainted due to its manipulative uses (the privileging of a selected group over the majority) and its differential application of Enlightenment principles in the colony—revealing the aporias of Republican colonialism.

While indigenous Muslims and Jews were subjected to French assimilation together, the incorporation of the Oriental Jew into the Occidental Jewish paradigm generated two parallel forms of assimilation—first, in relation to France as the emblem of the "universal" West; and second, in relation to France's emancipated European Jews (largely of Ashkenazi background), as the tokens of abandoned cultural particularity in favor of citizenship in the modern nation-state. Consequently, imperialized Jews began a process of losing their historical and cultural specificity within what could be termed a double assimilation process. Aiming to provide Jews with a universal education, assimilated French Jews, such as the politician Adolph Crémieux, actively participated in the civilizing mission, founding the *Alliance Israélite Universelle* schooling system not only in North Africa but also in the Middle East and the Balkans. The system embodied a pedagogical project that was simultaneously universalist (i.e., French) and particularist (i.e., Jewish-European). But by presumably becoming universal, the Orient's Jews were paradoxically transposed into the particularist idea of the assimilated French Jew. The Jew-in-the-colony was beginning to march on the same path as the emancipated European Jew. Orientalism's relatively unfamiliar non-European Jew was now becoming an intimate within the Humanist rescue vision, and even an internal ghost for an anti-Semitic discourse that was simultaneously Judeophobic and Arabophobic.

The spreading of the assimilationist vision by metropolitan French Jews, moreover, shaped a novel split in which the new Orientalist, the European Jew, reproduced the split that had already taken place in Europe, this time in the colony—i.e., a separation between the two intertwined indigenous Orientals, the Muslim and the Jew. With colonialist "emancipatory" practices such as the Crémieux Decree, the Oriental/Orientalist bifurcation, in other words, was taking shape outside of Europe even before the arrival of Zionism and the establishment of the State of Israel. Indigenous Jews in colonized Algeria had already been officially endowed with an ambiguous status that generated resentment on the part of Muslim-Algerians and disorientation on the part of the Jewish-Algerians themselves. Granted French citizenship and partially incorporated into the Enlightenment-colonial project, some Algerian Jews ended up identifying with the French, while others identified with the Algerians, at times even taking up arms with the nationalist movement. Others in the Maghreb, such as Albert Memmi, began by diagnosing the twinned pathologies of "the mind of the colonizer" and "the mind of the colonized" within an anti-colonial spirit but ended up seeing the necessity of Jewish nationalism.[42] In the context of the early 1970s, Muammar Qaddafi's call for the Arab Jews to return to their countries of origin was met with Memmi's vehement rejection of the possibility of such a return. This debate ultimately suggested a kind of burial of the very ontology of the Arab-Jew. Over a century of French domination of the Maghreb resulted in a Jewish/Muslim divide and physical displacement into *l'Hexagone*. Put differently, the colonizing mission of Enlightenment universalism gave way to seeking refuge in France's particularist form of supposedly race-blind republicanism.

With colonialism, Jewish Europeans also advanced their own version of the *mission civilisatrice*, exercising a new possessive hegemony in relation to their co-religionists in "the backwaters of the world." The modern schooling system of the *Alliance Israélite Universelle*, for example, attempted to displace indigenous Jewish methods of teaching, creating, and the transgenerational passing on of cultural practices. Religious/cultural artifacts also came under the usual colonial "rescue" rubric, for example, the centuries-long Arab-Jewish textual corpus—known as the *Geniza*—stretching from the Indian Ocean to the Atlantic. The initiative of rabbi and scholar Dr. Solomon Schechter to remove the documents from Ben 'Ezra Cairo synagogue to Cambridge University took place under Egypt's colonial authority, Lord Cromer. The dislocation reflected an increasingly dramatic Arab/Jewish split by which modern European Jews came to speak on behalf of all Jews, powerfully shaping Eurocentric representations of "Jewish History and Culture." The physical dislocation of the corpus of documents prefigured the demographic diasporization of the living bodies of the Arab Jews themselves in the wake of the Arab-Israeli conflict. Locating the split long before the actual partition of Palestine, in the colonial incursions into Muslim spaces, highlights the ways in which the colonial/modernity project triggered novel tensions and divisions. These antecedent fissures, prior to the emergence of Zionism—what could be regarded as the micro-ruptures before the macro-Rupture—foreshadowed the massive post-1948 dislocation of Arab Jews.

The initial fissures of these ruptures-before-the-Rupture resulted in the first serious splitting of "the Arab" and "the Jew," a splitting that became more pronounced, as we know, with the unfolding translation of the Zionist idea into a political reality. Already the fall of the Ottoman Empire, which triggered massive dislocations and consolidated ethno-national redefinitions of belonging, impacted the identity designations of indigenous Jews. Even after World War II, with decolonization and partitions, the process intensified, and life shifted for many communities, with population transfers that resulted in numerous transmutations of identity. The Jew-in-the-Orient, for the most part, continued to occupy the Oriental side of the bifurcation, but the signs of the cracks were increasingly more visible. The facts-on-the-ground *Yishuv* settlements, the 1917 Balfour Declaration, the UN resolution to partition Palestine, and the establishment of the State of Israel implemented a novel nationalist lexicon of Jews and Arabs. If Palestinians paid the price of Europe's industrialized slaughter of Jews, Arab Jews woke up to a new world order that could not accommodate their simultaneous Jewishness and Arabness. The anticipatory Orientalist split was to fully materialize only with colonial partition and its corollary of the dispossession of Palestinians and their dispersal largely to Arab zones, as well as with its concomitant dislocation of Arab Jews largely to Israel. While some, such as post-1948 Palestinians, have been shorn of citizenship for decades, others, like the Arab Jews, have partaken in forms of citizenship inhospitable to the complexities of their cultural identity. Today, the iconography of Muslims-killing-Jews reverberates with contemporary Islamophobic discourses. It evokes real and imaginary Jewish fears of Muslims that have persisted in the postcolonial diaspora in France, Israel, Canada, and elsewhere within Arab-Jewish exilic spaces. Such images are currently fetishized, however, as an "accurate" historical portrayal of a millennial Muslim persecution of Jews, within a self-fulfilling prophecy which suggests that the place of Jews can only be in their so-called "true land of origins," and thus, in a spatio-temporal leap, in the nation-state of Israel.

MUSLIM SPACES, JEWISH PASTS: THE QUESTION OF THE ARAB-JEW

Both as a historical community and as a contemporary critical topos, in sum, the "Arab-Jew" allows us to address the ambiguities of "the Jew" and "the Arab" within the Orientalist split—à la Said—into two Semites, one going the Oriental way, and the other the Orientalist way. Even prior to the formation of Zionism, with the traveling of Orientalism into the colony, the indigenous Jew-in-the-Orient disturbed the prevailing Orientalist classifications. The recognizable Jew-in-Europe, phantasmatically associated with distant Eastern origins, was replaced by a more palpably present, actually-existing Jew, decisively situated in the Orient. And if initially this newly "discovered" Jew-in-the-Orient was catalogued as simply Oriental, that same Jew—within a Euro-diffusionist minorities discourse—gradually came to occupy an ambivalent position vis-à-vis both the colonizer and the colonized. A de-Orientalized non-Muslim, the Arab-Jew nonetheless remained an Oriental non-European. For a post-Enlightenment trend which had already "elevated" Europe's assimilated Jew into the Orientalist/ White paradigm, the indigeneity of the-Jew-in-the-Orient became superfluous and uncontainable within the standard bifurcation. The portrayal of violent acts, which symbolically tore the Jew out of his/her Arab social landscape, underlined a broader de-indigenization of the Orient's Jew, now reframed as "in excess" of the Orient's geography. And while the position of "the native Jew"—as the Oriental—was being destabilized, that of the Muslim remained fixed within the terra firma of Oriental otherness.

The "native Jew" also remained Oriental vis-à-vis the European Jew. As a traditional Jew, he/she became increasingly subject to doubly assimilationist pressures, both carried under the banner of universalism, first from Europe's civilizing mission, and secondly from the modernization project carried out by the "emancipated Occidental Jew" in the name of the "modern Jewish values." Split off from the other Semite (the Arab), the assimilated European Jew was now empowered within the imperial process to spread the assimilationist project to the Jew in the colony. Fraternity among Jews was therefore no longer simply articulated within the enduring idiom of religious solidarity but more within a colonizing Enlightenment paradigm. In addition to a minorities-rescue discourse (about Jews) that was traveling to the colony, a shared religious affiliation (among Jews) facilitated a newly sub-colonial encounter between the European and the indigenous Jew. In this sense, the earlier de-Orientalization of the emancipated European Jew was now disseminated in the South and the East, as the Maghrebi/ Mashreqi Jew was remodeled according to a readymade post-Enlightenment blueprint. "Oriental Jews" had to be shorn of their "Orientalness"; within the new all-encompassing regime of de-Arabization, they could no longer be Arabs. The manufactured minorities discourse concerning the Middle East/North Africa region, supposedly intended to "save" the minority of Arab Jews, paradoxically, refashioned them as a new minority within a Eurocentrically conceived modern Jewishness. The imperial protecting-minorities endeavor, in tandem with the Jewish-metropolitan investment in emancipating their Oriental brethren, I have suggested, engendered a split-within-the split.

Colonial divide-and-rule strategy, along with Jewish-European assimilationist programs specifically directed at "the exotic Jews," then, played a crucial role in forming the ruptures prior to the post-partition Rupture. The imperial emancipation project displaced the longstanding designation, affiliation, and belonging of Jews within Muslim spaces. Thus already prior to Zionism and to the post-1948 demographic dislocation, their palimpsestic political, cultural, and affective indigeneity had been tangibly unsettled. The Orientalist bifurcation, formulated in post-Enlightenment Europe and now crossing over to the colony, only became magnified in the wake of Palestine's partition. Within this decolonizing genealogy, as the European-Jew has emerged de-Orientalized, and as the Muslim has been re-Orientalized, the Arab-Jew has dwelt in a kind of twilight zone. The question of the Arab-Jew has, then, to be persistently posed to complicate "the split," to more fully disassemble the essentialist Semitist idea and decolonize the conceptual divide. If the imagined Jew, within the split, forms a coherent unit, it would inevitably suggest that "the Jew" in question is defined, not according to a multi-regional religious affiliation, but in correspondence with a fixed nationalist paradigm.[43] Thus, a discussion of the splitting of "the Oriental" that speaks of "the Jew" without addressing a cultural geography, might implicitly reiterate: 1) a singular history, that of the European Jew; and 2) an ethno-nationalist redefinition of a previously religiously defined Jewishness. Such assumptions would subliminally impose a Eurocentric formulation both of Jewishness and of Arabness. To see the Arab-as-the-Oriental and the Jew-as-the-Orientalist, and to attempt to regroup the two under the pre-bifurcated category of "the Semite," may inadvertently reproduce the Arab-as-East and the Jew-as-West, thus reaffirming the very supposition that the critique of Orientalism seeks to dismantle.

A narrative of the fracturing into two Semites, which sidesteps or brackets the question of the Arab-Jew, may also risk a slippage into a stable nationalist lexicon of Jewishness and Arabness as irreconcilable. The question of the Arab-Jew, then, must continue to be posed if one is to avoid the conflation of Jewish religious with ethno-national formation. But a view that stresses the Arabness of the Arab-Jew, rather than "disappearing" that Arab-Jewishness into a single univocal form of Judeity, unsettles the ethno-nationalist Zionist narrative. After all, rather than subsume the Arab-Jew under the generic notion of a racialized European Jew, one could as well situate the same Arab-Jew on the Arab side of the bifurcation, within the larger colonialist Orientalization of the Arab. Indeed, within Arab anti-colonial discourse, the indigenous Jew, who initially also "went the Oriental way," formed part of an inclusive notion of Arabness. But with imperialism, and especially with Zionism, and in their wake with Arab nationalism's ambivalent gaze on the Arab-Jew, that affiliation began to fray. The Orientalist splitting of the Oriental was now compounded by a nationalist splitting. The connotation of the phrase "Arab-Jew" was transformed from being a taken-for-granted marker of religious (Jewish) and cultural (Arab) affiliation into a vexed question mark within competing nationalisms, each perceiving the "Arab-Jew" as "in excess." In a different fashion, the two nationalisms came to view one side of the hyphen in "the Arab-Jew" suspiciously. In the Arab world "the Jew" became out of bounds, while in the Jewish state, "the Arab" became out of bounds; hence, the "Arab-Jew," or the "Jewish-Arab," inevitably came to seem an ontological impossibility.

With the imperial and with subsequent Zionist seismic shifts, the long-standing Jewish feeling of "at-homeness" in the Arab world was thrown into doubt, thus giving way to a destabilizing sense of vulnerability, to the point that the post-1948 evacuation of Arab spaces, a century later, was gradually seen as historically inevitable. Thereafter, in postcolonial diasporic spaces, a sense of Arab belonging for Jews came to be narrated largely in the melancholic past tense. To revisit the imagined place of the Arab-Jew within the Orientalist bifurcation is thus vital precisely because the slippage in the definition of "the Jew"—between the religious and the ethno-national connotations—replicates the historical erasure of the Arabness of the Jew. Such slippage also undermines a more heteroglossic conceptualization of Arabness, which eschews an anxiously-voiced homogenous nationalism in favor of a prism of what might be called relational indigeneity. The (Arab) Jew, in other words, could be narrated as a differentiation within Arabness, without having to resurrect a pre-bifurcated Semitic figure, highlighting instead the complex overlay of cultures, a continuum of subtle differences and similarities. Within the long-term genealogy of what is often today considered the deep and presumably unhealable rift between Muslims and Jews, a different picture emerges when articulated through a de-Orientalizing genealogy that highlights a co-imbricated Judeo-Muslim cultural geography. As an empirical category and as a critical trope, then, the Arab-Jew, or Jewish-Arab, encourages us to go beyond the fait accompli of the violent ruptures, within a reconceived decolonizing framework of mutually constituted Jewishness and Arabness.

NOTES

This chapter is an abridged version of an essay of the same title published in *The Edinburgh Companion to the Postcolonial Middle East*, ed. Anna Ball and Karim Mattar, (Edinburgh: Edinburgh University Press, 2019).

1. For a critique of the "Aryan model," see Martin Bernal, *Black Athena: The Afroasiatic Roots of Classical Civilization*, vols. 1 & 2 (New Brunswick, N.J.: Rutgers University Press, 1987). For a critique of Eurocentrism as an epistemology, see Ella Shohat and Robert Stam, *Unthinking Eurocentrism* (London: Routledge, 1994) and *Race in Translation: Culture Wars Around the Postcolonial Atlantic* (New York: New York University Press, 2012).

2. It is commonly accepted that in the late eighteenth century, the German Orientalist August Ludwig von Schlözer first deployed the term "Semitic languages," which by the nineteenth century, in conjunction with racial classifications of people, largely replaced the previous term "Oriental languages." The notion of "Semitic languages," more generally, has reflected a sliding from linguistic categories, which themselves are hardly pure given the historical syncretism across languages, into originary ethno-national paradigms.

3. Voltaire, *The Works of Voltaire: A Contemporary Version with Notes, Vol. 12*, trans. William F. Fleming (London: E. R. Dumont, 1901), 32.

4. Voltaire, *An Essay on Universal History, the Manners, and Spirit of Nations*, trans. Mr. Nugent (London: J. Nourse, 1759), 49.

5. Ernst Renan, *Studies of Religious History and Criticism*, trans. O. B. Frothingham (New York: Carleton, 1864), 117, 154, 159.

6. G. W. F. Hegel, *The Philosophy of History*, trans. J. Sibree (Mineola, N.Y.: Dover Publications, 2004), 93. On the "Antinomies of the Enlightenment," see Shohat and Stam, *Unthinking Eurocentrism* and *Race in Translation*.

7. Edward Said, *Orientalism* (New York: Vintage, 1978), 307.

8. This thesis was advanced by Yitzhak Ben-Zvi and David Ben-Gurion.

9. For example, works by Keith W. Whitelam, Nadia Abu El-Haj, and Shlomo Sand.

10. See Shohat, *Israeli Cinema: East/West and the Politics of Representation* (Austin: University of Texas Press, 1989), 91–92 and also 2–3, 54–56, 71–76, 78–80, 100–103, 188–89; and in the second edition (London: I. B. Tauris, 2010), 253–55, 261–67, 295–96. On the relevance of Orientalist discourse to Arab Jews, and on their ambivalent place vis-à-vis Palestine, see Shohat, *Taboo Memories, Diasporic Voices* (Durham, N.C.: Duke University Press, 2006), 201–232.

11. Ella Shohat, *On the Arab-Jew, Palestine, and Other Displacements: Selected Writings* (London: Pluto, 2017), 3.

12. For several different critical engagements with the notions of the Semite and Semitism, see Gil Anidjar, *Semites: Race, Religion, Literature* (Palo Alto, Calif.: Stanford University Press, 2008); Joseph Massad, *Islam in Liberalism* (Chicago: University of Chicago Press, 2015), 312–342; and Gil Z. Hochberg, "'Remembering Semitism' or 'On the Prospect of Re-Membering the Semites,'" *ReOrient* 1, no. 2 (2016), 192–223.

13. Dehodencq's painting is also at times alternatively referred to as *L'exécution d'une juive au Maroc* (*The Execution of a Jewess in Morocco*).

14. Gabriel Séailles, *Alfred Dehodencq: L'homme & l'artiste* (Paris: Société de Propagation des Livres d'Art, 1910), 195.

15. Abraham Elmaleh, "Sol Ha-Tzadika," *Hed Hamizrah*, January 15, 1943, 6.

16. Maimonides, "Maamar Kiddush ha-Shem" (1165) in *Iggerot ha-Rambam*. https:// www.sefaria.org/Iggerot_HaRambam,_Maamar_Kiddush_HaShem?lang=bi.

17. See Erez Bitton, "Kasidat Solica" in *Naʿnaʿ: Shirim* (Tel Aviv: Eked, 1979), 27. For an English translation, see Ammiel Alcalay, ed., *Keys to the Garden: New Israeli Writing* (San Francisco: City Lights Books, 1996), 269–271. In this poem, Sol's experience can be read as an allegory for the Mizrahi/Moroccan experience in Israel, transposing the notion of being a minority Jew in Morocco to Israel. The bands Sfatayim ("Solica") and Droz ("Lalla Solica"), meanwhile, have adopted the Moroccan tradition into popular Mizrahi music. And recently, Beersheba Theater produced Maor Sabag and Tair Sibony's musical, *Sulica*, casting the Palestinian Nasreen Qadri as the heroine in an allegory of co-existence.

18. For two major comprehensive works on the case of Sol, see Sharon Vance, *The Martyrdom of a Moroccan Jewish Saint* (Leiden: Brill, 2011); and Juliette Hassine, *Soliḳah ha-tsadeḳet harugat ha-malkhut* (Jerusalem: Mosad Bialik, 2012).

19. Similarly, Jewish tour guides also highlight the blood relation between Moroccan Jews and Muslims (see darlett, "L'autre juive Solika la tsadika," DARNNA.com, December 13, 2007, http://www.darnna.com/phorum/read.php?13,120172, and "Lalla Soulika— Jewish martyr in the cemetery of Fez," YouTube, November 18, 2009, https://www .youtube.com/watch?v=qhCEjz5WNRQ [last accessed February 2, 2018]).

20. See, *Yahadut Maroco: Praqim be-Heker Tarbutam* (Jerusalem: Reuven Mas, 1975) and Josef W. Meri, *The Cult of Saints Among Muslims and Jews in Medieval Syria* (Oxford: Oxford University Press, 2002).

21. M. Léon Godard, *Description et histoire du Maroc* (Paris: E. Donnaud, 1860), 83. See also Issachar Ben-Ami, *Saint Veneration Among the Jews in Morocco* (Detroit: Wayne State University Press, 1998).

22. In recognition of Sol's grave as a holy site for both Jews and Muslims, the dome of the tomb is alternatively painted in the symbolic color of each religion, blue and green. The latter would seem to confirm a narrative of her embrace by Muslims. This syncretism is recognized in popular tourist sites (see, for example, Moshe Frigan, "Tfilat ha-ʿArviya be-Qever Suliqa," *Kikar ha-Shabat*, March 1, 2017, http:// www.kikar.co.il/223700.html [last accessed February 2, 2018] and Ruth Knafo Setton, "Searching for Suleika: A Writer's Journey," in ed. Emily Benichou Gottreich and Daniel J. Schroeter, *Jewish Culture and Society in North Africa* (Indianapolis: Indiana University Press, 2011), 226–238.)

23. This statement has been popularly attributed to Sol in Jewish-Moroccan culture and can also be found in texts: Eugenio Maria Romero, *El martirio de la jóven hachuel, ó la heroina hebrea* (Madrid: Diego Negrete, 1837), 10.

24. The exhibition *Les Juifs dans l'orientalisme (The Jews in Orientalism)* was held at the *Musée d'art et d'histoire du* Judaïsme in 2012 (see "Les Juifs dans l'orientalisme," *Musée d'art et d'histoire du Judaïsme*, October 19, 2015, http://www.mahj.org/fr /programme/les-juifs-dans-l-orientalisme-16049 [last accessed February 2, 2018]). In his review of the exhibition, Vladislav Davidzon uses the presence of Jews in Orientalist paintings to demonstrate the fallacy of Said's thesis (see Vladislav Davidzon, "The Ghosts of Edward Said," *Tablet*, July 2, 2012, http://www.tabletmag.com /jewish-arts-and-culture/105124/the-ghosts-of-edward-said [last accessed February 2, 2018]), echoing Robert Irwin, *For Lust of Knowing: The Orientalists and Their*

Enemies (London: Allen Lane, 2006). In contrast, I argue here that the imaging of Jews was on a continuum with that of Muslims. For the latter see Malek Alloula's *The Colonial Harem* (Minneapolis: University of Minnesota Press, 1986).

25. See *The Legacy of Islamic Anti-Semitism: From Sacred Texts to Solemn History*, ed. Andrew G. Bostom (Amherst, N.Y.: Prometheus, 2008).

26. For an analysis of the export of the Enlightenment Jewish minority discourse to the subcontinent, see Aamir Mufti, *Enlightenment in the Colony: The Jewish Question and the Crisis of Postcolonial Culture* (Princeton, N.J.: Princeton University Press, 2007).

27. Romero, *El martirio de la jóven hachuel*, 67.

28. See Lloyd P. Gartner, *History of the Jews in Modern Times* (Oxford: Oxford University Press, 2001).

29. The Alhambra Decree was officially overturned at the Second Vatican Council in 1968. Today, however, Spain and Portugal officially allow repatriation for Sephardi Jews but not for Andalusian Muslims.

30. For a historical study of Romero's liberal views, see Sharon Vance, "Sol Hachuel, 'Heroine of the Nineteenth Century': Gender, the Jewish Question, and Colonial Discourse," in ed. Emily Benichou Gottreich and Daniel J. Schroeter, *Jewish Culture and Society in North Africa* (Bloomington: Indiana University Press, 2011), 201–225. Elsewhere, Vance argues that European accounts "consistently portrayed relations between Muslims and Jews as characterized by animosity and violence. Any negative incidents in Morocco were used to reinforce arguments that Europeans should intervene" (Vance, *Martyrdom of a Moroccan Jewish Saint*, 70).

31. Sol's Sephardi origins are often referred to in contemporary popular sites (see for example *Hatchuel-Hatchwell: The Branches of Solika's Family*, http://hatchuel-hatchwell.net/ (last accessed February 2, 2018).

32. Sidestepping the spectacular *auto-da-fé*, the continuous repression of the *conversos* and, also, of the Moriscos, including after the 1492 fall of Granada, this Enlightenment-inspired discourse nonetheless elided the Inquisition's Tribunals and their public executions of Christian apostates, forgetting the many Sols to be found in the Iberia of the Reconquista. Romero's glorifying adjectives for the Hebrew heroine did stand in sharp contrast to the Inquisition, which did not name the executed Jews "martyrs" and "heroes" but "*marranos*" (pigs). In a different interpretation of Romero's omission, Sarah Liebovici argues that the text may implicitly criticize the expulsion from Spain in "Sol Hachuel la Tsaddikah ou la force de la foi," *Pardes* 4 (1986), 133–146.

33. Ruth Knafo Setton, *The Road to Fez* (Washington, D.C.: Counterpoint, 2001), 223, 224.

34. Interestingly, in Saïd Sayagh's novel, Sol attends a Jewish wedding, where she is surprised to encounter a European artist. The man is the French painter Eugene Delacroix, and Sol learns that he has received the rabbi's approval to portray the wedding. In this moment, the novel seems to evoke the anxiety around the visual imaging of the human figure, which it resolves through the rabbi's approval, presumably granted due to the mundane subject matter. Saïd Sayagh, *L'autre juive: Lalla soulika, La tsadika* (Paris: Ibis, 2009),72.

35. See Ella Shohat, "The Specter of the Blackamoor: Figuring Africa and the Orient," in *ReSignifications: European Blackamoors, Africana Reading*, ed. Awam Amkpa

(Rome: PostcArt, 2016), 95–115. In this sense, the French unveiled the Jewish woman before the Muslim.

36. Various moments in modern history have been read within what could be regarded as a "pogromization metanarrative," for example, the 1941 *Farhud* in Iraq. For a related critique of this persecution discourse in relation to the 1912 *Tritel* in Morocco, see Yigal S. Nizri, "On the Study of the Tritel in Fez," *Pe'amim* 136 (2012), 203–224.

37. Sharon Vance notes that neither forcible conversion nor the death sentence for apostasy were commonly deployed during the rest of the nineteenth century, indicating that the outcome of Sol's case was critically shaped by the French invasion of North Africa, which had "aroused religious outrage," exerting pressure on the Sultan to avoid any appearance of weakness (*Martyrdom of a Moroccan Jewish Saint*, 74).

38. On the debates over Berbers, see *Berbers and Others: Beyond Tribe and Nation in the Maghreb*, ed. Katherine E. Hoffman and Susan Gilson Miller (Indianapolis: Indiana University Press, 2010). In relation to Berber-Jews, see Majid Hannoum, *Colonial Histories, Post-colonial Memories: The Legend of the Kahina, a North African Heroine* (Westport, Conn.: Greenwood, 2001).

39. Sayagh, *L'autre juive*, 61; page references for citations from this book will henceforth be provided in the main text.

40. Montesquieu, "Another Origin of the Right of Slavery" in *The Spirit of the Laws* (1748), trans. Thomas Nugent (Kitchener, Ontario: Batoche, 2001).

41. Aimé Césaire, *Toussaint L'Ouverture: La Révolution Française et le Problème Coloniale* (Paris: Présence Africaine, 1981), 23.

42. Albert Memmi, *The Colonizer and the Colonized* (London: Souvenir Press, 1974). Despite his anti-colonial stance, Memmi took a Zionist position, which also led him to reject the notion of the Arab-Jew in "What Is an Arab Jew?," in *Jews and Arabs* (Chicago: J. Philip O'Hara, 1975). For a discussion of Memmi, see Gil Hochberg, *In Spite of Partition* (Princeton, N.J.: Princeton University Press, 2007), 20–43.

43. Within this Eurocentric perspective, as I argued in my earlier work, "Jew" and "Arab" were formulated as mutually exclusive categories and "the Arab-Jew" came to form an antinomy, an oxymoronic concept, which "necessitated" violent cultural de-Arabization. "Sephardim in Israel: Zionism from the Standpoint of its Jewish Victims," *Social Text* 19/20 (1988); "Dislocated Identities: Reflections of an Arab-Jew," *Movement Research* 5 (Fall 1991–Winter 1992), 8; and *Taboo Memories, Diasporic Voices*, 201–232, 330–359.

Chapter Five

RETURNING TO THE QUESTION OF EUROPE

From the Standpoint of the Defeated

HAKEM AL-RUSTOM

WRITING FROM A GRAY ZONE

It is widely understood that the "Jewish question" constitutes the lack of Jewish integration in European societies and the centuries-old anti-Semitism, racism, discrimination, denial of rights, and violence against Jews in Europe. It culminated in the genocide to annihilate European Jewry perpetrated by the German state under the Nazi regime during World War II in what came to be known as the *Holocaust*. Meanwhile, establishing an exclusively ethno-sectarian Jewish state in Palestine, dispossessing some 750,000 Palestinians, turning them into refugees, and depopulating and destroying over 400 of their villages in the aftermath of the Holocaust in what came to be known as the *Nakba*—the catastrophe—constituted the "Arab question."[1]

The definitions of each question give rise to a two-fold problem: first, where do Arab-Jews stand in this dichotomy? As part of the Arab question or the Jewish one? In other words, given their predicament, do they belong to the history of European anti-Jewish racism (known in European history as 'anti-Semitism') or to the Palestinian Arab displacement, to both, or neither? And aren't we ignoring their presence, experience, and potential for a critical intervention when they are obliterated from both the Arab and the Jewish questions? Where do we locate and historicize their forced migration and the dispossession of their properties and citizenship rights by Arab states? And how do we understand and situate the racist treatment and poor reception upon their arrival as second-class immigrant citizens in Ashkenazi-dominated Israeli state and society? The limited parameters of each question have silenced and subverted the displacement of Arab-Jews. This leads us to the second question: Why did the displacement of Arab-Jews and their erasure from history occur simultaneously by both Zionism and Arab nationalism and their respective historiographies? On a broader level, what does a point of agreement between supposedly enemy populations and opposing ideologies and histories tell us about their perception of their "self" and the "other(s)"? And what critical possibilities emerge from such an endeavor?

The chapter takes the silence about Arab-Jews in the Arab-Jewish engagement as a point of departure and an opportunity to launch a critique of the ways in which both the Arab and Jewish questions have been discussed and debated to date. Arab-Jews are Jewish communities of Arabic language and culture, who were labelled as *Mizrahim* (sing. *Mizrahi*; literally "Oriental" Jews in Hebrew) upon their migration to Israel.[2] Throughout this chapter, I refer to these diverse populations as "Arab-Jews" even though it has been a contested category by many Jewish communities from Arab societies mainly because their exclusion and expulsion were justified within Arab nationalist discourses. Yet, using the hyphenated category "Arab-Jews" is by no means endorsing the ideology of any nationalist regime or ideology, past or present. I have made this conscious decision because of its four political ramifications: to highlight their indigeneity to Arabic history and culture, broadly defined, that is not confined to a Muslim history since there have been Arab and Arabic-speaking Jews and Christians prior to both Islam and the rise of Arab nationalism; to account for their expulsion—both physical and symbolic—by Arab states and from Arab societies; to critique the ways in which they were racialized as "Arabs" and were subjected to intensive systematic de-Arabization policies upon their arrival in Israel; and finally as way to avoid the category "Mizrahim," which was invented by the Israeli-Zionist establishment in order to sever their connections with their home Arab societies, language, and culture. It is also notable that "Mizrahim" renders Arabness and Jewishness as mutually exclusive in the Zionist project, a view that many Arab nationalist regimes have adopted from Zionism.[3] By maintaining the designation "Arab-Jews," I aim to launch simultaneous critiques of both Zionist and Arab nationalisms and the subsequent Zionization of Arab and Jewish histories.

This chapter probes the principal parameters of each question, the Jewish and the Arab, and advocates for the inclusion of what Ella Shohat calls "the question of the Arab-Jew," which constitutes the predicament of Arab-Jews in both their home Arab societies and in Israel.[4] The separation of the three questions—the Jewish (in Europe), the Arab (in Palestine), and that of the Arab-Jew (in Israel and Arab states)—propagates Eurocentric and Zionist readings of history, and thus limits the possibilities of an integral engagement that is fully realized within the simultaneous critique of European anti-Semitism, European colonialism, and Arab nationalism. Following Walter Benjamin's concept of history, the chapter endeavors to move beyond binaries and identity-based insular histories to consider the three questions as constituents of a single catastrophic history of Europe from the standpoint of the three "defeated" populations.

The displacement of Arab-Jews from their home societies started in the wake of the establishment of the State of Israel as an exclusively Jewish state in Palestine with British colonial patronage. If we were to limit our discussion of the Jewish question to the predicament of European Jews, we risk falling into an engagement framed by Zionism because the state that Zionist elites have imagined is one that represents the political, cultural, and historical aspirations of the world's Jewry, thus limiting the diverse Jewish experiences to that of Europe and homogenizing the broad Jewish history to the long centuries of anti-Semitism in Europe.[5] This reductive approach to Jewish history ignores and systematically denies the diversity in histories, cultures, languages, and "geocultural spaces," which Jewish communities around the world were intrinsic parts of for over two millennia, as is the case with Arab-Jews.[6]

In an attempt to account for the history of violence against one population, the way each question is discussed continues to produce its own discourses of power and triumphalism where the civility of the self is conceived through narratives of victimhood and the barbarity of "others." This has not been the case for Arab-Jews, who were left voiceless, unaccounted for, and without a history as both the Zionist and Arab nationalist regimes silenced their experiences of dispossession. Considering the displacement of Arab-Jews as a question in its own right, coupled with the Jewish Holocaust and the Palestinian Nakba, puts us at the confluence of three, and not only two, questions that have been read separately, independently, and mostly, competitively.

The segregated approaches to histories of violence risks the trivialization of the suffering of "others," denies the complexity and interconnectivity of different histories, and confines us to intellectual ghettos in the historical narration. Such ghettos reflect categories established by colonial rule and the segregation in the imagination and policies in post-colonial nation-states, which produce dichotomous enmity between Arabs and Ashkenazi Jews (and later, all Jews). After all, both Arabs and Jews were categorized as "Semites" in European racist pseudoscience of the nineteenth century and were segregated in the twentieth century, which made Arab-Jews or any aspect of Jewish affiliation with Arab history and culture an impossibility, a point to which I return later.

In light of the essential Arab Jewish binary that emerged within colonial contexts and continues to be propagated by nationalisms, this chapter takes the impossibility of the Arab-Jew as an opportunity to interrogate history and conceive of a more integral future of an Arab Jewish engagement from a "gray zone." By *grayness* I mean the confusing, volatile, unanchored, multiple, opposite, borderless terrains—political as well as intellectual—that lay between the sharp identity divisions such as that between the *Jew* and the *Arab*, or the victim and the victimizer, which the stories around the two Egyptian synagogues in the next section reveal.

TWO CAIRO SYNAGOGUES

Despite the trilingual sign in Arabic, English, and French that the building was open, the doors were shut. When I asked the policeman stationed at the entrance if the building was open, he answered affirmatively. My three companions and I went to a police desk in the courtyard and asked if we could visit. "Sure, you can! Please present your passports." My companions were of non-Arab citizenship and this was their first visit to Cairo; luckily they had photocopies of their passports on them. Since I was the only Arabic speaker, I acted as a translator between my friends and the police officer. The passport details were copied in the police registry along with their hotel details.

Upon finishing, he looked at me and said, "Are you going in with them?" When I answered affirmatively, he asked for my passport as well. I replied, "Well, it is much simpler with me. Here is my Egyptian identity card." To my surprise, he said, "Sorry, sir! Only foreigners are permitted to visit the synagogue!" Confused and embarrassed in front of my friends, I asked, "What do you mean? Egyptians can't visit a synagogue in their own country? Churches and mosques are open to everyone, so why not the synagogues!" But there was no leeway. I tried to argue and rationalize, but it was to no avail. Nothing worked. They simply told me, "*Dih ta'limat*, these are the instructions we were given; we just follow orders." Furious, I said, "So if I were to bring a foreign passport, will you let me in?" "Yes, holders of any passport can enter," he explained, "except nationals of Arab states."

I was unable to figure out who the author of these *ta'limat* instructions was, since the Arabic phrase and the intonation of the speaker were vague and in the passive voice, which was meant to implement to impose a regime through ambiguity. More importantly, I questioned the motives behind such oversecuritization of Jewish sites in Egypt, which is also common throughout Europe. Are Jewish buildings vulnerable to Arab and Muslim "rage"? If that's the case, has the Egyptian state internalized Bernard Lewis's (along with his disciple, Samuel Huntington's) assumptions that Muslims are destined to clash with Jews and Christians? Or is it that Egyptian Jews—their past, their history, and their presence—were rendered in the realm of foreignness so much so that only non-Arab citizens are now allowed entry into this Cairo synagogue?

This encounter took place in October 2010 at Shaar Hashamayim Synagogue in downtown Cairo, decades after the (forced) migration, and in many instances, expulsion of Jews from Egypt and other Arab states. Such expulsion took place in the two decades following the Palestinian Nakba, which in itself occurred in the aftermath of the Jewish Holocaust in Europe. In this confluence of historical catastrophes, one may consider a visit to an Egyptian synagogue as a taboo place for Egyptians and Arabs as Jewish history and experience in Egypt have been placed in the realm of external-ity to the Egyptian collective past and present. European Zionist ideologues have also cleansed Arabs from their Eurocentric Jewish history and some Arab nationalist regimes obliterated Jews from theirs. However, such a displacement of peoples and histories from their regional geocultural space should be traced back to European interests in the region and race politics in the colonies during the nineteenth century.[7]

The displacement of Shaar Hashamayim from its Egyptian and Arab contexts in postcolonial Cairo speaks to a similar process that took place in nineteenth-century colonial Egypt at Ben Ezra, the only synagogue in Cairo open to all visitors. Ben Ezra housed the famous Geniza, a room of fragmentary documents that were collected over the centuries by Jewish Cairenes. The "discovery" of the Jewish documents (in both Arabic and Hebrew) in the Geniza is attributed to Count d'Hulst, who found them in 1889 during the synagogue's demolishing and rebuilding. D'Hulst's excavation mission was supported by the London-based Egypt Exploration Fund to find Coptic and Arabic antiquities in Cairo with the aim of increasing the Fatimid pottery collection of the British Museum. The Hebrew and Arabic documents that d'Hulst found in the Geniza constituted only one box out of the nine that d'Hulst sent to the Fund along with other fragments from Old Cairo that included, among other things, Kufic tombstones, coins, glass fragments, and pottery.[8]

It is in this context that Jewish antiquities were being sought along with Coptic, Muslim, and ancient Egyptian artifacts on behalf of scientific institutions in colonial centers. The discovery and uprooting—or in fact theft—of documents and antiquities within the European Enlightenment project gave Europeans legitimacy in transferring remains and ruins from the colonies to European colonial and scientific centers as a manifestation of the best values of the Enlightenment, namely progress, science, and universal humanism.[9] However, such colonial understanding of humanism reflects an embedded racism that suggests the native inhabitants of such territories do not have interest in or the capacity to appreciate their own past and interpret the wealth of knowledge buried underneath them.[10] It remains the duty of "white" Europeans to search, discover, and rescue them on their behalf, store artifacts and archives in European institutions, and interpret them for the scientific and literary circles in Europe. The "discovery" and uprooting of the Jewish documents of the Geniza, therefore, was part of a larger project to transfer documents and artifacts of antiquity to Europe for scholarship and commerce.[11] The Geniza documents, very much like all other displaced artifacts, were ideologically and physically displaced from their organic socio-historical context. It is notable that such displacements went on without posing basic questions about the ideological and hege-monic colonial regimes that degraded Egypt of the remnants of its past as well as many of its resources as a British "protectorate."[12]

The transfer of the Geniza proceeded in the context of an institutional and scholarly race on two levels: first, Oxford and Cambridge's university libraries were competing to expand their 'Oriental' collection; second, two rabbinic scholars, Adolf Neubauer and Solomon Schechter, were compet-ing to locate the missing Hebrew version of the book of Ecclesiasticus.[13] Following d'Hulst discovery, and in light of such competition, the Geniza documents made it to European libraries and private collections outside of Egypt. Reading the displacement of Egyptian and other Arab-Jews from their contexts, one is enticed to agree with Shohat's proposal that the dis-location of the Geniza documents "began a process of symbolic displace-ment of Jews from the East from their geocultural space" to Europe.[14] Such a displacement was a precursor to Zionism, an ideology that envi-sioned European Jewish culture as belonging to Europe, not the primitive Arab East. This process commenced in the colonial period and witnessed the displacement of almost all Egyptian Jews, the erasure of their history, the denial of their indigeneity, and even the banning of Egyptians from entering their synagogues in Cairo.[15] Meanwhile, successive nationalist regimes in Egypt and across the Arab world have justified policies of discrimination and racism against Jews and other religious and political minorities, the establishment of repressive police states, the criminalization of descent, and hindering the freedom of expression and thought all under the pretext of fighting Zionism, advocating Palestinian rights, and preserv-ing national security.[16]

"Colonialism did not pass over Egypt's Jewish community," making the displacement of documents not only between European colonialists and Egyptian natives, but also between European Ashkenazi Jewish scholars like Neubauer and Schechter on one hand and local Egyptian Jews on the other.[17] In this sense, coreligionists reflected the colonial relations that already existed between the European and the non-European as Ella Sho-hat explains: "British Jewish scholars, like their non-Jewish compatriots, cast an imperial gaze at the Egyptian Jews, the very people who had pro-duced and sustained the Geniza for almost a thousand years."[18] Yet the situ-ation was not strictly dichotomous, since such a transfer would not have been possible without the collaboration of local Egyptians who were selling artifacts to Europeans and the Egyptian Jewish elites who adopted European values of the Enlightenment that probably saw in the transfer of valuable documents to libraries such as Cambridge a common-sense good deed that was done out of good will to "salvage" treasures of knowledge from the oblivion of a stagnant and negligent Orient.[19]

It is imperative that, in light of this, we start looking at the diversity and power dynamics lurking underneath population categories. The displacement of the Geniza documents reveals that we cannot just use a category such as "Jewish" without considering that it is far from being a monolith: Egyptian Jews—like other Egyptians, were targeted by European colonialism, whose structure also included European Jews who, like Neubauer and Schechter, were also beneficiaries of colonial privileges to achieve scholarly aspirations on behalf of colonial institutions. Colonialism therefore targeted Egyptian Jews, as it targeted other Egyptians—alive and dead. Colonial domination is collective, and it is always preceded by a disciplined system of knowledge production that Said articulates in *Orientalism*.[20] Different segments of the population may therefore not have experienced colonial rule the same way, since colonial hegemony vary in the process of ruling the natives through dividing them into categories and subcategories.

Orientalist knowledge production displaces the temporal realities in a way that an event or a group of people are made to symbolize a distant past that is relevant for Europe's self-fashioning. This was made manifest in the invention and resurrection of dead languages and population categories; such was the case with the Phoenicians, the Hellenes, and the Palestinians to refer to the inhabitants of the Syrian coast, the Greek-speaking Ottomans, or southern Syrians, respectively, or their interest in the pasts of populations that continue to bear the same name, such as Egyptians. European interest in the dead cultures and peoples of the land they conquer almost always ignores that contemporary reality.[21] The interest in non-European and non-Christian literary traditions emerged in the context of the Renaissance and Reformation—including Oriental and Hebraist studies.[22] The case of Jewish and Hebraist studies, or "Hebraism," is noteworthy because it was important in reshaping European intellectual culture in the aftermath of the Reformation as Catholics and Protestants were drawn to reading scriptures in their original languages. While such affinity with Hebrew through biblical interpretations made the study of the language a relevant discipline for Europeans, it concurrently propagated racism with the exclusion of Jews from Europe for their presumed different faith, language, and "foreign" origin.[23]

Embracing Jewish studies and Hebrew literature while excluding Jews is symptomatic of Orientalism. It is mostly the dead of the Orient—the ancient, the Hebraic, and the classical—that have a civilizational value for Europeans, one that should be (re)discovered, studied, and salvaged from native hands. The actual and the contemporary of these populations is devalued and largely ignored in favor of the past "civilization" that is presumably buried underneath them. An exception to this practice occurs when the lived culture of a native population is posed to represent the primordialness of the lost culture and so becomes key to understanding a lost ancient past. An example of this is the Zionist rendering of Arab Palestinian culture as a carrier of a lost biblical Jewish culture and Arabs themselves as descendants of biblical Jews converted to Islam.[24] The practice of traveling, "discovering," and "salvaging" remnants of dead cultures and peoples, whether Hebraic or Oriental, or the transfer of documents and artifacts such as the Geniza documents of Old Cairo, are activities that could best be labelled as a kind of "voyeuristic necrophilia," to borrow Stathis Gourgouris's eloquent description.[25]

FROM THE STANDPOINT OF THE DEFEATED

The inclusion of the question of Arab-Jews in the discussion of the Arab and Jewish questions compels us to make a critical historical inquiry into the Arab and Jewish engagements that transcends the triumphalism embedded in the identarian binaries assumed in each question. I appeal to Walter Benjamin, whose concept of history, Michel Löwy writes, is one written "'from the standpoint of the defeated'—not just the history of the oppressed classes, but also that of women (half of humanity), of Jews, Gypsis, American Indians, Kurds, blacks, sexual minorities—in a word, of the pariah...of all ages and all continents."[26] Such a standpoint entices us to consider the Holocaust, the Nakba, and the question of the Arab-Jew as part of a single catastrophic European history and narrate against identity-based insular histories that promote hierarchical segregations of populations and bring to the foreground minor events, groups, and individuals.

In "Theses on the Philosophy of History" Walter Benjamin declares that "There is no document of civilization which is not at the same time a

document of barbarism."[27] Writing from the standpoint of multiple pari-
ahs abandons the civilization-barbarism binary symptomatic of the linear,
teleological, and triumphalist historical narratives. This enables a critique
on multiple ideological projects simultaneously and acknowledges the
"barbaric" chapter in every seemingly civilizational project, be it European
modernity, the civilizing mission behind European colonial conquest,
Zionism, or Arab nationalism. Since the construction of a historical narrative is always accomplished through a "bundle of silences," as Michel-Rolph
Trouillot observes, the document of civilization therefore could only be
forged through silencing the histories of the oppressed and the defeated,
especially the violence, conquest, and abuse practiced against them. Only
then could a document of civilization glitters with a moral higher ground,
devoid of the barbaric chapters through which victory was attained.[28]

Paul Klee's painting *Angelus Novus* became Benjamin's metaphor for the
angel of history who sees in multiple histories "one single catastrophe which
keeps piling wreckage upon wreckage."[29] Through the eyes of Benjamin's
angel we find that the Jewish and Arab questions are intertwined and the
Arab-Jewish question is inseparable from both. My aim here is to narrate
the experiences and histories of Arab-Jews in the midst of the competing
narratives of the events that happened in or within European contexts: the
Holocaust perpetrated by a *European* fascist regime, and the Nakba by *European* Zionism, under the auspices of British colonialism in the region, in
the aftermath of the Holocaust, which also took place on *European* soil in a
centuries-long sequence of anti-Semitism on the continent.

In *The Question of Palestine*, Said contrasts the "very well-known success" of European Zionism in bringing Jews to Palestine, "*and* the far less-
known disaster" that the Palestinian natives incurred in Palestine. Said
positions the centrality of the Palestine question as a challenge to the way
Zionism continues to be regarded as morally legitimate and politically
successful without any concern to what Zionism meant for the defeated:
namely, loss, dispersion, and catastrophe.[30] To shed more light on this fact,
Said quotes the following passage by Hannah Arendt, who herself escaped
the Nazi regime in Germany and France:

After the [Second World] war it turned out the Jewish question . . . was indeed
solved—namely, by means of a colonized and then conquered territory—but this
solved neither the problem of minorities nor the stateless . . . The solution of the

Jewish question merely produced a new category of refugees, the Arabs, thereby increasing the number of the stateless by another 700,000 to 800,000 people.[31]

This passage from Arendt's *The Origins of Totalitarianism* is perhaps the first to make the connection between the Jewish and Arab questions. Following Arendt's lead, Said articulates the Palestinian experience by seeing Palestinian Christians and Muslims as the "unhappy victims of the same movement [i.e., Zionism], whose whole aim is to end victimization of Jews by Christians in Europe," thus reading the Holocaust and the Nakba contextually—and not comparatively or competitively—as one leading to the other.[32] Said also advocates that the Palestinian Nakba was indeed an outcome of a Western European genocide against Jewish Europeans.[33] Following Said's critique, Ella Shohat sees the catastrophe of Arab-Jews as deeply entangled with the Nakba and advocates for the necessity of entertaining the "question of the Arab-Jew," following Said's "question of Palestine," considering it on its own right and especially that until recently it has been largely ignored in public and academic debates, Arab, Jewish, and Israeli alike.[34]

By demonstrating the ways in which the catastrophes of Arab-Jews and Palestinians are dually an outcome of European Zionism, Shohat's articulation of the experiences of Arab-Jews complicates the Jewish-Arab binary further. Thus, Shohat builds on Said's critical approach, yet critiques Said's discussion of the Jewish question as solely a European Ashkenazi one, ignoring Arab-Jews. If we were to move beyond the binary to write from the perspective of Benjamin's angel of history, we must probe into the implications of compiling the wreckage of the three events or questions within a single catastrophe originating in Europe on the Arab Jewish engagement. Accounting for their historical interconnectedness where the history of one cannot possibly be narrated without the others, is a methodological intervention that rids us of the binary between populations and their histories.[35] More importantly, the collective history of European Jews, Palestinians, and Arab-Jews cannot be fully critiqued as part of a single catastrophe unless it is grounded in a critique of the notion of progress that dominates European political and discursive hegemony.

One defies such cultural hegemony and triumphalism by challenging the purified narration of history of the victorious by presenting perspectives of the defeated groups. It is thus an imperative for critical historical inquiry to consider history from the standpoint of the defeated and the oppressed classes collectively, who in Benjamin's words are a "depository of historical knowledge."[36] To open such depositories, as Said says following Antonio Gramsci's commentary, is to compile an inventory from the fragmented traces that the past of the victimized and the defeated left for us and in us.[37] To explore the ramifications of the standpoint of the defeated on the future of the Arab Jewish engagement, I will now shed some light on Edward Said and Ella Shohat's critical practice of blurring the gap in reading Palestinians and Arab-Jews as simultaneously the defeated populations of the European Zionist nation-state building in Israel, that was realized in the aftermath of the Holocaust.

SOLIDARITY IN DEFEAT: ON PALESTINIANS AND ARAB-JEWS

Edward Said sees the Palestinian and Zionist struggle as one between presence and interpretation: the *presence* of the people who own and live on the land and the *interpretation* that transcends actual reality through ideology and narration. Interpretation is "controlled by portentous past and glorious potential future" and therefore the land belongs not to its inhabitants but to an imagined other, a more deserving people as prescribed by nationalist interpretation. The Arab's "negative personality" as Oriental, decadent, and inferior, rendered the Arab "a non-person" in Palestine and was replaced with a superior, modern, European Zionist who "became the only person" who should live on the land, Said explains.[38] The non-personhood of the Arab that Said discusses speaks of the elimination of the Arab, yet such elimination did not occur in the total absence of the Arab from the land (despite the expulsion of many), rather mainly in interpretation. In other words, Palestine was not to be guided by the actual realities of its inhabitants rather by a mythological interpretation authorized by a European colonial mindset on the level of interpretative narratives that accompanied colonial conquest. As naming is interpretive and "is itself a narrative of power disguised as innocence,"[39] the renaming of cities, villages, and landscape has been central to the Zionist nationalist conquest of Palestine with the aim of "effacement or replacement of the Palestinian Arab presence."[40] The geographical name "Palestine" was revived from biblical nomenclature going back to a designation in the Roman Empire and Arabs became "non-Jews" (as in the text of the Balfour Declaration), along with changing the names and historical significance of many sites, cities, and locals.[41] To quote Theodore Herzl, the father of political Zionism, who said in *New-Old World* (1902), a book Patrick Wolfe describes as an allegorical manifesto, "If I wish to substitute a new building for an old one, I must demolish before I construct."[42] The "demolition" that took place in Palestine was both on the interpretative and the physical levels, in order to deny and displace the Palestinian present in favor of a different reality stemming from ideological interpretations of Zionist nationalism, and indeed the manipulation of history and the past. One could not avoid seeing the resemblance among uprooting of artifacts in the colonies with the removal of the Geniza or the interest in Hebrew literature in post-Reformation Europe that paid little or no attention to the living Jewish people of those cultures. The artifacts and documents, just as the land of Palestine, were pursued without the people. Such reoccurrence of favoring the dead and depriving the living of their agency and sovereignty in the consumption of the arts, history, literature, and cultural production of non-Europeans is consistent with Orientalism as a discourse that guides a colonial way of seeing, interpreting, and authorizing knowledge over otherness.[43]

Interpretation was essential in the conquest of Palestine in order to write Zionism's own "document of civilization" while subverting its dark side. Several rationales try to justify the destruction of Palestinian society and the dispossession of Palestinians to deflect responsibility of the founding fathers of the Zionist state: the Arabs left while the Zionist forces told them to stay; those who stayed in Israel are better off than those who left for Arab countries; there is only one Jewish state (or twenty-two Arab countries) where Palestinians could go; the occupation of the West Bank was explained in terms of biblical prophecies; and Palestinians expelled were an exchange for the Jews who left Arab countries.[44] So when Said embarked on narrating what Zionism meant to its non-Jewish "victims" he was writing to give precedence to *presence* through his criticism of *interpretation* that displaced the indigenous Palestinians off their land, even if many physically remained on it.

Said's "Zionism from the standpoint of its victims" is meant to compile the rarely exposed inventory of what Zionism's "victims," and not its beneficiaries, have endured.[45] In that way he was constructing a contrapuntal history to unsettle what has already been known and perceived about Zionism, which has largely been regarded in the context of creating a state for European Jews in the aftermath of the Holocaust and rarely through the prism of its historical and ideological connections to European imperial-ism.[46] Due to the European remorse over the long history of anti-Semitism on the continent and the mass annihilation of Jews during the Holocaust, the conventional discourse among Europeans has silenced the dark side of Zionism, rendering the "victims" of the triumphant Zionist state as either unthinkable or deserving their predicament.[47]

Looking at Palestinians as "victims" of Zionism without a parallel inven-tory of its *Jewish* "victims" runs the risk of asserting a binary that this chap-ter scrutinizes. Published a decade after Said's similarly titled essay, Shohat's "Sephardim in Israel: Zionism from the Standpoint of its Jewish Victims" could be considered a response, a continuation to, and a critique of Said.[48] The essay's point of departure is critiquing the claim that Zionism was a "liberation movement for *all* Jews" by articulating the experiences of Arab-Jews, who bear more resemblance with the Palestinian predicament than with the European Jewish one. "Within Israel," Shohat says, "European Jews constitute a First-World elite dominating not only the Palestinians but also the Oriental Jews." In this sense, Arab-Jews, represent an *Orient* within an Israeli state and society dominated by Jewish Europeans and remain mar-ginal to the post-Holocaust Zionist narrative of liberation.[49]

As pertains to Jews and Jewish history, Zionist historiography has estab-lished two ideological assumptions. The first is denying the Arab and Mus-lim contexts of Jewish history, experience, and culture that evolved over the centuries in Southwest Asia, North Africa, and the Iberian Peninsula and the Ottoman Empire. The second assumes that Arab-Jews were erased through forcing them to put on the mask of the "universal" Jewish experi-ence centered in Europe.[50] Smadar Lavie went as far as to argue that Arab-Jews underwent "cultural genocide" and imposed self-destruction in order to resemble Ashkenazi Jews to fit the ideals of the Israeli national society as imagined by Jewish Europeans.[51] Many Arabs—Jews and non-Jews—adopted the Zionist paradigm that established Judaism as an equivalent to Zionism, and Arabness as an antonym to Jewishness, which put Arab-Jews in the position of having to choose between anti-Zionist Arabness and pro-Zionist Jewishness, without having the freedom to reject both or articulate themselves outside this colonial binary.[52] In other words, they had to choose between the two labels on both sides of their hyphenated identity—an unthinkable dichotomy that became only possible in the after-math of colonialism and nationalism. Arabness and Jewishness became antagonistic nationalist identities in the context of the Zionist racial and sectarian state-building project in Israel on one hand and the dominant stream of Arab nationalism on the other. Shohat reminds us that "Jewish and Arab nationalisms have shared . . . the notion of a single, authentic (Jewish or Arab) nation," thus the estrangement of Arab-Jews came to a full circle when Arabs equated *all* Jews (including Arab-Jews) to Zionism, regardless of their political inclinations, experience or geocultural origin;[53] they all became simply *Yahud* ("Jews"), which in many Arab contexts means also Israelis.[54] The de-Arabization of Arab-Jews was not only completed by Zionist and Israeli state systematic policies of erasure, but also Arab nationalist regimes who, like Zionists, shared the assumption that equated all Jews to Zionism, and Zionism to the Jewish state of Israel. For Zionist Ashkenazi Jews, the immigration of Arab-Jews to Israel was important to establish demographic majority after the failure of the Zionist movement to attract enough European Holocaust survivors to populate the newly established Jewish state; Arab-Jews were not desired in the formative years of Israeli state-building and were brought in only as a demographic necessity.[55]

In a connection to Said's analysis in *Orientalism*, Shohat demonstrates the ways in which Arab-Jews became the internal other of Zionism, who bore similar representational resemblance to the ways in which post-Enlightenment Europe represented, indeed invented, the orient: Arab-Jews were the inferior awaiting civilization and salvation from their Oriental Arab abyss. Here Shohat makes an important bridge between the Palestinian and Arab-Jewish questions within the long trajectory of Orientalism where denying the Eastern, Arab, and Muslim aspects of Jewish culture and history went hand in hand in denying the presence of Palestinians and their history and culture from Palestine. In European Zionist thought, Palestinians were the counternarrative as the evil of the East, while Arab-Jews represented the "good East" that waits Israel to cleanse them of their Arabness and Oriental residual.[56] Arab-Jews therefore were regarded as people frozen in history since biblical times. Their history, as is the case of other colonized peoples, started with contact with Europeans: upon their immigration to Israel, where they were perceived as passive, cheap labor and a mere replacement for Arab agricultural workers. Arab-Jews, therefore, constituted a "Jewish Third World people, from a semi-colonized nation-within-a-nation" and, therefore, their history and predicament in Israel have to be contextualized and critiqued within an anti-colonial framework akin to the way Said reads the history of Palestinians and other colonized peoples.[57] Here one could ponder the Geniza documents as a metaphor for Arab-Jewry, where they have been locked and accumulated in a room without change, and their "history" starts only when they are "discovered" and brought to colonial libraries to serve European—Jewish and non-Jewish— scholarship and archival accumulation.

Against this backdrop, the European approach to Jewish history confines the Jewish past to that of Europe and the Holocaust; Shohat clearly indicates that she takes an anti-colonial theoretical framework following mainly Said but also Aimé Césaire and Frantz Fanon in narrating "Zionism from the standpoint of its Jewish victims." It is therefore one of the first moments where Jewish history in the aftermath of the Holocaust is not confined to European genocidal violence and analyzed within the critiques of colonialism and other colonized peoples. As indicated earlier, relations between European Jews and Arab-Jews in Israel did not escape the racism of white supremacy manifested in the European colonial projects that positions the European in a superior relationship vis-à-vis the Arab.

Said and Shohat present the view from the standpoint of the "victims" in their respective essays on Zionism. In line with Benjamin's concept on history that transcends the victim-victimizer duality I have preferred to replace "victims" with "the defeated."[58] This is the case because victimhood insinuates a historical finality, a perpetual state that runs the risk of forging a triumphalist discourse for the victim population. On the other hand, defeat in the Benjaminian sense is inconclusive and productive in the way it goes beyond loss engendering dissent and solidarity with other groups who share similar catastrophic histories. The defeat of Palestinians and Arab-Jews through the success of Zionism was regarded as the triumph of Western liberal values, which subverts the barbaric elements of Zionism.[59] The consequences of this view is considering the history of Zionism as a "document of civilization" purified of its barbaric chapters, where on one hand European Jewish victims of the Holocaust could be conceived as victims of European fascism, which has a general consensus of being barbaric and vile. Palestinians and Arab-Jews, on the other hand, become the unthinkable victims of European Zionism, an ideology that enjoys the endorsement and support of the political and intellectual establishments in Western Europe and North America as being a liberation movement that seeks to bring Jewish victimhood to an end.[60]

The three questions formed around the defeated—that of the Holocaust, the Nakba, and the Arab-Jews—are constituent of a single catastrophe because they share an origin in Europe: the Holocaust perpetrated by a *European* Fascist regime and both the Nakba and the alienation of Arab-Jews by *European* Zionism in the aftermath of the Holocaust that also took place on *European* soil. As we consider the three questions as part of a single catastrophe, we must then return to Europe and ask as Anya Topolski does how and why Europe continues to produce "others" and turn them into problems?[61] The next section restarts the Arab Jewish engagement by probing the "question of Europe" where anti-Semitism and colonialism, as well as the "Arab" and the "Jew" as distinct categories, began.

RETURNING TO THE QUESTION OF EUROPE

Since the Nakba cannot be separated from the Holocaust, one wonders, as Andrew Rubin does, what prevents us from seeing the Holocaust and the Nakba as part of the historical process that is deeply rooted in German history? What prohibits us from entertaining the Palestinian past, present, and future within a discussion on German memory? More generally, why is this multifaceted catastrophe not debated within European history? The answer to these questions, Rubin tells us, lays in the same epistemic separation that prevents us from seeing that Orientalism and anti-Semitism stem from the same history of racism in Europe.[62] It is inevitable to make a detour to the European past to re-establish the common foundations of Orientalism and anti-Semitism as part of a single catastrophe to start contemplating the Arab Jewish engagement within the wider history of European fascism and colonial conquest.

European modernity was shaped around the formation of borders and boundaries, and therefore labelling, excluding, expelling, and annihilating populations that represented difference and otherness continue to be landmarks of modern European history.[63] The year 1492 witnessed a confluence for European confrontation with otherness: the expulsion of Jews and Muslims from the Iberian Peninsula by the Catholic kings, as well as the conquest followed by a genocide perpetrated against the indigenous populations in what Europeans came to call "the Americas."[64] What we ought to call "the age of conquest and expulsion"—and not the "age of discovery and exploration" by European colonial capitalism—was marked by the image of the "Jew" and "Muslim" as two internal others who lived in Europe with related theologies to Christianity. Such proximity tainted by the "narcissism of minor differences" (to use Freud's term) meant that while they lived in Europe, being non-Catholic Christians, they did not belong to it.[65] I say non-Catholic Christians because one could argue that the question of the other in Europe started much earlier with the rise of Islam as a political force in the sixth century, and this question also included Eastern Christians. Prior to cleansing Iberia of Jews and Muslims, Eastern Christians and Muslims were targeted by successive crusades starting in 1095. While the history of such encounters is beyond the focus of this chapter, it is noteworthy that unlike Eurocentric and Orientalist historiography, the crusades were not a mere struggle between Western-Christian "Crusades" versus Muslim "jihad," since the Crusaders targeted the Eastern Orthodox Church's control over historical sacred sites as well as Muslim rule over biblical lands with the political aim of capturing both under papal control.[66]

Yet with the 1492 expulsion of Jews and Muslims, Amnon Raz-Krakotzkin argues, "the modern consciousness" of Europe was created parallel to the "crystallization of Orientalism and Hebraism as fields of study."[67] Said diligently states in the early pages of *Orientalism* the historical and ideological connections between Orientalism and anti-Semitism; in fact, he sees Orientalism as "the Islamic branch of anti-Semitism":

I have found myself writing the history of a strange, secret sharer of Western anti-Semitism. That anti-Semitism and, as I have discussed it in its Islamic branch, Orientalism resemble each other very closely is a historical, cultural, and political truth that needs only to be mentioned to an Arab Palestinian for its irony to be perfectly understood."[68]

If we were to consider *Orientalism* as a study that "emerged out of a long, deep, and unsettling history . . . of silences," one of those silences is around how Orientalism is the "secret sharer" of anti-Semitism.[69] Said reiterated this point in a 1985 commentary titled "Orientalism Reconsidered" where he argued that the "hostility to Islam . . . has historically gone hand-in-hand with, has stemmed from the same source, has been nourished at the same stream as anti-Semitism." In the same essay, Said asserts the study of "Orientalism contributes to our understanding of the cultural mechanisms of anti-Semitism."[70] Said has therefore reestablished the severed connection between anti-Semitism and Orientalism as stemming from one ideological source rooted in European racial pseudoscience of the nineteenth century, which emerged in the context of European colonial conquest and capitalist expansion.

We could extend the relationship between anti-Semitism and Orientalism to the production of knowledge about the "Semitic" other in the fields of Orientalism and Hebraism. Here we see the persistence of the formula of excavating and "discovering" the treasures of the Orient while abandoning the Oriental person as stated earlier, leading us to an imposing question: What are the foundations that make anti-Semitism and Orientalism two branches stemming from the same ideological root? Following Said's method of understanding the theory and practice of Orientalism in philology, where he understands Orientalism "as a set of structures inherited from the past, secularized, redisposed, and re-formed by such disciplines a philology."[71] The "Semite" Joseph Massad reminds us is a philological classification unit was forged in eighteenth-century Europe as a linguistic category that included *both* Hebrew and Arabic and became a racial category in the nineteenth century.[72] Said therefore saw anti-Semitism and Orientalism as two branches of the same ideology since philologically Hebrew and Arabic were classified as "Semitic" languages, and the Hebraic and the Arabic represented together what Ernest Renan calls the "Semitic spirit," where the "Jew is like the Arab and vice versa."[73] When the category "Semite" was transformed from a linguistic category to a racial one, the speakers of Indo-European languages were also transformed into the racial category as "Aryans."[74] The very designation *Semite* was invited to assert the superiority of Indo-European (languages) and Aryan ("races"), so the very identification "Semitism" (to refer to Jews) and "anti-Semitism" (to refer to anti-Jewish racism) reproduce the very problematic and racist categorization that was invented especially to emphasize the superiority of white Europeans rendering both designations as inherently racist and "anti-Semitic" themselves.[75]

European self-definition was constructed as opposite to the Semite, the Oriental, and the native other. It was in Europe where the Jew and the Arab became inferior "others" under the broader category of the Semite, and both were enemies of Europe.[76] Yet both were not enemies of each other, a fact that is mostly forgotten and silenced. Since it is common to understand European hatred, racism, and violence against Jews as "anti-Semitism," with the Western European fear and hatred toward Islam, Muslims, and Arabs as "Orientalism,"[77] how do we understand the history of Arab-Jews as a product of anti-Semitism or Orientalism? Since the representation of Arabs, including Arab-Jews, fits the general structure of Orientalism, one is inclined to situate the experiences of Arab-Jews as an extension of Orientalism. Yet if we were to consider the three questions as part of the same catastrophic history, asking such a question would reproduce a binary between anti-Semitism and Orientalism. Instead, a critical reading would consider both as part of the same catastrophe whose wreckage keeps piling at the feet of Benjamin's angel of history.

The fact that the Zionist state was seen as a successful project in the aftermath of the Holocaust should not deny the fact that Palestinians experienced it through the arrival of European Holocaust survivors in Palestine, and not as ordinary refugees, but rather as a population with settler sovereignty, and such sovereignty negates that of Palestinians.[78] Arab-Jews, on the other hand, experienced Zionism in terms of racism and white supremacy, whose very migration to Israel was instigated when not enough European Jews immigrated there. The Zionist movement therefore resorted to Arab-Jews as a demographic reservoir necessary to create a Jewish majority in Israel in the early 1950s and their eventual dispossession from Arab states. From the perspective of the dual defeated populations of Zionism, Arab-Jews and Palestinians share the predicament of the colonized.[79]

A year following the publication of *Orientalism*, Said published *The Question of Palestine* in 1979, where he initiated a reading of European Jewish and Palestinian histories together to bring to the foreground the "intertwined history" of European Jewry as victims of anti-Semitism and Palestinians as victims of European colonialism and Zionism. In a piece that predates *The Question of Palestine*, Said bridges his argument in *Orientalism* where Oriental subjects or the natives were not given a voice to express their political will or aspirations, and Europeans determined these. He states, "The Zionists took it upon themselves as a partially 'Eastern' people emancipated from the worse Eastern excess to explain the Oriental Arabs to the West, to assume responsibility for expressing what the Arabs were really like and about, and never to let Arabs appear equally with them as existing in Palestine."[80]

While Said's reference here is to the Arab Palestinians, it could easily be a description of Arab-Jews, a population that became unwanted on both sides of the Arab-Jewish divide and remain outside the Arab Jewish engagement. It is only through abandoning the segregation between the three questions, and considering them as part of the same catastrophic history, that one could start an engagement that is not practiced on Eurocentric terms, does not take colonial categories for granted, and challenges narratives of moral triumphalism. Such measures are the first steps in the thorny terrain of decolonization—as a perpetual critique and not a goal since decolonization is an ongoing process without a possible end point.

It is notable that while some European Jews were a vehicle in the colonization of Palestine, they were also survivors of a genocide perpetrated by the German state. Michael Rothberg reminds us that the history of fascism and the Holocaust in Europe continue to be investigated separately from that of violent practices in European colonies against non-Europeans. Thus the "victims" of fascism in Europe and those of colonialism in the colonies lay in different histories and bodies of critique and rarely together.[81] Said also noted that many Western Marxists have been "blinded" to the critique of empire and imperialism, and that even the Frankfurt School of Critical Theory has been "stunningly silent on racist theory, anti-imperialist resistance, and oppositional practice in the empire."[82] Such observations however, are not recent. Writing in 1950, at the height of the wars of decolonization, Aimé Césaire observed that Europeans began to confront violence only when it was committed against white Europeans by Nazi Germany. Otherwise, violence was "until then had been reserved exclusively for the Arabs of Algeria, the 'coolies' of India, and the 'niggers' of Africa."[83] Such segregated perceptions of violence against Europeans and non-Europeans prevent us from seeing the Holocaust as the outgrowth of the same structure of violence that was committed against non-Europeans throughout the colonies, including the displacement of Palestinians and Arab-Jews.

In this spirit, the anthropologist and activist Smadar Lavie imagines crossing the Israel-Palestine border with Gloria Anzaldúa. Lavie invokes Anzaldúa's commitment for a south-south solidarity, saying, "The white elite wants us—people of the South—behind separate tribal walls. To pick us off one by one. To keep us prejudiced against each other. Stunned and apart."[84] Writing against insular histories of violence therefore opens up opportunities for critique to deepen the solidarity between the defeated populations that challenge the dichotomy between the "Arab" and "Jew," by considering simultaneously European fascism, colonialism, Zionism, and Arab nationalism, as ideologies and institutions that thrive on the defeat of oppressed populations. Countering racism and colonialism embedded in the European claims to universalism engenders solidarity among the oppressed and colonized peoples regardless on which side of a national border they ended up.

To write from the standpoint of the defeated is to swim against the political and intellectual currents where binaries, dichotomies, and hierarchies of suffering are the status quo. Benjamin's proposition that "every document of civilization is a document of barbarism" speaks of one document, and not two, where barbarism is an inseparable constituent of every claim to civilization and progress—including exclusive claims over "victimhood." In the aftermath of World War II, Europeans regarded Zionism as a movement that ultimately solved the Jewish question for Europe by transporting it to the Middle East while denying—politically, historically, and epistemically—any German or British responsibility of the Palestinian Nakba and its consequences on the displacement of Arab-Jews. The latter two were to become confined to their "Oriental" Middle Eastern contexts, and not seen as belonging to the catastrophic history of anti-Semitism and colonialism that originated in Europe and continues to be discussed exclusively on "white" platforms in Western Europe and North America. So if we were to engage the Holocaust, the Nakba, and the question of the Arab-Jew as part of a single catastrophe, it is imperative that we resume our critique by returning to question Europe.

NOTES

1. It is notable that while many survivors in Europe ended up in Palestine in the aftermath of the Holocaust, many chose not to immigrate to Palestine. The idea of establishing a Jewish homeland for European Jews outside of Europe predates the Holocaust and goes back to Theodor Herzl's 1896 proposal, *The Jewish State*, and was followed by Zionist immigration to Ottoman Palestine in the late nineteenth and early twentieth centuries.

2. On the history and context of Mizrahim, as an umbrella category for all non-Ashkenazi, European Jews, see Ella Shohat's "The Invention of the Mizrahim," *Journal of Palestine Studies* 29, no. 1 (Autumn 1999), 5–20.

3. Ella Shohat, "Sephardim in Israel: Zionism from the Standpoint of its Jewish Victims," *Social Text* 19/20 (Autumn 1988), 1. See also Shohat "The Invention of the Mizrahim." The fourth point I raise here is discussed by Yehouda Shenhav, *The Arab Jews: A Postcolonial Reading of Nationalism, Religion, and Ethnicity*. (Stanford University Press, 2006).

4. Ella Shohat has advocated for the "question of the Arab-Jew" in her "Introduction" to *On the Arab-Jew, Palestine, and Other Displacement* (London: Pluto, 2017), 1.

5. Shohat, "The Invention of the Mizrahim," 6.

6. I employ Ella Shohat's term "geocultural spaces" to refer to indigenous cultures that are specific to a particular geography. Thus, the displacement of people means also the displacement of culture, history, and language specific to a place and a population. See Ella Shohat, "Taboo Memories, Diasporic Visions: Columbus, Palestine, and Arab-Jews" in *Taboo Memories, Diasporic Voices* (Durham, N.C.: Duke University Press, 2006).

7. I invoke the term "displacement" from Shohat's "Introduction" to *On the Arab-Jew, Palestine, and Other Displacement*, where she extends the usage of term beyond the physical displacement of people, to include to the displacement of things such as documents, in addition to narratives and sense of belonging to place, whether one actually changed location or not.

8. This is according to a letter that d'Hulst sent to the Fund on February 16, 1890, quoted in Rebecca J. W. Jefferson, "A Genizah Secret: The Count d'Hulst and Letters Revealing the Race to Recover the Lost Leaves of the Original Ecclesiasticus" in *Journal of the History of Collections* 21, no. 1 (2009), 127. Jefferson's article details d'Hulst's role in finding and transferring the Geniza documents from Cairo to England. It is notable that the Egypt Exploration Fund was founded in 1882, the same year Egypt became a British protectorate, and one year after southern Syria (the area that the British called Palestine) became also a British protectorate.

9. Shohat, "Columbus, Palestine and Arab-Jews," 203–204.

10. Shohat, "Columbus, Palestine and Arab-Jews," 203–204.

11. Shohat, "Columbus, Palestine and Arab-Jews," 203.

12. In this paragraph, I am building on Shohat's critique in "Columbus, Palestine and Arab-Jews," 204.

13. Jefferson, "A Genizah Secret," 125.

14. Shohat, "Columbus, Palestine and Arab-Jews," 204.

15. For the history of Egyptian Jews, see Joel Beinin, *The Dispersion of Egyptian Jewry: Culture, Politics, and the Formation of a Modern Diaspora* (Berkeley: University of California Press, 1998), Najat Abdulhaq, *Jewish and Greek Communities in Egypt: Entrepreneurship and Business before Nasser* (London: I. B. Tauris, 2016), and Aimée Israel-Pelletier, *On the Mediterranean and the Nile: The Jews of Egypt* (Bloomington: Indiana University Press, 2018).

16. See Edward W. Said, *The Question of Palestine* (New York: Vintage, 1979), 88.

17. Shohat, "Taboo Memories, Diasporic Visions: Columbus, Palestine and Arab-Jews," 203.

18. Shohat, "Taboo Memories, Diasporic Visions: Columbus, Palestine and Arab-Jews," 204.

19. The Grand Rabbi of Egypt at the time, Aaron Raphael Ben Shim'on, along with the influential Jewish Cattaui family, supported Solomon Schechter's efforts to transfer

the documents out of Egypt. For details of the local collaborators and the involvement of the British Consul-General in Egypt, Lord Cromer, see Jefferson, "A Genizah Secret," 131.

20. Edward W. Said, *Orientalism* (New York: Vintage, 1978), 3, 22.

21. In *Orientalism*, 300, Said speaks of the Orientalist regard to abstractions about the Orient that bases knowledge production on older classical periods and not on the contemporary realities as one of the four dogmas of the Orientalist discourse.

22. Amnon Raz-Krakotzkin, "Orientalism, Jewish Studies and Israeli Society: A Few Comments," *Philological Encounters* 2 (2017), 242.

23. Raz-Krakotzkin, "Orientalism, Jewish Studies and Israeli Society," 242–43.

24. Susan Slyomovics, *The Object of Memory: Arab and Jew Narrate the Palestinian Village* (Philadelphia: University of Pennsylvania Press, 1998), 37. Also, Susan Slyomovics, "Who and What Is Native to Israel: On Marcel Janco's Settler Art and Jacqueline Shohet Kahanoff's 'Levantinism,'" *Settler Colonial Studies* (2013), 3.

25. Stathis Gourgouris, "*Orientalism* and the Open Horizon of Secular Criticism," *Social Text* 87, vol. 24, no. 2 (Summer 2006), 15.

26. Michel Löwy, *Fire Alarm: Reading Walter Benjamin's 'On the Concept of History,'* trans. Chris Turner (London: Verso, 2005), 23.

27. Walter Benjamin, "Theses on the Philosophy of History," in *Illuminations*, trans. Harry Zohn (New York: Schocken, 1968), 256 (Thesis VII).

28. Michel-Rolph Trouillot, *Silencing the Past: Power and the Production of History* (Boston: Beacon, 1995), 27.

29. Benjamin, "Theses on the Philosophy of History," 257–58 (Thesis IX).

30. Said, *The Question of Palestine*, xxxix.

31. Hannah Arendt, *The Origins of Totalitarianism* (New York: Harcourt Brace Jovanovich, 1973), 290, quoted in Said, *The Question of Palestine*, xxxix.

32. Said, *The Question of Palestine*, xxxix.

33. Andrew Rubin, "Orientalism and the History of Western Anti-Semitism: The Coming End of an American Taboo," *History of the Present* 5, no. 1 (Spring 2015), 105.

34. Shohat, "Introduction," *On the Arab-Jew*, 1.

35. Edward W. Said, *Culture and Imperialism* (New York: Verso, 1994), 72. Ella Shohat, *On Arab-Jews, Palestine, and Other Displacements* (London: Pluto, 2017).

36. Benjamin, "Theses on the Philosophy of History," 260 (Thesis XII).

37. I am here alluding to Edward W. Said's commentary on Gramsci's *Prison Notebooks*: see Said, *Orientalism*, 25, which he later invokes in *The Question of Palestine*, 73, to speak of an inventory of Zionism's victims.

38. Said, *The Question of Palestine*, 37.

39. Trouillot, *Silencing the Past*, 114.

40. Patrick Wolfe, "Settler Colonialism and the Elimination of the Native," *Journal of Genocide Research* 8, no. 4, (December 2006), 388. Wolfe here builds on the work of Maron Benvenisti, *Sacred Landscape: The Buried History of the Holy Land Since 1948* (Berkeley: University of California Press, 2000).

41. Said, *The Question of Palestine*, 8.

42. Wolfe, "Settler Colonialism and the Elimination of the Native," 388.

43. See Gourgouris, "*Orientalism* and the Open Horizon of Secular Criticism."

44. Said, *The Question of Palestine*, 45.

45. Said, *The Question of Palestine*, 73, 84.

46. Said, *The Question of Palestine*, 72.

47. I am here alluding to Trioullot's description of the Haitian Revolution as being unthinkability from the standpoint of European history of the time. Such history did not allow the Haitian "slaves" the agency and power to revolt against European colonial rule and succeed in the first slave-led revolution. See chapter 3 of Trouillot, *Silencing the Past*.

48. Shohat, "Sephardim in Israel."

49. Shohat, "Sephardim in Israel," 2.

50. Shohat, "The Invention of Mizrahim," 6.

51. Smadar Lavie, "Staying Put: Crossing the Israel–Palestine Border with Gloria Anzaldúa," *Anthropology and Humanism* 36, no. 1 (2011), 111.

52. Shohat, "The Invention of Mizrahim," 8.

53. Shohat, "The Invention of Mizrahim," 8, 11.

54. See Lavie, "Staying Put," 109.

55. Shohat, "The Invention of Mizrahim," 10. See also the testimonies presented in the documentary film *Forget Baghdad: Jews and Arabs—The Iraqi Connection*, dir. Samir, 2002.

56. Shohat, "Sephardim in Israel," 7–8.

57. Shohat, "Sephardim in Israel," 2. In this quote Shohat uses "Sephardim"; however, for the reasons, indicated earlier, I refer to them as Arab-Jews.

58 I am here following Michel Löwy's commentary on Benjamin's "Theses on the Philosophy of History" in Löwy, *Fire Alarm*, 23.

59. Said, *The Question of Palestine*, 37, 40. Said here refers to Palestinians, but I am extending the view of defeating Arabs to include Arab-Jews as well.

60. Said, *The Question of Palestine*, xxxix, 57.

61. Anya Topolski, "Good Jew, Bad Jew . . . Good Muslim, Bad Muslim: 'Managing' Europe's Others," *Ethnic and Racial Studies* 41, no. 12 (2017): 2179–96.

62. Rubin, "Orientalism and the History of Western Anti-Semitism," 102, 105.

63. Raz-Krakotzkin, "Orientalism, Jewish Studies and Israeli Society," 243.

64. Tzvetan Todorov, *The Conquest of America: The Question of the Other* (New York: Harper & Row, 1984), cited in Raz-Krakotzkin, "Orientalism, Jewish Studies and Israeli Society," 243.

65. Sigmund Freud, *Civilization and Its Discontents*, trans. and ed., James Strachey (New York: Norton, 1961), 61.

66. The first crusade was launched some four decades after the schism between the Eastern Orthodoxy and the Roman Catholicism in 1054. Even though the pope authorized military support to the Eastern Roman Empire ("Byzantium") to fight the advancing Ottoman invasions, that support was intended to reunite the two churches under Rome's authority. Starting with the first crusade, European Catholic military campaigns massacred Christians alongside Muslims, as was the case with the siege of the Syrian city of Antioch in 1097 and 1098; see Thomas Asbridge, *The Crusades: The War for the Holy Land* (New York: Simon and Schuster, 2012), 72–73. The fourth crusade sacked Constantinople, and Latin Catholic fighters destroyed many churches in the capital city of the Eastern Roman Empire; see Speros Vryonis, *Byzantium and Europe* (New York: Harcourt Brace and World, 1967), 152. Additionally, Eastern Christians fought alongside Muslim forces against Western Christian invasions. These details are important to problematize the Christian/Muslim dichotomy,

just as the Arab/Jewish dichotomy was probed by introducing the Arab-Jew to the debate. Therefore, this debate, I argue, needs the introduction of the Eastern and the Arab Christians to the question of Orientalism.

67. Raz-Krakotzkin, "Orientalism, Jewish Studies and Israeli Society," 243.

68. Said, *Orientalism*, 28.

69. Rubin, "Orientalism and the History of Western Anti-Semitism," 99. Rubin here brings to our attention that the term "secret sharer" is an allusion that Said makes to Joseph Conrad's short story of the same title.

70. Edward W. Said, "Orientalism Reconsidered," *Cultural Critique* 1 (Autumn 1985), 89–107.

71. Said, *Orientalism*, 122.

72. Joseph Massad, "Forget Semitism!," in *Living Together: Jacques Derrida's Communities of Violence and Peace*, ed. Elisabeth Weber (New York: Fordham University Press, 2012), 62.

73. Ernest Renan (1823–1892), cited in Gil Anidjar, *Semites: Race, Religion, Literature* (Stanford, Calif.: Stanford University Press, 2008), 32. Massad, "Forget Semitism!," 62, uses the same assertions of Renan in the context of arguing that the category "Semite" was invented in Europe.

74. Massad, "Forget Semitism!," 62.

75. Massad, "Forget Semitism!," 64–65.

76. Gil Anidjar, *The Jew, the Arab: A History of the Enemy* (Stanford, Calif.: Stanford University Press, 2003), xvii, xxv.

77. Anijdar, *The Jew, the Arab*, xvii.

78. Said, *The Question of Palestine*, 84.

79. For a discussion on the ways in which the Israeli state links Arab-Jews to Palestinians by arguing that the left properties of Iraqi Jews offsets those of Palestinian properties abandoned during the Nakba, see "What Do the Arab Jews and Palestinians Have in Common?," in Shenhav, *The Arab Jew*.

80. Said, "The Idea of Palestine in the West," *Middle East Research and Information Projects* 70 (September 1978), 5.

81. Michael Rothberg, *Multidirectional Memory: Remembering the Holocaust in the Age of Decolonization* (Stanford, Calif.: Stanford University Press, 2009).

82 Edward W. Said, *Culture and Imperialism* (New York: Vintage, 1994), 278.

83. Aimé Césaire, *Discourse on Colonialism* (New York: Monthly Review Press, 2000), 36. For a discussion of Césaire in the context of the Holocaust and decolonization, see Rothberg, *Multidirectional Memory*, chapter 3.

84. Gloria Anzaldúa, *Borderlands/La Froentera* (San Francisco: Aunt Lute, 1987), 86, quoted in Lavie, "Staying Put," 113.

Chapter Six

BETWEEN SHARED HOMELAND TO NATIONAL HOME

The Balfour Declaration from a Native Sephardic Perspective

YUVAL EVRI AND HILLEL COHEN

What was the position of the native Jews of Palestine toward the Balfour Declaration? Did they join the cheers of the Zionist movement? Did they notice that the declaration ignored the rights of the Palestinian Arabs? Did they see it positively or negatively? Did they mind that the declaration was intended for the Zionist organization and not for them, as residents of the country? Was there a general Sephardi, Mizrahi, or Arab-Jewish position toward the Balfour Declaration?[1]

These questions also arose in the contemporary Palestinian political and popular discourse. Prominent Palestinian leaders, such as Musa Kazim al-Husseini and Jamal al-Husseini, have emphasized that the Arab national movement never opposed the Jews and actually viewed the native Palestinian Jews as an integral component of the national movement. Based on this view, Arab political leaders argued that there was no reason for the native Jews to side with Zionism against the Arab national movement, and once declared that the Palestinian Arab national movement also represented the local Jews, as opposed to the Zionist immigrants—as was the case with the delegation that went to London in 1921 to fight the Balfour Declaration.

This "brotherhood concept" was presented by the president of the Palestine Arab Congress, Musa Kazim al-Husseini, to Winston Churchill, the secretary of state for the colonies, during his visit to Jerusalem in March 1921: "It is the idea of transforming Palestine into a home for the Jews that

Arabs resent and fight against. The fact that a Jew is a Jew never prejudiced the Arab against him. Before the war Jews enjoyed all the privileges of rights of citizenship." This was the basic demand of the Arab Executive: "First: that the principle of a National Home for the Jews be abolished. Second: a national government be created, which shall be responsible to a parliament elected by the Palestinian people who existed in Palestine before the war," i.e., including the Jews.[2]

Arab-Palestinian leaders voiced this rhetoric during the 1920s and 1930s. For example, on February 26, 1922, Jamal al-Husseini published an article in the newspaper *al-Sabah* calling the local Jews (*al-yahud al-wataniyin*) to join their Arab-Palestinian brothers: "Because you and we are the sons of the same homeland, whether the Zionists like it or not . . ." and thus "share the same rights and duties in our mother Palestine." From this shared and equal position as Palestinians "we are sorry for your persecution by the Zionists, for the denial of your rights, freedom, and ability to explore your goals and aspirations. We consider this to be an offense against the honor of the Palestinian nation, whose sons you are. Hence, your Muslim and Christian brothers strongly protest against these actions, extend their arms, and call you: come to us!"[3] Similarly, a year later al-Husseini issued an appeal on behalf of the Arab Executive urging the Palestinian Jews to distance themselves from the Zionist movement and join the Arabs' demand to abolish the Balfour Declaration and boycott the election for the legislative council.[4]

Two decades after the declaration was published, this perception had yet to disappear. On November 21, 1936, the Palestinian newspaper *Mirat al-Sharq* ran the following story on its front page: "Some longstanding Jewish residents of the country are interested in meeting with the Arab Higher Committee in order to discuss the general situation, and in particular, the subject of testifying before the Royal Commission; as we understand it, this is because they are not interested in recognizing the Balfour Declaration."[5] On page 7 of the same issue, the paper explained that, following the Arab revolt that broke out in 1936, and the subsequent British decision to dispatch the Peel Commission to Palestine, these veteran Jewish residents sought to present their position according to which they were, in fact, victims of Zionism. For many years, these Jews had lived side by side with local Arabs in peace and security, without demanding a national home or a Jewish state on the banks of the Jordan River, and were an indivisible part of Palestinian society. According to *Mirat al-Sharq*, the Balfour Declaration and Zionist immigration from Europe damaged their economic standing; moreover, the European immigrants were contemptuous of the Sephardic Jews of Palestine and kept them away from decision-making forums. The revolt, and the Arab boycott of the Jewish economy imposed from April 1936, mainly hurt the veteran Jewish community, and it became clear that the Zionist movement was unable and unwilling to help them. Thus, the paper argued, the local Jews had repudiated the Zionist movement and were preparing to appear before the Royal Commission.[6]

The distinction between the "foreign Jews" and "local Jews" was common in the Arab-Palestinian discourse during the late Ottoman Empire: the citizenship law, the concept of shared homeland, and the Arab national principle of separating state and religion altogether enhanced the idea of shared homeland in which local Jews—but not immigrants—are full partners.[7] It became a basic element in the early Arab political discourse after the war. The Syrian Congress—the postwar Arab national conference of May 1919—published a resolution against the Balfour Declaration and emphasized that "our Jewish brothers, the natives of the country, they are equal to us in their rights and in their duties." Similarly, leaflets that were distributed in Jerusalem during the visit of the King–Crane Commission the same year stated, "The Muslim, the Christian and the Jew are brothers and share [our desire for] independence."[8]

Arab statements regarding the anti-Zionist attitude of the Sephardi communities were sweeping generalizations, as we shall see below, but they were not completely baseless. Though the paper focuses on the intellectual discussion, an example from the old city of Jerusalem is also worth mentioning: in autumn 1929, following the bloody events of that summer, Arab activists convinced dozens of Maghrebi Jews in the old city of Jerusalem to sign an anti-Zionist petition in which they stated their rejection of the Zionist movement. Although Zionist activists stopped the circulation of the petition,[9] this activity might have strengthened the notion that there is a profound debate between native Jews and Zionists and that the former support the Palestinian-Arab national movement.

In the early 1920s, however, not all Palestinians shared the belief that native Jews would reject Zionism. Writers in the local Arabic newspapers *al-Karmil* and *Filastin* were rather skeptical about the probability of such an alliance. In a September 1921 article in *al-Karmil*, the writer declared, "Let the public not be deceived into thinking that the Arab Jews are on the side of their [Arab] brothers. The Arabs should learn the meaning of unity and mutual trust from the various sections of the Jews." It is the same rhetoric we find in the reaction to the Sephardi statement in *Filastin*. The writer emphasized the special historical relations between the Sephardi native Jews and the Arabs: the Sephardim found refuge in the Ottoman Empire after their persecution in Spain and were treated as equals to the Arab indigenous people in Palestine. But today, continues the writer, the Sephardim changed their loyalties from Ottoman or local patriotism to Zionist supporters:

Those Jews were known during the Ottoman rule for their opposition to the Zionist principle . . . [The Sephardi response] makes us believe that eventually every Jew is a Zionist. They ultimately align themselves with the winning side, the Zionists. Once they [the Sephardim] realized that the Zionists control the country, they turned away from the Arabs and joined their rivals, from their own race, in order to oppose the indigenous residents and their ambitions.[10]

These kind of conflicting statements and attitudes toward the Arab Jews in the Arab-Palestinian discourse reflect a broader social and political confusion in this historical moment of dramatic social and political changes, but it also reflects, as we will show later, the dynamic and transformative position of the native Palestinian Jews themselves in the new political structure that represented contradictory loyalties and affiliations.

Moreover, beyond the immediate political interest, we can find in these conflicting approaches in the Palestinian discourse an alternative map of alliances and political affiliations that underlay the post-Balfour Zionist-national perspective. Instead of national and social partitions based on binary separations between Jews and Arabs, the latter proposed a different set of distinctions between natives and settlers, between Zionists and Jews and between Europeans and Arabs or Easterners. Thus, they emphasized the Ottoman ethos of a shared homeland for native Arabs and Jews while rejecting the Zionist national claims for exclusive ownership of the land.

In the following pages we suggest a renewed reading of the reception of the Balfour Declaration by Sephardi Jews in Palestine. Contrary to the tendency in the literature to focus on the Zionist-British angle, we trace the reactions and interpretations of native Palestinians (Jews and Arabs) to the declaration and explore the tensions between the different identities.

We point out alliances that were proposed and rejected and examine a series of loyalties and partnerships that preceded the binary division between Jews and Arabs that was established at the time.

Moreover, revisiting this crucial moment in the history of Palestine through the prism of the native population opens for us new possibilities of framing and understanding the entangled history of the development of the main political questions of the time—the Palestine question and the Jewish question,[11] while also bringing to the fore another important (and neglected) question: the question of the Arab Jews.[12]

But here we have to go back and examine the basic Palestinian claim of Sephardic, Mizrahi, or Arab-Jewish resistance to the Balfour Declaration. The Sephardi community in Palestine were most affected and involved in the discourse around the declaration. Even though officially most of the political representatives of the community supported the declaration and the Zionist movement, close reading of their discourse reveals a more complex approach toward the declaration and its interpretation by the Zionist institutions and a large spectrum of interpretations and reactions, starting from official mainstream positions to more oppositional and critical point of views. Some of the Sephardi speakers and writers emphasized the connection between the declaration and the intensified tensions between Jews and Arabs in Palestine. Some also acknowledged the Arab Palestinians' frustrations regarding the declaration and their new political status. Few of them offered political solutions that aimed to amend the declaration as a symbolic gesture to reach out to the Arabs in Palestine or even announced their rejection of the declaration.

In these pages we focus on two native Sephardic intellectuals—Yosef Hayyim Castel and Hayyim Ben-Kiki—who had a critical approach toward the declaration. We examine their arguments and explain them against the background of the political and civic logic which developed during the end of the Ottoman period and which had a crucial role on their perception of Jewish-Arab relations in Palestine as well as on their attitude toward the European imperial superpowers.

Our argument is that in this critical point in time, when many Jews felt euphoric about the possibility of establishing a Jewish state that would make the Palestinian Arabs a minority within it, the local Sephardi Jews were trapped in a clash of loyalties between the idea of a shared homeland with the Arabs of Palestine and their sentiment of Jewish solidarity with the

European Zionists— between the ethos of civic partnership and the ideology of an exclusively Jewish state. This dilemma had emerged already at the end of the Ottoman era and aroused intense debate between Sephardic natives and the Ashkenazi immigrants and settlers over the nature of the Jewish national settlement. As we shall see, some Sephardic intellectuals imagined Palestine not as a separate "Jewish Western kingdom" or a European settlement but as a shared Jewish-Arab space that would be part of the new Middle East.[13]

THE JEWISH NATIVES OF THE LAND, THE BALFOUR DECLARATION, AND THE ARAB QUESTION

The role of the Sephardim in Palestine in the Zionist movement during the turn of the twentieth century was multifaceted and complex. While actively involved in Hebrew revivalism circles and in the Zionist circles in Palestine, they were also active in the Arabic Nahda cultural circles and the Ottoman political and cultural reformation (the Tanzimat) at a time when these movements were not yet seen to be contradictory or incompatible.[14]

During the late Ottoman era these Sephardi intellectuals perceived their involvement and affiliation with the Zionist movement as part of a larger cultural movement of Eastern modernization that included the Arab revival movement and the Ottoman reformations.[15] Figures such as Shimon Moyal, Ester Azari Moyal, Nissim Malul, and Yosef David Maman were an active force in the Hebrew and Arabic intellectual circles and promoted the idea of a shared Hebrew-Arabic literary and cultural space as a platform for a shared Jewish-Arab society in Palestine. This unique Zionist cultural and political approach was recently investigated in several research works that emphasized the alternative aspects of these options to mainstream Zionism. For example, Abigail Jacobson argued that the Sephardi option represented an "inclusive Zionist approach" toward the Arab Palestinians;[16] Michelle Campos pointed out their multiple loyalties and labeled them as representing "Ottoman Zionism";[17] and Behar and Ben-Dor Benite highlighted their Mizrahi and Middle Eastern political perspective, embodying different interpretation of Zionism and Hebrew modernization vis-à-vis the Palestinians and Arabs.[18] One main aspect that emerges from these important works is the crucial role played by the vision of Palestine as a "shared homeland" for Jews, Muslims, and Christians in the political and cultural vision of these Palestinian-Jewish intellectuals.[19] Our discussion relies on this literature and focuses on the last breaths of this vision.

The declaration regarding the establishment of a national home in Palestine appeared on the international stage at a time of crisis for the veteran Jewish community in the country.[20] World War I, the collapse of the Ottoman Empire, and the beginning of British rule formed crucial changes in the political and social status of the native Sephardi Jews. Their central role as mediators and representatives vis-à-vis the imperial rule was no longer needed, while their economic, legal, and political advantage over the new Jewish immigrants also disappeared.[21] The first few years after the British conquest were years of recovery and rebuilding for the community's institutions. From the beginning of this period, it was clear that the balance of power in the Yishuv had changed. The Sephardic Jewish communal committees and local activists lost their power and were replaced by representatives of the international Zionist movement. The standing of Chaim Weizmann in the global Zionist movement grew, and the foundation of the Zionist Commission also strengthened his position in Palestine. The Labor parties likewise became more powerful. The Jewish natives of the land were largely marginalized, and their influence on the reorganization of the Jewish community in Palestine, as well as on relations with the Palestinian Arabs, was peripheral. At that time they were already a minority among the Jewish population of Palestine due to the Second Aliyah of 1904–1914 and were weaker than ever due to the disintegration of the Sephardi institutions following internal conflicts.[22]

The leaders of the prewar Zionist labor movement, like the Zionist Commission after the war, did not view establishing relations with Palestine's Arab community as a necessity in the formation and growth of the Zionist Yishuv. Instead, they focused on building ties with the European powers and the Ottoman rulers (before the war) and the Hashemite family (after the war). This was the political thinking behind the Faisal–Weizmann negotiations of 1919.[23]

Unlike the formal Zionist leadership, the native Jews emphasized the importance of the native Arab population and the significance of creating a strong relationship with them. Such figures as David Avishar, Eliyahu Eliashar, Yosef Elyahu Chelouche, Isaaq Abadi, and Abraham Elmalh advocated for direct political and cultural dialogue with the local Arab Palestinians.[24] The native Sephardim had already warned of what was later called "the Arab question" during the end of the Ottoman period. In the early stages of Arab opposition to Zionism, they witnessed how the actions and attitudes of the new Jewish immigrants in Palestine affected their relations with the local Arab residents. In tens of articles published in the *Ha-Herut* newspaper between 1909 and 1914, they reported the criticism being voiced in the local Arab press of the Jewish Yishuv and the Zionist movement, and they pointed out the dangers inherent in this criticism to the political and social status of the Jewish community in Palestine. They also proposed strategies for action, criticized the arrogant and dismissive attitudes of the new Ashkenazi immigrants toward the Palestinian Arabs and their refusal to learn Arabic (the language of the land), and opposed the principle of "Hebrew labor" because of the harm it caused to local workers. They also published many articles in local Arab newspapers, in which they defended the Jewish Yishuv and the Zionist movement and argued with editors who had criticized them.[25]

The native Sephardim who supported the Zionist movement found themselves caught between the Zionist settlers and the native Arabs. Their liminal positions as native Palestinians and as members of the Jewish national community become untenable in light of the growing national tension. Some Zionists viewed the close relations between the Sephardim and the native Arabs with suspicion, mirroring Arab hopes that the Sephardim would indeed join them in opposing Zionism. Y. K. Silman, a Zionist journalist, wrote that the Sephardim were closer to the Arabs than to the Ashkenazim. In 1911, in a middle of a public dispute regarding the role of Arabic in the Jewish community in Palestine, Y. D. Maman heard from a European Zionist that "if you peel away the outer layer, the Sephardic Jew is just an Arab underneath." In 1913, Yaakov Rabinovich, who opposed the Sephardi initiative to establish an organization for Jewish Arabic teachers, believed that the Sephardic intellectuals "have absorbed nothing of the Hebrew culture . . . They are closer to the Arab effendi than to us . . . They may be dangerous for us if the natives [the Arabs] gain rights."[26]

Indeed, Sephardic native intellectuals tried to build a cultural and political platform that included the native Arabs and the Zionist immigrants. They offered a different political setting based on the logic of multiple loyalties instead of the logic of partition and separation.[27] This was meant to be understood as an attempt to preserve their own status as a local elite, as a product of their understanding of the needs and distress of both sides, and as a result of their conclusion that the inconsiderate behavior of the Zionists would necessarily lead to a long-running and bloody conflict.

After the war and the Balfour Declaration, the rules of the game changed dramatically. Their criticism of the Zionist movement died down, and the leading figures in that struggle faded away—some died, and the others like Nissim Malul, Elmalah, and Chelouche were pushed by the Zionist leadership to the fringes of public discourse. In the vacuum that remained, the writing of Hayyim Ben-Kiki stood out; in many ways, he continued the arguments made by the Sephardim before the war.

HAYYIM BEN-KIKI: MIZRAHI NATIONALISM

Hayyim Ben-Kiki was born in 1887 in Tiberias to a Sephardi Maghrebi family.[28] He studied at the town's communal schools, attained self-taught fluency in several languages, and began publishing articles in Hebrew and Arabic newspapers at a young age. In the early 1920s, Ben-Kiki served as the Haifa regional correspondent for *Doar Hayom* and as the secretary for the Sephardic Union in Haifa.

Although he did not publish many articles, in his writing he presented a well-formed and bold political stance. His articles stood out in light of the political and social euphoria that gripped the leadership of the Zionist Yishuv after the Balfour Declaration. Ben-Kiki's rhetoric contained a unique blend of indigenous critical analysis of the Western powers' actions in the Middle East together with a critique of the European foundations of the Zionist movement and its stance toward the Jewish and Arab East.[29]

In October 1920, he published an article in *Doar Hayom* in which he surveyed the different strategies by which European culture had penetrated the Arab countries of the East and the ways in which the European powers created differences between Jews, Christians, and Muslims for their own ends. He wrote from a native Ottoman perspective, rooted in suspicion of the actions of the European powers that threatened his ideal of Oriental unity. In the article, Ben-Kiki analyzed the Balfour Declaration and its consequences:

Even our new [Zionist] institutions and press helped to fan the flames of the misunderstanding between the Arabs and us. These institutions do not take into consideration anyone but the Jews and Europe, and totally ignore their [Arab] neighbors. They treated Arabs prejudicially and dismissed them, imitating the prevailing Western attitude toward the Arabs, even though the strong Europeans actually use different methods here in the region. It is two and a half years now that the Balfour Declaration has been on our mind. It is always present in our newspapers, meetings, and festivals, and it is entirely out of control.[30]

Ben-Kiki's harsh critique was unusual even among the local Sephardi intellectuals. He presented the Balfour Declaration as a framework that amplified the Jews' disregard for the Arab inhabitants of the country. In his view, the declaration was a symptom of foreign European meddling in native Oriental or Easterner society with no understanding of the cultural and political context of the Jewish and Arab native inhabitants. In many respects, Ben-Kiki continued the critical discourse of the Sephardi intellectuals at the end of the Ottoman era, as described in the previous section. In another article, published about a year later, he wrote about these efforts and the dismissive, mocking response it received from the Zionist Ashkenazi leaders:

True, before the Great War it was impossible to imagine that the [Arab] Question would develop into such a complicated matter. But still, the [Sephardi] natives of this Land felt that matters were not being well organized, and that all the noise—accompanied with that ringing, arrogant tone that came at us from outside—was inappropriate for both the time and the place. The [older] Sephardic Yishuv, a community that came to the lands of the East from an Eastern country—whose soul was forged and formed over several generations with the Arab peoples—sensed that something unpleasant was taking place here, and that all this movement [activity] was not being carried out decently. But the admonitions, criticisms, and warnings were considered meaningless. They stirred only ridicule and gave rise to accusations of assimilation. The new [European] settlers say that any Jew who speaks the language of his native country is an assimilating Jew."[31]

The way to dismiss the native perspective, Ben-Kiki explained, was to accuse the native Jews of assimilation with the Arabs—perhaps the worst possible accusation in Jewish and Zionist political lexicons. But this did not prevent Ben-Kiki from continuing and elaborating on his campaign against the Zionist movement. The Zionist enthusiasm for the Balfour Declaration was for him another proof of the European, colonial, and Orientalist character of the Zionist movement. He saw Zionism's European roots and its alliance with the imperialist Western powers as the source of the Jewish Yishuv's isolationist and condescending approach and, hence, what brought about Arab enmity. Readers can identify in Ben-Kiki's rhetoric elements of anti-colonial and settler critique. He made a clear distinction between native (Eastern) Zionism and settler (Western) Zionism, not just in terms of constituent communities, but as bearers of two different worldviews toward the land (Palestine) and its Arab inhabitants. Thus, while Western and settler Zionism is rooted in European culture, representing its values and exaggerating its sense of superiority over the East, and thus necessarily transforming into a colonialist foreign body, he suggested a different course that he termed "Eastern Zionism," which evolved out of an organic outgrowth of the local native Eastern context, embedded within it and not seeking to alter it, while at the same time also not opposing Jewish immigration to the country with the aim of integrating with its inhabitants.

This article, published in August 1921, was written in response to an article by the educator Yitzhak Epstein published in *Doar Hayom* some two weeks earlier, under the headline "The Question of Questions in the Yishuv." In it, Epstein continued the approach he outlined in his famous article, "A Hidden Question," published in *Hashiloah* in 1907, that pointed out the failures of the Zionist Yishuv in its attitude toward Arab residents, which led to the creation of the Arab question—that is, to the hostile and critical Arab attitudes toward the Zionist movement and the Yishuv.[32]

In the article Epstein proposed a number of steps for improving relations with the Arab inhabitants, including learning Arabic, establishing common associations, and creating special diplomatic channels. His approach is evocative of the rhetoric of the Sephardi Jews before the war. Epstein was also one of the founders of Brit Shalom in 1925 and one of the more sensitive and open leaders of the new Zionist Yishuv toward the Arabs.

Thus, Ben-Kiki's choice to respond critically to Epstein publicly was surprising. He chose to focus on the left flank of the Ashkenazi Zionist Yishuv, calling for it to refine its stance toward Zionist ideology and its attitudes toward the East and the eastern native, Jews and Arabs alike. Epstein did not understand, Ben-Kiki claimed, that his proposals contradicted the foundations of the Zionist project in Palestine, whose main goal was to create an isolated society separated from the Arabs. Thus, he missed the main issue—that central to any solution was a change in national Zionist ideology itself—from an isolationist European approach to one that seeks to integrate into local space as it is:

Epstein is furious that "our diplomatic work is rotten" . . . Yet the actual fact is that our culture is rotten! The root of evil in our work that produced the rupture with the Arabs is that we deserted our Oriental [Mizrahi] culture, whose basis is Arab culture, and brought in Western culture in its place. This new culture is completely opposed to the culture and mind of the people of this country—it turns us into a foreign, alien element that threatens to destroy the foundation of their [Arab] culture. It is that which makes them angry. . . . The principal condition for being good neighbors, as well as for mutual [Jewish-Arab] trust, before we come to propose to the Arab people what Epstein wants to offer to them (etc.), is one: return to our Oriental culture.

In other words, relations with the Arabs should not be pursued from a position of supposed superiority, but from the understanding that Palestine is located in the East, and that its inhabitants belong to Eastern culture (which has various points of contact with Western culture), and with a complete abandonment of the Western arrogance that has become a rooted feature of relations between the two peoples, as of internal Jewish relations.

AN ARAB BALFOUR DECLARATION: YOSEF HAYYIM CASTEL'S PROPOSAL

During the same months that Ben-Kiki composed these articles, Yosef Hayyim Castel was working on a plan for "A Solution to the Arab Question in Eretz Yisrael." On October 7, 1921, Castel submitted his plan to the head of the World Zionist Organization, Chaim Weizmann; he also sent a copy to Menachem Ussishkin, then head of the Zionist Commission.[33] This document stood out from the fairly large pool of proposals and documents written on the subject by Zionist activists in part because its writer was one of the Jewish natives of the land and because of the innovative ideas it presented. The seventeen-page paper contained a social-economic-political analysis of the Arab population of Palestine alongside concrete proposals for repairing relations between Jews and Arabs. Forming the background to the proposal was the wave of violence of May 1921 that brought many in the Yishuv to realize the centrality of the question of Arab relations. The Balfour Declaration had a prominent place in Castel's analysis.

Castel came from a well-known Hebronite-Jerusalemite family that arrived in Eretz-Israel, according to family lore, after the expulsion from Spain, and was named for their place of origin, Castile; he belonged to the group of Sephardic Jewish natives of the land who joined the Zionist movement in order to try to influence it from within. Born in Jerusalem in 1899, Castel joined the Ottoman army during the First World War and after it joined the public relations staff of the Zionist Commission, serving as secretary of its political department and head of the press bureau. He was later one of the founders of the Mizrahi Pioneers Union and a member of the editorial staff of *Haaretz*. His proposals should therefore be seen not as those of an oppositional figure but as an attempt to contribute to the Zionist movement from his position and experiences as a native of the land.

Castel's paper began with a detailed analysis of the political opinions among Palestinian Arabs, whom he believed were not of one mind regarding Jewish immigration and settlement. Some were stridently opposed, some supportive (mainly in secret), and many had no national consciousness. He listed several reasons behind the support of different Arab elements for Zionism. Some hoped for financial benefit from selling their lands to Jews; others thought that Zionism would lead to better education and improve circumstances in general; and some recognized the Jews' needs, or thought that it was God's will that the Jews return to their land. However, opposition to Zionism outweighed support, because the pro-Zionists were not organized, unlike their opponents, and also because there was no clear and consistent Zionist policy toward the Arabs. Castel subsequently went on to propose the outlines of such a policy. Before doing so, he emphasized the existence of Arab nationalism in Palestine and posits that, in spite of the claims made by Zionist public relations, "we can no longer deny the existence of a young Arab movement [in Palestine] with leaders educated in Istanbul and Europe, as a strand in the general Arab movement straddling all the Arab countries." This young movement, he continued, "is not fully formed, and it cannot be compared to European national movements or to our own, yet it continues to develop before our very eyes."[34]

Castel then moved on to a political analysis of the Arab opponents of Zionism, based on the assumption that their opposition was not immovable. Here he granted a central role to the Balfour Declaration: "As is known, the Balfour Declaration is the main barrier to collaboration with the Arabs; it frightens them by referring to 'a Jewish home in Palestine.' The second, restricting clause, that 'nothing shall be done which may prejudice the civil and religious rights of existing non-Jewish communities in Palestine,' does nothing to allay their fears. Yet many would agree to Jewish immigration if this declaration would not have been issued."

Like Epstein, Ben-Kiki, and others, he believed that the declaration and Zionist overcelebration of it became the main impediment to proper relations between Jews and Arabs in the country, but he added a claim no less important, the veracity of which is difficult to assess now: that the opposition of Arabs was not to Jewish immigration per se, but to the fact that it occurred in the context of the national home policy, that is, it made Palestine into a Jewish country, as had been declared by some Zionist leaders. Changing this policy, and recognizing that it was also an Arab country, would have reduced opposition.

Castel continued: "The leaders of their [the Arab] movement will never give up their demands for the Balfour Declaration to be annulled, even if they were convinced that these demands would go unanswered for generations. There is no doubt of this, and of course, our own leaders will never give up this vital historical document, particular the 'national home' phrase, that gives a 'home' to an itinerant people bereft of a homeland. Satisfying both of these demands is impossible."

In his analysis, Castel gave expression to a characteristic of his native Sephardi contemporaries: their understanding for the Arab national movement, its feelings and motives, without abandoning the Zionist perspective or their identification with "our movement" and the Jewish need for a homeland. But regarding the Balfour Declaration, the chasm between the two sides was so great as to be insurmountable. What, then, could be done? What could a man who identified with the Zionist movement, but fully understood and empathized with the Palestinian national movement, suggest?

Before making his proposal, Castel laid out his premises: since the Arabs were the majority in the country, and were there by right; since the British Mandate was in any case committed to improving the lives of Palestinian Arabs; and since "none of us would agree to Zangwill's proposal to drive them out," and the Zionist movement was not opposed to the cultural and economic development of the Arab population—then, he concludes, the Balfour Declaration should be revised to satisfy "both the sides warring over one country, who must, by historical decree, live together and develop in peace and harmony their two national homes in the same country that will one day be *a single state* [the emphasis is Castel's]." And what should the new version be? "Thus, the second, negative clause [stipulating that the rights of non-Jews should not be harmed] should be rewritten by Balfour himself, in a positive manner, such as, 'on condition that they develop the *existing national home of the other inhabitants* [our emphasis]—their education, agriculture, trade, and so on—and protect their legal rights to the land.'"[35]

This was an original and bold proposal from a Zionist perspective: Castel recognized that Palestine was the national home of the Arabs who lived there, and thus proposed that the British—via Balfour himself—declare that Palestine was also the national home of the Palestinian Arabs, and thus recognize their national rights to the land. This deviated from the dominant Zionist approach—and that of Balfour—according to which the Arabs had only civil and religious rights. He believed that recognizing the national rights of Palestinian Arabs would help reduce Arab hostility to Zionism and increase the possibility of cooperation between the two sides. And yet, he did not call for limiting the Zionist enterprise; on the contrary, he was careful to emphasize that Jewish immigration to Palestine would continue. But he did not ignore the fact that a binational framework would require extreme consideration for the Arab position. After revising the Balfour Declaration, as well as the Mandate document that was based on it, it would be possible to convene "a Jewish-Arab congress in Palestine and Israel to determine the terms for cooperation in all spheres of life, material and spiritual, including terms for immigration."[36] In Castel's proposal one can identify the Ottoman ethos of "Shared Homeland" that acknowledges the multiple affiliations and claims to the land. In its essence it differs from the spirit of the Balfour Declaration as well as of the Zionist dominant discourse of his time, which argued for one exclusive Jewish homeland. In that point we can find similarities between Castel and Ben-Kiki's arguments, which share the same point of view as Palestinian natives. But there is also a fundamental difference in their critique and analysis. While Ben-Kiki critiqued the foundation of Zionism in its colonial-settler framework and from that context analyzed the Balfour Declaration and suggested a radical transformation in the Zionist idea and practice, Castel's proposal offered a change of perception toward the native Arabs rather than a fundamental critique of Zionism.

Castel's proposal remains unanswered as far as we can trace; no one in the Zionist leadership responded to Castel's proposal, let alone changed Zionist attitudes toward the Balfour Declaration or the Arabs.

However, when Castel published his ideas in the Arab press two years later, he met a strong, direct opposition. This opposition followed another call by Jamal al-Husseini, the general secretary of the Arab Executive, to the native Jews, to oppose the Balfour Declaration and reject Zionism. It was in March 1923, the very month the Arab Executive succeeded in bringing about the cancellation of the election to the legislative council by arranging a massive boycott of it.

Castel believed that this rejection of the elections and of Zionism by the Arab anti-Zionist leaders was based on misconception, and in his article he offered his ideas on a shared homeland. In the cover letter Castel identified himself as a "Palestinian Jew who respects all nationalists, especially my neighbors because I myself am nationalist, i.e., Zionist," and added that all Palestinian Jews are Zionists like him.[37]

Castel presented three arguments to convince his readers. First, based on their long history of religious attachment and short history of settling and building in the country, Zionists, and actually all Jews, are native to the country and there is no distinction between native and non-native European Jews.

Second, he argued, it is a mistake to believe that the Zionist project can be stopped, "as long as the Israeli people are alive on earth and as long as he has national and religious sentiment."[38] In addition, he stated, there is no reason for any Jew to oppose the Balfour Declaration since it confirms their right to a national home in Palestine, thus al Husseini's call to oppose the Balfour Declaration would not be accepted by them.

So what should the Arabs do, according to Castel? They needed to understand that the Zionists improved the life of everyone who lived in the country, and they should accept the fact that Palestine was the homeland of both Jews and Arabs. What he suggested to them in return was his vision of a shared homeland that should be governed through a political system like in Switzerland or Belgium. Explicitly he presented it as the Zionist Organization political program.[39] In the second part of his article, published a week later, he focused on the achievements of the Zionist movement that improved the country's economy and focused on the international support the Zionist movement had, which made any opposition to it futile.[40]

Two critical responses to Castel were published in the following days. *Filastin*'s editor suggested a critical reading of Castel's piece. First, he argued, Castel was not a real Palestinian and actually could not write in Arabic. More pertinently, he refuted Castel's claim that all Jews are Zionists and mentioned the ultra-Orthodox anti-Zionist attitude as well as the views of the assimilating Jewish elites in France, Britain, and elsewhere. The Jews' rights in Palestine were only religious, and they had no national rights in the country. And as to the main proposal of Castel, the shared homeland, *Filastin*'s reaction was unequivocal: Palestine belonged to the Arabs and they were not going to share it with anyone nor give up their [full] rights over it. The editor concluded with an important note regarding the Arab attitude toward the local Jews: "You should know that the native population of the country started to view the native Jews like you [Castel] with suspicion, and the only way to end this state of suspicion is return to their minds and reject the outlandish Zionist movement which is going to harm not only the local Jews but Jews throughout the world."[41]

Another reply was sent to the paper by Mahmoud Jarkas of Jaffa. He also contended that Palestine was an Arab country in which the Jews had no right: "Until now you had never acknowledged us, and your leaders declared that they want Palestine to be as Jewish as England is English and America American, and now you accept us as your neighbors! Today you are ready to compromise and say that we are two brother nations that should share the homeland," he wrote sarcastically. "What generosity. This is a good result we were expecting, but do you think this is enough for us? No—because Palestine belongs only to us." The author was suggesting that the Jews would acknowledge the full, exclusive right of the Palestinian Arabs to the country, and then the Arabs might invite or accept some Jews to settle in the country if both sides could benefit from that. And as for Husseini's call to the local Jews to join the national movement—this was not because the country needed them but because it wanted to save them from losing their identity, he argued.[42]

Comparing Castel's rhetoric in Hebrew (in his proposal to Weizmann) and in Arabic (in his dialogue with the Arab-Palestinian intellectuals) illuminates his persistent advocacy of the shared homeland solution with stronger reference to binationalist models in Europe on the one hand while at the same time exposing the limitations of his proposal in post-Balfour Palestine and in light of the transformation in the Palestinian national

BETWEEN SHARED HOMELAND TO NATIONAL HOME

discourse. While Castel was trying to implement an Ottoman concept that emerged out of logic of multiple loyalties into a conflicted political context, the Arab-Palestinian response was already representing the logic of rejection of Zionist colonialism that became dominant in post-Balfour Palestine. Reading Castel's arguments regarding the Zionist claim to the land as natives only strengthens our understanding of the different approaches regarding Zionism between him and Ben-Kiki. While Ben-Kiki pointed out the differences between native Arab Jews and European settler Jews, Castel seem to erase the differences and presented them as one unit. In Castel's discourse in Hebrew and Arabic, readers can trace the roots of Sephardi ambivalence in post-Balfour Palestine.

CONCLUSION

The Balfour Declaration was a dramatic moment in the history of Palestine and a turning point in the Jewish-Arab conflict. For the Jewish and Arab natives of the country, who were not party to the formulation of the declaration, it symbolized in the starkest way possible the changing world order and the transformation of their political and social status. While the Arabs opposed the declaration and its consequences from the very beginning, demanding its annulment, the Sephardi natives of the land were caught between them and the Zionist movement and were expected to choose between the two. Their hyphenated identity as Palestinian-Jews exposed them to criticism from both sides: from the Arab-Palestinian leadership for their support of Zionism and their betrayal of their Arab neighbors (as was the case in the responses to Castel in the Arab press, and also to Elias Sasson, when he published his ideas of a Jewish-Arab alliance in the Arab press); and from Zionist activists, who sometimes viewed them as not Zionist enough. Their representatives tried to maneuver between their support for the Balfour Declaration and their identification with their Arab fellows and sought to mediate between the two. While the official representatives of the native Sephardic community adopted the official Zionist stance and repudiated the Palestinian claims that they opposed Zionism and the Balfour Declaration, Hayyim Ben-Kiki and Yosef Hayyim Castel stood out as they both, in their own ways, offered a critical analysis of the declaration. They also both proposed alternative courses of action regarding the Arab question.

Ben-Kiki took a more critical line toward the Zionist movement and its ideological foundations since he saw the declaration as another component of its overall approach, while Castel wrote an internal document for Weizmann and Ussishkin containing a concrete policy proposal, which was never meant to be published, and gained no response. Ben-Kiki's critique of Zionist ideas and actions (including Epstein's) also seemed to go unanswered. Furthermore, they both disappeared from the political and public spheres during the 1920s and 1930s. Ben-Kiki was fired from his role as secretary of the Sephardic Union of Haifa in 1923, seemingly on political grounds, and published no further articles until his tragic death in Aden in 1932. Castel continued as a clerk in the Zionist movement, before working for Hayim Nahman Bialik's publishing house and then founding a Palestine tourism company. He abandoned public and political life except for writing occasional newspaper essays.

What can we conclude from Ben-Kiki and Castel's analysis of the Balfour Declaration and its implications for the natives of Palestine? Ben-Kiki indeed had radical views and opted to change the Zionist web of alliances, but even Sephardi figures who responded positively to the Balfour Declaration were aware of its negative aspects and insisted on the need to take into consideration the Arab population of the country and its national and political rights.[43]

We can find similar approaches in the discourse of the Sephardi rabbinical leadership during the Mandate period. The first Sephardic chief rabbi, Yaacov Meir, made this statement in 1923:

No one will deny that Sephardi Jews, because they are native-born and know the language and customs of the Arabs, could be very helpful in this matter. Many of the country's prominent Arabs have requested me to work toward a peaceful and cooperative relationship between our peoples. It is still not too late to repair the situation by a renewed effort on the part of the Zionist leadership to reach out to all those able and willing to help us in building our national home.[44]

The binationalist option that emerged in the Zionist discourse around the creation of the Brit Shalom movement in 1925 and again in 1942 around the establishment of Ihud echoed in many ways the shared homeland ethos that the Jewish native intellectuals tried to promote. Thus, in the 1940s we can find a return to the spirit of the shared homeland in the discourse of some native Jewish leaders that was connected explicitly and implicitly with the Zionist binationalist movements. Thus, for example, the Chief Rabbi Ben-Zion Meir Hai Uziel responded in 1942 to a memorandum from Dr. Yaacov Tahun, proposing the establishment of two parallel autonomous national regimes:

While this proposal makes no mention of demands for a Jewish state, neither does it in any way deny the heritage of our ancestors in Eretz Yisrael or the hoped-for Kingdom of the House of David. But this proposal is based on the current realities, and the need to adapt to them at present. For it cannot be ignored that we live alongside the Arab people, who are many in number and have lived on large parts of the land for centuries, and justice and logic dictate that they have free autonomy in their own special affairs, and enjoy full and honest partnership in running the common affairs of the state that concern all its inhabitants.[45]

Uziel's recognition of Arab history and national rights in the country were noteworthy and grounded in his close familiarity with the country and its inhabitants. The yearning for redemption ("the hoped-for Kingdom of the House of David") perhaps forced him to treat this solution as only temporary, but still, it was a worthy political arrangement.

In the very same year, following the establishment of the Ihud ["unity"] movement, the head of the Sephardic Community Committee, Eliyahu Eliashar, wrote the following:

In the past, as today, the leadership of the Yishuv and the Zionist trade union [the Histradrut] neglected to draft . . . basic, clear plan for immediate action and for determining our policy and relationship with the Arabs in our country and in the neighboring countries. We have linked our entire destiny exclusively with the West—and this is notwithstanding the fact that the Jewish people originate in the East . . . . from the outset of our project in the Land we locked ourselves into a parochial working framework embodying unjustified and pointless arrogance. Intoxicated by the [Balfour] Declaration, we immersed ourselves wholeheartedly in building our material and spiritual home with love and dedication. . . . . Those who recently arrived in the Land brought with them a European lifestyle altogether different from the one prevailing in the Land. It was a fundamental error—indeed an unpardonable one—that we failed from the outset to establish contacts with our neighbors, to get to know them and to form cultural and economic relations with them. This state of affairs has led to the emergence of a deepening and fear-ridden alienation between our neighbors and us.[46]

It should be noted that this opinion was rooted in familiarity with Palestinian Arabs, and a desire to continue living with them rather than at their expense. In this sense, this is a "Mizrahi" approach, even though it was also taken by others who were not Mizrahi (such as Yitzhak Epstein). But these voices did not find an audience and were relegated to the margins of Zionist public discourse.

Ben-Kiki passed away before the establishment of the state. Eliyahu Eliashar continued seeking a middle path throughout his life, one between Jewish nationalism and the realities of the Middle East. His work in the Israel-Palestine Peace Council before his death in 1981 formed part of his continuing struggle for mutual recognition between the two peoples.

The views of Yosef Hayyim Castel, however, shifted. As the political realities changed, he abandoned his earlier ideas, along with recognition for the national rights of Palestinian Arabs. In an article he wrote two weeks before his death in 1968, titled "On the Liberated Territories," he presented widely accepted arguments against Israeli withdrawal from the West Bank. He noted that Transjordan was supposed to have been included in the borders of the Jewish national home but was parceled off by the British; that there had never been a Palestinian state; that the Arabs of Palestine had never formed a separate nation; that some believed that Palestinian Arabs were in fact descended from Jews; that the 1967 war was a defensive war; and that the Arabs had always refused any compromise—and thus reached the conclusion that "we have returned to our homeland, Western Eretz Yisrael, and it is clear that we have every right to fortify ourselves within it."[47]

It appears that the change in Castel's historical viewpoint indicates more than just a shift in one person's perspective. As we have shown in this chapter, the calls from some Jewish natives of the land to recognize Arab-Palestinian nationalism were very much outside the mainstream, including their own communities. The growing strength of the Zionist movement and of the Jewish Yishuv seemed to negate their claims that it was necessary to reach an understanding with Palestine's Arabs. Some of them continued to believe fully in the importance of such an accord; others abandoned their optimism and joined the main body of the Yishuv in its preference for the West over the East and for Zionist action over true dialogue.

Examining this neglected aspect in the history of Palestine at the turn of the twentieth century sheds new light on this key formative period in the creation of the Zionist-Arab conflict. Shifting the focus to the Sephardi natives enables us not only to trace back cultural and political options that materialized but also to reveal options that emerged at the time but were negated, marginalized, and forgotten. It also opens for us new paths to expose unexplored political options that aimed to transform and reshape social and cultural realities at a formative moment in the history of modern Palestine.

Thus, focusing on the role of the Sephardi Jews in this formative and dramatic period, helps us to understand the main political questions in both historical and contemporary Israel-Palestine beyond the logic of partition, which not only separates the question of Palestine from the Jewish question but also the histories and realities of the native Arabs and Jews of the land.

NOTES

Portions of our discussion here were published in our article: Yuval Evri and Hillel Cohen, "Shared Homeland or Jewish National Home: Sephardi Natives of the Land, Balfour Declaration and the Arab Question," *Theory and Criticism* 49 (2017): 291–304. The Van Leer Jerusalem Institute, Hakibbutz Hameuchad 2017 (Hebrew).

1. We decided not to confine ourselves to a single term such as "Sephardim" or "native Jews" but to illustrate the many terms used to mark the native-born in the Jewish and Arab discourse of the time. Throughout the chapter, we chose various combinations, such as "Mizrahi Jews," "Arab-Jews," "Palestinian Jews," or "local Jews"—mostly in accordance with the context in which they originally appeared. Similarly, we do not differentiate between "Oriental" and "Mughrabi." Due to the lack of space, we cannot discuss the various implications of these categories. For further details on the category of the native Jewish population at the turn of the twentieth century, see Yitzhak Bezalel, *Noladtem Ziyonim* [You Were Born Zionists] (Jerusalem: Yad Ben Zvi, 2008); Yuval Evri, *"Hashiva le-andalus: mahlokot al zehut ve tarbut yehudit-sefaradit ben arviut le ivriut"* (The Return to Al-Andalus: Disputes Over Sephardi Culture and Identity Between Arabic and Hebrew) Jerusalem: Magnes Press; Abigail Jacobson and Moshe Naor, *Oriental Neighbors* (Waltham, Mass.: Brandeis University Press, 2016).
2. Official Report: Deputation of the Executive Committee of the Haifa Congress Received by the Secretary of the Colonies," March 28, 1921. National Archives, file CAB 24/126, appendix 23, 145–146.
3. Jacobson and Naor, *Oriental Neighbors*, 22.
4. Jacobson and Naor, *Oriental Neighbors*: 22.
5. *Mirat al-Sharq*, November 21, 1936, 1.
6. *Mirat al-Sharq*, November 21, 1936, 7.

7. Michelle Campos, *Ottoman Brotherhood: Muslims, Christians, and Jews in Early Twentieth-Century Palestine* (Palo Alto, Calif: Stanford University Press, 2011); Neville J. Mandel, *The Arabs and Zionism Before World War I* (Berkeley: University of California Press, 1976), 225. See also Jonathan Gribetz, *Defining Neighbors* (Princeton, N.J.: Princeton University Press, 2014); Abigail Jacobson, *From Empire to Empire: Jerusalem Between Ottoman and British Rule* (Syracuse, N.Y.: Syracuse University Press, 2011); Rashid Khalidi, *Palestinian Identity: The Construction of Modern National Consciousness* (New York: Columbia University Press, 1997).

8. Abd al-'Al al-Bakouri, "Zionist-Israeli Propaganda and the Claim that 'the Arabs Want to Throw the Jews into the Sea,'" *Shuún Filastiniyya* 27 (1973), 172.

9. Letter from a member of the Jewish community to Y. Ben Tzvi of the Jewish Committee of Jerusalem, CZA, J1/149.

10. Jacobson and Naor, *Oriental Neighbors*, 21.

11. For more on the history of the development and intersection of these questions, see the introduction to this volume by Bashir and Farsakh.

12. Here we follow Ella Shohat's path; her groundbreaking article shows the intersection between the emergence of the question of Palestine and the emergence of the question of the Arab Jews (Shohat, *On the Arab-Jew, Palestine, and Other Displacements* [London: Pluto Press, 2017]).

13. On this Sephardi vision, see Moshe Behar and Zvi Ben-Dor Benite, *Modern Middle Eastern Jewish Thought: Writing on Identity, Politics, and Culture 1893–1958* (Waltham, Mass.: Brandeis University Press, 2013); Jacobson, *From Empire to Empire*.

14. For more on the multiple positions of the Sephardim, see Behar and Ben-Dor Benite, *Modern Middle Eastern Jewish Thought*; Bezalel, *Noladtem Ziyonim*; Campos, *Ottoman Brotherhood*; Jacobson, *From Empire to Empire*; Lital Levy, "The Nahda and the Haskala: A Comparative Reading of 'Revival' and 'Reform,'" *Middle Eastern Literatures* 16, no. 3 (2013), 300–316.

15. For more on this perception, see Moshe Behar and Zvi Ben-Dor Benite, "The Possibility of Modern Middle Eastern Jewish Thought," *British Journal of Middle Eastern Studies* 44, no. 1 (2014, 43–61; Levy, "Nahda and Haskala."

16. Jacobson, *From Empire to Empire*, 82–117.

17. Campos, *Ottoman Brotherhood*, 1–19.

18. Behar and Ben-Dor Benite, "Possibility of Modern Middle Eastern Jewish Thought," 43–61.

19. Behar and Ben-Dor Benite, "Possibility of Modern Middle Eastern Jewish Thought"; Bezalel, *Noladtem Ziyonim*; Campos, *Ottoman Brotherhood*, 1–19; Hillel Cohen, "Hayav u'moto shel ha-yehudi ha-aravi be-eretz yisrael u'mihutza la" ["The life and death of the Arab Jew in Eretz Yisrael and elsewhere"], *Studies in the Rebirth of Israel* 9 (2015), 171–200; Jacobson and Naor, *Oriental Neighbors*; Menachem Klein, "Arab Jew in Palestine," *Israel Studies* 9, no. 3 (2014), 134–153; Lital Levy, "Partitioned Pasts: Arab Jewish Intellectuals and the Case of Esther Azhari Moyal (1873–1948)," in *The Making of the Arab Intellectual (1880–1960): Empire, Public Sphere, and the Colonial Coordinates of Selfhood*, ed. Dyala Hamzah (London: Routledge, 2012), 128–163.

20. Before World War I, the total Jewish population in Palestine was between 60,000 and 85,000, out of a total population of 720,000. Only 10,000–12,000 lived in villages, nearly all of them in the more than forty agricultural colonies that had been established since 1878 (Khalidi, *Palestinian Identity*, 96–97).

21. Campos, *Ottoman Brotherhood*; , 224–244; Jacobson, *From Empire to Empire*, 82–117.

22. Ruth Kark and Joseph B. Glass, "The Jews in Eretz-Israel/Palestine: From Traditional Peripherality to Modern Centrality," *Israel Affairs* 5, no. 4 (1999), 73–107. See also Cohen, "Hayav u'moto"; Evri, "Paneha ha-merubot"; Jacobson and Naor, *Oriental Neighbors*.

23. For a survey of such negotiations, see Eliezer Tauber, "Jewish–non-Palestinian-Arab Negotiations: The First Phase," *Israel Affairs* 6 (2000), 3–4, 159–176; on the change of that policy, see Hillel Cohen, *Army of Shadows: Palestinian Collaborators in the Service of Zionism 1917–1948* (Berkeley: University of California Press, 2008), 19.

24. On the Sephardi involvement with the Arab question, see Yosef Eliyahu Chelouche, *Parashat Hayai 1870–1930* [*My Life, 1870–1830*] (Tel Aviv: Stroud, 1930); Cohen, "Hayav u'moto"; Eliyahu Eliashar, *Lihyot im yehudim* [*Living with Jews*] (Jerusalem: Y. Marcus, 1981); Jacobson and Naor, *Oriental Neighbors*.

25. Bezalel, *Noladtem Ziyonim*; Campos, *Ottoman Brotherhood*; Cohen, "Hayav u'moto"; Evri, "Paneha ha-merubot"; Jacobson, *From Empire to Empire*; Lital Levy, "Jewish Writers in the Arab East: Literature, History, and the Politics of Enlightenment, 1863–1914" (PhD diss., Berkeley: University of California, 2007).

26. Bezalel, *Noladtem Ziyonim*, 374, 381, 386.

27. On the logic of multiple loyalties, see Campos, *Ottoman Brotherhood*; Mandel, *Arabs and Zionism*.

28. Hayyim Ben-Kiki was born in Tiberias in 1887 to a well-known family of rabbis and for a number of years was the secretary of the Sephardic Union in Haifa and the northern correspondent for *Doar Hayom*. He died suddenly in the port city of Aden, on his way to India as an emissary of the Sephardic community in Tiberias in 1935. For more on Ben-Kiki, see Behar and Ben-Dor Benite, *Modern Middle Eastern Jewish Thought* and Behar and Ben-Dor Benite, "Possibility of Modern Middle Eastern Jewish Thought."

29. Behar and Ben-Dor Benite, *Modern Middle Eastern Jewish Thought*; Behar and Ben-Dor Benite, "Possibility of Modern Middle Eastern Jewish Thought."

30. Hayyim Ben-Kiki, "Ha-tarbut ha-eropit ba-mizrah," *Doar Hayom*, October 12–15, 1920, in Behar and Ben-Dor Benite, *Modern Middle Eastern Jewish Thought*, 97.

31. Hayyim Ben-Kiki, "Al she'elat ha-she'elot be-yishuv ha-aretz," ["On the question of questions regarding the settling of the land"], *Doar Hayom*, August 30, 1921, in Behar and Ben-Dor Benite, *Modern Middle Eastern Jewish Thought*, 103–104.

32. For further discussion of Epstein's article, see Alan Dowty, "A Question That Outweighs All Others: Yitzhak Epstein and Zionist Recognition of the Arab Issue," *Israel Studies* 6, no. 1 (2001), 34–54.

33. Yosef Hayim Castel, "Le-pitron she'elat ha-aravim be-eretz yisrael" ["Solving the Arab Question in Eretz Yisrael"], Central Zionist Archives, Z4/41245 (October 7, 1921).

34. Castel, "Le-pitron she'elat ha-aravim," 3.

35. Castel, "Le-pitron she'elat ha-aravim," 4–5.

36. Castel, "Le-pitron she'elat ha-aravim," 5.

37. Yosef Hayim Castel, *Filastin*, March 16, 1923, 3.

38. Castel, *Filastin*, March 16, 1923, 4.

39. Castel, *Filastin*, March 16, 1923, 4.

40. *Filastin*, March 20, 1923, 3.

41. *Filastin*, March 23, 1923, 1.
42. Mahmoud Jarkas, "The Native Jews and Zionism," *Filastin*, March 27, 1923, 2.
43. See Bezalel, *Noladtem Ziyonim*; Cohen, "Hayav u'moto"; Eliashar, *Liyhot im yehudim*; Jacobson and Naor, *Oriental Neighbors*.
44. Quoted in Eliashar, *Lihyot im yehudim*, 196.
45. Israel State Archives, file P 894/11.
46. Eliyahu Eliashar, "Yehudim ve-aravim" ["Jews and Arabs"], *Ha-Mizrah*, September 11, 1942, in Behar and Ben-Dor Benite, *Modern Middle Eastern Jewish Thought*, 133.
47. Yosef Hayim Castel, *Dapei Hayim* [Life Pages] (Tel Aviv, 1970), 47–48.

Chapter Seven

TOWARD A FIELD OF ISRAEL/PALESTINE STUDIES

DEREK PENSLAR

This volume is about the discursive entanglement of the "Jewish question" and the "Arab question" on the one hand and encounters between real Jews and real Arabs on the other. The success of the Zionist movement, the Palestinians' loss of their homeland, and the diminishing possibilities for Palestinian statehood have caused those encounters to be often hostile, and, particularly within Israel/Palestine, lethal. The editors and contributors to this volume unpack the interdependence of the Jewish and Arab questions and excavate the terrain of past symbioses between Jews and Arabs in order to promote new forms of constructive engagement. In this chapter, I consider scholars who work on these subjects as sources in and of themselves. I place scholarly work on Jewish-Arab encounters within the framework of the academic fields known as "Israel Studies" and "Palestine Studies" and explore whether these fields promote or impede the constructive encounters that we, the editors and contributors to this volume, valorize.

In today's world the most visible aspect of the Jewish and Arab "questions" is Israel/Palestine. The Israeli-Palestinian conflict generates waves of student and faculty activism. The public debate about Israel and Palestine at universities has rarely, however, integrated the academic teaching and research that lie at the center of a university's mission. This scholarship and teaching is often carried out in distinct academic fields such as Jewish, Israel, Middle Eastern, and Palestine Studies. This chapter examines the discourses on Israel/Palestine produced by these fields and assesses the effect of institutional separatism on the study of Jewish-Arab encounters. I am particularly interested in the institutional division between Israel and Palestine Studies.

The sources and methods employed by students of Israel Studies and Palestine Studies often differ, as do the questions they ask and the problems they seek to solve. These differences reflect the considerable divergence between Israel and Palestine's historic arcs and contemporary configurations. Relative to the Middle East, Israel is a regional superpower, whereas Palestine has achieved statehood in name only, and the Arab population within historic Palestine lives either under Israeli occupation (in the territories captured in 1967) or under discriminatory conditions within the state of Israel. Whereas Israel's foundational events, e.g., the 1948 and 1967 wars, were victories for Israel, for the Palestinians these wars were national disasters that resulted in the exile and dispersion of the bulk of the Palestinian people. Israel's narrative is of a suffering nation that has achieved redemption yet lives under constant threat; Palestine's is that of a people still living in exile and bondage yet determined to resist its oppressor.

In my teaching and research, I am constantly aware of these differences. As a graduate student during the 1980s, I came to the study of modern Israel through the fields of Jewish and European history. There was nothing explicitly apologetic or teleological about my educational formation, but it structured my thinking about the Zionist project in terms of modern Jewish politics and culture and European nationalism. I was also well aware, from the start of my graduate career, about Zionism's links with European colonialism. I wrote about those connections in my doctoral thesis and have returned to them over and again throughout my career. But in comparison with Jewish and European history, my engagement with modern Middle Eastern history has been more limited. Although I have read widely in Middle Eastern historiography I have not learned Arabic, nor have I spent significant amounts of time in the Arab world. In this sense, I am like many scholars of Israel Studies, who know Hebrew well, are native to or have lived for extended periods in Israel, and usually have a broad training in history or the social sciences, but who lack both academic expertise and intimate familiarity with the region in the midst of which the State of Israel is situated. My own subject position is thus the mirror image of those Middle Eastern historians who write on Palestine with scholarly and linguistic expertise but who do not know Hebrew and have a limited knowledge of the Jewish civilization from which the Zionist project emerged.

Fortunately, despite these vast geopolitical differences, there are increasing numbers of scholars who are intimately familiar with the history, languages, culture, and politics of both the state of Israel and the Palestinian people. In this chapter I will suggest how points of contact between those who identify themselves as students of modern Israel or Palestine can be enhanced. We must start with the fact that both Israel Studies and Palestine Studies focus on the same small territory—whether it is called historic Palestine or, in Zionist parlance, the land of Israel. In other ways, as well, there is a great deal of overlap between the two fields. Despite the Boycott, Divestment, Sanctions (BDS) movement and campaigns against the normalization of relations between Israeli and Palestinian scholars, practitioners of Israel Studies and Palestine Studies are often in conversation with each other. They frequently attend the same conferences and at times have close collegial relations. They seek out and read each other's work. Both fields can be politically charged with opposing polarities, but as I will show, the separation between the two fields is a product of institutional structures as well as political conviction. Most important, a generation of younger scholars, fluent in both Arabic and Hebrew, and committed to exploring the entangled nature of Zionist-Israeli and Palestinian history, is creating a new epistemological paradigm in which Israel/Palestine is being studied within an eponymous unified field.

Nonetheless, an *histoire croisée* of Israel and Palestine presents enormous challenges. Attempts to produce such work have at times fallen short of their methodological goals and treated Jews and Palestinians in separation.[1] In a joint history, core issues that lie at the heart of the conflict are consistently exposed, and clashing interpretations of Zionism, Palestinian peoplehood, the Palestinians' position within the Arab and Muslim worlds, and the relationship between anti-Zionism and antisemitism cannot be elided. Scholars who work on Israel/Palestine must decide, therefore, if it is their responsibility to engage in overt political advocacy, to cloak that advocacy under a pretense to Weberian neutrality, or to aspire to neutrality even if it is impossible to attain. They must decide whether "civility," that is, rational, respectful, and courteous conversation, is a relic from a bygone era, a screen for the concealment and maintenance of hegemony, or if it has continuing value as a means of fostering constructive communication with an often angry and fearful public. I believe that unlike the realms of political discourse and public opinion (now expressed via limitless and unchecked access to the internet), academic conversation about Israel/Palestine can and should refract, rather than reflect, the conflict. To continue with the optical metaphor, an academic field of Israel/Palestine studies can help not only scholars and students, but also a broad, global public, see the area in a new light.

DEFINING TERMS

The complexity of scholarly research and university-level teaching on Israel/Palestine is too great to justify simplistic divisions between faculty members who are "pro-Israel" or "pro-Palestine." These terms are at best ideal types or approximations of a rich and diverse discourse with enormous variations among those who would identify themselves as supportive of Israel, Palestine, or both. These terms must be used with caution and within specific contexts. In its broadest sense, to be "pro-Israel" means to believe that the establishment and future existence of Israel as a state with a prominent Jewish character are morally and historically justified. "Pro-Israel" is in this sense largely congruent with "Zionist," a word that has lost much of the depth of its original meanings, which were associated with a Jewish right to collective self-determination within historic Palestine, and it has all too often been tied to or associated with racist and exclusive forms of Jewish nationalism. One of the most important things one learns from the scholarly study of the Zionist project is that over the past 130 years "Zionism" has been more a matrix of concepts than a strictly-defined ideology. Within this capacious sentiment of yearning for Jewish self-determination, Zionism can incorporate binational, liberal, and non-statist approaches, or chauvinistic and territorially maximalist ones. One can thus be a Zionist and fully endorse or entirely reject Palestinian national rights. To be pro-Palestinian is similarly open-ended and can align with widely varying goals such as a Palestinian state alongside of Israel or a unitary state that may or may not be formally binational and may or may not welcome Jews as equals.

In general, "pro-Israel" is identified with opposition to the BDS movement, although there are Jews, both in Israel and abroad, who strongly consider themselves pro-Israel and who support a boycott limited to goods and services emanating from the occupied Palestinian territories. In turn, scholars who identify with the Palestinian cause have a wide range of views about the BDS movement, whose methods and tactics are themselves diverse, a product of it being, as BDS activist David Lloyd, puts it, a "decentralized, rhizomatic, and global civil society movement."[2] The Palestine Campaign for the Academic and Cultural Boycott of Israel has devised guidelines that draw a distinction between collaboration with individual Israeli academics, which is permitted, and institutional collaboration with Israeli universities or "complicit Israeli institutions or their support or lobby groups in various countries," which is forbidden.[3] The interpretation of these guidelines varies from person to person; for example, some scholars would define academic programs in Israel Studies as "support or lobby groups" for the state of Israel, whereas others would not. The terms "pro-Israel" and "pro-Palestinian" are therefore more revealing of an individual's self-understanding and self-representation than they are coherent categories of belief and behavior. The terms provide little indication of the precise questions posed and methods adopted by a scholar of modern Israel/Palestine.

CAMPUS ACTIVISM AND THE SCHOLARLY MISSION: OVERLAP AND DIFFERENCE

The current debates about Israel on university campuses are primarily the product of students, not academic staff. Instructors can have strong political views, and some have supported the BDS movement. The numbers, however, are small; at the largest and most prestigious research universities in the Anglophone world, (e.g., Oxford, Michigan, Berkeley, UCLA, Toronto) fewer than twenty individuals, including graduate students, post-doctoral fellows, and adjunct lecturers, have signed BDS petitions.[4] At most universities, a handful of academic staff regularly speak at pro-Palestinian events and take on a mentoring role to pro-Palestinian student activists. Advocacy on behalf of Israel is taken up by even smaller contingents of academic staff, some of whom organize into groups such as Scholars for Peace in the Middle East or the Canadian Academic Friends of Israel.

Most academics involved in pro-Palestinian and pro-Israeli campus activity are not experts in Middle Eastern or Israel Studies. After all, there are not many such experts in any university. By and large, support for the Palestinian cause comes from certain disciplines—not only Middle Eastern Studies, but also those fields within the humanities and social sciences that have, in recent decades, become closely identified with championing the oppressed, defending the dignity and autonomy of indigenous peoples, and challenging established authority. These fields include anthropology, postcolonial studies, gender studies, cultural studies, and English and comparative literature. Scholars in these fields see in critical theory a means of deconstructing what they would call discourses of domination.[5] In contrast, an engaged, pro-Palestinian approach is less common in the fields of political science and international relations, which engage directly with the exercise of state power and that, informed by variations of classic Realism, conceive of the state and conflict as sempiternal. (Scholars in security studies, a field that is deeply intertwined with the post-9/11 "war on terror," are more likely to reflect rather than challenge the often close relations between the Israeli and American military and intelligence services.)[6]

Whatever the nature of activism related to Israel/Palestine within the academy, the fact remains that the most visible and voluble debates among academics about Israel are occurring beyond the small clusters of scholars who have expertise in Israel/Palestine and its broader, Middle Eastern, context. Scholars of Israel Studies frequently, though by no means always, forge a meeting of minds with their colleagues who work on the Arab Middle East, Turkey, and Iran. It is not unusual for scholars of Israel and Middle Eastern Studies to disagree profoundly about the cause or interpretation of events but to respect each other's scholarly integrity and to defend their rights to freedom of inquiry and expression. To be sure, the relationship between the two fields can be fraught and filled with suspicion. On the other hand, the possibility of good professional relationships, respect, and dialogue assumes that in dialogues between people of different faiths or political viewpoints disagreement is the norm, not the exception. Moreover, Middle Eastern Studies is not the only academic field with which scholars of modern Israel find themselves both in contact and in tension. The other is, surprisingly, Jewish Studies. We can conceive of these three fields as points that constitute an isosceles triangle, with Israel Studies at the apex, resting upon yet removed from both of the others.

The Zionist project cannot be understood outside of the context of Jewish civilization, yet as an academic field, Jewish Studies is not well-suited to the study of modern Israel. A brief analysis of Jewish Studies' conceptual underpinnings will illuminate the problem. Since Jewish civilization is an ethno-religious collective, it has developed a secular as well as sacred lettered tradition, a political as well as ecclesiastical history. Scholars of Jewish Studies may be roughly divided between those are who are textualists and those who are contextualists. The former are scholars of Judaism, Jewish thought, and Jewish literature, while the latter are almost always historians, with some political scientists and an increasing number of scholars coming from a cultural studies perspective.

Israel Studies clearly lies in the contextualist camp, but its practitioners often ask a range of questions not within the ken of historians, social scientists, and cultural studies scholars of the Jews. Jewish Studies' contextualists think mainly about identity, community, and the mutual dynamic of Jewish and non-Jewish culture. Anti-Semitism and its effects on the Jewish world are of immense interest. Israel Studies scholars, on the other hand, are concerned with the accumulation and exercise by Jews of sovereign power, state formation and practice, diplomatic affairs, and ethnic conflict within the Israeli polity. Jewish Studies is the study of a globally diffuse population and does not have the tools to understand many aspects of a sovereign Jewish homeland. Paraphrasing Immanuel Kant, the Israeli historian Ehud Luz has observed that although throughout history Jews have at times wielded *Macht* (power) to shape their own religious and communal life, they have not exercised *Herrschaft* (domination) over another people.[7] Thus Israel's domination of the Palestinians is without historical precedent in Jewish history, and scholars of Jewish Studies are often hardpressed to make sense of it within the framework of their own academic training (and life experience). If Jewish Studies is about Jews, Israel Studies is about Israelis, most of whom are Jews, but a quarter of whom are not. Israel's occupation of the West Bank and control over the Gaza Strip bring almost to parity the number of Jews and Arabs whose lives fall within the purview of a scholar of Israel Studies.

Palestine Studies' connection with Middle Eastern Studies is less fraught than that between Israel Studies and Jewish Studies. Since antiquity, Palestine has been a focal point of the Mashriq, and the same methods and approaches that a scholar would bring to bear on the study of modern Syria or Lebanon can be brought to the study of Palestine. Nonetheless, one can discern tensions between Palestine Studies and Islamic Studies. Middle Eastern Studies and Islamic Studies are not synonymous, given the long history of Christian Arab communities and of non-Arab, non-Muslim minorities in the region, but the Arab Middle East, including Palestine, has been predominantly Muslim, and, given Jerusalem's status as one of the most holy sites in the Islamic world, Palestinian politics has been steeped in Islamic rhetoric and imagery. Yet scholarship on modern Palestine often underplays this connection. Major scholars of Palestinian history (e.g., Salim Tamari, Beshara Doumani, Rashid Khalidi, Zachary Lockman, Michelle Campos, and Sherene Seikaly) have offered detailed analyses of Palestinian political movements and social and economic life in the late Ottoman and Mandate periods.[8] There is a sizable literature on the history and political activity of Israel's Palestinian citizens (e.g., recent work by Oded Haklai, Amal Jamal, and Shira Robinson), while a growing body of literature, pioneered by Yezid Sayigh, examines post-1967 Palestinian politics within the Occupied Territories, the Middle East, and the international arena.[9] Several scholars have examined the relationship between religion and politics in modern Palestine,[10] but the most senior and influential scholars at the major centers of graduate training in modern Middle Eastern history in the United States (e.g., NYU's Lockman, Columbia's Khalidi, and Stanford's Joel Beinin) do not deal directly with religion in their own work, and this orientation is reflected in the work of their doctoral students. Perhaps this lacuna is the product of a Marxist (or more broadly radical) historical approach that emphasizes the primacy of material factors over ideology, or perhaps it reflects a secular ethos that is widespread among many practitioners of the historical and social sciences in North America.

In previous generations, scholars of Israel Studies were very much influenced by the hegemonic secular Zionism of the mid-twentieth century, but in recent years the field has become more open to conceptions of late Ottoman Palestine's population as divided along religious rather than ethnic lines.[11] The field has also paid increasing attention to the significance of religion among Israel/Palestine's communities of Jews of Middle Eastern origin.[12] In these and other ways, the fields of Israel and Palestine Studies, which developed in isolation from each other, are beginning to merge, even if their practitioners are not always aware of it.

ISRAEL STUDIES AND PALESTINE STUDIES: GENESIS AND DEVELOPMENT

In the nineteenth and first half of the twentieth centuries, historical and social scientific scholarship frequently served as the handmaiden of national awakening and as a fundamentally state-supporting tool. Since the Second World War, the scholarship has become increasingly critical, that is, operating outside of the conceptual and political system that is the subject of analysis, expunging its terminology from the observer's analytical vocabulary, and striving to maintain independence from the elites currently governing the states or nations under the scholar's microscope. This critical ethos characterizes the development of Israel Studies as an academic field. By the 1970s, Israeli universities had produced and hired scholars of Israel's history and society, and some of them, particularly sociologists at the University of Haifa, had a pronouncedly critical approach to such sensitive issues as immigration and Ashkenazi-Mizrahi relations. The founders of the Association for Israel Studies (1985) included farsighted social scientists such as Ian Lustick and Baruch Kimmerling, who placed Israel within broader frameworks of comparative state expansion and contraction and whose ideas were widely adopted across the field.

In the early 2000s, Israel Studies began to experience rapid growth, primarily in North America and the United Kingdom. Many of the new teaching posts were funded from general university resources, but some, particularly at the most senior level, were funded by private benefactors who were Jewish, sympathetic with Israel, and concerned with what they perceived to be an unfairly negative depiction of Israel on university campuses. These new positions generated concerns throughout academia, particularly in Middle Eastern Studies, that the scholars hired to fill these posts would use them as vehicles for apologetics and advocacy. These concerns were in part a response to the transformation of many public universities' funding model from state support to a constant search for external funding, at the possible cost of the sacrifice of academic freedom. As universities began to accept funding for endowed positions in ethnic or national studies, it was not uncommon for members of ethno-religious communities funding such posts to become irate about the chairholders' scholarship or publicly expressed opinions that did not accord with cherished collective memories of victimization and unresolved grievances against other nationalities.

In Israel Studies as well there has been the possibility for disharmony between benefactors and scholars, between community interest and scholarly striving for disinterest, and between a yearning for certainty and affirmation and the scholar's obligation to interrogate and critique. Notably, however much suspicion the field of Israel Studies has evoked among scholars of Middle Eastern studies, the individuals hired for these new positions have rarely been the objects of attack. That is, there has been opposition to Israel Studies per se yet not to the actual scholarship produced by the individuals hired to fill these posts. Middle Eastern Studies scholars have usually been cordial, and at times close, to faculty members and doctoral students in Israel Studies. That is not to deny the powerful sense of grievance toward Israel and its chief patron, the United States, which can be found in Middle East Studies departments. That grievance can manifest itself in splenetic language, which I have at times felt to be discomfiting and disturbing, yet over the course of my thirty-five-year career I recall only two occasions where a colleague in Middle Eastern Studies spoke to me in language that I considered to be unequivocally anti-Semitic. More common, in my experience, has been a substantial measure of civility, which is an important mechanism for the management of disagreement and not something to be taken lightly or for granted.

I am aware that civility can be invoked to obscure or dilute a political cause. According to all sides a right to be heard can have the pernicious effect of enforcing an epistemological and, by extension, political status quo. Even worse, it can, as seen in recent controversies about "free speech" in the United States, be a strategy for justifying the airing of hateful and racist views. In my view, "civility" neither tolerates incendiary speech nor endorses passivity, circumlocution, or a refusal to argue vigorously for one's position. Civility, rather, enables intelligent conversation, without which there can be no response to conflict other than emotional manipulation and the appeal to brute force. To the extent that debate about Israel/Palestine ceases to be civil, it ceases to have informational value. To the extent that faculty colleagues in Israel and Middle Eastern Studies are civil with one another, they can teach each other's students and frankly discuss how differing political positions influence the questions scholars ask, the methods they employ to answer them, and the answers they derive.

Not only political perspectives, but also deep-seated structural factors, account for the parallel development of "Israel Studies" and "Palestine Studies" as separate fields, even though they both examine the same 11,000-square-mile patch of land, the same people, and the same situations. Israel Studies emerged within a sovereign state possessed of longstanding political and economic institutions. When the first institutions and journals for the study of Zionism and Israel were founded at Israeli universities during the 1960s and 1970s, the Yishuv (Palestine's pre-1948 Jewish community) and Israel were epistemologically constructed as objects with an existence separate from the Israeli–Palestinian conflict. Alongside of, yet distinct from, the historians who first began to chronicle the history of the Yishuv and early State of Israel arose a cohort of Middle East or security experts, often with backgrounds in military intelligence, who studied Arab affairs from the perspective of "knowing the enemy."[13] Israel's political, social, and economic history was thus hived off from that of the Arabs, even those who lived within the state, not to mention the refugees who were just beyond its borders. In contrast, in Palestine Studies there has been much less of a separation between self and other, the nation and its enemy, in that Palestine is simultaneously a historical reality and an as-yet unachieved political aspiration. There is a vast body of literature on Palestinian society, culture, and politics in the late Ottoman and Mandate periods, but it is difficult to write a history of post-1948 Palestine that is not intertwined with Israel given that millions of Palestinians live under Israeli rule or occupation, or as refugees in neighboring lands, from which Palestinian guerrillas have launched raids or fired rockets into Israel, and whom Israeli armed forces have attacked with massive force.

The lopsided relationship between the fields of Israel and Palestine Studies, wherein the former conceives of itself as self-sufficient, while the latter, however reluctantly, acknowledges that the two are intertwined, dates back to the time when the history of both groups was largely written by activists and functionaries rather than university-based scholars. On the one hand, the Zionist labor movement and Israel Defense Force produced works like the multivolume history of the Israel Defense Force, *Sefer Toldot ha-Haganah* (1954–1972). On the other, the Institute for Palestine Studies, established in Beirut in 1963, and the Palestine Liberation Organization Research Center, founded, also in Beirut, two years later, produced a vast corpus of published material that combined polemics with what Jonathan Gribetz, in his current book project on the PLO Research Center, calls "highly sophisticated pieces of academic, if engaged, research."[14] The PLO Research Center's early publications included studies of Israel's hegemonic political party, Mapai, the Israeli economy, the kibbutz, and women in Israeli society. The Institute for Palestine Studies translated selections from the writings of David Ben-Gurion, as well as from works of Israeli official historiography, into Arabic.[15] Particularly in its early years, *the Journal of Palestine Studies* devoted considerable attention to Israeli domestic politics and foreign and military affairs that directly affected Palestinians throughout the world.

The extent to which Palestinian scholars have accurately "known the enemy" has varied, in part because many do not know Hebrew and/or have never been to the State of Israel (as opposed to what for many was their birthplace in Ottoman and British Palestine). Moreover, engaged scholarship produced in nationalistically oriented venues, without the oversight of peer review or the rigorous documentation of sources, can be of limited benefit. For example, in 1968, when Anis Sayigh, director-general of the PLO Research Center, published translated portions of Theodor Herzl's diaries into Arabic, he did so in order to prove that "the Zionist movement is a colonial movement," that it adopted "unethical methods" such as bribery and deceit to attain its goals, and that it was anti-socialist.[16] Sayigh argued that the diaries were a far more valuable historical source than the *Protocols of the Elders of Zion*, whose inauthenticity Sayigh disturbingly did not clearly deny. He also made unsubstantiated and erroneous claims that the Zionist movement attempted to suppress publication of the diaries. Sayigh was correct, however, to point out that the diaries clearly laid out Herzl's aspirations for colonial alliances, as well as his lack of consideration of the rights of a future Jewish state's native population, which, at one point early in his dairies, he considered transferring to neighboring lands.[17]

The story of the Arabic translation of Herzl's diaries illustrates the interdependence between parties to a conflict upon sources produced by both their own brethren and their antagonists. The question of sources is particularly painful and urgent for Palestinian scholars. The Zionist movement and the State of Israel have produced well-stocked and well-ordered archives, in which generations of documentation has accumulated, and which is usually made available to scholars regardless of provenance, although access can be difficult, if not impossible, for Palestinians, depending on their citizenship and the nature of the material they have requested. Access to the Israel State Archive has of late been stymied by two, possibly unrelated, events: a mammoth digitization project has effectively closed the archives' reading room and recent legislation has ruled that files from any government ministry may not be released without written approval from that ministry. (It is conceivable that the current government wishes to slow down scholarly access to information that might put the state's previous acts and policies in a bad light.) Even before these developments, access by any scholar to files dealing with security and military affairs was uneven and unpredictable. Nonetheless, compared with scholarly research on Israel, research on Palestine has been seriously hindered by the destruction, dispersion, or sequestration of Palestinian archival sources as well as the hermeneutic of suspicion assumed by Arab state archives toward the public. For these reasons, Palestinian scholars have depended heavily on family or local archives as well as oral history.[18]

Whereas Israeli scholars have until recently had the luxury of access to troves of local archival sources, Palestinian scholarship has had to look elsewhere: to archives scattered throughout the world, printed Arabic sources, and oral history. It has also relied on Israeli scholarship. When in 1988 Benny Morris wrote of the "New History" of the 1948 war, he insisted that he and a few of his peers were the first to enter the relevant archives, where they found abundant evidence that Israel fought the 1948 war from a position of strength, not weakness, and that the forced flight of over half of historic Palestine's Arabs was, directly or indirectly, Israel's responsibility. But these claims were hardly new; they had been adumbrated by earlier scholarship by the eminent Palestinian scholar Walid Khalidi, co-founder of the Institute for Palestine Studies. And although Khalidi did not have access to archival sources, he made constructive use of published Israeli sources for his seminal article of 1961 on the Haganah's Plan D, which Khalidi called a "master plan for the conquest of Palestine."[19] In Khalidi's work, Palestine Studies depended on Israeli sources, sources that were admittedly read against the grain, but the engagement with which demonstrates the blurriness of distinctions between Israel and Palestine Studies.

Khalidi based his argument on two histories of the war written from a strongly Zionist perspective, Jon and David Kimche's *A Clash of Destinies* and Netanel Lorch's *The Edge of the Sword*. The former book alluded to Plan D, while the latter mentioned it explicitly. Khalidi then made extensive use of two Hebrew-language works published by the Israel Defense Force: an official history of the battles of 1948 (*Kravot 1948*) and *Sefer Ha-Palmach*, the official history of the Palmach, the Haganah's elite strike force. *Kravot 1948* explicitly claimed that in the spring of 1948 the Haganah aspired to conquer land beyond the UN-approved borders of the Jewish state, and *Sefer Ha-Palmach* provided copious data on Israeli arms production. These

Israeli sources, Khalidi claimed, demonstrated Israeli military superiority over the Palestinians and a clearly aggressive intent that led to a spring military offensive designed to not only conquer Palestine but to denude it of its Arab population. In 1988, Khalidi republished his article of 1961, claiming that the findings of the Israeli "new historians" had confirmed his original argument. In the 1988 version, Khalidi added English translations of the unabridged text of Plan D, which in 1972 had been reproduced in volume 3 of the official history of the IDF, *Sefer Toldot ha-Haganah*.

In scholarship produced over the past thirty years, Israeli historians have continued to acknowledge the importance of Plan D, but they also have been sensitive to the imperfect connection between strategy formulated by the highest echelons, battlefield decisions made by unit commanders, and events whose causes are obscured by the fog of war. The fact remains that a combination of a diligent search for, and a critical reading of, Israeli sources enabled Khalidi, a Palestinian scholar with explicit commitments to the Palestinian cause, to make a powerful, evidence-based argument about Zionist goals during the 1948 war.

No less significant is the fact that Israeli official historiography provided this information, that neither Israel's military preparedness nor Plan D were deep secrets, but published and made available to anyone who knew Hebrew. It is not difficult to understand why a Palestinian scholar would turn to Hebrew sources to ferret out Israeli intentions and actions in 1948, but to what do we attribute the inclusion of Plan D in *Sefer Toldot ha-Haganah*? It was not a scholarly enterprise but rather a work of official historiography that was intended to document a nationalistic historical narrative and inculcate patriotism among Israeli Jews. That is, the volumes formed a mirror image of the "enemy studies" produced by the Institute for Palestine Studies and the PLO Research Center.

I believe that there was nothing in the document about which the guardians of the IDF's historical branch would feel ashamed. Evidence to support this view comes from Ben-Tsion Dinur, Israel's minister of education between 1951 and 1955, in his long introductory essay to *Sefer Toldot ha-Haganah*. Zionism, he claims, was faced from the outset with the problem of how to "insert [the Jews] into a settled land, upon which another people dwelled . . . indeed, there dwelled in the land a people who conquered it 1,200 years or more before. And it struck roots in it, became an organic component of its landscape, and, as if, (*ke-ilu*) identified itself with the land." Dinur quotes approvingly the words of Yitzhak Rülf, the Chief Rabbi of Memel, in 1883: "'At this point we speak of settlement and only settlement. That is our immediate goal. We speak of it and only of it.' But clearly, 'England is for the English, Egypt for the Egyptians and Judea is for the Jews. In our land there is room for us. We will say to the Arabs: move on! If they do not agree, if they oppose with force—we will force them to move. We will smite them upon their heads, and we will force them to move.'" Dinur continues: "Thus there were no illusions. Indeed, some things were not to be mentioned [*liba lepuma la galya*]. But all knew that the way was long and that weighty campaigns awaited that generation and generations to follow."[20]

Dinur was writing about the entire history of the Zionist project from the perspective of the 1950s and the aftermath of the 1948 war. Dinur firmly believed that decades of violence between Palestinians and Jews had left no alternative to forced flight and blocked repatriation of Palestinian refugees. It was precisely his investment in, and acceptance of, Zionist ideology that allowed him to make his candid reference to Rabbi Rülf, or that would enable his successor as chief editor of the history, Yehuda Slutzky, to reproduce Plan D in the work's third volume.

These statements and actions by agents of Israel's older, official history suggest that there has long been more agreement between Israeli and Palestinian historians than one might think about the Palestinians' flight or expulsion during the war and the State of Israel's refusal to let the vast majority of them return after the war was over. To be sure, there is disagreement about what happened, but more about why it happened and who was culpable. Even on these questions there is an at times unwitting consensus between scholars on opposite sides of the Israel-Palestine divide.

For example, scholars whom one could type as hawkish-Zionist, such as Benny Morris and Ephraim Karsh, or deeply sympathetic to the Palestinians, such as Rashid Khalidi and Ilan Pappé, or profoundly (yet eruditely) ambivalent, such as Hillel Cohen, have all presented Palestine's Arabs in 1947–1948 as mostly peaceful and uninterested in armed struggle against the Zionists.[21] Itamar Radai, an Israeli scholar sympathetic to Zionism, has documented the strength of Palestinian civil society in Jerusalem in 1948 in his meticulous analysis of the collapse of Arab Jaffa and the ability of most of eastern Jerusalem's Palestinians to stay in place.[22] Avi Shlaim, who is highly critical of Israeli actions against Palestinians in 1948, denies there was a "smoking gun," that is, a general expulsion order, in 1948, but avers

that expulsion was in the air, was not punished or discouraged, and was consolidated after the war through the refusal to allow refugees to return.[23] On
this point the staunchly Zionist Morris and the anti-Zionist Shlaim agree.

For a unified field of Israel/Palestine studies to take form, this tacit
agreement needs to become active and self-conscious. Regardless of differing political sensibilities and points of view, scholars must acknowledge the
catastrophic events and consequences of 1948 for the Palestinian people.
A further requirement for the advancement of Israel/Palestine Studies is
abandoning the approach, taken by earlier generations of Israeli scholars,
to posit a clear-cut separation between Jews and Arabs in historic Palestine.
More than twenty years ago, Zachary Lockman broke down that barrier
in his classic work on Jewish and Arab laborers in Mandate Palestine.[24]
Over the past ten to fifteen years, the "relational paradigm" that Lockman
proposed has been incorporated into the research of a sizable cohort of
scholars, trained in Middle Eastern Studies but intimately familiar with
Zionist-Israeli history, commanding Hebrew and Arabic alike, and adept
at archival research. Dissolving the border between the study of the Zionist
project and Palestinian politics and society throws new light on the internal
histories of both national movements and the deep and many-layered relations between them. As Michelle Campos, Jonathan Gribetz, Moshe Naor,
Abigail Jacobson, Menachem Klein, and Yair Wallach have shown, social
and economic contacts between Jews and Arabs in pre-1948 Palestine were
rich and dense. Jews of Sephardic or Middle Eastern origin, who spoke
native Arabic and were comfortable with local Arab cultures, put themselves forward within the Yishuv as mediators between the Jewish and Palestinian communities, but their aspirations for leadership were thwarted by
Ashkenazic newcomers.[25]

Taken as ideal type, the Arab Jew has become a focal point for scholars seeking to study Israel/Palestine as a unit and to imagine new forms
of peaceful coexistence within the frameworks of a unitary or binational
state. I would caution, however, against the romanticization of historical
experience. In pre-1948 Palestine, Arabophone Jews were not necessarily
any less nationalist in orientation than Ashkenazim, and their self-identification as mediators was in part a claim to authority, an expression of
desire to recover the influence that they had held before World War I, after
which they were displaced by Jewish immigrants from eastern Europe. As
Jacobson and Naor have pointed out, many of the Oriental Jewish activists

during the Mandate period who claimed they could bring comity between Jews and Arabs wound up working for the Haganah's security services as Arab "experts." In late Ottoman and Mandatory Palestine, contacts between Jews and Arabs were not always happy ones, nor were they necessarily on equal terms. Hillel Cohen's study of collaboration between Palestinian and Zionist elites during the Mandate period is a story of broken Zionist promises of nonaggression, just as his book on the 1929 riots is as much about hatred and bloodshed as it is about brotherhood and rescue of members of one community by the other.[26]

The possibilities for a unified field of Israel/Palestine Studies are pushed forward by the increasing popularity of the relational paradigm as well as Palestine Studies' longstanding openness to the employment of Israeli sources and incorporation of Israeli scholarship. This joint venture does face a serious challenge, however. As I remarked at the outset, the political divide between those who are empathetic to the one side and not the other is not an insurmountable problem. Empathy is not a requirement for sound scholarship. Sympathy—the ability to recognize what others are thinking and feeling—is sufficient, and all but the most passionately engaged scholars are capable of sympathizing with the various parties to the Israeli–Palestinian conflict. Writing from the perspective of a scholar of Israel Studies, I see a different core issue, one that deeply frustrates many Israel Studies scholars, even those who are highly sympathetic to the Palestinian cause, while most scholars of Palestine Studies do not see it as an issue at all. I am referring to the relationship between Zionism and colonialism. My chapter concludes, therefore, with a look backward, to the very beginnings of the Zionist enterprise, and it suggests a way forward that could be of benefit to not only scholarship but the broader academic environment in which debates about the Israeli-Palestinian conflict area taking place.

REIMAGINING ZIONISM AND COLONIALISM

Palestinian characterizations of Zionism as a form of European colonialism date back to the 1920s, and in Palestinian scholarship references to Zionism as a colonial ideology or Israel as a colonial state have been ubiquitous. Associations between Zionism and colonialism gained worldwide currency in the 1970s, when the Soviet and the non-aligned blocs linked

Zionism with racism, apartheid, and colonialism, as exemplified by United Nations General Assembly Resolution 3375 in 1975. Two years previously, the French scholar Maxime Rodinson had published a short and influential book titled *Israel: A Colonial-Settler State?* In 1979, Edward W. Said's canonical article, "Zionism from the Standpoint of Its Victims," transmitted the Palestinian critique of Zionism as colonialist to a global academic audience.[27] Ever since, scholars from a wide range of disciplines have characterized Israel as a settler-colonial state, that is, one that transports people from one territory to another in order to create permanent settlements and expropriates the native population.[28]

This approach has merit, but it can also be simplistic and crude. It can have the paradoxical effect of thwarting, rather than stimulating, understanding of the dynamics between the various forms of Zionism and modern Palestinian collective identities, and between the state of Israel and the Palestinians under its authority. A model is a heuristic, a starting point for an investigation whose outcome should not be predetermined.

Links between Zionism and colonialism are numerous and obvious. Early Zionist leaders explicitly and repeatedly spoke of the linkage between Zionism and European colonialism. The Zionist movement was, from the start, heavily dependent upon the European Great Powers for recognition and support. Had it not been for the Balfour Declaration of 1917 and the British Mandate for Palestine, under which hundreds of thousands of Jews were allowed to enter Palestine and to develop autonomous political, economic, and military institutions, there would have been no State of Israel. Recent scholarship on Israeli rule over Palestinians during the 1950s and on Israel's settlement of the Occupied Territories since 1967 demonstrates continuity of policies for the expropriation of native land and its settlement by Jews.[29] Last but not least, Zionist and Israeli discourse routinely speak of a Jewish state as an island of civilization to the benighted Orient—what in 1896 Herzl called a "rampart of Europe against Asia, an outpost of civilization as opposed to barbarism," and Ehud Barak described exactly a century later as a "modern and prosperous villa in the middle of the jungle, a place where different laws prevail."[30]

Comparisons between attitudes and policies regarding land, labor, and native populations in Israel, on the one hand, and the likes of pre-1994 South Africa, pre-1962 French Algeria, or North America across the sweep of its modern history, on the other, can be illuminating.[31] But situating

Zionism and Israel solely within this set of comparands, and solely within the framework of settler colonialism, reduces the history of Israel/Palestine to one of exogenous colonizers and indigenous colonized. It obscures essential aspects of the Jews' historic and religious links with Palestine, the variegated origins of the Yishuv's and Israel's Jewish population, and the young State of Israel's similarities with postcolonial states, similarities that were widely perceived throughout much of the developing world during Israel's first decades.

It is paradoxical but nonetheless the case that Israel emerged due to the contraction of the same British Empire that, at its zenith, recognized and promoted the Zionist project through the Balfour Declaration and Mandate for Palestine. Israel's creation was a catastrophe for the Palestinians and for the entire Arab world, yet it was connected with the general phenomenon of post-1945 anti-colonial struggle and decolonization. Palestine's pre-1948 Jewish community could be seen as a classic frontier society: a collective of indigenized colonials, fighting with a native people for possession of the land, fiercely independent and critical of the Western world yet at the same time culturally dependent upon it. Palestine's Jews, however, also resembled colonized peoples of the era in their striving for sovereignty and development of effective political and military institutions, even when under considerable duress.

Between 1948 and 1967, Israel presented itself to the world, and outside of the Middle East it was often perceived as the product of an anti-colonial rebellion against the United Kingdom and as a model of postcolonial state development. Although Israel was cold shouldered from the Bandung Conference of nonaligned states in 1955, Israel enjoyed close relations with sub-Saharan African countries, whose leaders explicitly referred to Israel's anti-colonial origins.[32] The 1956 collusion between Israel and the waning colonial powers of France and the United Kingdom was much more damaging to Israel's international image than the 1948 war itself. After 1967, the identification of Israel as a colonial state accelerated not only because of Israel's conquests but also due to global geopolitical changes throughout the developing world.

The settler-colonial paradigm is problematic for more than historical reasons. Its choice of comparands—that is, the saltwater empires of western European powers—makes little sense given that since the end of World War II the expropriation of indigenous peoples and settlement in those people's patrimony of members of the dominant nationality has been a global practice, referred to by Johannes Becke as "post-colonial state expansion."[33] Going back a bit further in time, one finds the most spectacular and horrific case of settlement colonialism in the twentieth century, neither in Western Europe's overseas empires nor in Palestine, but rather in Soviet Kazakhstan during the 1930s. Under enforced agricultural collectivization over two million people, some half of the native population, died or were driven into exile and were replaced by members of minority nationalities from across the USSR.[34] There are good reasons to place Israel within a settler-colonial framework, but that framework requires considerable expansion, both geographic and conceptual, beyond what is currently found in the literature.

Writing from the perspective of a scholar of the Zionist project, I have highlighted the obstacles that a simplistic association of Zionism with colonialism places in the way of the formation of a common field of Israel/ Palestine studies. I hope that Palestinian scholars will respond favorably to my critique, for within the settler-colonial paradigm, the category of "native" is, in fact, no less complex and variable as that of the colonizer. Since settler-colonial practices have varied so widely, and elicited a vast range of responses and outcomes, the usefulness of the settler-colonial paradigm is limited to framing a set of questions without predetermined answers. If there is to be a meeting of minds between scholars of Israel and Palestine Studies, they will need to formulate a more precise vocabulary to describe Zionism's goals and practices, including mechanisms of oppression, occupation, and resistance within the State of Israel and the Occupied Territories.

A unified field of Israel/Palestine Studies is a necessity because scholars of Israel and of Palestine scrutinize the same small bit of land, the same events, and often the same people. They have much to learn from each other. Yet the field will remain an impossibility so long as its would-be practitioners remain wedded to conceptual frameworks that are Procrustean beds—which, as the legend has it, destroy those who lie on them. A field of Israel/Palestine Studies demands that its practitioners consistently engage each other, argue rigorously and substantiate their claims, and be open to alternative perspectives and the possibility of error. As the Palestinian legal and political theorist Raef Zreik has recently argued, Zionism's essence is national as well as colonial, and it can be explained in terms of historical circumstances particular to the Jews as well as the practices of legacies of Western imperialism. Zreik further contends that the colonized Palestinians have an obligation to understand (in his words, "theorize") the Israeli-Jewish colonizer.[35] This approach makes scholarly conversation possible because Zreik separates the realms of analysis (what Zionism is and why Israel behaves as it does) from prescription ("one-state," "two-state," or other long-term scenarios for Israel/Palestine). Scholars of Israel/Palestine may come to agree on the former yet still differ regarding the latter.

There is nonetheless a utilitarian aspect to Zreik's approach because blinkered mutual conceptions hinder an accurate diagnosis of one's opponent's behavior and how it might be changed. For example, one does not need to accept Zionist self-justifications to find fault in analogies between it and apartheid. Rather, as Zreik has observed, the radical difference between the spatial and geopolitical terrains of subjugated South African blacks and dispossessed Palestinians problematizes the comparison.[36] As I have argued elsewhere, there are abundant cultural as well as structural disparities between apartheid South Africa and Israel, and these disparities illuminate Israel's cohesiveness and ability to resist external threats and pressures.[37]

The critique of the Israel-South Africa comparison, and the fact that Zreik's work and my own find common ground despite our different subject positions, constitutes a small step toward a greater goal. Other hopeful signs may be found throughout this volume and in a variety of institutional initiatives throughout the United States and the United Kingdom. In 2015, the University of Colorado at Boulder filled a newly endowed position in Israel/Palestine Studies, and in 2016, at Brown University, the Holocaust historian Omer Bartov, supported by Brown's Watson Center for International and Public Affairs, initiated a multiyear series of conferences on "Israel and Palestine—Lands and Peoples."[38] At many universities, including NYU, UCLA, Birkbeck, and Oxford, scholars of Israel Studies and Jewish Studies routinely reach out to Palestinian scholars. For reasons I have discussed, these invitations often evoke distrust or run afoul of the boycott movement. Yet without direct engagement between scholars, within universities, conferences, meetings of professional societies, and active research collaborations, a unified field of Israel/Palestine Studies will remain an aspiration.

NOTES

1. For example, Ilan Pappe's *A History of Modern Palestine: One Land, Two Peoples* (New York: Cambridge University Press, 2004) examines each community in separate sections. Tom Segev's *One Palestine, Complete: Jews and Arabs Under the British Mandate* (New York: Henry Holt, 2001) intertwines the stories of Jews and Arabs in an engaging manner but lacks an analytical framework for understanding those interactions. Later in this chapter I explore more recent and more conceptually sophisticated attempts at a joint Zionist-Palestinian historiography.

2. David Lloyd, "Anthropologists Speak Out for Justice in Palestine," *Jadaliyya*, November 25, 2015, http://www.jadaliyya.com/pages/index/23249/anthropologists-speak-out-for-justice-in-palestine.

3. See PACBI Guidelines for the International Academic Boycott of Israel, https://bdsmovement.net/pacbi/academic-boycott-guidelines, accessed January 4, 2018.

4. The most successful petition to date, "Anthropologists for the Boycott of Israeli Academic Institutions," gained more than 1,300 signatures worldwide, but virtually all research institutions in North America and the United Kingdom contributed between five and twenty signatures; the University of Chicago, with twenty-eight signatures, was an outlier. See https://anthroboycott.wordpress.com/signatories/, last updated September 30, 2015; accessed February 6, 2017.

5. Academics from these fields who hold pro-Palestinian views have attempted to mobilize support for pro-BDS positions within their professional associations. Between 2013 and 2015, the Association of Asian American Studies, the American Studies Association, and the National Women's Studies Association all passed pro-BDS motions. In 2016, the American Anthropological Association narrowly rejected a BDS resolution, while multiple attempts to pass such motions within the Modern Languages Association and the American Historical Association have failed: Elizabeth Redden, "Another Association Backs Israel Boycott," *Inside Higher Ed*, December 1, 2015, https://www.insidehighered.com/news/2015/12/01/national-womens-studies-association-joins-israel-boycott-movement; "Boycott of Israeli Academic Institutions," American Studies Association, December 4, 2013, https://www.theasa.net/about/advocacy/resolutions-actions/resolutions/boycott-israeli-academic-institutions; Elizabeth Redden, "Anthropology Group Won't Boycott Israel," *Inside Higher Ed*, June 7, 2016, https://www.insidehighered.com/news/2016/06/07/anthropology-group-rejects-resolution-boycott-israeli-academic-institutions (all accessed February 11, 2018).

6. Professional schools of business, engineering, and medicine tend to avoid overt politicization but often establish close relations with Israeli academics due to Israel's technological and entrepreneurial prowess. In 2013, a BDS motion was defeated by a 3–1 margin at the annual meeting of the American Public Health Association. See the *American Jewish Year Book 2014* (New York: American Jewish Archive, 2014), 149.

7. Ehud Luz, *Wrestling with an Angel: Power, Morality and Jewish Identity* (New Haven, Conn.: Yale University Press, 2003), 24–25.

8. Beshara Doumani, *Rediscovering Palestine: Merchants and Peasants in Jabal Nablus, 1700–1900* (Berkeley: University of California Press, 1995); Rashid Khalidi, *Palestinian Identity* (New York: Columbia University Press, 1996); Zachary Lockman, *Comrades and Enemies: Arab and Jewish Workers in Palestine, 1905–1948* (Berkeley: University of California Press, 1996); Salmi Tamari, *Mountain Against the Sea: Essays*

on Palestinian Society and Culture (Berkeley: University of California Press, 2008); Michelle Campos, *Ottoman Brothers: Muslims, Christians, and Jews in Early Twentieth-Century Palestine* (Stanford, Calif.: Stanford University Press, 2010); Sherene Seikaly, *Men of Capital: Scarcity and Economy in Mandate Palestine* (Stanford, Calif.: Stanford University Press, 2015).

9. Yezid Sayigh, *Armed Struggle and the Search for State: The Palestinian National Movement, 1949–1993* (New York: Oxford University Press, 1999); Hillel Cohen, *Good Arabs: The Israeli Security Agencies and the Israeli Arabs, 1948–1967* (Berkeley: University of California Press, 2010); Amal Jamal, *Arab Minority Nationalism in Israel: The Politics of Indigeneity* (London: Routledge, 2011), Shira Robinson, *Citizen Strangers: Palestinians and the Birth of Israel's Liberal Settler State* (Berkeley: University of California Press, 2013); Oded Haklai, *Palestinian Ethnonationalism in Israel* (Philadelphia: University of Pennsylvania Press, 2013); Nadim Rouhana and Sahar Huneidi, eds., *Israel and its Palestinian Citizens: Ethnic Privileges in the Jewish State* (Cambridge: Cambridge University Press, 2017).

10. See, for example, Philip Matar: *The Mufti of Jerusalem: Al-Hajj Amin al-Husayni and the Palestinian National Movement* (New York: Columbia University Press, 1988); Ted Swedenburg, *Memories of Revolt: The 1936–1939 Rebellion and the Palestinian National Past* (Fayetteville: University of Arkansas Press, 2003). For a more contemporary analysis of political Islam in the occupied territories, see the important work of Sara Roy, most recently *Hamas and Civil Society in Gaza: Engaging the Islamist Social Sector* (Princeton, N.J.: Princeton University Press, 2011); and Tareq Baconi, *Hamas Contained: The Rise and Pacification of Palestinian Resistance* (Stanford, Calif.: Stanford University Press, 2018).

11. See in particular the pioneering work of Jonathan Gribetz, *Defining Neighbors: Religion, Race, and the Early Zionist-Arab Encounter* (Princeton, N.J.: Princeton University Press, 2015).

12. See Moshe Behar and Zvi Ben-Dor Benite, eds., *Modern Middle Eastern Jewish Thought: Writings on Identity, Politics, and Culture, 1893–1958* (Waltham, Mass.: Brandeis University Press, 2013).

13. On the growth of *misrahanut* ("Oriental," or Middle Eastern, Studies) in Israeli military and academic institutions, see Gil Eyal, *The Disenchantment of the Orient: Expertise in Arab Affairs and the Israeli State* (Stanford, Calif.: Stanford University Press, 2006).

14. Thanks to Jonathan Gribetz for sharing with me his unpublished draft manuscript, "The Founding of the PLO Research Center, 1965–1967," from which this quotation is taken.

15. Thanks to Johannes Becke for allowing me read his unpublished manuscript, "Hebrew in Beirut: Studying Israel at the 'Institute for Palestine Studies.'"

16. *Yawmiyyat Hertzal* (Beirut: PLO Research Center, 1968).

17. Derek J. Penslar, "Theodor Herzl and the Palestinian Arabs: Between Myth and Counter-Myth," *Journal of Israeli History* 24 (2004), 65–77.

18. For a brief introduction to the significance and varieties of archival research undertaken by scholars of modern Palestine, see Beshara Doumani, "Archiving Palestine and the Palestinians: The Patrimony of Ihsan Nimr," *Jerusalem Quarterly* 36 (2009), 3–12.

19. Walid Khalidi, "Plan Dalet: Master Plan for the Conquest of Palestine," reprinted in *The Journal of Palestine Studies* 18 (1988), 4–33. Plan D was a military strategy

developed by the Zionist militia Haganah in March 1948 in the wake of three months of Zionist-Palestinian fighting that had cut off rural Zionist settlements from the main cities of the Yishuv (Palestine's Jewish community). Also, since February, access to Jerusalem from the west had been blocked by Palestinian forces. Given the imminent British withdrawal from Palestine, Plan D was a mechanism to secure the entirety of the territory accorded by the United Nations to the Jewish state as well as to (as the document reads) "areas of Jewish settlement and concentration which are located outside the borders [of the Hebrew state] against . . . forces operating from bases outside or inside the state." The primary area referred to here is Jerusalem, which under the UN partition resolution was to be internationalized.

20. Ben-Tsion Dinur, chief ed., *Sefer Toledot Ha-Haganah* (Jerusalem: Ha-sifriyah ha-tsiyonit, 1954), I, 4–5.
21. Rashid Khalidi, "The Palestinians and 1948: The Underlying Cause of Failure," in *The War For Palestine*, ed. Eugene Rogan and Avi Shlaim (New York: Cambridge University Press, 2001), 12–26; Ilan Pappé, *The Ethnic Cleansing of Palestine* (Oxford: Oneworld, 2007); Hillel Cohen, *Army of Shadows. Palestinian Collaboration with Zionism, 1917–1948* (Berkeley: University of California Press, 2008); Benny Morris, *1948: A History of the First Arab-Israeli War* (New Haven, Conn.: Yale University Press, 2008); Ephraim Karsh, *Palestine Betrayed* (New Haven, Conn.: Yale University Press, 2010).
22. Itamar Radai, *Palestinians in Jerusalem and Jaffa, 1948: A Tale of Two Cities* (London: Routledge, 2015).
23. Avi Shlaim, *The Iron Wall: Israel and the Arab World* (New York: Penguin, 2014).
24. Lockman, *Comrades and Enemies.*
25. Campos, *Ottoman Brothers;* Jonathan Gribetz, *Defining Neighbors: Religion, Race, and the Early Zionist-Arab Encounter* (Princeton, N.J.: Princeton University Press, 2015); Menachem Klein, *Lives in Common: Arabs and Jews in Jerusalem, Jaffa, and Hebron* (New York: Oxford University Press, 2014); Moshe Naor and Abigail Jacobson, *Oriental Neighbors: Middle Eastern Jews and Arabs in Mandatory Palestine* (Hanover, N.H.: University Press of New England, 2016); Yair Wallach, "Jerusalem Between Segregation and Integration: Reading Urban Space Through the Eyes of Justice Gad Frumkin," in *Modernity, Minority, and the Public Sphere: Jews and Christians in the Middle East*, ed. S. R. Goldstein-Sabbah and H. L. Murre-van den Berg (Leiden: Brill, 2016), 205–233.
26. Cohen, *Army of Shadows;* Hillel Cohen, *Year Zero of the Arab-Israeli Conflict: 1929* (Hanover, N.H.: Brandeis University Press, 2015).
27. Maxime Rodinson, *Israel: A Colonial-Settler State?* (Atlanta: Pathfinder Press, 1973); Edward W. Said, "Zionism from the Standpoint of Its Victims," *Social Text* I (1979), 7–58.
28. Lorenzo Veracini, who has written widely on settler-colonialism, places Israel within this paradigm in his book *Israel and Settler Society* (London: Pluto Press, 2006). Since its founding in 2011, the online journal *Settler Colonial Societies* has devoted three special issues and numerous standalone articles to Israel/Palestine. The settler-colonial paradigm features prominently in Palestinian scholarship on the recent history and current situation of Palestinians in the Occupied Territories, e.g., Leila Farsakh, "Palestinian Economic Development: Paradigm Shifts Since the First Intifada," *Journal of Palestine Studies* 45, no. 2 (2016), 55–71; Adam Hanieh,

"Development as Struggle: Confronting the Reality of Power in Palestine," *Journal of Palestine Studies* 45, no. 4 (2016), 32–47; Nadim Rouhana and Areej Sabbagh-Khoury, "Memory and the Return of History in a Settler-Colonial Context," in Rouhana and Huneidi, *Israel and Its Palestinian Citizens*, 393–432.

29. Avi Raz, *The Bride and the Dowry: Israel, Jordan, and the Palestinians in the Aftermath of the June 1967 War* (New Haven, Conn.: Yale University Press, 2012); Robinson, *Citizen Strangers*.

30. Theodor Herzl, *The Jewish State* (New York: American Zionist Emergency Council, 1946), 96; Ehud Barak, "Address to the National Jewish Community Relations Advisory Council, February 11, 1996," https://mfa.gov.il/mfa/mfa-archive/1996/pages/fm%20barak-%20address%20to%20njcrac%20-%20feb%2011-%201996.aspx. Accessed May 31, 2020.

31. The comparative literature on Israel and settler-colonialism takes two different forms. The more common variety focuses on the relationship between Zionist political and economic practices and those of settler communities or states, e.g., Baruch Kimmerling, *Zionism and Territory* (Berkeley: University of California, International and Area Studies, 1983) and Gershon Shafir, *Land, Labor, and the Origins of the Israeli-Palestinian Conflict, 1882–1914* (New York: Cambridge University Press, 1988). A second type engages in the comparative study of identity formation, e.g., Donald Akenson, *God's Peoples: Covenant and Land in South Africa, Israel, and Ulster* (Ithaca, N.Y.: Cornell University Press, 1992) and Uriel Abulof, *The Mortality and Morality of Nations: Jews, Afrikaners and French Canadians* (Princeton, N.J.: Princeton University Press, 2015).

32. Anat Mooreville, "Eyeing Africa: The Politics of Israeli Ocular Expertise and International Aid, 1959–1973," *Jewish Social Studies* 21, no. 3 (2016), 31–71. See also Daniel Kupfert Heller, "Israeli Aid and the 'African Woman': The Gendered Politics of International Development, 1958–73," *Jewish Social Studies* 25, no. 2 (2020): 49–78.

33. Johannes Becke, "Towards a De-Occidentalist Perspective on Israel: The Case of the Occupation," *Journal of Israeli History* 33 (2014), 1–23. See also Oded Haklai and Noephytos Loizides, eds., *Settlers in Contested Lands: Territorial Dispute and Ethnic Conflicts* (Stanford, Calif.: Stanford University Press, 2015); Awet Tewelde Weldemichael, *Third World Colonialism and Strategies of Liberation: Eritrea and East Timor Compared* (Cambridge: Cambridge University Press, 2013).

34. Kate Brown, chapter 7 in *A Biography of No Place: From Ethnic Borderland to Soviet Heartland* (Cambridge, Mass: Harvard University Press, 2004).

35. Raef Zreik, "When Does a Settler Become a Native? (With Apologies to Mamdani)," *Constellations* 23 (2016), 351–364.

36. Raef Zreik, "Palestine, Apartheid, and the Rights Discourse," *Journal of Palestine Studies* 34, no. 1 (2004), 68–80.

37. Derek J. Penslar, "What If a Christian State Had Been Established in Palestine?," in *What Ifs of Jewish History: From Abraham to Zionism*, ed. Gavriel Rosenfeld (New York: Cambridge University Press, 2016), 142–164.

38. "Israel-Palestine, Lands and Peoples: An Initiative Led by Omer Bartov," https://watson.brown.edu/research/2019/israel-palestine-lands-and-peoples-initiative-led-omer-bartov, accessed June 5, 2020.

PART III

Stubborn Realities and Alternative
Visions for Palestine/Israel

Chapter Eight

APOCALYPSE/EMNITY/DIALOGUE

Negotiating the Depths

JACQUELINE ROSE

Running through the core of this volume is a vexed question: are Arab-Jewish, and Jewish-Arab, understanding—the latter being, in the words of our editors, "rare as well as conceptually problematic"—characterized by what might be described as a constitutive blindness? Indeed, in the discussions at the Bruno Kreisky Forum for International Dialogue out of which this book arose, it soon became clear that we were dealing with a radical asymmetry: on the one hand, the Palestinian Arabs, and Arabs more widely, have had no choice but to engage with the Jews, who would build a nation-state in Palestine; on the other, the Jews who arrived in Israel and indeed in the diaspora either failed to see the Arabs completely or have mostly done so through a lens prescribed by the rules of national self-determination, then conquest and occupation. From the outset, therefore, this led to an internal bifurcation in terms of who would predominate and who—politically and culturally—would be seen and unseen. Edward Said puts it as follows in just one of his many statements that go to the heart of the matter:

Everything that did stay to challenge Israel was viewed not as something *there*, but as something *outside* Israel and Zionism bent on its destruction—from the outside . . . In his body and being, and in the putative emotions and psychology assigned to him, the Arab expressed whatever by definition stood *outside, beyond* Zionism.[1]

What this meant was that Israel could not, or refused to, see as political and fully human the people who—whether in refugee camps on the borders (the putative Palestinian state), inside the country (the Israeli-Arabs), or scattered all over the world (the Palestinian diaspora)—were and still are, psychically as well as politically, *in its midst*. They could not see the people with whom, to use a term from the introduction, they would be "entwined."

If this was true in the 1970s and 1980s when Said made his comment, it has emerged as no less true in the course of the new century, a situation summarized by Yair Lapid's now notorious remark at the time of the 2015 Israel elections, before the results were even announced, that he would not "join a blocking majority with Hanin Zuabis"—meaning he would not align with any Arabs. As a *Ha'aretz* leader put it, his remarks gave off an unmistakable racist, "nationalist stench."[2] At the same time, the so-called center of this new political landscape could be traced to middle-class social anxieties and a complete silence on the occupation (there was not one mention of Operation Pillar of Defense, the army's assault on Gaza in November 2012, by a politician in the entire election campaign). In a 2013 article "The Invisibility of the Palestinians" in the *New York Times*, Roger Cohen spoke of a "systematic blindness" of Israel "willing abnormality into invisibility" (which is why, for Cohen, the nation will never achieve the normality it craves). During a recent visit to the settlement of Gush Etzion, he had watched a Palestinian boy holding a ladder for his father as he repaired a café awning, both of them completely ignored by the Israelis sipping Turkish coffee and flirting over pastries beneath.[3]

For me, this poses a specific ethical demand: the demand to explore the question of Jewish engagement with the Arabs by looking inward, inside the thought of Zionism itself, to try to grasp in what this constitutive blindness might consist. In this chapter, and in the context of the apparently intractable and deteriorating situation in Israel-Palestine, I therefore start by asking what might be the motives, often unconscious, that—on the side of Israel—obstruct the path to understanding, serving as a blockage in something I will risk calling "the national mind." Such motives, I suggest, have formed the recurrent subtext to "the aggressive and ongoing colonization of Palestine" and of the Palestinians under occupation (see the introduction) who, in the recent words of Hagai el-Ad, executive director of B'Tselem, are today living "a bare life, with neither land nor ballot, court nor justice."[4] I then ask what role literature might have to play in creating an alternative path to understanding. Israel today is locked in what seems a spiral of destruction toward the Palestinian people and toward itself, not least because it fails to see the link that binds them—that is, the utter inter-dependency of the two peoples on each other.

In some sense, my writing on Zionism can be read as a footnote to Edward Said's plea—or demand—that we enter, without inhibition, into the mindset out of which Zionism was historically forged. Zionism, he writes, suffers from an internal "bifurcation" or splitting: "between care for the Jews and an almost total disregard for the non-Jews or native Arab population."[5] For Said, this splitting, which can be traced back to the very beginning of the conflict, is not only unjust but also self-defeating. In the eyes of the Arabs, Zionism became nothing other than an unfolding design "whose deeper roots in Jewish history and the terrible Jewish experience was necessarily obscured by what was taking place before their eyes."[6] Sigmund Freud spoke of the "blindness of the seeing eye" (or in the words of James Joyce, "shut your eyes, and *see*").[7] Zionism, we could say, has done itself a major disservice. So fervently has it nourished the discrimination between Jew and non-Jew and the rationale of its dispossession of the Palestinians that, while it may have seized the earth, it has also snatched the grounds for understanding from beneath its own feet, hence the Palestinian inability to understand the *inner* force of Zionism, that is, the "internal cohesion and solidity" of what it is up against. It is the affective dimension, as it exerts its pressure historically, that has been blocked from view. Said—although assessments of his work rarely go there—was analyzing a trauma: "an immensely traumatic Zionist effectiveness" (he meant traumatic for the Palestinians, but I would want to add traumatic also for the Jews).[8] Crucially for this argument, none of this detracts from the "benevolent and humanistic" impulse of Zionism toward its own people. What if the key to understanding the catastrophe for the Palestinians, of 1948 and after, were to be found in the love that the Jewish people—for historically explicable reasons—lavish on themselves? We have entered the most stubborn and self-defeating psychic terrain, where a people can be both loving and lethal, and their most exultant acts toward—and triumph over—an indigenous people expose them to the dangers they most fear.[9]

It should not need stating that to enter into this only partly conscious terrain is in no sense a form of disparagement. Psychoanalysis starts from the premise that the part of our minds that does not fall under the aegis of reason is worthy of the most serious attention, not to say respect. I described it that way in the preface to the Hebrew edition of *The Question of Zion*, which provoked outrage in some circles where the idea of a nonrational dimension to the national history of the Jews was felt as an affront:

Zionism, as a collective movement, has been shaped by vocabularies whose very power have often blinded it to the potential outcomes of its own desires and actions—outcomes whose bleakness for Israel as a nation and injustice for the Palestinians grow more and more visible by the day.

To understand this fully, I believe we need psychoanalysis which has always been for me a crucial part of critical thought. *The Question of Zion* is not, however, a psychoanalysis of Zionism. Rather it deploys Freud's ideas to try to enter into some of the most deeply held convictions of a movement that was itself more than happy to describe itself as the fulfilment of an impossible dream. For psychoanalysis, collective movements, like individual subjects, are bound to be partially driven by forces that go beyond the rational dimension of any singular destiny. Freud devoted a crucial part of his studies to the understanding of collective life, although this part of his work is not well known. In discussions of nationalism today it has in fact become commonplace to argue that it is the imaginative element which secures the cohesion of the group. To this extent Zionism is no different from any other movement (certainly not "uniquely pathological," in the words of one hostile reviewer of this book in Britain). The strongest critical responses to *The Question of Zion* have come from those who have felt it somehow demeaning to tar Zionism with the brush of the nonrational, to suggest as I do in the first chapter that, even in secular Zionism, there is a messianic fervor which has both inspired and endangered the nation to this day. But to try and understand the specific psychic components or fantasies that play their part in one group or identity is neither to accuse, insult nor degrade it. The founding principle of psychoanalysis is that no one is—*ever*—demeaned by the unconscious. Restoring the "dignity"—*die Würde*—of the psyche was Freud's stated aim in interpreting dreams.[10]

For psychoanalysis, to be a member of a group is to share a passion. And for psychoanalysis, the passion of the group (like all passion, we might say) is always a violent, potentially murderous affair. In my investigations of Zionism, I have been struck over and over again by the warnings that were issued by Jewish thinkers—Zionist and non-Zionist—who, in the buildup to 1948, did not want the Jewish homeland to become a nation-state: Martin Buber, Ahad Ha'am, Hannah Arendt. Each of them in their different ways could be seen as exemplary, in the words of the introduction, of "the possible productive relationships between the Arab and Jewish Questions." But it was only recently that I noticed that for Hannah Arendt, one of the foremost of these thinkers, Zionism contained a perilous self-sacrificial strain. For her, the political blindness of Herzl would have suicidal effects. Not just in the potentially disastrous consequences of what was for her a fully political mistake—creating a Jewish state in the midst of a hostile world that would be utterly dependent on a far-off nation, the United States, to survive, but more as emblem or residue of a wrong version of history inside the mind of the new nation. By presenting the destiny of the Jewish people in terms of an eternal anti-Semitism, Herzlian Zionism failed to give the Jewish people their full role in national historical and contemporary political life. Disempowering them, it left them at once powerless, ruthless, and desolate. For her, the view of anti-Semitism as eternal was a dangerous mystification that rendered the Jews defensive only, walled off from the people and nations surrounding them, in retreat. "Today," she wrote in 1946, "reality has become a nightmare . . . horrible beyond the scope of the human imagination."[11] As Herzl had always insisted, the Jewish people now saw themselves as surrounded by eternal enemies. But, she continued, "Our failure to be surprised by this development does not make Herzl's picture truer—it only makes it more dangerous."[12]

For Arendt, this vision of the Jews as always on the verge of being destroyed was in danger of being inscribed on the heart of the nation-state. Herzl himself had not hesitated to appeal to anti-Semitism, notably in the attempt to gain support inside Europe for the idea of a Jewish homeland, thereby ridding Europe of most of its Jews. Now the confidence that anti-Semitism could be helpful to the Jews had been destroyed. "Herzl's doctrine can only encourage suicidal gestures," she wrote, "for whose ends the natural heroism of a people who have become accustomed to death can be easily exploited."[13] The reference to suicide seems to me crucial. For Arendt, the trauma of the Jewish people was leading to a vision of a nation beset by eternal danger as the ultimate—and in some versions cosmic—justification for its existence. This spelled at once a blindness to the political reality of Palestine—the reality of the Arabs—a refusal to belong in the real world, and a corresponding sacrificial impulse lurking behind a language of optimism in the face of all odds. "Some of the Zionist leaders," she wrote, "pretend to believe [note the 'pretend'] that the Jews can maintain themselves in Palestine against the whole world and that they themselves can persevere in claiming everything or nothing against everybody and nobody."[14] Behind this "spurious optimism," she felt "lurks a despair of everything and a genuine readiness for suicide that can become extremely dangerous should they grow to be the mood and atmosphere of Palestinian politics."[15] Omnipotence was a false cover for despair. Even at their most ruthless—especially at their most ruthless—the Zionists were carrying into their future a vision of their own doom. Arendt was not alone in this view. To cite the introduction once more, Vladimir Jabotinsky, founder of Revisionist Zionism, saw the attempts by moderate Zionist to address the Arab question, as "either naïve (buying consent and loyalty through money) or suicidal."

For me, this vision is one of the deep-rooted obstacles within Zionism to Jewish-Arab engagement or dialogue. Look forward from Arendt to Zionism in the new century, and we can see how far it has perpetuated itself inside the nation's struggle with self-definition and its failure to engage with anything even vaguely resembling a true dialogue with the Palestinian people. To understand this fully, I suggest we move from the center to the periphery where some of the darkest versions of the Zionist imagination have taken hold. In "A Mounting Sense of Urgency," a December 2004 article in *Ha'aretz*, Nadav Shragai recounted a visit by dozens of agents of the Shin Bet security service to the home of Rabbi Yisrael Ariel, who was the head of the Temple Institute in the Jewish Quarter of Jerusalem's Old City at the time. "They came," he writes, "not to arrest him but to listen to him."[16] Ariel, one of the settlers from the Northern Sinai settlements demolished by Israel before the area was returned to Egypt in 1982, had for many years been making vessels for the Third Temple Mount. These settlers, as Shragai pointed out, fringe settlers although Ariel's books about the Third Temple, together with the prayer books for the Jewish holidays published by the Institute, are bestsellers among the religious national public, and Ariel himself is still vocal to this day. On June 2, 2019, "Liberation Day," he addressed visitors to the Mount and spoke about his part in its liberation in the 1967 war.

The year 2004 was the buildup to the Gaza disengagement. Shin Bet was concerned above all with the practical aspects of Ariel's doctrine. Ariel believed that the pullout from Gaza was a punishment for neglect of the Temple Mount—a belief he shared with Rabbi Yisrael Rosen, identified with the National Religious Party (he was head of the Zomet Institute for technology and *halakah* at the settlement of Alon Shvut), and with Rabbi David Dudkevich, the rabbi of many of the "hilltop people" of Samaria. "If there is a weakness in the heart," Rosen stated, "this is manifested in organs that are far from the source of vitality, at the extremities, such as in Gush Katif and the Gaza district."[17] "Weakness at the place of the temple," Dudkevich echoed, "is projected to the external organs."[18] Shin Bet's question was whether there were Jews, as there had been in 1982, who as a consequence of the disengagement plan would try to blow up the mosques on the Temple Mount.

At the time of the Gaza disengagement, Torah scribe Elitzur Segal, who was living in Ofra, one of these hilltop settlements, issued a *halakhic* article dealing with the concept of *mesirut hanafesh* (self-sacrifice) during war, entitled "Suicide for the Sake of Heaven." Segal writes, "In every war situations arise in which a person must knowingly place himself in a situation where his death is certain, and anyone who volunteers for such an operation is a holy hero." He then continues: "It is permitted to carry out an action that causes death, as people in the outposts in Sinai did in the Yom Kippur War and in other wars in which they fought the enemy to the death, even though they could have saved themselves, or as the holy person, Dr. Baruch Goldstein did in Hebron, but it appears that even a more certain death, such as blowing oneself up with a hand grenade together with the enemies—a case in which death is certain—is also without a doubt permitted and a commandment."[19] Baruch Goldstein shot and killed 29 Muslim worshippers at a Hebron mosque before being killed by others at the site in 1994. Attorney Naftali Wertzberger, who regularly represented Kach members and hilltop residents who fall foul of the law, referred to him as a *shaheed*, or martyr for the cause. Goldstein's grave at Hebron, visited today by Jews from all round the world, is a shrine.

It could be argued that the rabbis of the hilltops were definitively discredited by the pullout from Gaza, its relative peacefulness, and—given the many who prophesied it would not come to pass—by its having happened at all. Indeed it was a prevalent view that the pullout from Gaza was the start of the detachment of Israeli civil society from the religious right.[20]

If I was always somewhat wary about this analysis, however, it is not just because the place of the Orthodox parties in Israel's political landscape has if anything intensified since then but because of the accompanying political narrative, which argues that the pullout was the first crucial stage in a renewed impetus towards peace. As became crystal clear within months and has been abundantly reinforced since then, Ariel Sharon's plan was to annex most of the West Bank and hence to destroy any viable possibility of Palestinian statehood (within less than a year after the pullout, double the number of settlers who left Gaza had moved into the West Bank). Not to speak of the continuing economic crippling of Gaza, and its effective transformation into a prison—the stranglehold on the movement of the people that Israel continues, with a few minor recent modifications, to operate.

And if this is the case, then we are being confronted with a discourse of reason that still denies its own violent, sometimes unconscious, although in Sharon's case, manifestly conscious, intent. This is not of course historically exclusive to Zionism. As Ernst Renan argued in his famous 1882 lecture, "What Is a Nation?," nations are characterized by the speed with which, in relation to what is most often a founding and constitutive violence, they forget.[21] Nonetheless, it is as if the pullout were being presented as one stage of Israel's path toward a rational and reasoned transcendence of the fringe or extreme elements of itself; at the same time as the political reality continues to reflect the hostility toward the Palestinians that the settlers of Judea and Samaria are exceptional only in being so willing to articulate. For while the settlers' main grievance is with other Jews, the Arabs are the targets of their hate. In September 2003, one group—the Bat Ayin underground—had planned to detonate a cart filled with explosives next to a school in the Arab neighbourhood of A-Tur in Jerusalem. (Bat Ayin teenagers are regularly arrested for making such plans.)

Perhaps, then, if we want to understand the persistence of this hatred, we need to turn the dominant rhetoric of progression toward peace, and the final victory over religious radicalism, on its head. And we need to suggest that what we are witnessing in such arguments is another chapter in Israel's attempt to repress knowledge of the violence of the state *as intention*. In *The Suppression of Guilt*, former journalist and media analyst Daniel Dor argued that the Israeli media, including its left wing and critical elements, were nonetheless united in the project of shielding Israel from blame.[22] The result is that Sharon's activities, even at their worst, were never seen as deliberately or coherently planned. The key to understanding his actions could not be named. In this context, marginalizing the settlers might be seen as, to use Freud's famous concept, *over-determined* in its origins and effects—at once a genuine attempt at self-transformation for the majority of Israelis and, at the same time, part of the rhetoric of denial based on a misguided will-to-belief: that reason has prevailed and that the religious mandate for the nation has submitted to the reason of the state. For anyone thinking in psychoanalytic terms, we should be skeptical of the idea that reason rules. Israel would then be one of the very few nations, if not the only nation, that has attained the domain of rationality in public affairs. Like all exceptionalisms, of which critics of Israel are routinely accused, this would be a form of radical self-deceit. As Gerschom Sholem put it, in a formula resonant with psychoanalytic insight, "Reason is a dream, but no reality. It is the longing of the dumb."[23]

Arendt, I suggest, was right. There is a part of Zionism that carries self-sacrifice inside itself as a form of sacred belief, part of the deepest level of what constitutes—or "coheres," to use Said's expression—the national aspirations of the Jewish people. Writing to Arnold Zweig, who had just returned from a visit to Palestine in 1932, Freud describes it as a "tragically mad land . . . that has never produced anything but religions, sacred frenzies, presumptuous attempts to overcome the outer world of appearance by the inner world of wishful thinking."[24] We can read this as Orientalism—Europe as civilization versus the fanaticism of the East—but we should remember that Freud, as one of the harshest critic of civilization, could hardly or innocently subscribe to a binary such as this. Zweig moved to Palestine the following year. In this context, I see Freud saying something far more subtle and closer to what I am describing here. Do not make the mistake of thinking that, by entering into the national aspirations of the Jewish people, however much they can and must be seen as the reasoned response to historic persecution, you will avoid the perils of collective life. Look to Palestine if you want to see one of the most powerful embodiments of the dangers of the group mind. Zweig would eventually agree. Against the whole drift of the Jews of Europe, he left Palestine to return to Germany in 1948.[25]

For me the brilliance of Arendt's analysis is that it is at once political and psychological. A people, brought to despair, blind themselves to the real political nature of the opposition that they face since all obstacles come to be seen as the fulfilment of, or another chapter in, a potentially tragic destiny. Thus armed with their own fear, they cannot see the justifiable antagonism that they face on the part of the Palestinian people. In a potentially lethal combination, the nation is brushed at once with the colours of triumph and suicide. In Jerusalem, poet Yehuda Amichai writes in his long poem "Jerusalem, 1967" that "large desires for horrible death are well cared-for."[26] Such a vision is not confined to Amichai. To take another famous example, A. B. Yehoshua's "Facing the Forests,"[27] which is often taught in schools. It was brought to my attention by the Israeli literary critic Sidra deKoven Ezrahi in order to persuade me that knowledge of the violence toward the Arabs in the founding of the state was not repressed inside Israel (it was, she agreed, one of very few exceptions to the general rule). In fact, Yehoshua's story brilliantly displays the logic that Arendt so dreads. A disillusioned young Israeli, struck with *anomie* in the city, looking for a purpose in life, turns to Jewish history and decides to write a thesis on the Crusades: "For isn't mass suicide," he muses, "a wonderful and terrible thing?"[28] In search of calm, he leaves the city for the forests where he becomes a firewatcher. Slowly, as he sinks into the vacancy and isolation of his leafy retreat, he discovers that the trees he protects are planted on an Arab village deserted in 1948. In response to this knowledge, he starts to yearn for the fire whose prevention at all costs is his very reason for being there. "I am," he observes, "still awaiting a conflagration"; "a dry flow of desert wind," he muses, "may rouse the forest to suicide."[29] An apocalyptic, suicidal strain lights on the earth and sets fire to the very trees whose new planting was intended to symbolise the rebirth of the Jewish nation.

Crucially, Yehoshua and Amichai, like Arendt, make the links between the political imagination, as scarred by traumatic history, and the fledgling nation's investment in a violence carried out toward the other, but which also—unconsciously at least—carries the meaning of its own death. In his famous exhortation to Polish Jews on the eve of the Shoah, Ze'ev Jabotinsky proclaimed, "What else I would like to say to you on this day of Tisha B'Av [the day of the destruction of the Temple] is whoever of you will escape from the catastrophe, he or she will live to see a great Jewish wedding—the rebirth and rise of a Jewish state." At its simplest, we can simply note the intimate relation between catastrophe and redemption, between extermination and divine marriage, between death and the nation-state.[30] And we might ask—I think this is Arendt's question or warning—whether redemption of this intensity will not always harbor somewhere the violence from which it is fleeing, at its own core. Throughout this analysis, there is therefore a simple, but far-reaching political point to be made. We cannot assign to the Palestinians a monopoly on martyrdom as a political tool any more than we can ignore the extent to which self-sacrifice is inscribed in complex and disturbing ways at the heart of the Zionist imagination. Because of the tragic historic conditions for the Jewish people under which it was founded, and the violence toward the Arabs that was its partially blind, partially cognizant, consequence, Israel as a nation-state is "wedded"(Jabotinsky's word) to its own violent redemption.

In 1971, Gershom Scholem asked this still-pertinent question: "Can Jewish history manage to re-enter concrete reality without being destroyed by the messianic claim which [that re-entry] is bound to bring up from its depths?"[31] None of this of course has gone away. Benjamin Netanyahu takes his inspiration from his father, the historian Benzion Netanyahu, whose work and ideas harkened back to the messianic writings of the fifteenth-century Jewish figure Don Isaac Abravanel, for whom the worst is always yet to come. "More than anything else," writes Avner Ben-Zaken in Ha'aretz in May 2015, "[he] adopted from Abravanel the approach of integrating political thought into the history of catastrophism."[32] It was Abravenel who fixed in conservative political thought the connection between apocalypse (history), state of emergency (law), and sovereignty (politics). From this, Netanyahu the younger has taken the creed that the Jewish political consciousness can only be preserved by "maintaining, sustaining, and managing a potential catastrophe."[33] Some orthodox factions go so far as to claim that the Lubavitcher Rebbe told Netanyahu, "You will be the final prime minister and you will be the person to transfer the leadership to the Messiah."[34] In this terrifying vision Israel does not only destroy the possibility of any viable political existence for the Palestinian people; as a political entity, it also sublates or effaces itself. At the time of the Gaza pullout, Sarah Roy concluded an article in the *London Review of Books* with chilling prescience:

Israel and the United States worry that the Islamists will take over [in Gaza]. But the real threat lies deeper . . . By taking so much more away from the

Palestinians than any other agreement since the occupation began, the Disengagement Plan will prove disastrous for everyone, including Israel.

The question then becomes: where do we look for engagement and— potentially—understanding? Where might we find the possibility of breaching the wall? Other contributors to this volume write about the earliest beliefs in binationalism, the form of deep economic and cultural cooperation that, at least up to the founding of the state and in some circumstances after its creation, existed between Arabs and Jews, forms of connection that are being fostered by dissident voices and organizations inside and outside Israel to this day.[35] Others suggest literature might also have a role to play. For me, two anecdotes taken from my teaching stand out for me as symmetrical with one another and take us to the heart of the matter. For over a decade, I taught a course on Israeli and Palestinian history and fiction at Queen Mary University of London, which is situated in Mile End, which was historically and still is today the migrant center of the city. The course attracted students from the most varied backgrounds. Among the students taking the course one year were three British Muslims, three half-Egyptians, one Muslim from Brunei, one Palestinian, one Polish emigré, and three Jewish Americans. One of the American students shared during our personal introductions that she had been educated to idealize Golda Meir. The Muslim from Brunei had been raised to hate the Jehudi [the Jews]—to even take the course, which started by entering deep into the Zionist imagination, was therefore already a brave move.

My first anecdote involves the American student who chose to do a presentation on the story briefly alluded to above, "Facing the Forests," by A. B. Yehoshua, the story of the young man who retires to the forest in crushing dissociation from the ideals of the nation. It is important that the story was written in 1963, between independence and the 1967 war, when those ideals were still at their height, unsullied by the occupation that began four years later. Yehoshua's protagonist was therefore already anomalous for a nation that did not yet feel—not consciously at least—that it had any need to question itself. Crucially, the story turns on the possibility and failure of dialogue between Arab and Israeli Jews—the young man only discovers that the forest he has been hired to protect was built over a Palestinian village when his Arab attendant sets fire to the trees. The Arab is mute, his tongue cut out during the war (in the words of Rachel Feldhay Brenner, the fire watcher and the gesticulating Arab "exchange stories in languages incomprehensible to one another").[36] It is a shocking story that violates just about every shibboleth of Israeli national self-imagining. Planting trees was of course from the beginning, and in many ways has never ceased to be, an Israeli ideal. As a young Jewish schoolgirl growing up in London in the 1950s, I too helped raise money for Israel to plant trees. In the middle of her presentation, the student stopped and paused: "I have planted trees in Israel," she commented. "I am now wondering what on earth I was planting them on."

The second moment involves the student from Brunei who had been brought up to hate the Jews. In that strange way that often draws us to the one thing most designed to disturb our most cherished, deeply held beliefs, she chose to do her presentation on David Grossman's famous 1989 novel, *See Under: Love*, which tells the story of an Israeli boy's attempt to understand the Holocaust and how its traumatic presence inside his family is personified by the unwelcome return of his grandfather, who was believed to have perished in the camps.[37] Only Momik, the grandson, loves, relates, and talks to his long-lost grandfather, whose arrival dismays the boy's already haunted parents, whose screams increase in the night. *See Under: Love* is a novel about how Israel cannot fully recognize a trauma to which it also, many would say, owes its political existence, and on which— as so cogently analyzed by Avhaham Burg—it also cannot leave behind.[38] It is therefore is a novel about how a nation deals, or fails to deal, with its past. Grossman has explained how he wrote this novel in order to understand a story he was never told, an experience that, although it was not directly his own, had seared the coming-into-being of his generation and his nation. No one ever speaks to Momik about what happened "over there" so uncovering the truth then becomes the young boy's most fervent mission.

Nothing could have been more pertinent for this student, whose hatred of the Jews was backed, as she then told us, by a complete ignorance of Jewish history. Learning about the Holocaust in the voice of someone struggling to understand might therefore have been the only way she could listen. "No one," she said, "told us about this." In tears, she described how she had phoned her 17-year-old sister in Brunei to tell her that she had to read this book. Like Yehoshua's "Facing the Forests," *See Under: Love* is a story about blindness, about the lengths that people—a people—will go in order to remain ignorant, to blot out a too-painful political reality, to forget. In both cases, history has been silenced. But speaking it brings no solace. It sets the world on fire and tears the heart to shreds. Instead of solving anything, telling an untold story—as both these works suggest— is where the psychological and political work needs to begin. These are moments of unanticipated insight, moments when the fervor of politi- cal and psychic identities—and for me the two are always inseparable— unexpectedly break. But I think they also demonstrate the intensity of emo- tional investment, the need to understand the power of resistance and the barriers to engagement that such moments are up against. Or in the words of the Palestinian poet Mahmoud Darwish—Said and Darwish were of course the closest of interlocutors and friends—"The Israelis are not the same as they were when they came, and the Palestinians are not the same people either. Each dwells inside the other . . . The other is a responsibility and a test . . . Will the third emerge out of the two? This is the test?"[39]

Literature is one of the places where the forms of death-dealing logic and imagination discussed so far are, for me, most radically undone. To take another example, S. Yizhar's famous story "The Prisoner," which stages the utter abjection and humiliation of the Arab shepherd, thrown into the back of an Israeli military truck where, it is made more or less explicit, he is being taken to be tortured.[40] He becomes, in Gil Anidjar's reading, the Musulman.[41] He is therefore a Jew. In this reading, the story is therefore a repetition, an echo of the Jewish tragedy in Europe, to which the Israeli soldier's guilty, well-meaning struggle is woefully unequal: in the last pages of the story the narrative voice splits as he engages in a fraught internal dialogue as to whether he should let the prisoner go. Although, as Anidjar points out, the Hebrew does not use the phrase of the English translation "rot of humanity" in its description of the Arab village; it is a radical dehu- manization, or "absolute subjection" in Anidjar's words that we are talking about.[42] I agree with this reading but would add another dimension, crucial to our topic in this collection, which is the ironizing, the invisible quota- tion marks, around the narrator's voice in this story. From the beginning, this voice is unsteady: "A whirlpool of gleaming mountain fields, olive hills and a sky ablaze with an intense silence blinded us for moments and so beguiled our hearts that one longed for a moment of redeeming joy."[43] How can silence blind and beguile? And what is this longing for redeeming joy other than a veiled confession, against the whole impetus of the fledgling nation in 1948, that redemption is yearned for but not guaranteed, that it might already be endangered by the scene that is about to unfold?

We are therefore, I suggest, the witness to this voice that is anxious even before the story begins. I do not think we are being asked to identify with it. I think we are meant to be appalled by the inhuman, degrading way the soldier, in collective mode, describes the world of the Arabs (I think we are also meant to see that degradation as the sign of the violent expulsion to come). In his introduction to the English translation, Robert Alter universalizes the message of "The Prisoner" as a sign of the dehumanization of war. Alter is a Jewish scholar I learn from and respect, but this reading depoliticizes the story: we should not, he suggests, assume the Israeli soldier's behavior is "in any way typical"; it takes only a little historical imagination, he argues, to understand the feelings of young Jews in Palestine—they are calling out to beat the shepherd—subject to "repeatedly murderous Arab incursions."[44] In fact, we find that it is the soldier himself who offers no such excuse or rational but who himself suggests that what they are doing is typical: "It's your duty to break free of this habitual swinishness." Right at the heart of his internal dialogue, as he wrestles with the question of whether he should set the prisoner free, the narrator inculpates the whole army in the behavior of animals (this is not a simile since the verbal equation between army and swine is unqualified). The distinction between animal and human, one of the historically attested rhetorical licenses for brutality, collapses. It is the Arabs, not the Israeli army, who are meant to be beyond the pale of the human. On his capture, the shepherd lurches forward "like a trapped gazelle."[45] "What a laugh! What fun!" is the gleeful exclamation that immediately follows, but we are hardly meant to take their spirit at its word. "The Prisoner" is a story of self-indictment, about radical ambivalence that is also historically precise. There is no redemption. Instead, the ugly reality of what the nascent nation is doing to the Arab prisoner literally splits open the voice of the text and cuts the Israeli to the quick.[46]

Let's return to Darwish, to the wondrous poem "As He Draws Away," which serves as the epigraph to Gil Anidjar's book *The Jew, the Arab*.[47] One moment in particular struck me: "Were it not for the gun, / Our flutes would have merged." What exactly does this mean? That if not for our hatred, we would make music together (which seems like pure sentimentality or at least crushingly banal). Or, before there was violence, there was a shared task of labor: crafting the instruments of peace? This reading comes close to Buber's idea of a shared covenant between the two peoples based on the sacred tasks of daily life held in common, which he evokes in his essay "Zionism and 'Zionism,'" another key text written in 1948.[48] Or that the gun conceals from us a fundamental identity, a merging of the two peoples that gives a lie to the enmity binding them. And, if so, is this a lost possibility, a way of harking back to a bygone age of harmony— Andalusia, for instance, which Darwish regularly invokes—or a desire for the future, or both? The same diverse readings, each one offering a form of dialogue, can be asked of the lines already quoted from Darwish: "Each dwells inside the other . . . The other is a responsibility and a test . . . Will the third emerge out of the two?"[49] Looking at several translations, I found as alternatives to "our flutes would have merged" "our flutes would have played a duet," and "were it not for the gun the flute would pass into the flute."[50] It is this last translation by Jeffrey Sacks—"the flute would pass into the flute"—that comes closest to what I have been trying to evoke in this chapter. Not a merging, certainly not a duet, but the conditions under which one people make their agonizing and self-wrenching passage back into the other who—deep inside their histories, inside their minds, past the debris and the wreckage—is already there.

Still not happy, however, with any of these solutions, I then wrote to Mohammad Shaheen, who has translated Darwish before and helped with the original Arabic of poems I have been working on, and who, it turns out, at the request of Darwish before he died, was just putting the final touches on his retranslation of *Why Did You Leave the Horse Alone?*, the anthology from which this poem is taken. In his translation the line now reads this way: "Were it not for the pistol, / Reed-pipe would blend with reed-pipe." "There are," he says, "two main problems with the existing translations"

One is that "alnāi" in Arabic is by no means the "flute" in English, and they are never the same musical instrument . . . "Emerge" is definitely not the word, and "pass" is better though it is not a faithful rendering . . . Yet the major problem in the act of translating the two lines mentioned is the Arabic word "yakhtalit," which in classical Arabic is positive and in modern Arabic is negative; one suggests intimacy, the other confusion. The three translations mentioned capture the positive sense, so they are more than halfway through.[51]

That the translation omits, or cannot render, the radical ambiguity of "yakhtalit" as positive and negative goes to the heart of what I have been trying to describe: it sits somewhere between intimacy and confusion—or "entwinements" to use Bashir Bashir and Leila Farsakh's term in the introduction. If the confusion of tongues that is literature can allow us to glimpse this possibility for a moment, the gist of the rest of this chapter has been to evoke—as everything in today's harsh and deteriorating political climate in Israel, and not just in Israel, confirms—just how difficult, once the external and internal battle lines are drawn, it is to do so.

NOTES

1. Edward W. Said, "Zionism from the Standpoint of Its Victims," in *The Question of Palestine* (London: Vintage, 1979), 88–89.
2. Ha'aretz Editorial, "Yair Lapid's Mental Block," *Ha'aretz*, January 25, 2013.
3. Roger Cohen, "The Invisibility of Palestinians," *New York Times International Weekly*, February 3, 2013.
4. Hagai el-Ad, "Netanyahu exploits the Holocaust to Brutalise the Palestinians," *Ha'aretz*, January 23, 2020.
5. Said, "Zionism from the Standpoint of Its Victims," 83.
6. Said, "Zionism from the Standpoint of Its Victims," 83.
7. Sigmund Freud, *Studies on Hysteria, 1893–1895*, in *The Standard Edition of the Complete Psychological Works of Sigmund Freud*, 24 vols. (London: Hogarth, 1955), 2: 117n; James Joyce, *Ulysses* (Harmondsworth, UK: Penguin, [1922]1971), 42.
8. Said, "Zionism from the Standpoint of its Victims," 83.
9. Shay Fogelman, "Mission Impossible," *Ha'aretz*, January 25, 2013.
10. Jacqueline Rose, *The Question of Zion* (Princeton, N.J.: Princeton University Press, 2005); Hebrew Edition, trans. Oded Wolkstein, with new preface (Tel-Aviv: Resling Press, 2007), 11–12.
11. Hannah Arendt, "The Jewish State: Fifty Years After—Where Have Herzl's Politics Led?," in *The Jew as Pariah*, ed. Ronald H. Feldman (New York: Random House, 1978), 174.
12. Arendt, "The Jewish State," 175.
13. Arendt, "The Jewish State," 176.
14. Arendt, "The Jewish State," 176.
15. Arendt, "The Jewish State," 176.
16. Nadav Shragai, "A Mounting Sense of Urgency," *Ha'aretz*, December 30, 2004.
17. Nadav Shragai, "A Mounting Sense of Urgency."
18. Nadav Shragai, "A Mounting Sense of Urgency."
19. Nadav Shragai, "A Mounting Sense of Urgency."
20. For both sides of this argument see Uri Ram, "From Nation-State to Nation—State: Nation, History and Identity Struggles in Jewish Israel," and Avishai Erlich, "Zionism, Anti-Zionism, Post-Zionism," in *The Challenge of Post-Zionism: Alternatives to Israeli Fundamentalist Politics*, ed. Ephraim Nimni (London: Zed Books, 2003).

Ram suggests this narrative of redemption is under challenge in a potentially post-Zionist world; Erlich argues that secular Zionism has, if anything, been increasingly usurped by religion as the source of political legitimation for the state.

21. Ernst Renan, "What Is a Nation?," in *Nation and Narration*, ed. Homi Bhabha, (London: Routledge, 1990), 8–22.

22. Daniel Dor, *The Suppression of Guilt:Israeli Media and the Reoccupation of the West Bank* (London: Pluto, 2005).

23. Gershom Scholem, *Lamentations of Youth: The Diaries of Gershom Scholem*, ed. Anthony David Skinner (Boston: Harvard University Press, 2008) entry of January 29, 1915, 50.

24. Sigmund Freud, *The Letters of Sigmund Freud and Arnold Zweig*, ed. Ernst L. Freud, trans. Elaine Robson-Scott and William Robson-Scott (New York: Harcourt Brace, 1970), 40.

25. For a fuller discussion of Arnold Zweig's and Freud's engagement with Palestine, see Rose, "The Last Resistance," chapter 1 in *The Last Resistance* (London: Verso, 2007), 17–38.

26. Yehuda Amichai, stanza 13 of "Jerusalem," (1967), in *Selected Poems*, ed. and trans. Chana Bloch and Stephen Mitchell (Harmondsworth, UK: Penguin, 1986), 47–55.

27. A. B. Yehoshua, "Facing the Forests," in *Modern Hebrew Literature*, ed. Robert Alter (Springfield, N.J.: Behrman House, 1975).

28. Yehoshua, "Facing the Forests," 368.

29. Yehoshua, "Facing the Forests," 382, 271.

30. See Idith Zertal, *Israel's Holocaust and the Politics of Nationhood*, trans. Chaya Galai (Cambridge: Cambridge University Press, 2005).

31. I discuss the links between Zionism and messianism in more depth in Rose, Chapter 1 in *The Question of Zion* (Princeton, N.J.: Princeton University Press, 2005).

32. Avner Ben-Zaken, "The Father, the Son, and the Spirit of Catastrophe," *Ha'aretz*, May 22, 2015.

33. Ben-Zaken, "The Father, the Son, and the Spirit of Catastrophe."

34. Ben-Zaken, "The Father, the Son, and the Spirit of Catastrophe."

35. In 2015, Independent Jewish Voices in the UK, a network of dissident Jewish voices, held a conference in London under the title "Equal Rights for All—A New Path for Israel-Palestine," which was cosponsored by the Kreisky Forum for International Dialogue out of which this collection arose. The conference, which brought together a range of speakers from both sides of the divide, including Sam Bahour, Moustafa Barghouti (by link), Salma Karmi-Ayoub, Leila Shahid, Avrum Burg, Philippe Sands, and Avi Shlaim, is widely considered to have succeeded in producing a space for dialogue between Arab and Jews impossible inside Israel itself. See https://www.kreisky-forum.org/wp-content/uploads/2019/04/Equal-Rights-for-All-Conference-Proceedings.pdf.

36. Rachel Feldhay Brenner, *Inextricably Bonded: Israeli-Arab and Jewish Writers Re-Visioning Culture* (Minneapolis: University of Wisconsin Press, 2003), 183.

37. David Grossman, *See Under: Love*, trans. Betsy Rosenberg (New York: Simon and Schuster, 1989).

38. Avraham Burg, *The Holocaust Is Over—We Must Rise from Its Ashes* (New York: Palgrave Macmillan, 2008).

39. Feldhay Brenner, *Inextricably Bonded*, 117.

40. S. Yizhar, "The Prisoner," in *Modern Hebrew Literature*, trans. V. C. Rycus and ed. Robert Alter (West Orange, N.J.: Behrman House, 1975), 291–310.

41. Gil Anidjar, *The Jew, the Arab—A History of the Enemy* (Stanford, Calif.: Stanford University Press, 2003), 114–119.

42. Anidjar, *The Jew, the Arab*, 115.

43. Yizhar, "The Prisoner," 294.

44. Alter, introduction to "The Prisoner," 292–293.

45. Yizhar, "The Prisoner," 295.

46. For further discussion of the writers discussed in this chapter, see chapters 2 and 3 in Jacqueline Rose, *Proust Among the Nations: From Dreyfus to the Middle East* (Chicago: University of Chicago Press, 2011).

47. Anidjar, *The Jew, the Arab*, viii–ix.

48. Martin Buber, "Zionism and 'Zionism,'" in *A Land of Two Peoples: Martin Buber on Jews and Arabs*, ed. Paul Mendes-Flohr (New York: Oxford Universities Press, 1983), 220–223.

49. Cited Feldhay Brenner, *Inextricably Bonded*, 112.

50. Mahmoud Darwish, *Why Did You Leave the Horse Alone?*, translated from the Arabic by Jeffrey Sacks (New York: Archipelago, 2006), 194; Darwish, "As He Walks Away," trans. Sargon Boulos, *The Adam of Two Edens*, ed. Munir Akash and Daniel Moore (New York: Syracuse University Press, 2000), 52.

51. Personal communication from Mohammed Shaheen, March 2, 2014.

Chapter Nine

COMPETING MARXISMS, CESSATION OF (*SETTLER*) COLONIALISM, AND THE ONE-STATE SOLUTION IN ISRAEL-PALESTINE

MOSHE BEHAR

Oslo set the stage for separation, but real peace can come only with a binational Israeli-Palestinian state.

—EDWARD SAID, "THE ONE-STATE SOLUTION" (1999)

Are the "Jewish Question" and the "Arab Question" best interpreted as *colonial* or *national* questions in their manifestation in Israel-Palestine? In exploring post-1967 entanglements with—and juxtaposition of—these twin questions, the argument put forward here is twofold. I first analyze the competing Marxist conceptualizations fashioned by (i) the post-1967 Popular Front for the Liberation of Palestine (PFLP) and (ii) Israel's Matzpen group and the respective pathways they each offered to terminate colonialism and resolve the Israel-Palestine question. My second part investigates the extent to which this "old" intra-Marxist disagreement remains relevant to post-Oslo debates over the vision of a single non-partitioned state in Israel-Palestine—debates that have chiefly developed following the 1999 publication of Edward Said's seminal essay "The One-State Solution."

Observers should firstly recognize that for many Palestinians and Arabs, for decades Euro-Zionism has remained an illegitimate colonial movement and the State of Israel an abnormal implant in the Middle East. Yet primary and secondary sources pertaining to the Palestine question have remained cloudy about the *precise* meanings, implications and consequences of such phrases as "the liberation of Palestine," "decolonization," and "anti-colonialism." It does not come as a complete surprise that "Pathways of

Settler Decolonization" (a special issue of *Settler Colonial Studies* published in 2017) barely included anything about the Israel-Palestine case, contrary to what the journal usually publishes.[1] This fogginess is similarly found in what are otherwise the finest analyses, including the pioneering 1965 one by Fayez Sayegh:

The people of Palestine, notwithstanding all their travails and misfortunes, still have undiminished faith in its future. And the people of Palestine know that the pathway to that future is *the liberation of their homeland*. It was in this belief that the Palestinian people—after sixteen years of dispersion and exile, during which the people had reposed their faith in returning to their country in world conscience and international public opinion, in the UN, or in the Arab states—chose at last to seize the initiative. . . . Only in *the liberation of Palestine*, spearheaded by Palestinians prepared to pay the price [for what *precisely?*—M.B.], can the supreme sacrifices of past generations . . . be vindicated, and the visions and hopes of living Palestinians be transformed into reality.[2] (italics added)

Atypically for the pre-1967 period, Sayegh comprehended Euro-Zionism as a form of *settler* colonialism—rather than of what I term here "standard" colonialism, that is, a form of *non*-settler colonialism (Americans in Vietnam, British in India). Yet Sayegh's classic essay—like countless others before or after him—does not explain what is to be done with the colonial settlers, nor what decolonization (of *settler* colonialism, that is) precisely means or entails. Unclear is the extent that this process differs, or is supposed to differ, from decolonization of "standard" (*non*-settler) colonialism. In what follows I attempt to exemplify, defend, and historicize these opening contentions.

1917–1949: A REAPPRAISAL

The principal Palestinian or Arab view of the Euro-Zionist movement and ideology as illegitimate—and, by extension, of the ensuing Israeli state as an abnormal colonial entity—predated 1917.[3] Yet the year 1917, when Britain issued the Balfour Declaration, is a productive *terminus a quo* for interrogating the concept of decolonization. For reasons that one can explore elsewhere,[4] the British opted to regard Jews as a collection of dispersed individuals who nonetheless comprise a modern *national* collectivity. That meant that the British, essentially in the footsteps of Christian and non-Christian Zionists, neither viewed Jews merely as individual (religious or secular) members of the religion called "Judaism," nor even as "the *People* of Israel," as Jews have continued to be signified collectively in Christian-informed discussions. In 1917 Britain stipulated officially that the fourteen million Jews who back then lived worldwide comprise a national collectivity, albeit diasporic.[5] Politicians were of the persuasion that Jews deserved a territorial homeland as a collective historic right; this was predictably understood to suit British interests *and* comprise a proper pathway for "fixing" the scattered existence of "wandering" Jews and the vulnerability their minority position has so often entailed (in Europe).

The paragraph-long Balfour Declaration nonetheless avoided specifying a precise configuration for its envisioned "Jewish National Home," nor detailed its territorial size or borders. The reason for this imperial vagueness and caution was awareness that prospects were slim for the declaration to be viewed favorably by Arab Palestinians or non-Palestinians. The word "State" was thus excluded from the declaration notwithstanding Zionist efforts to inject into earlier drafts terms stronger than a "Jewish National Home" (consult draft of July 12).[6] I contend this: the phrasing of the Balfour Declaration left wide open the principal possibility for the "Jewish National Home" to assume a *sub*state configuration. Saturated with non-contingent teleological reasoning, coupled with ex-post-facto rationalizations, Zionist and anti-Zionist historiographies have exhibited little patience to discuss (post-1917) reasons that might have underlie such substate paths not taken.

These foundational clarifications are crucial because they seldom inform studies of the historical dynamics that have underpinned the Israel-Palestine question (to date). As a consequence, substate possibilities for securing collective rights in order to alleviate, and possibly even resolve, the Israel-Palestine situation are not discussed in any depth. By way of illustration, consider the aftermath of the Nakba beginning on November 29, 1947, when the UN General Assembly affirmed Resolution 181. Imprecise framing typifies effectively countless studies of the crucial 1947–1949 period. Scholarly and activist discussions alike present and frame Palestinian-Arab opposition chiefly as resistance to (i) territorial partition of the homeland, (ii) the notion of a two-state solution, and (iii) the creation, legitimacy, and international sanction of a Jewish state on 55 percent of Arab Palestine (that would become 77 percent following the armistice agreement).

I suggest that that this hegemonic framing is imprecise and, as such, inevitably skews comprehensions of Israel-Palestine dynamics—again, to this very day. That is so because *none* of the above three points was the principal locus for Palestinian opposition and resistance to Euro-Zionism. This locus was not opposition to a Jewish state, incidentally irrespective of its potential size. It was, instead, opposition to the notion of granting in Palestine a collective right for Jews including in a non-statist (or substate) form. Consequently, commonly brushed aside is that most Palestinians and Arabs—incidentally in harmonious concert with Zionists—rejected outright in 1947 the "Minority Plan" that United Nations Special Committee on Palestine members Iran, Yugoslavia, and India brought to the UN General Assembly. That plan rejected the formation of partitioned Arab and Jewish states. It urged the establishment of a single federated state whereby Palestine's sizable Jewish minority (33 percent)—and not Jews worldwide—would be granted a collective right in a substate federative configuration. It was therefore that type of resolution of the Palestine discord that Palestinians (and Zionists) rejected between 1917 and 1948—and not partition, a Jewish state, or a two-state arrangement.

It should become apparent momentarily why it still remains entirely unviable—in the twenty-first century—to arrive at a satisfactory comprehension of the Israel-Palestine matrix without the surgical differentiation I offer here between dissimilar manifestations of Palestinian-Arab opposition and resistance to competing types of resolutions of the Palestine situation. Yet before I head there I must first hasten to emphasize that Palestinians had every right to oppose the granting of collective rights to Palestine's Jews, the majority of whom were recent arrivals, refugees of the Nazi genocide included. Such Palestinian opposition was neither racist nor anti-Jewish by definition (although it could have been, and occasionally was, among far-right secular and religious constituencies). This kind of opposition was certainly anti-Zionist; it enjoyed as such some support from orthodox, liberal, and Marxist Jews (who must never be labeled "self-hating" to explain away their conscious non-Zionism).

From the vantage point I propose here to explore post-1917 paths taken *and untaken*, 1948 can be conceptualized not only in its more customary terms of ethnic cleansing[7] but, additionally, as an unsuccessful "standard" anti-colonial undertaking (unlike the Vietnamese, Algerian, Indian, etc.). I should mention that the formula of granting a collective right to Palestine's Jews in a substate form within a single Palestinian-Arab state was the foundation of the British 1939 White Paper, rejected by Zionists and Palestinians. Non-partitioned formulas affording collective rights to Jews in substate configurations were proposed—and also rejected by Zionists and Palestinians—in 1945 and 1946. These may have all been contingent bi-national paths *not* taken.

1949-1967: PALESTINIAN UNDERSTANDING OF ZIONISM AS (*NON-SETTLER*) COLONIALISM AND ITS IMPLICATIONS

For Arab nationalism generally, and the PLO specifically, Zionism was part of European colonialism; Palestine's colonial reality was viewed as unjust and required correction. Until 1967 the principal thrust powering Palestinian (and Arab) nationalism was to materialize in Lilliputian Palestine what I termed above as "standard" anti-colonial struggle vis-à-vis Euro-Zionism and its ensuing Israeli state; that is "anti-colonialism 101," which means decolonization of the robbed land to ends similar to those of Asian and African anti-colonial movements including the Indian, Algerian, or Vietnamese: the destiny of colonizers is to withdraw or relocate. In this context, the year 1917 constituted the departure lounge and frame of reference for the Palestinian-Arab anti-Zionist struggle; pre-1967 Marxists and nationalists mobilized for decolonization and restoration of the homeland to a 1917 state of (pre-colonial) affairs. Owing to space constraints, one simple way to exemplify this anti-Zionist and anti-colonial reasoning and activism is to revisit the PLO's 1964 Charter. Article 6 for example makes this stipulation:

The Palestinians are those *Arab* citizens who were living *normally* in Palestine up to 1947, whether they remained or were expelled. Every child born to a Palestinian

Arab father [and mother—M.B.] after this date, whether in Palestine or outside, is a Palestinian. (italics added)

While I consciously choose to tiptoe here around the mammoth conundrum of "who is an Arab"[8]—Article 6 conveyed clearly that *non*-Arabs present in 1964 Israel-Palestine are *not* Palestinians while their residence in the territory is viewed as abnormal, i.e., colonial. Providing the struggle's historical framing, including a working definition of the adversary party, Article 18 of the Charter established this:

The Balfour Declaration, the Palestine [pre-1948] Mandate System, and *all that has been based on them* are considered *null and void*. The claims of historic and spiritual ties between Jews and Palestine are not in agreement with the facts of history or with the true basis of sound statehood. Judaism, because it is a divine religion, is not a nationality with independent existence. Furthermore, the Jews are not one people with an independent personality because they are citizens to their states. (italics added)

Save for the bizarre questioning of "spiritual ties," the above is a standard notion of anti-Zionism (not anti-Semitism); there were back in 1964, and remain today, Jews who adhere to it. Article 7 of the Charter stipulated that "Jews *of Palestinian origin* are considered Palestinians if they are willing to live peacefully and loyally in Palestine" (italics added). "Palestinian origin" meant ethnic-cultural-lingual more than geographical-territorial. Until 1967 terminating Palestine's colonial-Zionist reality entailed two principal ingredients: (i) establishment of an Arab-Palestinian state in lieu of Israel; (ii) the notion that such a state will normalize on an individual-personal basis the position and presence in the territory of post-1964 Jewish Israelis whose historical lineage in Palestine pre-dated 1917 (officially documented Palestinian Jews such as myself). By the Charter's default, Ashkenazi and Mizrahi Israelis lacking a pre-1917 Palestinian lineage—already the vast majority of Israelis in 1964—were effectively akin to Algeria's Pieds-Noirs. Most crucially, in pre-1967 Palestinian-Arab framings by nationalists and Marxists, Euro-Zionism was analyzed as a manifestation of "standard" colonialism; it was *not* conceptualized in any rigorous manner as a form of *settler* colonialism.

FIGURE 9.1 The 1903 Ottoman Certificate confirming the Jerusalem residency of my great-grandfather, Nissim Behar Effendi (1854–1917). According to pre- and post-1967 Palestinian charters, this certificate defines him and his descendants as Palestinians.

POST-1967 INTRA-MARXIST DIVIDE

Several variables conjoined to produce profound modifications to the pre-1967 anti-colonial Palestinian position and (popular armed) struggle. To begin with, the global context changed. The emergence of the New Left, coupled with the modernist, secularized, libertarian spirit of the 1960s, meant that radical young people worldwide were forward looking, interested chiefly in modifying the politics and culture of their present (and future) along progressive, inclusionary, democratic, and internationalist lines. They dismissed nostalgic conservative views and customs concerning women, LGBTQ, immigrant, indigenous, and religious minorities (Jews included). For many non-Arab leftists worldwide it was not too taxing to think that Ashkenazi Israelis—foremost descendants of the Nazi genocide—did not really have a viable "home" to return to in Poland, Hungary, and possibly Nazi-collaborationist Western Europe as well. Zionists thus appeared as colonialists of a peculiar type while the two-decades-old Israeli state seemed to have been successful in transforming itself into a (new) home for such Jewish Europeans.

Second, Israel's 1967 victory over conventional Arab armies—and its consequent control over entire Mandatory Palestine—appears to have shrunken somewhat Palestinian-Arab prospects for realizing "anti-colonialism 101"—again, removal of colonial settlers from occupied territories. Consequently, for the first time, systematically and comprehensively, Palestinian activists and intellectuals began viewing Zionism as a form of settler colonialism rather than of "standard" colonialism. This entailed gigantic revisions in analyses of the conflict's history, evolution, and current state.[9] Chief among those was that 1948 replaced 1917 resolutely as the year providing the organizing frame of reference for the anti-Zionist undertaking.

Agonizing as it surely was for Palestinian nationalists and Marxists, the implication was weighty: that the roughly 2.3 million Mizrahi and Ashkenazi Israelis in 1967 Palestine were probably there to stay; developments between 1882 and 1967 were not akin to a (non-settler) colonial carpet that can be rolled back (as happened in 1962 in Algeria and was shortly going to be the case in Vietnam, for example). It was at this exact post-1967 junction that the competing Marxist schools of Matzpen and PFLP surfaced. To grasp productively the intra-Marxist disagreement—let alone what I will suggest is its truly profound relevance to twenty-first-century Israel-Palestine debates—the elementary Marxist theorization vis-à-vis the national question (globally) must be revisited.

During the early twentieth century, Marxists faced the tenacity of nationalist sentiments and their fragmenting impact over European workers, who during World War I would go on to slaughter each other by the millions in the service of their respective national bourgeoisie. Additionally attempting to address how the Bolsheviks should deal with the Russian Empire's many ethno-national minorities, the 35-year-old Joseph Stalin—not yet a mass murderer—was commissioned to address these issues systematically. In his *Marxism and the National Question* (1913), Stalin postulated that "a nation is a historically constituted, stable community of people, formed on the basis of a common language, territory, economic life, and psychological makeup manifested in a common culture." Stalin curiously spotlighted Jews to exemplify his definition's applicability:

Bauer [1809–1882] speaks of the Jews as a nation, although they "have no common language"; but what . . . national cohesion is there, for instance, between the Georgian, Daghestanian, Russian, and American Jews, who are completely separated from one another, inhabit different territories and speak different languages?

For most Marxists, Jews inside or outside (Ottoman) Palestine did not constitute a nation.[10] It so happened that the opening footnote in Stalin's otherwise thematic-conceptual-global analysis refers to Euro-Zionism. Zionism for him was "a reactionary nationalist trend of the Jewish bourgeoisie, which had followers among the intellectuals and the more backward sections of the Jewish workers. The Zionists endeavor to isolate the Jewish working-class masses from the general struggle of the proletariat."

Three years later, Vladimir Lenin added critical formulations to the Marxist reading of the phenomenon nationalism worldwide. In *The Working Class and the National Question* (1916) he elaborated:

The national question must be *clearly considered and solved* by all class-conscious workers. . . . Advanced countries, Switzerland, Belgium, Norway and others, provide us with an example of how *free nations under a really democratic system live together in peace or separate peacefully from each other.* Today [WW1] the bourgeoisie fears the workers and is seeking an alliance with . . . reactionaries, and is betraying democracy, advocating oppression or unequal rights *among nations* and corrupting the workers with *nationalist* slogans. In our times the proletariat alone upholds the real freedom of nations and the unity of workers of all nations. For different nations to live together in peace and freedom . . . a full democracy, upheld by the working class, is essential. *No privileges for any nation or any one language*! Not even the slightest degree of oppression or the slightest injustice in respect of a *national minority*—such are the principles of working-class democracy. (italics added)

Impressive over a century later is Lenin's appreciation of European states that future social scientists will recognize as federative-consociational democracies, i.e., systems well-versed in the notion of collective rights enshrined in law in a substate form—contrary liberal democracies.

Let me simplify the Marxist procedure formulaically: (i) observe as empirically or dispassionately as possible every place or situation on earth and test against it the definition of "a nation"; (ii) based on such "scientific" observation determine whether a "National Question" is in existence. Unlike atomized liberals, Marxists have long possessed an enormous body of reasoning to deal with the National Question (globally); it is within these terms that the competing Marxisms of Matzpen and PFLP must be analyzed.[11]

PFLP'S READING

The PFLP was established after the 1967 defeat. As detailed, the Palestinian struggle began to be guided at that time by a 1948 frame of reference. The Vietnamese and Algerian anti-colonial model was replaced by what I call here the African National Congress (ANC)'s "inclusive" South African anti-colonial model. The newer thesis was to establish an inclusive, secularized democratic state throughout Mandatory Palestine;[12] the status of colonial Jewish Israelis—now irrespective of their historic, geographic, or ethnic lineage—was to be normalized individually as citizens who are members of a religious minority group.

In 1971, Ghassan Kannafani was a 35-year-old PFLP leader who drafted its lengthy Marxist-Leninist program. He was interviewed in the *New Left Review* by the 25-year-old Fred Halliday, who would become a world-renowned scholar of the Middle East. Halliday asked him this question:

Do you think there is such a thing as an Israeli nation? The [Israeli] Matzpen group and others [notably French-Marxist historian Maxime Rodinson, 1915–2004] have argued that there may not originally have been a Jewish nation, but the migrants who have come to Palestine have established there a new community, which can be called the Israeli nation.[13]

Kannafani replied:

That is the Rodinson solution [1968]. It is a fantastic intellectual compromise. It means that any group of colonialists who occupy an area and stay there for a while can justify their existence, by saying they are developing into a nation.

Halliday asked, "So you don't think the Israelis are a nation?" and Kannafani replied:

No, I don't. It is a *colonialist* situation. What you have is a group of people, brought for several reasons, justified and unjustified, to a particular area of the world. Together, they all participate in a *colonialist* situation, while between them there are also relations of exploitation. I agree that Israeli workers are exploited. But this is not the first time this has happened. The Arabs in Spain were in the same position. There were classes among them but the main contradiction was between the Arabs in Spain as a whole and the Spanish people (italics added).

For the Marxist-Leninist PFLP, a National Question in Israel-Palestine did *not* exist in relation to 2.5 million Hebrew-speaking Israelis; a colonial setting *alone* existed. (A National Question obviously did exist in relation to colonized or exiled Palestinians). Yet correcting this Zionist state of colonial affairs was possible and no longer required "standard" anti-colonialism or decolonization; PFLP conceptualized Mizrahi and Ashkenazi Israelis in a way resembling the ANC's analysis of white South Africans rather than Algeria's National Liberation Front's conceptualization of Pieds-Noirs. Following the demolition of Israeli-Zionist political-legal apparatus, Israelis could stay (like white South Africans). As is otherwise the mundane case in liberal democracies, the Marxist-Leninist PFLP would remove Palestine's colonial imposition and restore normalcy by extending *individual* rights to Jewish-Israelis in a secularized Palestinian-Arab democratic state. Put otherwise, PFLP dismissed binationalism in a way that resembled earlier dismissals of the non-partitioning 1939 White Paper and the 1947 federative "Minority Plan."

MATZPEN'S MARXISM (BEFORE AND AFTER 1967)

The line of interview Halliday pursued with Kannafani was doubtlessly influenced by Israel's anti-Stalinist dissidents who, nine years earlier (1962), were expelled from the Communist Party. They co-founded the Israeli Socialist Organization, better known by the title of its journal, *Matzpen* (Compass). Known members included Jabra Nicola (1912–1974), Akiva Orr (1931–2013), Oded Pilabski (1932–2011), Haim Hanegbi (1935–2018); Moshé Machover (b. 1936), and Aharon Bachar (1942–1987). While *Matzpen* was minuscule in macro-sociopolitical terms, its members were analytically sophisticated in their reading of the Israel-Palestine trajectory when assessed vis-à-vis Zionist or Arab analyses.

It was before 1967 that *Matzpen* laid (in Hebrew and Arabic) the principal explanatory framework for analyzing Zionism as a manifestation of settler colonialism (rather than of what I called "standard" colonialism). In doing so *Matzpen*'s analysis differed from pre-1967 manifestations of Arab Marxism. Knowingly or latently, subsequent works applying a settler-colonial framework to the Israel-Palestine case have departed from *Matzpen*'s foundational formulations.[14] I can think of Sayegh's 1965 analysis (quoted above) as coming close to *Matzpen*'s pre-1967 writings in terms of rigor, yet Sayegh never articulated a real way out for Israel-Palestine beyond declarative generalizations such as "the liberation of Palestine" or its "decolonization." In May 1967, Machover and Nicola made this argument:

As a result of Zionist colonization, a Hebrew nation with its own national characteristics (common language, separate economy, etc.) has been formed in Palestine. This nation has a capitalist class structure—it is divided into exploiters and exploited, a bourgeoisie and a proletariat. That this nation has been formed artificially and at the expense of the indigenous Arab population does not change the fact that it exists. It would be a disastrous error to ignore this fact. . . . Nationalist Arab leaders who call for the liberation of Palestine ignore the fact that even if Israel would be defeated militarily and cease to exist as a State, a Hebrew nation will still exist. If the problem of the existence of this nation is not solved correctly, a situation of dangerous and prolonged national conflict will be re-created which will cause endless bloodshed and suffering. . . . It is no coincidence that the [Arab] leaders who advocate such a "solution" are also incapable of solving the Kurdish problem.[15]

While the PFLP was not yet in existence, pre-1967 Marxist-informed intellectuals and activists associated with Arab nationalism adhered to an Algerian-type anti-colonialism and decolonization. PFLP's modified thesis following 1967—Kannafani's above-cited 1971 articulation included—probably encouraged Matzpen members to rearticulate their pre-1967 reading of the National Question vis-à-vis Israel-Palestine. In May 1973—contrary to PFLP's Marxist dominancy—Nicola and Machover reemphasized that "the idea that Israeli Jews do not constitute a nation is a myth, a piece of wishful thinking based on lack of familiarity with the actual facts."[16] For PFLP, Stalin and Lenin's theses on the National Question were inapplicable to Israelis: the colonial setting alone existed in relation to them.

During the early 1970s—yet to some extent nowadays, too—an intriguing dialectic converged the bottom-line analyses of four forces: the Marxist Arab left; the Arab conservative-nationalist current; the religious Arab right; and—lastly—Zionist Israelis and non-Israelis. All four schools maintained that a Hebrew-speaking national collectivity was nowhere to be found between the river and the sea. Machover summarized the Zionist view: "Zionist ideology denies . . . that a new Hebrew nation has come into existence because its self-legitimation depends on the fiction that all Jews around the world are one nation that has an eternal right over its God-given homeland."[17] In 2014, Israel's Supreme Court ruled that an Israeli nation does not exist.[18] Albeit via a different trail, the court reached the same mountain peak that Kannafani described in 1971.

CROSSROADS INTO THE TWENTY-FIRST CENTURY

I argue that the terms underlying the intra-Marxist Matzpen-PFLP divergence are profoundly relevant to controversies among post-Oslo constituencies that evolved following the publication of Edward Said's 1999 essay "The One-State Solution"; these twenty-first-century constituencies either reject in principle, or no longer view as realistic or viable, the notion of a two-state solution in Israel-Palestine and consequently entertain alternatives to partition.[19] Matzpen-PFLP's divergence is unquestionably relevant to the post-2010 textual deluge in settler-colonial studies.

Since detailed analysis of the 1974–2000 period is inconsequential to my argument here, I will now telegraphically summarize it for bridging purposes alone.

For non-PFLP and non-Marxist nationalist constituencies within the PLO, foremost the Fatah majority faction, 1974–2000 can be interpreted as an attempt to transform Israel-Palestine by a reference to a (post-1967) notion of a two-state solution. The process started in 1974 during the twelfth gathering of the Palestine National Council (PNC) that concluded with a ten-point program stipulating that "the PLO will employ all means, and first and foremost armed struggle, to liberate Palestinian territory and to establish the independent national authority for the people over *every part* of Palestinian territory liberated"[20] (italics added). PFLP opposed this plan as well as Viennese initiatives to bring the PLO to peace negotiations.[21] George Habash (1926–2008) elaborated:

One day truth will be clear to all that there is no peace in the area with the existence of a fascist, racist [Israeli] state based on a reactionary [Zionist] doctrine and with the aim of serving the imperialist interest. The slogan of a democratic society in Palestine raised by the Palestinian revolution is the only road to freedom and progress for the entire people of the area, including the Jews, and is the road to permanent and durable peace.[22]

Among non-PFLP factions clearer endorsements of the principle of a two-state partition dominated the 1988 PNC meeting in Algiers. Whereas 253 PNC delegates voted for the notion of partition (Edward Said included[23]), 46 voted against and 10 abstained; the latter two groups included PFLP Marxists. From 1988 the (non-PFLP) leading anti-colonial Palestinian stream ceased being "standardized" unequivocally when compared to its preceding pre-1967 and pre-1988 positions, let alone when studied vis-à-vis Asian and African anti-colonial struggles. Explicitly informed now by a 1967 frame of reference—rather than a 1917 one or a 1948 one (as was the case before 1967 and 1988 respectively)—this meant that an offer to rectify Palestine's settler-colonial setting was extended to Mizrahi and Ashkenazi Israelis both individually and collectively. Moreover, this entailed a principal PLO consent to normalize the existence of Jewish Israelis not only as an officially recognized substate social collectivity but in an independent state west of the 1949 Green (armistice) Line.[24]

PLO's recognition of the possibility of a two-state partition became more explicit in September 1993 upon signing the Oslo Accords. The Oslo process rested on endorsement of UN Security Council Resolution 242 (1967) and 338 (1973) that lent legitimacy to an Israeli state on the pre-1967 territory (while effectively rendering obsolete the UN partition lines of 1947). Israel's legitimacy west of the Green Line was additionally stipulated by the International Court of Justice in its 2004 ruling on the illegality of Israel's Wall when erected east of the Green Line (together with the entire settlement apparatus). Yet the ruling's supporters are commonly unaware of the fact that had Israel erected a wall on the Green Line, the International Court of Justices would have produced a blank report.

And last, as far as this bridging summary of the 1974–2000 period is concerned, many studies documented the disintegration of the Oslo process and the consequent outbreak of the "second intifada." As these pre-2000 processes are peripheral to this article, I simply consider them givens. What conversely *is* critical is that in the twenty-first century these processes gave birth to a vigorous debate between two schools. The first consists of scholars or activists who remained of the view that only territorial partition to two states is capable of securing stability and peace for everyone in Israel-Palestine.

The second includes those who either reject in principle the notion of a two-state partition or cease viewing it as viable due to the Oslo debacle. Probably the best example for this is Edward Said's transformation from his 1988 vote for a two-state partition to his support of one (bi-national!) state in 1999. During the 1990s Said increasingly mentioned individuals and groups who opposed with sophistication the concept of partition, including Brit Shalom during the 1920s or Ihud (Union) during the 1940s.[25] What has come to be known in the twenty-first century as the one-state solution is comprised of scholars and activists who promote alternatives to partition. It is vis-à-vis this non-homogenous group that the intra-Marxist Matzpen-PFLP disagreement remains potently relevant.

LIBERALISM, BINATIONALISM, INDIVIDUAL VERSUS COLLECTIVE RIGHTS

During the twenty-first century two main alternatives to the Oslo logic, and its notion of partition, emerged from the non-religious end of the spectrum.[26] Advocates of the first school promote the constitution of a single unitary state in Israel-Palestine. Extensive scrutiny of websites and writings by this school reveals that this proposed alternative reproduces the ideal type of the modern state envisioned by the English spectrum from John Locke to John Stuart Mill, i.e., a liberal democratic state—aspiring in earnest to be ethnic-, religious-, racial- and color-blind—whose chief raison d'être is securing equal individual rights for all its citizens.

Those advocating for the second alternative—to partition—uphold some notion of a federated binational state. This means that, in addition to their insistence on securing equal individual rights for everyone, members of this school recognize explicitly the social existence of collectivities. This leaves them little choice other than to grapple with notions of collective rights, which, as an analytic category, also includes national rights. Unsurprisingly, both schools disregard 1967 as a launchpad for alternative proposals vis-à-vis the concept of partition (contra the two-state school); both schools are guided by a 1948 frame of reference (unlike, for example, post-1988 PLO). This concurrently means that it is not only 1967 but—equally crucially—1917 that does not serve as a frame of reference of the two schools' reasoning and proposals for resolving the Israel-Palestine question. Be it nominally or substantively, members of both non-partition schools have chosen to shelve "standard" anti-colonialism, i.e., decolonization of the Algerian or Vietnamese type. Both aim to restore normalcy in twenty-first century Palestine in a manner that is inclusive of roughly seven million Mizrahi and Ashkenazi Israelis otherwise viewed as colonialists. The remainder of the chapter offers my reading of these two schools.

THE LIBERAL SINGLE UNITARY STATE

Of various twenty-first-century schools promoting alternatives to partition, the liberal one-state school is undoubtedly the single most globally dominant, vibrant, known, active, and organized. The prime accomplishment that the school's envisioned state is supposed to materialize is "one-person, one-vote." Equal individual rights and citizenship are the corner stones while the limitations are rarely addressed.[27] Notions of collective rights are overall bypassed; the axis around which the thesis revolves is the maxim "ethnicity and nationalism OUT—citizenship IN": the (global) phenomenon of ethno-nationalism is effectively brushed aside.

A comprehensive early articulation of the liberal one-state thesis rejecting vehemently the notion of binationalism was published in 2005 by Virginia Tilley.[28] The year 2007 witnessed a potent linkage (in London and Madrid) between scholarship and advocacy in the form of the "London One State Group." Coauthored by fourteen intellectual activists, and later endorsed by dozens, the six-hundred-word "Madrid Declaration" summarized:

Palestine belongs to all who live in it and to those who were expelled or exiled from it since 1948, regardless of religion, ethnicity, national *origin* or current citizenship status; any system of government must be founded on the principle of equality in civil, political, social and cultural rights for all citizens. Power must be exercised with rigorous impartiality on behalf of all people in the diversity of their identities."[29] (italics added)

The word "national" appears twice more in the declaration. Once again in the phrase "national *origin*" and for the third time in the phrase "national experience." While the word "Israel" is predictably bypassed, coauthors appear to have paid surgical attention to avoid hinting at the possibility that, post-1882, Hebrew-speaking Israelis may comprise (in 2007, that is) a collectivity that has acquired *national* characteristics—rather than solely political, social, or cultural. While the coauthors are all scholarly members of the constructivist social science school, it is unclear whether their avoidance of such a hint resulted from empirical observation of 2007 Israel-Palestine or from an a priori ideological choice brought to the meeting from home. The declaration ultimately recommended "the creation of a non-sectarian state that does not privilege the rights of one ethnic or religious group over another and that respects the separation of state from all organized religion"; a consideration of national dimensions is absent. In an Al-Shabaka policy brief, the Declaration's coauthor Ali Abunimah elaborated:

The concept that a settler-colonial community is entitled . . . to participate in self-determination, not as a distinct national group, but as legitimate residents, accords fully with international law and with precedents in other decolonizing countries including South Africa, Namibia, Northern Ireland and Mozambique. Omar Barghouti, a leader in the Palestinian BDS campaign on Israel, has argued strongly against recognizing Israeli Jews as forming a national community in Palestine. Barghouti warns that "recognizing national rights of Jewish settlers in Palestine cannot but imply accepting their right to self-determination."[30]

Abunimah understated the settlement reached in Northern Ireland follow-ing the 1998 Good Friday agreement; the agreement's most important con-sequence was not securing equal individual rights for local Catholic Irish and Protestant English settlers (many of whom are actually Scottish and Welsh ethnically). Profoundly more critical is that the consociational agree-ment secures collective rights for both groups. These rights are enshrined in law and rest on a strict notion of power-sharing in running Northern Ireland regardless of groups' numerical-demographic ratio. North Ireland's (Protestant) settlers thus do not merely "participate in self-determination" of indigenous (Catholic) Irish, to cite Abunimah, as this is a gigantic under-statement of their case and position.

Abunimah was sensible to quote verbatim a 2009 essay by a coau-thor of the 2007 "Madrid Declaration," Omar Barghouti, an essay that led Abunimah himself to ditch his former commitment to binationalism;[31] Barghouti explained:

A binational solution . . . other than its inherent logical and legal flaws, cannot accommodate the right of return as stipulated in UNGA Resolution 194, not to mention the fact that it infringes, by definition, the inalienable rights of the indig-enous Palestinians on part of their homeland, particularly the right to self-deter-mination. Recognizing national rights of [Ashkenazi and Mizrahi] Jewish settlers in Palestine cannot but imply accepting their right to self-determination, other than contradicting the very letter, spirit and purpose of the universal principle of self-determination primarily as a means for "peoples under colonial or alien domi-nation or foreign occupation" to realize their rights, may, at one extreme, lead to claims for secession or Jewish "national" sovereignty on part of the land of Pales-tine. A Jewish state in Palestine, no matter what shape it takes, cannot but infringe the basic rights of the land's indigenous Palestinian population and perpetuate a system of racial discrimination that ought to be opposed categorically.[32]

It is unclear what the precise foundation is to Barghouti's thesis that bina-tionalism and UN General Assembly Resolution 194 are mutually exclusive by definition. A popular proponent of the liberal one-state school among Euro-American activists and scholarly associations, Barghouti is logical and principled. Like his other writings, this 2009 essay is free of hesitations, reevaluations, or hindsight introspections. That is so in relation to, for example, the Palestinian leadership's dismissal of the 1939 White Paper or of the United Nations Special Committee on Palestine's 1947 "Minority Plan."

Cognizant of the Nakba as it empirically materialized, Barghouti held in 2009 what is essentially a 1939 view that rejects the possibility of a unitary federative state in Palestine. That is his democratic right, all the more so as Palestinian. But, as a thought experiment, suppose that for whatever reason a post-2010 Israel would have agreed to the return of all exiled Palestinians and to the relinquishing of its armed forces in exchange for maintaining control over, say, one Tel-Aviv skyscraper, designated to constitute one of the two territorial pillars of a single binational federation. Principled Barghouti would reject such option since "recognizing national rights of Jewish settlers in Palestine cannot but imply accepting their right to self-determination and this . . . may . . . lead to claims for secession or Jewish "national" sovereignty on *part* of the land of Palestine" (one skyscraper included).

Barghouti's choice to bypass the possibility that seven million post-2009 Jewish-Israelis may comprise a national collectivity grows out of his single furthest projection that they (might) seek self-determination from a (futuristic) binational federation. That is why Jewish-Israelis can be regarded only as individuals. At the very same time, Barghouti annuls anti-colonialism of the Algerian or Vietnamese type (at least declaratively). Zionist colonialists can remain on occupied Palestine. Barghouti's annulment of "anti-colonialism 101" is apparently driven by an anti-Fanonite ethical or moral benevolence toward Ashkenazi and Mizrahi colonialists that, as such, permits the normalization of their presence as individuals absent of a collective ethno-national affiliation:

A secular, democratic unitary state in British Mandate Palestine is the most just . . . solution . . . because it offers the best hope for reconciling . . . the *inalienable* rights of the indigenous Palestinians, particularly the right to self-determination, and the *acquired* rights of the colonial settlers to live in peace and security, individually and collectively. Specifically, the secular democratic state is the only one among discussed alternatives that promises ethical coexistence between the natives and the settlers. (italics in the original)[33]

It is unclear on whose mandate Barghouti requires that colonized Palestinians abdicate "standard" anti-colonialism and instead grant rights to colonizers settled on their lands. Be that as it may, in cases where liberal one-staters write down the word "collectively" in relation to Jewish-Israelis—

in the above-cited 2007 declaration included—this means that Jewish-Israelis comprise a (non-national) religious or linguistic collectivity. (Since Ashkenazi, Mizrahi, Ethiopian, and other Jewish-Israelis share no "ethnicity" they do not comprise an ethnic collectivity.)

For more hesitant observers of on-the-ground Israel-Palestine agonies—and surely for colonialism or nationalism scholars—one question is whether the student should factor in, merely as an additional variable, the empirical self-view of Jewish-Israelis themselves on these puzzles. Regardless of one's verdict, it seems safe to suggest that the self-identification of Jewish-Israelis is likely to approximate more of a national collectivity than an ethnic or lingual one. Does this inevitably mean that such collectivities must possess a state? Binationalists are among those who answer in the negative.

I must lastly add that the outbreak of the Arab Spring modified the one-state school's principal thesis of "secular democratic state":

In the past the main slogan of the left was "secular democratic state." Today [2013] the main slogan is "one democratic state." Yes, this is a concession of the secular left. It reflects the need, in the conditions of the Arab Spring, to cooperate with Islamic movements in the struggle for democracy. The left should examine critically its own history and the history of the region, remember what was done in the name of the left and on behalf of secularism, and understand the need for flexibility and the central role of democracy in the region's political agenda in this period.[34]

If the organizing modernist principles of the democratic system are by definition secular, then the whiteout of "secular" may not be much more than a nominal, sematic, or heuristic appeasement. Moreover, of the critiques leveled against such states as Israel and Pakistan, one is that religion is excessively fused there with the state. which is argued, in turn, to affect unfavorably prospects for democratic consolidation. Be these as they may, the core thesis of the liberal one-state school is this: the colonial presence of Ashkenazi and Mizrahi Israelis in Palestine can be normalized but solely on a subnational individual basis.

THE FEDERAL OR BINATIONAL SCHOOL

The second school promoting a post-Oslo alternative to the 1947 or 1967 versions of partition is federal or binational. It (re)emerged in Israel around the 1991 founding of Brit Shivyon (Covenant of Equality) from which Israel's Palestinian party Tajamu consolidated in 1995. The school is disproportionally inhabited by Israel's Palestinian-Arab citizens than by other Palestinians; early articulations were made by Azmi Bishara, Amnon Raz-Krakotzkin, As'ad Ghanem, and others.[35] The school entertains the extension of collective substate rights to Jews in Israel-Palestine by establishing a single federative or consociational democratic state of its citizens. Sorrowful as it is for Palestinian-Arab members of the school, they still view twenty-first -century Jewish-Israelis as comprising a collectivity that since 1882 has acquired subjective and objective national characteristics (revisit Stalin's definition above). Honaida Ghanim explained: "Israeli Jews who propose binationalism don't give up on the most central ingredient of Zionist ideology whereas Palestinians who accept binationalism give up on the dream of 'liberating the homeland' and accept the principle of sharing their homeland with colonialists."[36]

So long as colonialists are physically present—individually or collectively—on the land, then Ghanim's stipulation regarding "native-colonialist sharing" shall stand intact by definition; only Algerian or Vietnamese "anti-colonialism 101" can overcome the condition she typifies. It remains historically possible that the Israel-Palestine question is ultimately a zero-sum game between the rival parties.[37] In this context, the defining feature of the federative or binational school diverges from two other schools: the first includes Zionist Christians and non-Christians who adhere to heterogeneous notions of a Jewish State; the second school is composed of liberals proposing a unitary state that extends national recognition to only one collectivity (Palestinian Arabs). A document that conveys the thrust of the binational school is the co-authored "Haifa Declaration," which was published in May 2007 (five months before the aforementioned "Madrid Declaration"):

Our vision for the future relations between Palestinian Arabs and Israeli Jews . . . is to create a democratic state founded on equality between the two *national* groups. This solution would guarantee the rights of *the two groups* in a just and equitable manner. This would require a change in the constitutional structure and a change in the definition of the State of Israel from a Jewish state to a democratic state established on *national* and civil equality between the two national groups. . . . This historic reconciliation also requires us, Palestinians and Arabs, to recognize *the right of the Israeli Jewish people to self-determination* and to life in peace, dignity, and security with the Palestinian and the other peoples of the region. . . . We firmly believe that the fulfillment of all the conditions for a reconciliation between the *two peoples, the Jewish Israeli and Arab Palestinian*, which requires the recognition of the right of the Palestinian people to self-determination, and the realization of the rights of the Palestinians in Israel as a homeland minority, will create political circumstances that will enable the creation of confidence, cooperation, and mutual respect between two independent and democratic states: the State of Palestine and the State of Israel. We further hope that this will open up new horizons in which agreements and treaties will be concluded between them in the economic, scientific, and cultural fields that guarantee free and reciprocal movement, mobility, residence, and employment for the citizens and residents of the two states. (italics added)

The "Haifa Declaration" atypically upheld the possibility for a Palestinian state to exist next to a non-Jewish binational Israel west of the Green Line. Among the declaration's sixty coauthors were Professor Nadim Rouhana, director of Mada al-Carmel (Arab Center for Applied Social Research), Members of Knesset Ayman Odeh and Haneen Zoabi, Law professor Nadera Shalhoub-Kevorkian, and Ameer Makhoul, former director of Ittijah (Union of Arab Community-Based Organizations) and—since 2010—a political prisoner. Matzpen's reasoning during the 1960s influenced thematically (and otherwise) twenty-first-century articulations of the binational school (notwithstanding Matzpen's profound skepticism about prospects to resolve nonregionally the Israel-Palestine question).[38] Before I turn to conclude with what I view as affinities between PFLP's post-1967 thesis and the twenty-first-century liberal one-state school, I will compare, contrast, and juxtapose the few elements that typify the competing liberal and binational schools.

My impression is that the thrust underlying the adherence of members of the federative or binational school to the year 1948 as a launching pad for their proposed alternative is more genuine and rigorous when compared to the parallel thrust underlying the adherence to 1948 of the liberal one-state school. In the case of the former, the agonizing decision to put to ultimate rest "standard" anti-colonialism and decolonization comes across as an introspective, voluntary choice that is strategically driven, rather than merely utilitarian or tactical. The decision grows out of what I view as a cool-headed analysis, however heartbreaking, of the domestic, regional, and international sociopolitical dynamics that produced the tumultuous

1947–1949 chapter and, more crucially, its tangible social consequences during the ensuing seven decades.

These same issues differ in the case of the liberal one-state school. Here, the adherence to 1948, the introduction of the notion of "acquired rights" to individual colonialists, and the burial of anti-colonialism of the Algerian or Vietnamese type do not seem as outgrowths of willful choice or lucid deliberation of the post-1948 Zionist-Arab trajectory. Instead, the abandonment of 1917, the adherence to 1948, and the construction of "acquired rights" notion seem to be outcomes of a structural imposition forced upon liberal adherents of the one-state school entirely from outside. This external enforcer is the bombardment that Euro-Zionism has managed to inflict upon a rather poorly led post-1939 Palestinian anti-colonial movement.

Laying 1917 to rest as the frame of reference of the anti-colonial struggle generates a flamboyant type of half-baked, declarative anti-colonialism. Coupled with the (involuntary) introduction of "acquired rights" to colonialists, this ensemble comes across as more of an evasive maneuver than a genuinely strategic choice to resolve the Israel-Palestine question viably. Recognizing seven million Jewish Israelis as atomized or religioned individuals alone appears like lip service to empirical history and sociology. This heuristic generosity may well result from one simple awareness: had genuine commitment to anti-colonialism been openly declared as it was surely desired in people's hearts, enough global observers would have viewed it as anachronistic. It is therefore that dynamic that is the chief reason for the (otherwise undesired) shift in frame of reference from 1917 to 1948 among the liberal one-state school and for its clinging to what is effectively a Eurocentric salvation in the form of messianic liberalism—ostensibly incapable of detecting more than one national collectivity in 2016 Palestine.

Furthermore, the idea to grant individual rights to Jewish Israelis seems more anachronistic than an honest *public* commitment or adherence to the "standard" form of anti-colonialism based on 1917 (whereby colonialists are expected to exit, as was the case in Algeria, Vietnam, India, etc.). The reason is that the liberal one-state's shift from 1917 to 1948 does not seem to rest on a thorough consideration of such consequential variables as the Middle East's four hundred years of Ottoman social and organizational legacy (in the form of a non-liberal, Millet-based communitarian-collectivism), or the vast imbalance of forces between the Palestinian and Israeli-Jewish collectivities.

Compared to the unitary, liberal one-state school in terms of influence on the global discourse on Israel-Palestine, the federative or binational school seems frail, immobilized, and insignificant. Its members occasionally come across as fearing their own shadows. One reason is the sizable overlap between the one-state school idea and the Boycott, Divestment, Sanctions (BDS) movement (even if no shred of inherent contradiction exists between binationalism and BDS tactics). One-state and BDS associates do not seem too tolerant of not only advocates of a two-state partition—think of the semi-excommunicated Norman Finkelstein or Noam Chomsky—but of binationalists, too. For example, a lecture by binational thinker and Tajammu member Amnon Raz-Krakotzkin during the pioneering "Challenging the Boundaries: A Single State in Israel-Palestine" (SOAS, November 17–18, 2007) met with intolerant derision. Similar dynamics transpired in 2012 vis-à-vis the Israeli Committee Against House Demolitions's Jeff Halper.[39] Liberal one-state advocates essentially deem binationalism a form of Zionism; if that is indeed so, then binationalism is a form of normalization (of the unjust that is).

An end result of these dynamics is that affiliates of the binational school are cautious to express views as vigorously or publicly as otherwise required to affect global discourse, mobilization, and activism; this reluctance may partially grow out of concerns about being branded normalizers. The risks of "guilt by association with normalization" are formidable, particularly in obedient, conformist academia. Yet the intra-Palestinian phenomenon of labeling ideological opponents collaborators with Zionism is old: already the 1936–1939 anti-colonial revolt witnessed hundreds of Palestinians killed by others who branded them collaborators, traitors, or normalizers[40] and similar dynamics took place in the 1970s. Mutual intra-Palestinian exclusions undoubtedly assisted in a profound manner the Zionist historical triumph.[41]

An additional and more prosaic reason for the comparative weakness of the binational school is that leading members of the liberal one-state school—including Barghouti, Abunimah, and Pappé—wisely work tirelessly in public advocacy while admirably investing energy and time in activism. As a worldview and frame of reference, binationalism remains elitist: for Euro-American students and activists its reasoning is considerably more complex than that of atomized western liberalism. Consequently, binationalism has no translation at all to grassroots activism across Euro-America.

CONCLUSION

Should the twenty-first-century, liberal one-state school be understood as a 180-degree turn back to the PFLP's post-1967 (anti-binational) one-state thesis? Honaida Ghanim is skeptical:

The new take on a one-state solution is fundamentally different from those that preceded it, be it in terms of context, organizing and referential ideas, tools, and approach. The PLO enterprise was formulated . . . with intimate reference to decolonization principles and methodology; it called for the removal of Zionist colonization and its symptoms and restoration of the indigenous people's stolen rights through a revolutionary armed resistance . . . . The normative-political ethos was . . . concretized in the form of political-institutional programs by the proposition of a single democratic state . . . whereby Jewish settlers may live in Palestine as equals to the indigenous counterparts. From a Palestinian viewpoint, the discourse was seen as moral and generous—offered by the indigenous population to the colonizer . . . to enable a form of living together. . . . The Palestinians' vocabulary was inspired by that found in international liberation movements and struggles. In contrast, contemporary Palestinian voices calling for the "one-state solution" depart from a different international purview. . . . Its vocabulary is inspired by . . . the . . . reality that Israel has imposed in *Historic Palestine*. . . . The old intellectual and political elites advocated the *single democratic state* as a forward-looking national liberation enterprise, through which decolonization is achieved, whereas the new/current political elites advocate the one-state solution as an oppositional project; an acknowledgement of the defeat of the nationalist enterprise, Israel's success, . . . as well as the failure of the coordinated national struggle. . . . The one-state solution that dominates the semi-official political discourse nowadays is engendered in the context of Oslo Accords, not in the critical discourse that Edward Said and others reintroduced . . . in 1999. The latter still viewed decolonization . . . as the means that would realize the single democratic state, whereas the formers focus primarily on citizenhood and equality without discussing decolonization. Consequently, today's one-state discourse brackets the question of decolonization to a large extent and leans towards *egalitarian citizenhood* as a possible alternative. (italics in the original)[42]

To start with, Ghanim did not highlight resolutely that Edward Said supported binationalism unequivocally—and that is in complete opposite of *both* one-state schools. That aside, Ghanim overstates the differences between the two one-state schools (notwithstanding the certainly real difference between armed struggle and non-violent resistance); Ghanim additionally romanticizes the pre-1974 years while oddly still not clarifying to her readers what decolonization precisely meant, or means. Underemphasized by Ghanim is the substantive similarity between the two one-state schools that outweighs their differences: both envisioned a South African-inspired liberal vision that aimed to terminate Palestine's colonial setting by extending individual rights to everyone inclusively and national rights to one collectivity (the Palestinian Arabs).

While the two one-state schools are in my reading similar conceptually, the difference that does divide them is considerably greater than—yet different from—the one that Ghanim highlighted. My contention is this: while the "older," post-1967 one-state school was undoubtedly historical—the twenty-first-century liberal one-state school is ahistorical. This may amount to a Palestinian exemplification of Karl Marx's dictum from *The Eighteenth Brumaire of Louis Napoleon* (1852): "History repeats itself, first as tragedy [1939, 1947, 1971—M.B.], second as farce [twenty-first century—M.B]." To elaborate:

(1) During 1947 the overwhelming majority group, under the leadership of Haj-Amin al-Husseini (1897–1974), rejected outright both Marxist and liberal versions of a single federal, non-partitioned, binational state. Back then Jews numbered 650,000, comprised 33 percent of the population, were recent (European) arrivals, spoke Hebrew sporadically, and possessed minimal ingredients that could be said to constitute "national culture" (revisit Stalin's definition). Haj-Amin's leadership contra a single federated state may have been insufficiently wise strategically, yet it cannot be said to have been unreasonable, ergo, it was in Marxist terms a historical moment of "history as tragedy."

(2) In 1971 the PLO, PFLP, and Kanafani rejected binationalism outright; they identified in Palestine only individual colonialists and no (second) national collectivity. By that time Jewish Israelis numbered 2.5 million, spoke Hebrew as a nationally unifying language, produced countless manifestations of Hebrew culture and literature, and possessed a state with world-leading universities, an army, as well as about fifty atomic bombs. In 1971 Marxist definitions for nation and nationalism turned more relevant to Jewish-Israelis than was the case in Haj-Amin's White Paper of 1939 or the "Minority Plan" of 1947; ergo, the 1967–1974 period also appears as "history as tragedy."

(3) In 2017 the Balfour Declaration turned 100 years old, 1947 was 70, Israel's control of entire Mandatory Palestine had lasted 50 years, and the First Intifada was 30 years in the past. Jews numbered seven million while comprising 50 percent of the population between the Jordan River and the Mediterranean Sea. To be incapable in 2017 of witnessing more than a single national collectivity in Palestine—as in a 1947/1971 carbon copy—came across as Marx's history repeating itself as (ahistorical) farce; such disposition disregarded the fundamentals underlying the school known as social constructivism. Upsetting as it surely is, even outright criminal rape can occasionally produce an offspring.

So what sense to make of binationalism in 2017? To begin with, binationalism *and* the liberal one-state school are both attempts to terminate colonialism, normalize the presence and status of colonialists, and resolve the Israel-Palestine conflict. I nonetheless find it difficult to witness in twenty-first-century Israel-Palestine anything other than binationalism. Ignoring the binational elephant in the room remains as permissible in the twenty-first century as it was in 1971, 1947, or 1939; such choice, however, appears to leave its devotees little room other than to reintroduce into their analyses the Crusades analogy (notwithstanding that the latter did not possess two hundred nuclear bombs).

Put differently, the democratic tenets of Locke and Mill's individual liberalism—their consequent one-person, one-vote notion included—are prerequisites for every settlement in Israel-Palestine. Yet application of the liberal thesis is unlikely to suffice in order to resolve inter-communal relationships in post-Ottoman Israel-Palestine (or, for that matter, also in such neighboring countries as Syria, Iraq, Lebanon, and Yemen). Eyes cannot be wide shut vis-à-vis the twenty-first-century (global) phenomenon of ethno-nationalism, as this may be as messianic or escapist as the denial of global warming.

NOTES

1. Rachel Busbridge, "Israel-Palestine and the Settler Colonial 'Turn': From Interpretation to Decolonization," *Theory, Culture and Society* 35, no. 1 (2018), 91–115.
2. Fayez A. Sayegh, *Zionist Colonialism in Palestine* (Beirut: Research Center, Palestine Liberation Organization, 1965), reprinted in *Settler Colonial Studies* 2, no. 1 (2011), 206–225.

3. Rashid Khalidi, *Palestinian Identity: The Construction of Modern National Consciousness* (New York: Columbia University Press, 1997); Emanuel Beška, *From Ambivalence to Hostility: The Arabic Newspaper* Filastīn *and Zionism, 1911–1914* (Bratislava: Slovak Academic Press, 2016).

4. James Renton, *The Zionist Masquerade: The Birth of the Anglo-Zionist Alliance, 1914–1918* (New York: Palgrave Macmillan, 2007); Victor Kattan, *From Coexistence to Conquest: International Law and the Origins of the Arab-Israeli Conflict, 1891–1949* (London: Pluto, 2009); Jonathan Schneer, *The Balfour Declaration* (London: Bloomsbury, 2010).

5. "Jewish Population in the World and in Israel," *Statistical Abstract of Israel*, 62/2, 163.

6. Maryanne Rhett, *The Global History of the Balfour Declaration: Declared Nation* (Abingdon, UK: Routledge, 2015), 23, 34, 36.

7. Ilan Pappé, *The Ethnic Cleansing of Palestine* (Oxford: Oneworld, 2006).

8. Moshe Behar, "What's in a Name? Socio-Terminological Formations and the Case for 'Arabized-Jews,'" *Social Identities* 15, no. 6 (2009), 747–771; Abeed Dawisha, *Arab Nationalism in the Twentieth Century: From Triumph to Despair* (Princeton, N.J.: Princeton University Press, 2014).

9. See also Sune Haugbolle, "The New Arab Left and 1967," *British Journal of Middle Eastern Studies* 44, no. 4 (2017), 497–512.

10. Around 1939, when Jews comprised 29 percent of Palestine's population, some non-Arab Marxists started to introduce some revisions to the principal thesis.

11. Both groups made a significant regional analysis of the question of Palestine; owing to space constraints it is not studied here.

12. Leila Farsakh "A Common State in Israel–Palestine: Historical Origins and Lingering Challenges," *Ethnopolitics* 15, no. 4 (2016), 380–392.

13. Ghassan Kannafani, "On the PFLP and the September Crisis," *New Left Review* I, no. 67 (May–June 1971).

14. See Gershon Shafir, *Land, Labor and the Origins of the Israeli-Palestinian Conflict, 1882–1914* (Cambridge: Cambridge University Press, 1989) and what in the twenty-first-century is termed the "settler-colonial turn" in the research.

15. "The Palestine Problem and the Israeli-Arab Dispute," May 18, 1967, at https://matzpen .org/english/1967-05-18/the-palestine-problem-and-the-israeli-arab-dispute/.

16. Reprinted in Moshé Machover, *Israelis and Palestinians: Conflict and Resolution* (Chicago: Haymarket, 2012), 22–24. While PFLP's weaker and smaller splinter group "Democratic Front for the Liberation of Palestine," formed in 1969, came closer to Matzpen, I lack space to address this.

17. Machover, *Israelis and Palestinians*, xii.

18. Appeal of the NGO "I'm an Israeli" via "Uzi Ornan vs. the State of Israel," Israeli High Court, CA 8573/08 (October 3, 2013). On this issue and the court's ruling, see: https://versa.cardozo.yu.edu/opinions/ornan-v-ministry-interior.

19. Bashir Bashir and Azar Dakwar, eds., *Rethinking the Politics of Israel/Palestine: Partition and Its Alternatives* (Vienna: Bruno Kreisky Forum and S&D Group, 2014); Bashir Bashir, "The Strengths and Weaknesses of Integrative Solutions for the Israeli-Palestinian Conflict," *Middle East Journal* 70, no. 4 (2016), 560–578.

20. Palestine Liberation Organization, "Political Program for the Present Stage of the Palestinian National Organization Drawn by the Palestinian National Council, Cairo, June 9, 1974," *Journal of Palestine Studies* 3, no. 4 (1974), 224 (italics added)

21. George Habash, "Liberation no Negotiation," *PFLP Bulletin* 9, no. 6–7, and 10, no. 4–5 (1974).
22. "George Habash Outlines PFLP Policy," *PFLP Bulletin* 13, no. 10–11 (1974).
23. Edward Said, "From Intifada to Independence," *Middle East Report* 158 (1989), 14–16.
24. This decision was voted on without necessarily extending PLO recognition to Israel's self-definition as "Jewish" since this would mean acceptance of non-Jewish Palestinians as second-class citizens in their homeland. Israel's "Jewishness" was generally understood by the PLO to be an internal Israeli affair that Jewish and non-Jewish citizens should have the right to oppose.
25. Like most Israel-Palestine scholars, Said did not know much about ideas of non-Ashkenazi intellectuals during these periods on matters such as coexistence. Consult Moshe Behar and Zvi Ben-Dor Benite, *Modern Middle Eastern Jewish Thought: Writings on Identity, Politics and Culture, 1893–1958* (Waltham, Mass.: Brandeis University Press, 2013) and "The Possibility of Modern Middle Eastern Jewish Thought," *British Journal of Middle Eastern Studies* 41, no. 1 (2014), 43–61.
26. See Leila Farsakh, "The One-State Solution and the Israeli-Palestinian Conflict: Palestinian Challenges and Prospects" *Middle East Journal* 65, no. 1 (2011), 55–71. Religiously informed post-Oslo alternatives—including those of Hamas or Israeli settlers—exceed this article's mandate. Also not discussed is the initiative "Two-States/One-Homeland," which proposes confederation as the alternative to partition; one reason for bypassing it here is that 1967 remains a significant frame of reference for the initiative.
27. See Stathis Kouvélakis, "The Marxian Critique of Citizenship: For a Rereading of *On the Jewish Question*," *South Atlantic Quarterly* 104, no. 4 (2005), 707–721.
28. Virginia Tilley, *The One-State Solution: A Breakthrough for Peace in the Israeli-Palestinian Deadlock* (Detroit: University of Michigan Press, 2005).
29. "The One-State Declaration," reprinted in *The Electronic Intifada*, November 29, 2007, https://electronicintifada.net/content/one-state-declaration/793.
30. Ali Abunimah, "Reclaiming Self-Determination," Al-Shabaka policy brief (May 2010) http://al-shabaka.org/policy-brief/politics/reclaiming-self-determination
31. Ali Abunimah, *One Country: A Bold Proposal to End the Israeli-Palestinian Impasse* (New York: Metropolitan, 2006).
32. Omar Barghouti, "Re-imagining Palestine," July 29, 2009, https://zcomm.org/znetarticle/re-imagining-palestine-by-omar-barghouti/.
33. Omar Barghouti, "A Secular Democratic State in Historic Palestine: Reconciling the Inalienable Rights of the Indigenous with the Acquired Rights of the Settlers," *Israel/Palestine: Mapping Models of Statehood and Paths to Peace* (Toronto: York University, June 22–24, 2009).
34. Ilan Pappé, "One Democratic State," 2013, https://freehaifa.wordpress.com/2013/01/28/ilan-pappe-in-haifa-the-arab-spring-puts-israel-against-the-historical-trend/.
35. Graham Usher, "Bantustanisation or Bi-nationalism? An Interview with Azmi Bishara," *Race & Class* 37, no. 3 (1995), 43–49; As'ad Ghanem and Sara Ozacky-Lazar, "Towards an Alternative Israeli-Palestinian Discourse, Instead of 'Two States for Two Peoples,'" *Palestine-Israel Journal* 3, no. 3 (1996), at https://www.pij.org/articles/525/towards-an-alternative-israelipalestinian-discourse; Amnon Raz-Krakotzkin, "Exile Amidst Sovereignty: Critique of the Negation of the Exile in Israeli Culture," *Theory and Criticism* 4 (1993), 23–55 [Hebrew]; *News from Within* issues during the 1990s.

36. Honaida Ghanim, "On Indigeneity, Ghosts and Shadows of Destruction," *Indigeneity and Exile in Israel/Palestine*, ed. Shaul Setter (Tel Aviv: Tel Aviv University, Minerva Center, 2014), 17–24. [Hebrew]

37. Moshe Behar, "Past and Present Perfect of Israel's One-State Solution," in *Israel and Palestine Alternative Perspectives on Statehood*, ed. John Ehrenberg and Yoav Peled, (London: Rowman & Littlefield, 2016), 243–270.

38. Consult Moshe Behar, "One-State, Two-States, Bi-National State: Mandated Imaginations in a Regional Void," *Middle East Studies Online Journal* 5, no. 2 (2011), 97–136.

39. Teodora Todrova, "Reframing Bi-nationalism in Palestine-Israel as a Process of Settler Decolonisation" *Antipode* 47, no. 5 (2015), 1367–1387. It seems that Halper was ultimately unable to sustain the pressure, possibly for concerns he might experience a fate similar to that of Finkelstein and Chomsky. He eventually opted to slide away from his former binationalism toward liberalism.

40. Hillel Cohen, *Army of Shadows: Palestinian Collaboration with Zionism, 1917–1948* (Berkeley: University of California Press, 2008); Maha Nassar, *Brothers Apart: Palestinian Citizens of Israel and the Arab World* (Stanford, Calif.: Stanford University Press, 2017).

41. Issa Khalaf, *Politics in Palestine: Arab Factionalism and Social Disintegration, 1939–1948* (Albany: State University of New York Press, 1991).

42. Honaida Ghanim, "Between Two 'One-State' Solutions: The Dialectics of Liberation and Defeat in the Palestinian National Enterprise," *Constellations* 23, no. 3 (2016), 340–341.

Chapter Ten

DIALECTIC OF THE NATIONAL IDENTITIES IN PALESTINIAN SOCIETY AND ISRAELI SOCIETY

Nationalism and Binationalism

MARAM MASARWI

Identity, personal or national, isn't merely something you have like a passport. It is also something you discover daily again. Like a strange country. Its core is not something solid, like a mountain. It is something molten, like magna.

WILLIAM MCILVANNEY

One well-known paradox in early Greek philosophy is called the Ship of Theseus, named for the mythical founder-king of ancient Athens. Theseus and the ship returned from Crete after Theseus had vanquished the Minotaur. Greek philosopher and historian Plutarch wrote that, because of the ship's importance, the Greeks preserved it for a very long time. Over the years, however, as the wood disintegrated, they were obliged to replace one wooden plank after another, until the entire original ship had been replaced with new wood. Plutarch asked whether the ship, having had all its parts replaced, was or was not still the same ship. That philosophical paradox is the point of departure of this chapter, in which I examine questions about how we define and redefine an identity as it undergoes continual disassembly and reconstruction, and consider potential benefits presented by this process of change and redefinition.[1]

Although it seemingly maintains a fixed shape and is apprehended as given and distinct, national identity, like any other social identity, is a product of ongoing social construction and constantly changes. My aim in this chapter is to examine the dialectic between the national identities in two societies, Palestinian and Israeli, in terms of the national model and the binational model.

My main argument is that, under certain conditions, a binational model and its various components could challenge the national model by opening up fresh new horizons for analysis and highlighting important values in a new way. Such a challenge could have direct and profound influence on the structure and content of the identities of which these nations are comprised, prompting the evolution of an alternative, or even subversive, dialectic of identities.

NATIONAL IDENTITY AND ITS IMPLICATIONS

In recent decades, the notion of "identity" has captured a central place in the cultural and academic arena mainly because it reshuffles earlier traditional categories of discourse both in academic practice and political thought.[2] The leading modern collective identity is national identity—among the most elusive and controversial identities.

These days it is difficult to define any (non-national) collective identity that has not borrowed elements from national identity and national movements.[3] The issue of collective political identity is complex because of the lack of clarity in the definition of the term and because there is no unequivocal definition. Yet identity has intrinsic and internal content, defined by the common origin or common structure of experiences, whereby both are usually relative and defined by their distinctiveness from other identities and processes.[4] Other scholars like Peter Oakes refer to the meaning of identity as imparting meaning to affiliation or belonging.[5]

Benedict Anderson added the construction dimension of national identity. In his opinion, nationality replaces religion and tribal-communal relations as the basis of identity. Nationalism has established a different connection between people who do not necessarily know each other, and is based on language, territory, and culture, national consciousness, and a sense of partnership with people with whom one does not even come into contact.[6]

This structural approach relates to the construction of a program of national and cultural identity, as well as to the manner in which these contents are represented by individuals and their interactions. The group identity (cultural, national) is defined by a large-group identity—whether it refers to nationality, ethnicity, religion, or political ideology—as the subjective experience of thousands or millions of people who are linked by a persistent sense of sameness, even while simultaneously sharing some characteristics with people who belong to large foreign groups. In such large groups, most of the individuals will never meet during their lifetimes.

They would not even know of the existence of many others who belong to the same entity. Yet they will share a sense of belonging, usually a language, sentiments, nursery rhythms, songs, dances, and representations of history.[7] Norms and beliefs about the specific cultural and historical pasts are such that, historically, the latter move along a spectrum of trauma, resurrection, and fortitude, mixed with chauvinism, anxiety, messianic religion or political faith.[8] Scholars whose research focuses on national identity in Ireland and Slovakia have concluded that it is possible to classify people's attitudes regarding their identity as either primordial or situational. With a primordial identity, identity is understood as fixed and determined, having existed since time immemorial and meant to continue as it is into the distant future. By contrast, a situational approach to identity perceives the ethnic-national identity as not fixed but as a product of social construction during a given period, evolving for complicated reasons, and serving complex interests.[9]

The longstanding Jewish-Israeli-Palestinian-Arab conflict and the reality of occupation have brought these two group identities into a dialectic that encompasses dynamics of power and competition, along with systems by which each of the former nourishes and sustains the other.[10]

COMPETITION

Competition between these national identities, Palestinian and Israeli, does not revolve around independence, territory, and resources alone. Rather, the competition extends over to narratives, ethos, trauma, and victimization, all of which are at the center of this chapter. Competition over these components helps us understand their main role in shaping the two national identities and the dichotomy that exists between them, produced in the collective consciousness of each of the two identities.[11]

My argument is based on Yehouda Shenhav, who claims that, undoubtedly, some of the attitudes in the political arena are more the outcome of covert struggles over identity and less about the content itself.[12] This struggle illuminates, for example, the need for a cultural and historical narrative justifying the struggle over a conflictual reality. Both identities, Palestinian and Israeli, prompt a tremendous need to provide a political and cultural narrative that can bolster survival, both individual and collective.[13] From the depths of that consciousness, embodying both of these identities, emerged narratives and ethos that were utilized by various social agents to reshape and rebuild the components and characteristics of the respective national identities. All large groups have ritualistic rec-ollections of events and heroes whose mental representations include a shared feeling of success and triumph among group members. The events and persons appearing in such recollections are heavily mythologized over time, with these mental representations evolving to become large-group markers that I call chosen glories.[14] The two national narratives not only contradict one another but also compete over content, sources, val-ues, and worldviews. Deep in the consciousness of both identities is an image of the victim: the victim of the Holocaust on the Israeli side and of the defeated Palestinian in the wake of the Nakba and Naksa (1948 and 1967, respectively), on the Palestinian.[15] The mythical figure of the *sabra* was counterpoised to the figure of the indigenous Palestinian, the Israeli fighter to the Palestinian rebel *feda'i*, a diaspora of dispersion to a dias-pora of refugees. Gradually a unified national narrative emerges on each side, aided by the collective memory constructed by that society as part of its nation's emergent history. This involves history, specific heroes, battles for independence won and lost, songs and poems, language and dialect, memory, but also forgetting, erasure, and repression, as well as other spe-cific facets of the two groups.[16] A nation's biography, written as its national culture emerges, resembles an individual's biography: certain memories are presented and others erased.[17]

Amnon Raz-Krakotzkin, for example, illustrates how this idea was adopted by the Zionist movement. He points to the Zionist movement's attempt to cast Jewish history as a history of the victors, unlike the diaspora perspective. The Holocaust signifies the excluded "diaspora as negative" mindset and bolsters the legitimacy of the colonialist agenda in the occupied territories.[18]

As Zionism strives to elide diaspora from the emergent national consciousness, the Palestinian dispersal is lodged ever deeper in Palestinian collective memory. Trauma is thus utilized, if differently, by both societies. Zionism co-opted the Holocaust to justify the occupation; the Palestinian leadership enlisted the refugee narrative of the past for the sake of the future dream of return and independence.[19] The approximate developmental stage when a traumatized society analyses its traumas helps explain the purpose of a culture of death. To construct a collective consciousness that can restore, process, and reconstruct difficult past events, as experienced both individually and collectively, a society creates a relevant worldview, concepts, and representations adopting the past, which leads to the resurrection. Using trauma as the glue for national identity has been effective, even crucial, for both sides, fueling their ideologies of entitlement.[20]

WHO ARE YOU, DAVID?

The Palestinians' goal is resurrection; for Israelis, past trauma explains the need for and connection with power as the competition involves historical ownership of the territory but also the theological dimension of ownership claims. The parties compete over the mythical figure of the fighter in reality but also pursue a theological competition over the mythic hero figure in the sources of the two identities.[21]

One of the ways in which diversity of national, religious, and cultural content is expressed in the group identity is the adoption of the heroes of the theological stories. Many such stories were reanimated to serve this competition.[22] The story of the binding (sacrifice) of the son, the Masada ethos of an honorable death over slavery, David and Goliath, and the story of Samson provided inspiration and were enlisted in shaping the ethos of sacrifice and heroism in Israeli society; likewise, they played a significant role in the construction of national identity.

These scriptural narratives were part of the formation of the new Israeli national identity that sought to ensure that the new native identity would have none of the diaspora identity in it.[23]

After the occupation of 1967, this process was amplified in a concrete manner through land theft and control practiced over another people.[24] Like the mythical heroes and theologians of Israeli national identity, Palestinian identity, also an "identity of resurrection," was involved in competing over its mythic figures; sometimes both societies would even share the same figures. To illustrate this process, I will present some examples in which the national hero went beyond the boundaries of legends. Yasser Arafat's legendary phrase, *"sh'ab aljabbareen"* ("the nation of heroes"), which served the idea of resurrection in Palestinian society, is instructive as to this process. "Aljabbareen," the Arafatian metaphor, is the people of Amalek,[25] which historically represented a threat to the existence of the Jewish people for generations. This threat linked to the figure of the Palestinian national hero, his face masked and a rifle on his shoulder—although later on the rifle gave way to stones hurled by hand—brought about the invention of the new Palestinian Goliath, a dramatic role reversal.[26]

Shlomo Sand relates to this story by noting that the heroes of the biblical account appear twice in the same country; however, this second time around, the Palestinians are David and the Israeli military is Goliath.[27] On the Israeli side, ample use was made of this story to describe the events of 1948; in the history books and in real life, Israeli society saw itself as David (a minority) that had beaten the Palestinian-Arab Goliath (the majority). Not only did David and Goliath receive this representation, but the story of the Abrahamic house was treated with special attention and the story of Abraham's sacrifice of his son was also adopted for the Palestinian revolution. In his poem, "The Sacrifice," written in the midst of the second intifada, Mahmoud Darwish describes the former situation:

> . . . Go on alone,
> Past the stone altar,
> Around you the priests waiting for the instruction of God,
> You are the sacrifice, the sacrifice of the burnt offering.

Likewise, the heroic figure of the biblical Samson has inspired much disagreement and created an arena for quarrels moving between the axis of attribution and appropriation in the face of distancing and separateness. Anyone familiar with the "political suicide" culture cannot ignore the similarities with and inspiration from Samson's biblical story.[28]

In his film *Avenge But One of My Two Eyes*, Avi Mograbi argues that the first act of political suicide in history was carried out by Samson. In the film, Mograbi addresses the question of how the story of Samson and the story of Masada were enlisted by the Zionist movement to create the new mythic figure of the Jewish fighter, and to cast the Palestinian Arab culture as a culture of suicide. The stories of Masada and Samson, the scriptural stories so admired by the Jews, might be the parallel of the Arab culture of suicide.[29]

A similar connection to what Mograbi did between Samson and the State of Israel was done by the journalist Seymour Hersh. In his book dealing with Israel's nuclear weapons, *The Samson Option*, Hersh shows that since the establishment of the nuclear project, several of its senior officials, including David Ben-Gurion and Ernst David Bergman, who was the father of the Israeli nuclear bomb, are determined that no future enemy will be able to inflict another Holocaust on Israel. Just as the biblical Shimshon (Samson) brought down the temple of Dagon in Gaza against its Philistine enemies, so Israel will destroy all those who try to destroy it.[30] Gil Anidjar was swept into the political dimension inspired by the Samson story and used the term "suicide state" as a metaphor for the State of Israel: he claims that the state contemplates and enacts its own destruction. The state of Israel is a state at war with itself. It is the suicide state.[31] In this sense, the well-known play by Ze'ev Jabotinsky about Samson is instructive regarding the Zionist vision, the culture of the Land of Israel, and the idea of a Hebrew army, as Jabotinsky saw them. The nationalist religious ideology of Jabotinsky and others established the idea of the State of Israel as holy, "chosen," and of the Jewish people, and is the ideology behind the notion that the Arab adversary can be seen by Jews as their ancient and eternal enemy, the Amalekites.[32] The Palestinian side draws its mythological figures from the same sources.[33] In contrast to Jabotinsky, Ibrahim Abbas argues in an article published in the newspaper *Al-Ittihad* that Israelis perceive the story of Samson as a model for emulation and look to it as a source of inspiration and as the rationale for their cruelty toward the Palestinian people.[34] Ala Allami considers Samson the Hebrew, the murderer of the Palestinians, the spiritual and military father of those who carry out the Salafi suicide operations of our time.[35] Other scholars and writers like Mu'in Bseiso deal with Samson's mythological figure. In his play "Samson and Delilah," he argues that historians and critics of Arabic literature have given the Jewish Samson an entrée into their own history and folklore.[36] Therefore, whether Samson is enlisted to serve the Zionist movement or the Palestinian revolution, whether he is Jewish or Palestinian, and whether the Amalekites are the Palestinian Arabs or the Israeli army, this argument expresses the dialectic between the two identities, one that involves a competition for courage, courage that contains the need for growth, construction, self-creation, resurrection, and the ability to grow out of the defeat and trauma that the two nations have undergone. Additionally, it is also a competition for victimhood and the preservation and usage of trauma and sacrifice.[37]

BECOMING THE SAME?

Both national identities, Palestinian and Israeli, are ranged along this axis.

Mahmoud Darwish expresses this dialectic very well; in his poem "He Is Quiet and I Am Like Him," he hints of the trauma and victimhood in the encounter between the two identities:

He is quiet and I am like him,
he sipping his lemon tea and I my coffee
that is the essential difference between us.
He is dressed like me in a flowing striped shirt[38]

He continues with this parallel all the way through the poem and ends it with the line, "I think maybe this is about a murderer, or perhaps he is just a passerby who thought that I was a murderer. He is afraid, and so am I."[39]

The mirroring process presented by Darwish in this poem cannot help but resonate with the Hegelian view, which sees identity as a subject that is revealed only through the ongoing interaction (movement) occurring in existence itself. In the Israeli-Palestinian case, it is about the relationship between one consciousness and another, the struggle over authority and recognition. Each identity tries to build and actualize itself and achieve recognition from the other side without acknowledging what is human in the other. Over the years, these identities have become some other things, mirrors for one another. In hot and deadly or chronic international realities like the Israeli-Palestinian one, suitable targets of externalization do not remain permanent, safe, effective, and distant reservoirs "out there." Thus, psychologically speaking, the psychological structures of both large groups, to a certain degree, become the same.[40]

My opinion is that, so long as the national model that follows the logic of essentialism, closure, victimhood, and ethnic exclusivity is the frame, negative dynamics will always predominate over positive dynamics in the dialectic between these two identities. At the same time, I would point to the dialectic relations that reinforce each of the respective identities and cause them to draw on sources from the same theological, historical, and national materials and even compete for ownership of those sources.[41] Both groups take these materials for their identities while interpreting them differently.[42]

I see these dialectic relations as multidirectional—each national identities is affected by these processes and also affects and is affected by the other. Both are complex and divided national identities, full of internal contradictions and mutually contradictory contents that pull in different directions and access relations of rebellion, adoption, resistance, and mirroring. The adoption of a nationalist ideology on both sides' societies manage most of the time to bridge the gaps and the internal contradictions within each society and are able to obscure the collective differences and gaps and place the national ethos and interests above the differences in these identities.[43]

Such is the case even if we argue that hegemony always has fissures, and that there will always be identities and sub-identities coming into being that will undermine the existing political discourse. In the asymmetrical political reality of Israel-Palestine, when it comes to the reality of an occupation in which Israel controls, oppresses, and abuses the Palestinian side, there is very little prospect that these identities will succeed in undermining, or in detaching themselves from, the worldview inherent in the national viewpoint.[44] Under conditions of real conflict, the boundaries of the mixed groups are more strictly maintained, and breaches of those boundaries are punished more severely.[45] The dialectic of identities will continue happening in the realm of the "old politics," given that it serves the classic national framework in which both sides are functioning, and it will mainly be influenced by the continuation of the Israeli occupation.[46]

Thus far, I have addressed the dialectic of identities as they exist in the shadow of the national model. Here I will go on to argue that the binational model could, under certain conditions, challenge the existing dialectical boundaries between these identities, which could lead to the emergence of an alternative discourse of identities and to the creation of hybrid identities that could challenge and even, under certain circumstances, subvert the national model.

THE BINATIONAL PARADIGM

The political impasse with the continued failure of peace negotiations between Israel and Palestine has prompted an increase in calls for a binational model as an alternative solution to the national model.[47]

The literature offers several binational models referencing South Africa, Ireland, Belgium, and Switzerland. My interest here is in the conceptual aspects of a binational approach rather than in a specific model. I will adopt the definition given by Raz-Krakotzkin of a binational model: Binationalism is not a declaration in favor of a particular type of political solution. It is not about binationalism per se as the term is used in political jargon. Binationalism is an analytical stance based on values and signifies, first and foremost, the dialogical dimension in the reality of the two peoples involved.[48] Binationalism, in the Israeli-Palestinian case, involves a consociational arrangement in which political equity is assumed and social and economic equity aimed at. Equity regarding immigration is also required both for Jews and Palestinians from their respective diasporas, a "law of return" for both Jews and Palestinians.[49]

The binational stance is crucial to any arrangement, the aim of which is an egalitarian partnership, whether between two separate states or otherwise. The dilemma regarding one state versus two states is not earth-shattering; it is merely a choice between a vertical distribution (territorial) and a horizontal distribution (sharing the governing).[50] The crucial question is not which is the better option but what values underlie the option chosen. Is the distribution to be based on equality and mutual respect, meaning respect for the identity and ethos of both societies? Is the idea of this equality to afford civil and national rights to both identities, with the recognition of full rights of the Palestinian people on its land and beyond?

As people become more aware and examine their world more critically, they come to view ethnic-national identity as situational. Generally, people in that case employ a discourse that includes aspects from both identities, primordial and situational. Conflicts evoke a tendency for members of a group under threat to reclaim the primordial identity with the sense of stability and certainty it affords. I have argued that, under the binational concept proposed, both the Israeli national identity and the Palestinian national identity can be understood as situational identities. Like the definition of situational identity, the structural approach to the study of identity gives prominence to environmental, socio-political, and historical components and their function in defining an ethnic group.[51] The structural approach argues that the boundaries of ethnic identity are not stable and fixed but stabilize themselves continually through interaction with the environment. Viewed this way, ethnic identity is in fact determined both by boundaries and by cultural content, as these define one another through their interaction.[52]

Seeking the binary poles in the identity of the occupier and the occupied produces hybrid categories, which allow us to talk about a circumstantial identity that is dynamic, shaped, and changes in reciprocity. The current hybrid discourse seeks to reassure the very possibility of critical discussion in the intermediate situations; it assumes that a limited critical discussion of binary categories (such as nationality and nationalism) limits and restrains the range of cultural possibilities.[53]

I argue that under the binational model, hybrid existence is a tentative existence—a conditional existence. It dictates practices of concealment and discovery and requires an appearance that emphasizes each other as an aspect of collective identity, in accordance with the expectation inherent in its social context. Hybrid existence opposes the concept of identity, that is, a definition that is identical to it, and which is imposed entirely on the subject from the outside. When a particular body responds to contradictory identity demands, it becomes committed to a changing performance, quantitatively in character, in which it must externalize a single element of its identity and conceal the opposite element.[54]

This is not a theoretical position: it is a theatrical practice of life, which takes place against its will, in order to achieve visibility in a public space, linking the visibility option with basic assumptions, fantasies, and narratives that are connected to each of the conflicting aspects of identity. Furthermore, it allows for a game of fluidity and inconsistency, which has a real potential of colorful appeal to the distinctions that permit the existence of the ongoing identity order.

Hybrids have the potential to redefine the criteria by which cultural consciousness gives marks in its details. Derrida describes the hybrid horizon in his words by asserting, "What hatred of culture is not to be identical to itself."[55]

Under the classical national paradigm, the various elements will not be integrated into one body but will undermine the perception of reality. For example, we would find it hard to accept a gender perception of a Palestinian woman without understanding the oppressive and authoritarian relations that take place in the shadow of the ongoing occupation. Alternately, we will find it difficult to see the connection between different sexual and ethnic categories and the social context that does not allow for an orderly perception of the creatures of the transgressors. The binational model under a critical national epistemology can stretch the boundaries of various identities and create coalitions that cannot occur under the national model. Palestinian and Mizrahi Israeli Jews, for example, could find themselves in a reality in which their ethno-cultural identity might outweigh their national identity, a thing which is nearly impossible to imagine as a broad phenomenon under the national model. Similarly, an economic and religious coalition could outweigh the national identity. This discourse of identities and the politics that typifies it should be taken seriously as the public space is always flooded with projects seeking to reinvent identities, or to block identities, and some are even turned into subversive protest projects.[56] While some aspects of this process are liable to be dangerous, it is still crucial to examine it under the binational perspective I am proposing.

CONCLUDING REMARKS

The discourse of identity in this mode could enable political changes and create new geographical and moral spaces. New communities could be created there to offer their members new meanings. New cultural repertoires and alternative cognitive maps could appear to nourish once again the need for organizing on the basis of values. Mainly, the process could potentiate a discourse of identities that would create new categories.[57] Hence, the perception of binationalism examines the role of narratives as produced by the media, political institutions, and academia: in the making of history and its place in the construction of identities, in the Israeli and Palestinian societies.

Stephen Reicher, Nick Hopkins, and Kate Harrison reveal how narratives shape identities, perception, and action, including who is seen as a member of the national community and who is not, and on what basis. In other words, identity is less a matter of attitude and more a matter of action, if and when circumstances arise.[58] In my judgment, the dialectic of identities under the binational model as proposed here calls for granting legitimacy to existing collective identities and could challenge the social and traditional boundaries of both societies, reorganizing them in terms of time and space. Moreover, the use of the notion of identity allows us to talk again about history and memory and connect them to reconciliation and forgiveness.[59] Therefore, a binational perception enables us to analyze the discourse of identity under the national and the binational models in an alternative way; using it will allow us to utilize this additional analytical stage to develop a point of view beyond the perspective that has fostered the national outlook. This observation may devour the boundaries of "us" and "them" and lead to a redefinition of national identity. This point of view, for example, disturbs the dichotomous nationalist separation between Jews and Arabs. It can also create new categories.

In my view, the binational model has the ability to reconceptualize hybrid desire as an asymmetrical imagination, and opens possibilities of an "ability to act," that is, of encouraging practices of resistance, acceptance, or re-dialectical creation of identity categories.

Undoubtedly, in the Israeli-Palestinian reality, the issue of hybrids addresses complex lifestyle practices that include objections, contradictions, and deceptions. The two cultures still seek to build a unified national identity for themselves while simultaneously predicting the violent consequences of imposing a uniform national identity on its details and discussing the diversity that the binational model suggests is more substantive than the discussion of the uniformity of the national model. And it has the potential to promote the growing discourse of representations of hybrid politics.

NOTES

1. Hana Herzog and Anat Lapidot-Firilla, "Paradox Sfenat Tezeos: Megdar, Dat ve-Leom" [Theseus's Paradox: Gender, Religion and State] (Jerusalem: Hakibbutz Hameuchad, Van-Leer, 2014), 7–23. [Hebrew]
2. Frank Bechhofer and David McCrone, "National Identity, Nationalism, and Constitutional Change," in *National Identity, Nationalism, and Constitutional Change*, ed. Frank Bechhofer and David McCrone (London: Palgrave Macmillan, 2009), 1–16.
3. Hana Herzog and Anat Lapidot-Firilla, "Paradox Sfenat Tezeos: Megdar, Dat ve-Leom," 7–23. [Hebrew]
4. Henri Tajfel and John Turner, "The Social Identity Theory of Intergroup Behavior," in *Political Psychology: Key Readings*, ed. John Jost and James Sidanius (New York: Psychology Press, 2004), 276–293.
5. Peter Oakes, "The Root of All Evils in Intergroup Relations: Unearthing the Categorization Process," in *Blackwell Handbook of Social Psychology: Intergroup Processes*, edited by Robert Brown and Samuel Gaertner (Malden, Mass.: Blackwell, 2001).
6. Benedict Anderson, *Imagined Communities: Reflections on the Origin and Spread of Nationalism* (London: Verso, 1997), 5–7.
7. Vamik Volkan, "Psychoanalysis and Diplomacy: Part III. Potentials for and Obstacles against Collaboration," *Journal of Applied Psychoanalytic Studies* 1, no. 4 (1999): 305–318.
8. Bernardo Ferdman and Gabriel Horenczyk, "Cultural Identity and Immigration: Reconstructing the Group During Cultural Transition," in *Language, Identity and*

Immigration, ed. Elite Olshtain and Gabriel Horenczyk (Jerusalem: Hebrew University Magnes Press, 2000), 81–100; Vamik Volkan, "Transgenerational Transmissions and Chosen Traumas: An Aspect of Large Group Identity," *Group Analysis* 34, no. 1 (2001), 79–97.

9. Peter Weinreich, Vira Bacova, and Nathalie Rougier, "Basic Primordialism in Ethnic and National Identity," in *Analysing Identity: Cross-culture, Social and Clinical Context,* ed. Peter Weinreich and Wendy Saunderson (New York: Routledge, 2002), 115–171.

10. Nava Sonnenschein, "Dealog Meatger Zehout" [Dialogue-Challenging Identity] (Haifa: Pardes, 2008), 35–84.

11. Paul Scham, "Competing Israeli and Palestinian Narratives," in *The Routledge Handbook on the Israeli–Palestinian Conflict,* ed. Peters Joel and David Newman (New York: Routledge, 2013), 33–45.

12. Yehouda Shenhav and Hannan Hever, "Megamot cmehkar hapost Koloniali" [Trends in postcolonial research], in *Colonialism and Post-colonial Reality,* ed. Yehouda Shenhav (Jerusalem: Van Leer and Tel-Aviv: Hakebutz Hameohad, 2004).

13. Abdul-Rahim Al-Shaikh, "Falasten Alhawia wa al Kadia: al jamiaa waeadat benaa al sardya al watania al falastenia" [Palestine Identity and Story: The University and the Reconstruction of Palestinian narrative], *Bab Elwad,* November 2, 2017; Idith Zertal, *Israel's Holocaust and the Politics of Nationhood* (Cambridge: Cambridge University Press, 2005).

14. Volkan, "Psychoanalysis and Diplomacy."

15. Zertal, *Israel's Holocaust and the Politics of Nationhood,* 157–174.

16. Yael Zerubavel, *Collective Memory and the Making of Israeli National Tradition* (Chicago: University of Chicago Press, 1995).

17. Anderson, *Imagined Communities,* 5–7.

18. Amnon Raz-Krakotzkin, "Exile and Binationalism: From Gershom Scholem and Hannah Arendt to Edward Said and Mahmoud Darwish," Carl Heinrich Becker Lecture of the Fritz Thyssen Stiftung, with an introduction by Wolf Lepenies (Berlin: Wissenschaftskolleg zu Berlin, 2011).

19. Abdul-Rahim Al-Shaikh, "The Political Darwish," *Journal of Arabic Literature* 48, no. 2 (2017): 93–122; Amnon Raz-Krakotzkin, "Exile Within Sovereignty for Criticism of the Deprivation of Exile in Israeli Culture" [in Hebrew], *Theory and Criticism* 2, no. 5 (1994), 113–130.

20. Zertal, *Israel's Holocaust and the Politics of Nationhood,* 157–174. A chosen trauma may change function as it passes from one generation to the next. In one generation, it may support the large-group identity as a victimized group. In another generation, it may be used to give the group an identity as avengers. A chosen trauma may also remain dormant in a group's collective "memory." At times of stress, when the group's identity is threatened, it gets reactivated and can be used by leaders to inflame the group's shared feelings about themselves and their enemy. A time collapse occurs and the chosen trauma is then experienced as if it had happened only yesterday: feelings, perceptions, and expectations associated with a past event and past enemy heavily contaminate those related to current events and current enemies, leading to maladaptive group behaviour, irrational decision-making, and resistances to change. See Volkan, "Transgenerational Transmissions and Chosen Traumas," 79–97.

21. Yael Zerubavel, *Collective Memory and the Making of Israeli National Tradition* (Chicago: University of Chicago Press, 1995).
22. Yehezkel Landau. *Healing the Holy Land: Interreligious Peacebuilding in Israel/ Palestine* (Washington, D.C.: United States Institute of Peace, 2003).
23. Talal Asad, *On Suicide Bombing* (New York: Columbia University Press, 2007).
24. *Avenge But One of My Two Eyes*, directed and written by Avi Mograbi (Israel/France: Les Films Du Lesange, 2005).
25. The giants (Hebrew: Amalek, Amalek) or the Amalekites were one of the oldest inhabitants of southern Syria and the descendants of Esau. They lived in the beginning near Kadesh, southwest of Homs. They were spread out in Palestine when the Hebrews came from Egypt. The Israelis used to call them the Amalek tribes, according to their great grandfathers, and called themselves the children of Israel according to their grandfather Jacob (Israel). The Jewish books mentioned the people of Amalek many times and mentioned the names of some of their leaders and cities; they experienced the entry and exit of the Israelites to and from Egypt and collided with them in several battles in Gaza and Sinai after their departure from Egypt. Furthermore, according to Jewish books, David killed their king, Goliath. The Palestinian leader Yasser Arafat used the term *"sh'ab aljabareen"* ("the nation of heroes") as a metaphor for the Palestinian people.
26. Al-Shaikh, " Falasten Alhawia wa al Kadi."
27. Shlomo Sand, "Daoud Alfalasteni wa Jouliat Al-yahudi." [The Palestinian David and the Jewish Goliath]. *Al-Masri Alyoum*, February 4, 2009. http://today.almasryalyoum .com/article2.aspx?ArticleID=197621.
28. Asad, *On Suicide Bombing*; Riaz Hassan, *Suicide Bombings* (New York: Routledge, 2011).
29. Mograbi, *Avenge But One of My Two Eyes*.
30. Seymour Hersh, *The Samson Option: Israel's Nuclear Arsenal and America's Foreign Policy* (New York: Random House, 1991).
31. Gil Anidjar, "The Suicide State," *Boundary 2* 44, no. 4 (November 2017), 57–75.
32. Asad, *On Suicide Bombing*, 75.
33. In the course of a bible study session during Hanukkah in November 2017 hosted by Israeli prime minister Benjamin Netanyahu at his home, he reminded his guests that the Hasmonean kingdom had survived for only eighty years and that he was working to ensure that the State of Israel would last at least one hundred years. He added that the existence of Israel was not self-evident. Observing Netanyahu's words, one may understand that the State of Israel exists in the Middle East on borrowed time. His words may further strengthen the researchers' claims regarding the suicidal dimension that exists in the State of Israel. See "Netanyahu as Hasmoneant," *Haaretz*, October 11, 2017, https://www.haaretz.co.il/opinions/editorial-articles/.premium -1.4511026.
34. Ibrahim Abbas, "Shimshon wa Dalila Senaat Al Ostoura aw Astarat al Siyasa" [Samson and Delilah, the myth creation or mythologizing politics], *Al-Itihad*, February 23, 2011.
35. Ala Allami, "The Historical Roots of the Suicide Bomber Phenomenon" [in Arabic]. *Al-Akhbar*, March 18, 2014, http://www.al-akhbar.com/node/202798.
36. Mu'in Bseiso, "Shamshon Wa Dalila" [Samson and Delilah] (Beirut: Dar al-Odeh, 1997). [Arabic].

37. Al-Shaikh, "Falasten Alhawia wa al Kadia"; Zertal, *Israel's Holocaust and the Politics of Nationhood*, 157–174.

38. The stripes may be an allusion to the clothing worn by Holocaust internees and a reference to collective trauma. A man is clothed in his trauma.

39. Mahmoud Darwish, "La Taatather Amma Faalt" [Do not apologize for your actions] (London: Dar El-Raies, 2004), 87–88.

40. Volkan, "Psychoanalysis and Diplomacy," 305–318.

41. Daniel Bar-Tal and Gabiel Salomon, "Israeli-Jewish Narratives of the Israeli-Palestinian Conflict: Evolvement, Contents, Functions and Consequences," in *Israeli and Palestinian Narratives of Conflict: History's Double Helix*, ed. Robert Rotberg (Bloomington: Indiana University Press, 2006).

42. Thomas Juneau and Mira Sucharov, "Narratives in Pencil: Using Graphic Novels to Teach Israeli-Palestinian Relations," *International Studies Perspectives* 11, no. 2 (2010): 172–183.

43. Volkan, "Psychoanalysis and Diplomacy," 305–318.

44. Yehouda Shenhav, "Zehut Behevra Post Leoomit."

45. Susan Olzak, *The Dynamics of Ethnic Competition and Conflict* (Stanford, Calif.: Stanford University Press, 1992).

46. Yehouda Shenhav, "Zehut Behevra Post Leoomit."

47. Neve Gordon and Yinon Cohen, "Western Interests, Israeli Unilateralism, and the Two-State Solution," *Journal of Palestine Studies* 41, no. 3 (2012): 6–18.

48. Amnon Raz-Krakotzkin, "Exile and Binationalism: From Gershom Scholem and Hannah Arendt to Edward Said and Mahmoud Darwish," Carl Heinrich Becker Lecture of the Fritz Thyssen Stiftung 2011, with an introduction by Wolf Lepenies (Berlin: Wissenschaftskolleg zu Berlin, 2011).

49. Teodora Todorova, "Reframing Bi-nationalism in Palestine-Israel as a Process of Settler Decolonisation," *Antipode* 47, no. 5 (2015), 1367–1387.

50. Meron Benvenisti, "Haloum Hatzavar Halavan" [The White Sabra Dream: An Auto-biography of Disillusionment] (Tel-Aviv: Keter, 2012) [Hebrew]; Todorova, "Reframing Bi-nationalism in Palestine-Israel as a Process of Settler Decolonisation."

51. Sonnenschein, "Dealog Meatger Zehout," 35–84.

52. Ferdman and Horenczyk, "Cultural Identity and Immigration"; Volkan, "Transgenerational Transmissions and Chosen Traumas," 79–97.

53. Mati Shmuelof, Shahar Garfunkel, and Omri Herzog, "Zoakeem et shemcha bekama leshonot: al zehoot hebredit bysrael" [Shouting your name in many languages: About hybrid identity in Israel]," *Hakevon Mezrach* 14 (2010), 1–111.

54. Shmuelof al el., "Zoakeem et shemcha bekama leshonot."

55. Jacques Derrida, "On Forgiveness," in *Cosmopolitanism and Forgiveness* (London: Routledge, 2001), 27–60.

56. Shenhav, "Zehut Behevra Post Leoomit"; Homi Bhabha, *The Location of Culture* (New York: Routledge, 1994).

57. Derrida, "On Forgiveness."

58. Stephen Reicher, Nick Hopkins, and Kate Harrison, "Social Identity and Spatial Behaviour: The Relationship Between National Category Salience, the Sense of Home, and Labour Mobility Across National Boundaries," *Political Physiology* 27, no. 2 (2006), 247–263.

59. Shenhav, "Zehut Behevra Post Leoomit."

BIBLIOGRAPHY

Abdulhaq, Najat. *Jewish and Greek Communities in Egypt: Entrepreneurship and Business Before Nasser*. London: I. B. Tauris, 2016.

Abulhwa, Susan. *Mornings in Jenin: A Novel*. New York: Bloomsbury, 2010.

Abulof, Uriel. *The Mortality and Morality of Nations: Jews, Afrikaners and French Canadians*. Princeton, N.J.: Princeton University Press, 2015.

——. "National Ethics in Ethnic Conflicts: The Zionist 'Iron Wall' and the 'Arab Question.' " *Ethnic and Racial Studies* 37, no. 14 (2014): 2653–2669.

Abunimah, Ali. *One Country: A Bold Proposal to End the Israeli-Palestinian Impasse*. New York: Metropolitan, 2006.

——. "Reclaiming Self-Determination." *Al-Shabaka* policy brief (May 2010). http://al-shabaka.org/policy-brief/politics/reclaiming-self-determination.

Achcar, Gilbert. *The Arabs and the Holocaust: The Arab-Israeli War of Narratives*. Trans. G. M. Goshgarian. New York: Metropolitan, 2010.

——. *The People Want: A Radical Exploration of the Arab Uprising*. Berkeley: University of California Press, 2013.

Akenson, Donald. *God's Peoples: Covenant and Land in South Africa, Israel, and Ulster*. Ithaca, N.Y.: Cornell University Press, 1992.

al-Bakouri, Abd al-'Al. "Zionist-Israeli Propaganda and the Claim that 'The Arabs Want to Throw the Jews into the Sea.'" *Shu'un Falastiniyya* 27 (1973): 167–196. [Arabic]

Al-Madhoun, Rabai. *Destinies: Concerto of the Holocaust and the Nakba*. Beirut: Arab Studies Institute; Haifa: Kul-Shee Library, 2015. [Arabic]

Al-Shaikh, Abdul-Rahim. "The Political Darwish." *Journal of Arabic Literature* 48, no. 2 (2017): 93–122.

Alcalay, Ammiel. *After Jews and Arabs: Remaking Levantine Culture*. Minneapolis: University of Minnesota Press, 1993.

Allami, Ali. "The Historical Roots of the Suicide Bomber Phenomenon." *Al-Akhbar*, March 18, 2014, http://www.al-akhbar.com/node/202798. [Arabic]

Amichai, Yehuda. *Selected Poems*. Ed. and trans. Chana Bloch and Stephen Mitchell. Harmondsworth, UK: Penguin, 1986.

Anderson, Benedict. *Imagined Communities: Reflections on the Origin and Spread of Nationalism*. London: Verso, 1997.

Anidjar, Gil. "The Dignity of Weapons." *Law, Culture and the Humanities* (2015): 1–11.

——. *The Jew, the Arab: A History of the Enemy*. Stanford, Calif.: Stanford University Press, 2003.

——. *"Our Place in al-Andalus": Kabbalah, Philosophy, Literature in Arab Jewish Letters*. Stanford, Calif.: Stanford University Press, 2002.

——. *Semites: Race, Religion, Literature*. Stanford, Calif.: Stanford University Press, 2007.

——. "The Suicide State." *Boundary* 2 44, no. 4 (2017): 57–75.

Arendt, Hannah. "The Jewish State: Fifty Years After—Where Have Herzl's Politics Led?" In *The Jew as Pariah*, ed. Ronald H. Feldman, 164–177. New York: Random House, 1978.

——. *The Origins of Totalitarianism*. New York: Schocken, 1951.

Asad, Talal. *On Suicide Bombing*. New York: Columbia University Press, 2007.

Asbridge, Thomas. *The Crusades: The War for the Holy Land*. New York: Simon and Schuster, 2012.

Aydin, Cemil. *The Muslim World: A Global Intellectual History*. Cambridge, Mass.: Harvard University Press, 2017.

Baconi, Tareq. *Hamas Contained: The Rise and Pacification of Palestinian Resistance*. Stanford, Calif.: Stanford University Press, 2018.

Bar-Tal, Daniel, and Gabiel Salomon. "Israeli-Jewish Narratives of the Israeli-Palestinian Conflict: Evolvement, Contents, Functions and Consequences." In *Israeli and Palestinian Narratives of Conflict: History's Double Helix*, ed. Robert Rotberg. Bloomington: Indiana University Press, 2006.

Barghouti, Omar. "A Secular Democratic State in Historic Palestine: Reconciling the Inalienable Rights of the Indigenous with the Acquired Rights of the Settlers." *Israel/Palestine: Mapping Models of Statehood and Paths to Peace*. Toronto: York University, June 22–24, 2009.

Bashir, Bashir. "The Strengths and Weaknesses of Integrative Solutions for the Israeli-Palestinian Conflict." *Middle East Journal* 70, no. 4 (2016): 560–578.

Bashir, Bashir, and Rachel Busbridge. "The Politics of Decolonization and Binationalism in Israel/Palestine." *Political Studies* 67, no. 2 (2019): 338–405.

Bashir, Bashir, and Azar Dakwar, eds. *Rethinking the Politics of Israel/Palestine: Partition and Its Alternatives*. Vienna: Bruno Kreisky Forum and S&D Group, 2014.

Bashir, Bashir, and Amos Goldberg. "Deliberating the Holocaust and the Nakba: Disruptive Empathy and Binationalism in Israel/Palestine." *Journal of Genocide Research* 16, no. 1 (2014): 77–99.

——, eds. *The Holocaust and the Nakba: A New Grammar of Trauma and History*. New York: Columbia University Press, 2018.

Bashkin, Orit. *New Babylonians: A History of Jews in Iraq*. Stanford, Calif.: Stanford University Press, 2012.

Bechhofer, Frank, and David McCrone, eds. *National Identity, Nationalism and Constitutional Change*. London: Palgrave Macmillan, 2009.

Becke, Johannes. "Towards a De-Occidentalist Perspective on Israel: The Case of the Occupation." *Journal of Israeli History* 33, no. 1 (2014): 1–23.

Behar Moshe. "One-State, Two-States, Bi-National State: Mandated Imaginations in a Regional Void." *Middle East Studies Online Journal* 5, no. 2 (2011): 97–136.

———. "Past and Present Perfect of Israel's One-State Solution." In *Israel and Palestine Alternative Perspectives on Statehood*, ed. John Ehrenberg and Yoav Peled, 243–270. Rowman & Littlefield, 2016.

———. "What's in a Name? Socio-terminological Formations and the Case for 'Arabized-Jews." *Social Identities* 15, no. 6 (2009): 747–771.

Behar, Moshe, and Zvi Ben-Dor Benite. "The Possibility of Modern Middle Eastern Jewish Thought." *British Journal of Middle Eastern Studies* 41, no. 1 (2014): 43–61.

———. eds. *Modern Middle Eastern Jewish Thought: Writings on Identity, Politics, and Culture*. Waltham, Mass.: Brandeis University Press, 2013.

Beinart, Peter. *The Crisis of Zionism*. New York: Picador Paper, 2013.

Benjamin, Walter. "Theses on the Philosophy of History." In *Illuminations* (Thesis IX).

Benvenisti, Maron. *Sacred Landscape: The Buried History of the Holy Land Since 1948*. Berkeley: University of California Press, 2000.

Ben-Kiki, Hayyim. "Al she'elat ha-she'elot be-yishuv ha-aretz" [On the question of questions regarding the settling of the land]. *Do'ar Hayom*, August 30, 1921.

———. "Ha-tarbut ha-eropit ba-mizrah" [European culture in the Orient]. *Do'ar Hayom*, October 12–15, 1920.

Ben-Yehuda, Omri. "Kafka's Muslim: The Politics of Semitism." *Tel Aviver Jahrbuch für deutsche Geschichte* 45 (2017): 211–233.

Ben Yehuda, Omri. "'In Quest of *Du*': Dialogue in Kafka and Agnon." *Prooftexts* 37, no. 3 (2019): 553–577.

Ben-Zaken, Avner. "The Father, the Son, and the Spirit of Catastrophe." *Ha'aretz*, May 22, 2015.

Berghahn, Klaus L., ed. *The German-Jewish Dialogue Reconsidered: A Symposium in Honor of George L. Mosse*. New York: Peter Lang, 1996.

Bernal, Martin. *Black Athena: The Afroasiatic Roots of Classical Civilization, Volumes 1 & 2*. New Brunswick, N.J.: Rutgers University Press, 1987.

Beška, Emanuel. *From Ambivalence to Hostility: The Arabic Newspaper* Filastin *and Zionism, 1911–1914*. Bratislava: Slovak Academic Press, 2016.

Bezalel, Yitzhak. *Noladtem Ziyonim* [You Were Born Zionists]. Jerusalem: Yad Ben Zvi, 2008.

Bhabha, Homi. *The Location of Culture*. New York: Routledge, 1994.

Bishara, Azmi. "The Arabs and the Holocaust: An Analysis of the Problematical Nexus." *Zmanim* 13, no. 53 (1995): 54–71. [Hebrew]

Bishara, Azmi, et al. *The Sectarian Question and the Manufacturing of Minorities in the Arab World*. Beirut: Centre for Research and Policy Studies, 2017. [Arabic]

Bishara, Marawn. "Trump's 'Peace Plan': The Farce, the Fraud, and the Fury." *Aljazeera*, January 29, 2020.

Blanchot, Maurice. *The Infinite Conversation*. Trans. Susan Hanson. Minneapolis: University of Minnesota Press, 1993.

———. "The Pain of Dialogue." Trans. Charlotte Mandell. In Maurice Blanchot, *The Book to Come*. Stanford, Calif.: Stanford University Press, 2003.

Blum, Mark. E. *Kafka's Social Discourse: An Aesthetic Search for Community*. Bethlehem, Pa.: Lehigh University Press, 2011.

Bodemann, Michal. "Ideological Labour: Theses on Jewish and Non-Jewish Theatres of Memory in Germany." In *Desintegration: A Congress of Contemporary Jewish*

Positions, ed. Max Czollek and Sasha Marianne Salzmann, 33–60. Berlin: Kerber, 2017.

Botros, Atef. *Kafka: Ein jüdischer Schriftsteller aus arabischer Sicht*. Wiesbaden, Germany: Reichert, 2009.

Boulbina, Seloua Luste. *Le singe de Kafka et autres propos sur la colonie*. Lyon: Sens Public, 2008.

Bouteldja, Houria. *Whites, Jews, and Us: Toward a Politics of Revolutionary Love*. Trans. Rachel Valinsky. South Pasadena, Calif.: Semiotext(e), 2017.

Boyarin, Jonathan. *Storm from Paradise: The Politics of Jewish Memory*. Minneapolis: University of Minnesota Press, 1992.

Brown, Kate. *A Biography of No Place: From Ethnic Borderland to Soviet Heartland*. Cambridge, Mass.: Harvard University Press, 2004.

Brown, Wendy. *States of Injury: Power and Freedom in Late Modernity*. Princeton, N.J.: Princeton University Press, 1995.

Bruce, Iris. *Kafka and Cultural Zionism: Dates in Palestine*. Madison: University of Wisconsin Press, 2007.

Bseiso, Mu'in. "Shamshon Wa Dalila" [Samson and Delilah]. Beirut: Dar al-Odeh, 1997.

Buber, Martin. "The Bi-national Approach to Zionism." In *Toward Union in Palestine: Essays on Zionism and Jewish-Arab Cooperation*, ed. Martin Buber, J. L. Magnes, and E. Simon. Jerusalem: Ihud (Union) Association, 1947.

——. *Ich und Du*. Heidelberg, Germany: Lambert Schneider, 1983.

——. "Zionism and 'Zionism.'" In *A Land of Two Peoples: Martin Buber on Jews and Arabs*, ed. Paul Mendes-Flohr, 220–223. New York: Oxford Universities Press, 1983.

Budeiri, Musa. "The Palestinians; Tensions Between Nationalist and Religious Identities." In *Rethinking Nationalism in the Arab Middle East*, ed. James Jankowski and Israel Gershoni, 191–206. New York: Columbia University Press, 1997.

Burg, Avraham. "The End of Zionism." *The Guardian*, September 15, 2003.

——. *The Holocaust Is Over: We Must Rise from Its Ashes*. New York: Palgrave Macmillan, 2008.

Busbridge, Rachel. "Israel-Palestine and the 'Settler Colonial Turn': From Interpretation to Decolonisation." *Theory, Culture and Society* 35, no. 1 (2018): 91–115.

Butler, Judith. *Parting Ways: Jewishness and the Critique of Zionism*. New York: Columbia University Press, 2012.

Byrnes, Sholto. "The Rise of Islamophobia in Europe Is Being Normalized by Intellectuals— But They Are Pushing at an Already Open Door." *The National*, June 4, 2018.

Campos, Michelle. *Ottoman Brotherhood: Muslims, Christians, and Jews in Early Twentieth-Century Palestine*. Palo Alto, Calif.: Stanford University Press, 2011.

Caplan, Neil. *Palestine Jewry and the Arab Question, 1917–1925*. New York: Frank Cass, 1978.

Case, Holly. *The Age of Questions: Or, A First Attempt at an Aggregate History of the Eastern, Social, Women, American, Jewish, Polish, Bullion, Tuberculosis, and Many Other Questions in the Nineteenth Century, and Beyond*. Princeton, N.J.: Princeton University Press, 2018.

Césaire, Aimé. *Discourse on Colonialism*. New York: Monthly Review Press, 2000.

——. *Toussaint L'Ouverture: La Révolution Française et le Problème Coloniale*. Paris: Présence Africaine, 1981.

Chelouche Yosef Eliyahu. *Parashat Hayai 1870–1930* [My Life, 1870–1830]. Tel Aviv: Stroud, 1930.

Cohen, David. "Les Nationalistes Nordafricains face au Sionisme (1929–1939)." *Revue francaise d'histoire d' outre-mer*, 76–87 (1989/1990–2000).

Cohen, Hillel. *Army of Shadows. Palestinian Collaboration with Zionism, 1917–1948.* Berkeley: University of California Press, 2008.

———. *Good Arabs: The Israeli Security Agencies and the Israeli Arabs, 1948–1967.* Berkeley: University of California Press, 2010.

———. "Hayav u'moto shel ha-yehudi ha-aravi be-eretz yisrael u'mihutza la" [The life and death of the Arab Jew in Eretz Yisrael and elsewhere]. *Studies in the Rebirth of Israel* 9 (2015): 171–200.

———. *Year Zero of the Arab-Israeli Conflict, 1929.* Hanover, N.H.: Brandeis University Press, 2015.

Cohen, Roger. "The Invisibility of Palestinians." *New York Times International Weekly*, February 3, 2013.

Cole, Joshua. "Constantine Before the Riots of August 1934: Civil Status, Anti-Semitism, and the Politics of Assimilation in Interwar French Algeria." *Journal of North African Studies* 17, no. 5 (2012): 839.

Darwish, Mahmoud. *The Adam of Two Edens.* Ed. Munir Akash and Daniel Moore. Trans. Sargon Boulos. New York: Syracuse University Press, 2000.

———. "As He Walks Away." Trans. Sargon Boulos. In *The Adam of Two Edens*, ed. Munir Akash and Daniel Moore (New York: Syracuse University Press, 2000).

———. "La Taatather Amma Faalt" [Do not apologize for your actions]. London: Dar El-Raies, 2004.

———. "A Ready Script." Trans. Fady Joudah. *American Poetry Review 37*, no. 6. (November/December 2008): 11.

———. *Why Did You Leave the Horse Alone?* Trans. Jeffrey Sacks. New York: Archipelago, 2006.

Dawisha, Adeed. *Arab Nationalism in the Twentieth Century: From Triumph to Despair.* Princeton, N.J.: Princeton University Press, 2003.

Derrida, Jacques. "Interpretations at War: Kant, the Jew, the German." Trans. Moshe Ron. In Derrida, *Acts of Religion*, ed. Gil Anidjar. New York: Routledge, 2002.

———. "On Forgiveness." Trans. Mark Dooley and Michael Hughes. In *Cosmopolitanism and Forgiveness*, 27–60. London: Routledge, 2001.

———. "Violence and Metaphysics." Trans. Alan Bass. In *Writing and Difference*. Chicago: University of Chicago Press, 1978.

Di-Capua, Yoav. *No Exit: Arab Existentialism, Jean-Paul Sartre, and Decolonization.* Chicago: Chicago University Press, 2018.

Dor, Daniel. *The Suppression of Guilt: Israeli Media and the Reoccupation of the West Bank.* London: Pluto, 2005.

Doumani, Beshara. "Archiving Palestine and the Palestinians: The Patrimony of Ihsan Nimr." *Jerusalem Quarterly* 36 (2009): 3–12.

———. "Palestine Versus the Palestinians? The Iron Laws and the Ironies of a People Denied." *Journal of Palestine Studies* 36, no. 4 (2007): 49–64.

———. *Rediscovering Palestine. Merchants and Peasants in Jabal Nablus, 1700–1900.* Berkeley: University of California Press, 1995.

Dowty, Alan. "'A Question That Outweighs All Others': Yitzhak Epstein and Zionist Recognition of the Arab Issue." *Israeli Studies* 6, no.1 (2001): 34–54.

Dubiel, Helmut. "The Remembrance of the Holocaust as a Catalyst for a Transnational Ethic?" *New German Critique* 90 (2003): 59–70.

Eliashar, Eliyahu. *Lihyot im yehudim* [Living with Jews]. Jerusalem: Y. Marcus, 1981.

——. "Yehudim ve-aravim" [Jews and Arabs]. *Ha-Mizrah*, September 11, 1942. In *Modern Middle Eastern Jewish Thought: Writing on Identity, Politics, and Culture, 1893–1958*, ed. Moshe Behar and Zvi Ben-Dor Benite, 133. Boston: Brandeis University Press, 2013.

El-Ad, Hagai. "Netanyahu Exploits the Holocaust to Brutalise the Palestinians." *Ha'aretz*, January 23, 2020.

Eliot, T. S. *Selected Poems*. London: Faber & Faber, 1954.

Elmaleh, Abraham. "Sol Ha-Tzadika." *Hed Hamizrah*, January 15, 1943 : 6.

Epstein, Yitzhak. "The Question of Questions." *Doar Hayom*, August 17, 1921: 1. [Hebrew]

Erlich, Avishai. "Zionism, Anti-Zionism, Post-Zionism." In *The Challenge of Post-Zionism: Alternatives to Israeli Fundamentalist Politics*, ed. Ephraim Nimni, 63–97. London: Zed, 2003.

Evri, Yuval. "Paneha ha-merubot ve-ha-mishtanot shel ha-'sfaradiyut' be-mifneh ha-meah ha-esrim" ["The many and changing faces of "Sephardiness" at the turn of the twentieth century"]. PhD diss., Tel Aviv University, 2014.

——. "Translating the Arab-Jewish Tradition: From al-Andalus to Palestine/Land of Israel." In *Essays of the Forum Transregionale Studien*, 17–23. Berlin: Forum Transregionale Studien, 2016.

Eyal, Gil. *The Disenchantment of the Orient: Expertise in Arab Affairs and the Israeli State*. Stanford, Calif.: Stanford University Press, 2006.

Farsakh, Leila. "A Common State in Israel-Palestine: Historical Origins and Lingering Challenges." *Ethnopolitics* 15, no. 4 (2016): 380–392.

——. "The One-State Solution and the Israeli-Palestinian Conflict: Palestinian Challenges and Prospects." *Middle East Journal* 65, no. 1 (2011): 55–71.

——. "Palestinian Economic Development: Paradigm Shifts Since the First Intifada." *Journal of Palestine Studies* 45, no. 2 (2016): 55–71.

——. "The 'Right to Have Rights': Partition and Palestinian Self-Determination." *Journal of Palestine Studies* 47, no.1 (Autumn 2017): 56–68.

Feldhay Brenner, Rachel. *Inextricably Bonded: Israeli-Arab and Jewish Writers Re-Visioning Culture*. Madison: University of Wisconsin Press, 2003.

Ferdman, Bernardo, and Gabriel Horenczyk. "Cultural Identity and Immigration: Reconstructing the Group During Cultural Transition." In *Language, Identity and Immigration*, ed. Elite Olshtain and Gabriel Horenczyk, 81–100. Jerusalem: Hebrew University Magnes Press, 2000.

Flapan, Simha. *Zionism and the Palestinians*. London: Croom Helm, 1979.

Fleischacker, Samuel, ed. *Heidegger's Jewish Followers: Essays on Hannah Arendt, Leo Strauss, Hans Jonas, and Emmanuel Levinas*. Pittsburgh, Pa.: Duquesne University Press, 2008.

Fogelman, Shay. "Mission Impossible." *Ha'aretz*, January 25, 2013.

Freud, Sigmund. *The Letters of Sigmund Freud and Arnold Zweig*. Ed. Ernst L. Freud. Trans. Elaine Robson-Scott and William Robson-Scott. New York: Harcourt Brace, 1970.

——. *Studies on Hysteria, 1893–1895*. In volume 2 of *The Standard Edition of the Complete Psychological Works of Sigmund Freud*, 24 vols. London: Hogarth, 1955.

——. *Totem and Taboo: Some Points of Agreement Between the Mental Lives of Savages and Neurotics*. New York: Routledge, 2004.

Friedman, Isaiah. *The Question of Palestine, 1914–1918*. London: Routledge, 1973.
Funkenstein, Amos. "The Dialectics of Assimilation." *Jewish Social Studies* NS 1: 2 (Winter 1995): 1–14.
——. *Perceptions of Jewish History*. Berkeley: University of California Press, 1993.
Gartner, Lloyd P. *History of the Jews in Modern Times*. Oxford: Oxford University Press, 2001.
Ghanim, Honaida. "Between Two "One-State" Solutions: The Dialectics of Liberation and Defeat in the Palestinian National Enterprise." *Constellations* 23, no. 3 (2016): 340–341.
——. "On Indigeneity, Ghosts, and Shadows of Destruction." In *Indigeneity and Exile in Israel/Palestine*, ed. Shaul Setter, 17–24. Tel Aviv University: Minerva Center, 2014. [Hebrew]
Ghazal, Amal. "An Ottoman Pasha and the End of Empire: Sulayman al-Baruni and the Networks of Islamic Reform." In *Global Muslims in the Age of Steam and Print*, ed. James L. Gelvin and Nile Green. Berkeley: University of California Press, 2013, 40–58.
——. "Counter-currents: Mzabi Independence, Pan-Ottomanism, and WWI in the Maghrib." *First World War Studies* 7, no. 1 (2016): 81–96.
——. "Tensions of Nationalism: The Mzabi Student Missions in Tunis and the Politics of Anti-Colonialism." *International Journal of Middle East Studies* 47 (2015): 47–63.
Gilman, Sander. *Franz Kafka: The Jewish Patient*. New York: Routledge, 1995.
Goldberg, David Theo. "Racial Europeanization." *Ethnic and Racial Studies* 29, no. 2 (2006): 331–64.
Gordon, Neve, and Yinon Cohen. "Western Interests, Israeli Unilateralism, and the Two-State Solution." *Journal of Palestine Studies* 41, no. 3 (2012): 6–18.
Gordon, Peter E. *Continental Divide: Heidegger, Cassirer, Davos*. Cambridge, Mass.: Harvard University Press, 2010.
Gourgouris, Stathis. "*Orientalism* and the Open Horizon of Secular Criticism." *Social Text* 87, 24, no. 2 (Summer 2006): 11–20.
Gribetz, Jonathan Marc. *Defining Neighbors: Religion, Race, and the Early Zionist-Arab Encounter*. Princeton, N.J.: Princeton University Press, 2015.
Grossman, David. *See Under: Love*. Trans. Betsy Rosenberg. New York: Simon and Schuster, 1989.
Ha'am, Ahad. *Al Parashat Derahim* [At the crossroads]. Berlin: Judischer, 1921.
Habash, George. "George Habash Outlines PFLP Policy." *PFLP Bulletin* 13 (10–11), 1974.
——. "Liberation no Negotiation." *PFLP Bulletin* 9 (6–7) and 10 (4–5), 1974.
Haddad, Mahmoud. "The Rise of Arab Nationalism Reconsidered." *International Journal of Middle East Studies* 26, no. 2 (1994), 201–222.
Haklai, Oded. *Palestinian Ethnonationalism in Israel*. Philadelphia: University of Pennsylvania Press, 2013.
Haklai, Oded, and Noephytos Loizides, eds. *Settlers in Contested Lands: Territorial Dispute and Ethnic Conflicts*. Stanford, Calif.: Stanford University Press, 2015.
Hammerschlag, Sarah. *The Figural Jew: Politics and Identity in Postwar French Thought*. Chicago: University of Chicago Press, 2010.
Hanebrink, Paul. *A Specter Haunting Europe: The Myth of Judeo-Bolshevism*. Cambridge, Mass.: Harvard University Press, 2018.

Hanieh, Adam. "Development as Struggle: Confronting the Reality of Power in Palestine." *Journal of Palestine Studies* 45, no. 4 (2016): 32–47.

Hannoum, Majid. *Colonial Histories, Post-colonial Memories: The Legend of the Kahina, a North African Heroine*. Westport, Conn.: Greenwood, 2001.

Hanssen, Jens. "Kafka and Arabs." *Critical Inquiry* 39, no. 1 (2012): 167–197.

Harel, Naama. *Kafka's Zoopoetics: Beyond the Human-Animal Barrier*. Ann Arbor: University of Michigan Press, 2020.

Harrison, Olivia C. *Transcolonial Maghreb: Imagining Palestine in the Era of Decolonization*. Stanford, Calif.: Stanford University Press, 2015.

Hassan, Riaz. *Suicide Bombings*. New York: Routledge, 2011.

Haugbolle, Sune. "The New Arab Left and 1967." *British Journal of Middle Eastern Studies* 44, no. 4 (2017): 497–512.

Hegel, G. W. F. *The Philosophy of History*. Trans. J. Sibree. Mineola, N.Y.: Dover Publications, 2004.

Hersh, Seymour. *The Samson Option: Israel's Nuclear Arsenal and America's Foreign Policy*. New York: Random House, 1991.

Herzl, Theodor. *The Jewish State: An Attempt at a Modern Solution of the Jewish Question*. London: Henry Pordes, 1993.

Herzog, Hana, and Anat Lapidot-Firilla. "Paradox Sfenat Tezeos: Megdar, Dat ve-Leom" [Theseus's paradox: Gender, religion, and state]. Jerusalem: Hakibbutz Hameuchad, Van-Leer, 2014.

Hilal, Jamil. "Imperialism and Settler Colonialism in West Asia: Israel and the Arab Palestinian Struggle." *Utafi* 1, no. 1 (1976): 51–70.

Hochberg, Gil. *In Spite of Partition: Jews, Arabs, and the Limits of Separatist Imagination*. Princeton, N.J.: Princeton University Press, 2007.

——. "'Remembering Semitism' or 'On the Prospect of Re-Membering the Semites.'" *ReOrient* 1, no. 2 (2016): 192–223.

Hoffman, Katherine, and Susan Gilson Miller, eds. *Berbers and Others: Beyond Tribe and Nation in the Maghreb*. Indianapolis: Indiana University Press, 2010.

Irvine, Richard. "Israel's Cynical Campaign to Pit Arab Jews Against Palestinian Refugees." *The Electronic Intifada*, July 1, 2012.

Jabotinsky, Vladimir. "The Iron Wall." *The Jewish Herald*, November 26, 1937.

Jacobson, Abigail. *From Empire to Empire: Jerusalem Between Ottoman and British Rule*. Syracuse, N.Y.: Syracuse University Press, 2011.

——. "Sephardim, Ashkenazim, and the 'Arab Question' in Pre-First World War Palestine: A Reading of Three Zionist Newspapers." *Middle Eastern Studies* 39, no. 2 (2003): 105–130.

Jacobson, Abigail, and Moshe Naor. *Oriental Neighbors*. Boston: Brandeis University Press, 2016.

Jamal, Amal. *Arab Minority Nationalism in Israel: The Politics of Indigeneity*. London: Routledge, 2011.

Jarkas, Mahmoud. "The Native Jews and Zionism." *Filastin*, March 27, 1923.

Jefferson, Rebecca J. W. "A Genizah Secret: The Count d'Hulst and Letters Revealing the Race to Recover the Lost Leaves of the Original Ecclesiasticus." *Journal of the History of Collections* 21, no. 1 (2009): 125–142.

Joyce, James. *Ulysses*. Harmondsworth, UK: Penguin, [1922]1971.

Judt, Tony. "From the House of the Dead: An Essay on Modern European Memory."
In *Postwar: A History of Europe Since 1945*, 803–831 New York: Penguin, 2005.
——. *Postwar: A History of Europe Since 1945*. New York: Penguin, 2005.
Juneau, Thomas, and Mira Sucharov. "Narratives in Pencil: Using Graphic Novels to
Teach Israeli-Palestinian Relations." *International Studies Perspectives* 11, no. 2
(2010): 172–183.
Kafka, Franz. "Jackals and Arabs." Trans. Willa Muir and Edwin Muir. In *The Complete
Stories and Parables*, ed. Nahum N. Glatzer, 407–411. New York: Quality Paperback
Book Club, 1983.
Kalmar, Ivan Davidson, and Derek J. Penslar, eds. *Orientalism and the Jews*. Waltham,
Mass.: Brandeis University Press, 2005.
Kamil, Omar. *Der Holocaust im Arabischen Gedächtnis: Eine Diskursgeschichte, 1945–1967*.
Göttingen, Germany: Vandenhoeck and Ruprecht, 2012.
Kanafani, Ghassan. "On the PFLP and the September Crisis." *New Left Review* 1, no.
67 (1971).
——. *Returning to Haifa*. In *Palestine's Children: Returning to Haifa and Other Stories*.
Trans. Barbara Harlow and Karen E. Riley, 149–196. London: Heinemann, 1984.
Kark, Ruth, and Joseph B. Glass. "The Jews in Eretz-Israel/Palestine: From Traditional
Peripherality to Modern Centrality." *Israel Affairs* 5, no. 4 (1999): 73–107.
Karmi, Ghada. *Married to Another Man: Israel's Dilemma in Palestine*. London: Pluto,
2007.
Karsh, Ephraim. *Palestine Betrayed*. New Haven, Conn.: Yale University Press, 2010.
Kattan, Victor. *From Coexistence to Conquest: International Law and the Origins of the
Arab-Israeli Conflict, 1891–1949*. London: Pluto, 2009.
Katz, Ethan B. *The Burdens of Brotherhood: Jews and Muslims from North Africa to
France*. Cambridge, Mass.: Harvard University Press, 2015.
Kauffmann, R. Lane. "The Other in Question: Dialogical Experiments in Montaigne,
Kafka, and Cortázar." In *The Interpretation of Dialogue*, ed. Tullio Maranhão,
157–194. Chicago: University of Chicago Press, 1990.
Khalaf, Issa. *Politics in Palestine: Arab Factionalism and Social Disintegration, 1939–1948*.
Albany: State University of New York Press, 1991.
Khalidi, Rashid. *The Hundred Years' War on Palestine: A History of Settler Colonialism
and Resistance, 1917–2017*. New York: Metropolitan, 2020.
——. "The Palestinians and 1948: The Underlying Cause of Failure." In *The War for
Palestine*. Ed. Eugene Rogan and Avi Shlaim, 12–26. New York: Cambridge University
Press, 2001.
——. *Palestinian Identity*. New York: Columbia University Press, 1996.
——. *Palestinian Identity: The Construction of Modern National Consciousness*. New
York: Columbia University Press, 1997.
Khalidi, Rashid, Lisa Anderson, Muhammad Muslih, and Reeva S. Simon, eds. *The
Origins of Arab Nationalism*. New York: Columbia University Press, 1991.
Khalidi, Walid. "Plan Dalet: Master Plan for the Conquest of Palestine." *Journal of
Palestine Studies* 18 (1988): 4–33.
Khayr Bek, Bushra Ali. *Mawqif al-Harakat al-Wataniyya fi Aqtar al-Maghrib al-`Arabi
(Tunis—al-Jaza'ir—al-Maghrib) min Qadiyyat Filastin bay al-`Amayn 1917–1939*.
Damascus: Manshurat al-Hay'a al-`Amma li al-Kitab, 2015.

Khoury, Elias. *Children of the Ghetto: My Name Is Adam* [Awlad el-ghetto: Esmi Adam]. Beirut: Dar Al-Adab, 2016.

———. *Gate of the Sun* [Bab al-Shams]. Trans. Humphrey Davies. New York: Archipelago, 2006.

Kia, Mana. "Indian Friends, Iranian Selves, Persianate Modern." *Comparative Studies of South Asia, Africa, and the Middle East* 36, no. 3 (2016): 398–417.

Kimmerling, Baruch. *Zionism and Territory*. Berkeley: University of California, Berkeley, International and Area Studies, 1983.

Klein, Menachem. "Arab Jew in Palestine." *Israel Studies* 9, no. 3 (2014): 134–153.

———. *Lives in Common: Arabs and Jews in Jerusalem, Jaffa, and Hebron*. New York: Oxford University Press, 2014.

Klug, Brian. "The Collective Jew: Israel and the New Antisemitism." *Patterns of Prejudice* 37, no. 2 (2003): 117–38.

———. "Interrogating 'New Anti-Semitism.'" In *Racialization and Religion: Race, Culture and Difference in the Study of Antisemitism and Islamophobia*, ed. Nasar Meer, 84–98. London: Routledge, 2014.

———. "The Myth of the New Anti-Semitism." *The Nation* 278, no. 4 (2004): 23–29.

———. "To Flee or Not to Flee: Is That the Question?" *International Journal of Public Theology* 10 (2016): 338–353.

Kouvélakis, Stathis. "The Marxian Critique of Citizenship: For a Rereading of 'On the Jewish Question.'" *South Atlantic Quarterly* 104, no. 4 (2005): 707–721.

Kramer, Martin. "Arab Nationalism: Mistaken Identity." *Daedalus* (Summer 1993): 171–206.

Landau, Yehezkel. *Healing the Holy Land: Interreligious Peacebuilding in Israel/Palestine*. Washington, D.C.: United States Institute of Peace, 2003.

Laqueur, Walter. *A History of Zionism: From the French Revolution to the Establishment of the State of Israel*. New York: Random House, 2003.

Lavie, Smadar. "Staying Put: Crossing the Israel–Palestine Border with Gloria Anzaldúa." *Anthropology and Humanism* 36, no. 1 (2011): 101–121.

Lerman, Antony. "Antisemitism Redefined: Israel's Imagined National Narrative of Endless External Threat." In *On Antisemitism: Solidarity and the Struggle for Justice*, ed. Jewish Voice for Peace, 7–20. Chicago: Haymarket, 2017.

Levene, Mark. "The Balfour Declaration: A Case of Mistaken Identity." *English Historical Review* 107, no. 422 (1992): 54–77.

Leventhal, Robert. "The Jewish Physician as Respondent, Confidant, and Proxy: The Case of Marcus Herz and Immanuel Kant." In *On the Word of a Jew: Religion, Reliability, and the Dynamics of Trust*, ed. Nina Caputo and Mitchell Hart, 222–244. Bloomington: Indiana University Press, 2018.

Levy, Lital. "The Arab Jew Debates: Media, Culture, Politics, History." *Journal of Levantine Studies* 17, no. 1 (2017): 79–103.

———. "Jewish Writers in the Arab East: Literature, History, and the Politics of Enlightenment, 1863–1914." PhD diss., University of California, Berkeley, 2007.

———. "The Nahda and the Haskala: A Comparative Reading of 'Revival' and 'Reform.'" *Middle Eastern Literatures* 16, no. 3 (2013): 300–316.

———. "Partitioned Pasts: Arab Jewish Intellectuals and the Case of Esther Azhari Moyal (1873–1948)." In *The Making of the Arab Intellectual (1880–1960): Empire, Public Sphere, and the Colonial Coordinates of Selfhood*, ed. Dyala Hamzah, 128–163. London: Routledge, 2012.

——. *Poetic Trespass: Writing Between Hebrew and Arabic in Israel/Palestine*. Princeton, N.J.: Princeton University Press, 2014.

Librett, Jeffrey S. *The Rhetoric of Cultural Dialogue: Jews and Germans from Moses Mendelssohn to Richard Wagner and Beyond*. Stanford, Calif.: Stanford University Press, 2000.

Liska, Vivian. *German-Jewish Thought and Its Afterlife: A Tenuous Legacy*. Bloomington: Indiana University Press, 2017.

Lockman, Zachary. *Comrades and Enemies: Arab and Jewish Workers in Palestine, 1905–1948*. Berkeley: University of California Press, 1996.

Lustick, Ian. "Abandoning the Iron Wall: Israel and 'the Middle Eastern Muck.'" *Middle East Policy* 15, no. 3 (2008): 30–56.

Luz, Ehud. *Wrestling with an Angel: Power, Morality and Jewish Identity*. New Haven, Conn.: Yale University Press, 2003.

Machover, Moshé. *Israelis and Palestinians: Conflict and Resolution*. Chicago: Haymarket, 2012.

Maier, Charles S. "Consigning the Twentieth Century to History: Alternative Narratives for the Modern Era." *American Historical Review* 105, no. 3 (2000): 807–31.

Mandel, Maud S. *Muslims and Jews in France: History of a Conflict*. Princeton, N.J.: Princeton University Press, 2014.

Mandel, Neville J. *The Arabs and Zionism Before World War I*. Berkeley: University of California Press, 1976.

Massad, Joseph. "Forget Semitism!" In *Living Together: Jacques Derrida's Communities of Violence and Peace*, ed. Elisabeth Weber, 59–79. New York: Fordham University Press, 2012.

——. *Islam in Liberalism*. Chicago: University of Chicago Press, 2015.

——. "The Persistence of the Palestinian Question." *Cultural Critique* 59 (2005): 1–23.

Matar, Philip. *The Mufti of Jerusalem: Al-Hajj Amin al-Husayni and the Palestinian National Movement*. New York: Columbia University Press, 1988.

Matzpen. "The Palestine Problem and the Israeli-Arab Dispute." May 18, 1967. http://www.matzpen.org/english/1967-05-18/the-palestine-problem-and-the-israeli-arab-dispute/.

McDougall, James. *History and the Culture of Nationalism in Algeria*. Cambridge: Cambridge University Press, 2008.

McIlvanney, William. "Freeing Ourselves from Inner Exile." *The Herald* (Glasgow), March 5, 1999.

Meer, Nasar, ed. *Racialization and Religion: Race, Culture and Difference in the Study of Antisemitism and Islamophobia*. London: Routledge, 2016.

Meier, Heinrich. *Carl Schmitt and Leo Strauss: The Hidden Dialogue*. Trans. J. Harvey Lomax. Chicago: University of Chicago Press, 1995.

Memmi, Albert. *The Colonizer and the Colonized*. London: Souvenir Press, 1974.

——. "What Is an Arab Jew?" In *Jews and Arabs*. Chicago: J. Philip O'Hara, 1975.

Mendes-Flohr, Paul. "Ambivalent Dialogue: Jewish-Christian Theological Encounter in the Weimar Republic." In *Divided Passions: Jewish Intellectuals and the Experience of Modernity*, 133–167. Detroit, Mich.: Wayne State University Press, 1991.

——. *Martin Buber: A Life of Faith and Dissent*. New Haven, Conn.: Yale University Press, 2019.

——. "Martin Buber and Martin Heidegger in Dialogue." *Journal of Religion* 94, no. 1 (2014): 2–25.

Mendes-Flohr, Paul, and Jehuda Reinharz, eds. *The Jew in the Modern World: A Documentary History*. Oxford: Oxford University Press, 1995.

Mograbi, Avi. *Avenge But One of My Two Eyes*. Israel/France: Les Films Du Lesange.

Morris, Benny. *1948: A History of the First Arab-Israeli War*. New Haven, Conn.: Yale University Press, 2008.

Moses, A. Dirk. "The Contradictory Legacies of German Jewry." *Leo Baeck Institute Yearbook*, 54 (2009): 36–43.

Mooreville, Anat. "Eyeing Africa: The Politics of Israeli Ocular Expertise and International Aid, 1959–1973." *Jewish Social Studies* 21, no. 3 (2016): 31–71.

Mufti, Aamir. *Enlightenment in the Colony: The Jewish Question and the Crisis of Postcolonial Culture*. Princeton, N.J.: Princeton University Press, 2007.

Musallam, Akram. *A Girl from Shatila [Bent Min Shatila]*. Amman, Jordan: Al-Dar Al-Ahlia, 2019.

Myers, David. *Between Jew and Arab: The Lost Voice of Simon Rawidowicz*. Hanover, N.H.: Brandeis University Press, 2009.

Nafi, Basheer. *Arabism and Islamism and the Palestine Question, 1908–1941: A Political History*. Reading, UK: Ithaca, 1998.

Naor, Moshe, and Abigail Jacobson. *Oriental Neighbors: Middle Eastern Jews and Arabs in Mandatory Palestine*. Hanover, N.H.: University Press of New England, 2016.

Nasir, Muhammad. *Abu al-Yadhan wa Jihad al-Kalima*. n.p., 1979.

——. *Al-Maqala al-Sahafiyya al-Jaza'iriyya: nash'atuha, tatawwuruha, a`lamuha*. Vol. 1. Algiers: al-Sharika al-Wataniyya li al-Nashr wa al-Tawzi`, 1978.

——. *Al-Shaykh Ibrahim Atfiyyash fi Jihadihi al-Islami*. Muscat, Oman: Maktabat al-Damiri, 1992.

Nassar, Maha. *Brothers Apart: Palestinian Citizens of Israel and the Arab World*. Stanford, Calif.: Stanford University Press, 2017.

Nathan, Emmanuel, and Anya Topolski, eds. *Is There a Judeo-Christian Tradition? A European Perspective*. Berlin: De Gruyter Mouton, 2016.

Nizri, Yigal S. "On the Study of the Tritel in Fez." *Pe'amim* 136 (2012): 203–224.

Oakes, Peter. "The Root of All Evils in Intergroup Relations: Unearthing the Categorization Process." In *Blackwell Handbook of Social Psychology: Intergroup Processes*, ed. Robert Brown and Samuel Gaertner. Malden, Mass.: Blackwell, 2001.

Olender, Maurice. *The Languages of Paradise: Aryans and Semites, a Match Made in Heaven*. Trans. Arthur Goldhammer. New York: Other, 2003.

Özyürek, Esra. "Export-Import Theory and the Racialization of Anti-Semitism: Turkish-and Arab-Only Prevention Programs in Germany." *Comparative Studies in Society and History* 58, no. 1 (2016): 40–65.

Palestine Liberation Organization. "Political Program for the Present Stage of the Palestinian National Organization Drawn by the Palestinian National Council, Cairo, June 9, 1974." *Journal of Palestine Studies* 3, no. 4: 224.

Pappé, Ilan. *The Ethnic Cleansing of Palestine*. Oxford: Oneworld, 2007.

——. *A History of Modern Palestine: One Land, Two Peoples*. New York: Cambridge University Press, 2004.

Penslar, Derek J. "Theodor Herzl and the Palestinian Arabs: Between Myth and Counter-Myth." *Journal of Israeli History* 24 (2004): 65–77.

——. "What If a Christian State Had Been Established in Palestine?" In *What Ifs of Jewish History: From Abraham to Zionism*, ed. Gavriel Rosenfeld, 142–64. New York: Cambridge University Press, 2016.

Presner, Todd S.. *Mobile Modernity: Germans, Jews, Trains*. New York: Columbia University Press, 2007.

Provence, Michael. "Ottoman Modernity, Colonialism, and Insurgency in the Interwar Arab East." *International Journal of Middle East Studies* 43 (2011): 205–225.

Qualey, Marcia Lynx. "True Histories: Renaissance of Arab Jews in Arabic Novels." *The Guardian*, October 29, 2014.

Radai, Itamar. *Palestinians in Jerusalem and Jaffa, 1948: A Tale of Two Cities*. London: Routledge, 2015.

Ram, Uri. "From Nation-State to Nation-State: Nation, History and Identity Struggles in Jewish Israel." In *The Challenge of Post-Zionism: Alternatives to Israeli Fundamentalist Politics*, ed. Ephraim Nimni, 20–41. London: Zed, 2003.

Ravid, Barak. "Netanyahu Launches Blistering Attack on EU: 'Their Behavior Toward Israel Is Crazy,'" *Haaretz*, July 19, 2017.

Raz, Avi. *The Bride and the Dowry: Israel, Jordan, and the Palestinians in the Aftermath of the June 1967 War*. New Haven, Conn.: Yale University Press, 2012.

Raz-Krakotzkin, Amnon. "Binationalism and Jewish Identity: Hannah Arendt and the Question of Palestine." In *Hannah Arendt in Jerusalem*, ed. Steven E. Aschheim, 165–180. Berkeley: University of California Press, 2001.

——. *The Censor, the Editor, and the Text: The Catholic Church and the Shaping of the Jewish Canon in the Sixteenth Century*. Trans. Jackie Feldman. Philadelphia: University of Pennsylvania Press, 2007.

——. "Exile Amidst Sovereignty: Critique of the Negation of the Exile in Israeli Culture." *Theory and Criticism* 4 (1993): 23–55. [Hebrew]

——. "Exile and Binationalism: From Gershom Scholem and Hannah Arendt to Edward Said and Mahmoud Darwish." Carl Heinrich Becker Lecture of the Fritz Thyssen Stiftung 2011. Berlin: Wissenschaftskolleg zu Berlin, 2012.

——. "Jewish Peoplehood, 'Jewish Politics,' and Political Responsibility: Arendt on Zionism and Partitions." *College Literature* 38, no. 1 (2011): 57–74.

——. "Orientalism, Jewish Studies, and Israeli Society: A Few Comments." *Philological Encounters* 2, no. 3–4 (2017): 237–269.

——. "Secularism, the Christian Ambivalence Toward the Jews, and the Notion of Exile." In *Secularism in Question: Jews and Judaism in Modern Times*, ed. Ari Joskowicz and Ethan B. Katz, 276–298. Philadelphia: University of Pennsylvania Press, 2015.

Reicher, Stephen, Nick Hopkins, and Kate Harrison. "Social Identity and Spatial Behaviour: The Relationship Between National Category Salience, the Sense of Home, and Labour Mobility Across National Boundaries." *Political Physiology* 27, no. 2 (2006): 247–263.

Renan, Ernest, *Studies of Religious History and Criticism*. Trans. O. B. Frothingham. New York: Carleton, 1864.

——. "What Is a Nation?" In *Nation and Narration*, ed. Homi Bhabha, 8–22. London: Routledge, 1990.

Renton, James. *The Zionist Masquerade: The Birth of the Anglo-Zionist Alliance, 1914–1918*. New York: Palgrave Macmillan, 2007.

Renton, James, and Ben Gidley, eds. *Antisemitism and Islamophobia in Europe: A Shared Story?* London: Palgrave Macmillan, 2017.

Rhett, Maryanne. *The Global History of the Balfour Declaration: Declared Nation*. New York: Routledge, 2015.

Roberts, Sophie B. *Citizenship and Anti-Semitism in French Colonial Algeria, 1870–1962*. Cambridge: Cambridge University Press, 2017.

Robertson, Ritchie. *The German-Jewish Dialogue: An Anthology of Literature Texts, 1749–1993*. Oxford: Oxford University Press, 1999.

——. *Kafka: Judaism, Politics, and Literature*. Oxford: Clarendon Press, 1985.

Robinson, Shira. *Citizen Strangers: Palestinians and the Birth of Israel's Liberal Settler State*. Berkeley: University of California Press, 2013.

Robson, Laura. *States of Separation: Transfer, Partition, and the Making of the Modern Middle East*. Berkeley: University of California Press, 2017.

Rodinson, Maxime. *Israel: A Colonial-Settler State?* Atlanta: Pathfinder Press, 1973.

Romeyn, Esther. "Anti-Semitism and Islamophobia: Spectropolitics and Immigration." *Theory, Culture and Society* 31, no. 6 (2014): 77–101.

——. "Liberal Tolerance and Its Hauntings: Moral Compasses, Anti-Semitism, and Islamophobia." *European Journal of Cultural Studies* 20, no. 2 (2017): 1–18.

Rose, Jacqueline. *The Last Resistance*. London: Verso, 2007.

——. *Proust Among the Nations: From Dreyfus to the Middle East*. Chicago: University of Chicago Press, 2011.

——. *The Question of Zion*. Princeton, N.J.: Princeton University Press, 2005.

Rothberg, Michael. *Multidirectional Memory: Remembering the Holocaust in the Age of Decolonization*. Stanford, Calif.: Stanford University Press, 2009.

Rouhana, Nadim. "The Palestinian National Project: Towards Restoring the Settler Colonial Paradigm." *Majjalat al-Dirasat al-Filistiniyah (Journal of Palestine Studies)* 19 (2014): 18–36. [Arabic]

Rouhana, Nadim, and Sahar Huneidi, eds. *Israel and Its Palestinian Citizens: Ethnic Privileges in the Jewish State*. Cambridge: Cambridge University Press, 2017.

Rouhana, Nadim, and Areej Sabbagh-Khoury. "Memory and the Return of History in a Settler-Colonial Context." In *Israel and Its Palestinian Citizens: Ethnic Privileges in the Jewish State*, ed. Nadim Rouhana and Sahar Huneidi, 393–432. Cambridge: Cambridge University Press, 2017.

Roy, Sara. *Hamas and Civil Society in Gaza: Engaging the Islamist Social Sector*. Princeton, N.J.: University Press. 2011.

Rubin, Abraham. "The 'German-Jewish Dialogue' and Its Literary Refractions: The Case of Margarete Susman and Gershom Scholem." *Modern Judaism* 35, no. 1 (2015): 1–17.

——. "Reading Kafka, Debating Revelation: Gershom Scholem's Shadow Dialogue with Hans-Joachim Schoeps." *Literature & Theology* (2016): 1–21.

Rubin, Andrew. "Orientalism and the History of Western Anti-Semitism: The Coming End of an American Taboo." *History of the Present* 5, no. 1 (Spring 2015): 95–108.

Rubinstein, William C. "Kafka's 'Jackals and Arabs.'" *Monatshefte* 59, no. 1 (1967): 13–18.

Said, Edward W. *Culture and Imperialism*. New York: Verso, 1994.

——. *Freud and the Non-European*. London: Verso, 2003.

——. "From Intifada to Independence." *Middle East Report* 158 (1989): 14–16.

——. "The Idea of Palestine in the West." *Middle East Research and Information Projects* 70 (September 1978): 5.

——. "The One-State Solution." *New York Times Magazine*, January 10, 1999.

——. *Orientalism*. New York: Vintage, 1978.

——. "Orientalism Reconsidered." *Cultural Critique* 1 (Autumn 1985): 89–107.

——. *The Question of Palestine*. New York: Vintage, 1980.

——. "Zionism from the Standpoint of Its Victims." *Social Text* 1 (1979): 7–58.

Sayagh, Saïd. *L'autre juive: Lalla soulika, La tsadika*. Paris: Ibis Press, 2009.

Sayegh, Anis. *Palestine and Arab Nationalism*. Beirut: Palestine Liberation Organization Centre, 1970.

Sayegh, Fayez A. *Zionist Colonialism in Palestine*. Beirut: Research Centre, Palestine Liberation Organization, 1965.

Sayigh, Yezid. *Armed Struggle and the Search for State: The Palestinian National Movement, 1949–1993*. New York: Oxford University Press, 1999.

Scham, Paul. "Competing Israeli and Palestinian Narratives." In *The Routledge Handbook on the Israeli–Palestinian Conflict*, ed. Peters Joel and David Newman, 33–45. New York: Routledge, 2013.

Schneer, Jonathan. *The Balfour Declaration*. London: Bloomsbury, 2010.

Scholem, Gershom. "Against the Myth of the German-Jewish Dialogue." Trans. Werner J. Dannhauser. In *On Jews and Judaism in Crisis: Selected Essays*, ed. Werner J. Dannhauser, 61–64. New York: Schocken, 1976.

——. *Lamentations of Youth: The Diaries of Gershom Scholem*. Ed. Anthony David Skinner. Cambridge, Mass.: Harvard University Press, 2008.

——. "On Kafka's The Trial (1926)." Trans. Jonathan Chipman. In *On the Possibility of Jewish Mysticism in Our Time and Other Essays*, ed. Avraham Shapira. Philadelphia: Jewish Publication Society, 1997.

Séailles, Gabriel. *Alfred Dehodencq: l'homme & l'artiste*. Paris: Société de Propagation des Livres d'Art, 1910.

Segev, Tom. *One Palestine Complete: Jews and Arabs Under the British Mandate*. New York: Henry Holt, 2000.

Seikaly, Sherene. *Men of Capital: Scarcity and Economy in Mandate Palestine*. Stanford, Calif.: Stanford University Press, 2015.

Sela, Avraham. "The Wailing Wall Riots (1929) as a Watershed in the Palestine Conflict." *The Muslim World* 84, no. 1–2 (1994): 60–94.

Setton, Ruth Knafo. *The Road to Fez*. Washington, D.C.: Counterpoint, 2001.

Shafir, Gershon. *Land, Labor, and the Origins of the Israeli-Palestinian Conflict, 1882–1914*. New York: Cambridge University Press, 1988.

Shenhav, Yehouda. *The Arab Jews: A Postcolonial Reading of Nationalism, Religion and Ethnicity*. Stanford, Calif.: Stanford University Press, 2006.

Shenhav, Yehouda, and Hannan Hever, "Megamot cmehkar hapost Koloniali" [Trends in postcolonial research]. In *Colonialism and Post-colonial Reality*, ed. Yehouda Shenhav. Jerusalem: Van Leer and Tel-Aviv: Hakebutz Hameohad, 2004.

Shlaim, Avi. *The Iron Wall: Israel and the Arab World*. New York: Norton, 2000.

Shmuelof, Mati, Shahar Garfunkel, and Omri Herzog. "Zoakeem et shemcha bekama leshonot: al zehoot hebredit bysrael" [Shouting your name in many languages: About hybrid identity in Israel]. *Hakevon Mezrach* 14 (2010): 1–111.

Shohat, Ella. "The Invention of the Mizrahim." *Journal of Palestine Studies* 29, no. 1 (Autumn 1999): 5–20.

——. *Israeli Cinema: East/West and the Politics of Representation*. Austin: University of Texas Press, 1989.

——. *On the Arab-Jew, Palestine, and Other Displacements*. London: Pluto, 2017.

——. "Rupture and Return: Zionist Discourse and the Study of Arab-Jews." In *Taboo Memories, Diasporic Voices*, 330–358. Durham, N.C.: Duke University Press, 2006.

———. "Sephardim in Israel: Zionism from the Standpoint of Its Jewish Victims." *Social Text* 19/20 (Autumn 1988): 1–35.

———. "The Specter of the Blackamoor: Figuring Africa and the Orient." In *ReSignifications: European Blackamoors, Africana Reading*, ed. ed. Awam Amkpa, 95–115. Rome: Postcart, 2016.

Shohat, Ella, and Robert Stam. *Race in Translation: Culture Wars Around the Postcolonial Atlantic*. New York: New York University Press, 2012.

———. *Unthinking Eurocentrism*. London: Routledge, 1994.

Shumsky, Dimitry. "Czechs, Germans, Arabs, Jews: Franz Kafka's 'Jackals and Arabs' Between Bohemia and Palestine." *AJS Review* 33, no. 1 (2009): 71–100.

Shragai, Sharagai. "A Mounting Sense of Urgency." *Ha'aretz*, December 30, 2004.

Sidi Moussa, Nedjib. "A Contingent Nationhood: The Jewish Question and the Palestinian Cause Within the Algerian Independence Movement." *Hamsa: Journal of Judaic and Islamic Studies* 4 (March 2018): 105–118.

Silverstein, Paul A. "The Context of Antisemitism and Islamophobia in France." *Patterns of Prejudice* 42, no. 1 (2008): 1–26.

———. *Postcolonial France: Race, Islam and the Future of the Republic*. London: Pluto, 2018.

Slyomovics, Susan. *The Object of Memory: Arab and Jew Narrate the Palestinian Village*. Philadelphia: University of Pennsylvania Press, 1998.

———. "Who and What Is Native to Israel: On Marcel Janco's Settler Art and Jacqueline Shohet Kahanoff's 'Levantinism.'" *Settler Colonial Studies* 4, no. 1 (2013): 27–47.

Sonnenschein, Nava. "Dealog meatger zehout" [Dialogue-challenging identity]. Haifa: Pardes, 2008. [Hebrew]

Spector, Scott. *Prague Territories: National Conflict and Cultural Innovation in Franz Kafka's Fin de Siècle*. Berkeley: University of California Press, 2000.

Stein, Leonard. *The Balfour Declaration*. New York: Simon and Schuster, 1961.

Stein, Sarah. *Saharan Jews and the Fate of French Algeria*. Chicago: Chicago University Press, 2014.

Sternhell, Zeev. "Here Is the Proof That Zionism Can Achieve Its Goals Within the Green Line." *Haaretz*, October 3, 2015.

Sutcliffe, Adam. *Judaism and Enlightenment*. Cambridge: Cambridge University Press, 2003.

Swedenburg, Ted. *Memories of Revolt: The 1936–1939 Rebellion and the Palestinian National Past*. Fayetteville: University of Arkansas Press, 2003.

Tajfel, Henri, and John Turner. "The Social Identity Theory of Intergroup Behavior." In *Political Psychology: Key Readings*, ed. John Jost and James Sidanius. New York: Psychology Press, 2004.

Takriti, Abdel-Razzaq. *Monsoon Revolution: Republicans, Sultans, and Empires in Oman, 1965–1976*. Oxford: Oxford University Press, 2013.

Tamari, Salim. *Mountain Against the Sea: Essays on Palestinian Society and Culture*. Berkeley: University of California Press, 2008.

Tauber, Eliezer. "Jewish–Non-Palestinian-Arab Negotiations: The First Phase." *Israel Affairs* 6 (2000): 3–4, 159–176.

Tilley, Virginia. "After Oslo, a Paradigm Shift? Redefining 'Peoples,' Sovereignty, and Justice in Israel-Palestine." *Conflict, Security and Development* 15, no. 5 (2015): 425–53.

———. *The One-State Solution: A Breakthrough for Peace in the Israeli-Palestinian Deadlock*. Detroit: University of Michigan Press, 2005.

Todorov, Tzvetan. *The Conquest of America: The Question of the Other*. New York: Harper & Row, 1984.

Todorova, Teodora. "Reframing Bi-nationalism in Palestine-Israel as a Process of Settler Decolonisation." *Antipode* 47, no. 5 (2015): 1367–1387.

Topolski, Anya. "Breaking the Post-Shoah Silence About Race in Europe: Whiteness, Antisemitism, and Islamophobia." *Critical Philosophy of Race* 6, no. 2 (2018): 280–286.

——. "Good Jew, Bad Jew . . . Good Muslim, Bad Muslim: 'Managing' Europe's Others." *Ethnic and Racial Studies* 41, no. 12 (2017): 2179–2196.

Traverso, Enzo. *The End of Jewish Modernity*. London: Pluto, 2016.

Trouillot, Michel-Rolph. *Silencing the Past: Power and the Production of History*. Boston: Beacon, 1995.

Usher, Graham. "Bantustanisation or Bi-nationalism? An Interview with Azmi Bishara." *Race & Class* 37, no 3 (1995): 43–49.

Vance, Sharon. *The Martyrdom of a Moroccan Jewish Saint*. Leiden: Brill, 2011.

——. "Sol Hachuel, 'Heroine of the Nineteenth Century': Gender, the Jewish Question, and Colonial Discourse." In *Jewish Culture and Society in North Africa*, ed. Emily Benichou Gottreich and Daniel J. Schroeter, 201–225. Bloomington: Indiana University Press, 2011.

Veracini, Lorenzo. *Israel and Settler Society*. London: Pluto, 2006.

Vereté, Mayir. "The Balfour Declaration and Its Makers." *Middle Eastern Studies* 6, no. 1 (1970): 48–76.

Volkan, Vamik. "Psychoanalysis and Diplomacy: Part III. Potentials for and Obstacles Against Collaboration." *Journal of Applied Psychoanalytic Studies* 1, no. 4 (1999): 305–318.

——. "Transgenerational Transmissions and Chosen Traumas: An Aspect of Large Group Identity." *Group Analysis* 34, no. 1 (2001): 79–97.

Voltaire. *An Essay on Universal History, the Manners, and Spirit of Nations*. Trans. Mr. Nugent. London: J. Nourse, 1759.

——. *The Works of Voltaire: A Contemporary Version with Notes*, vol. 12. Trans. William F. Fleming. London: E. R. Dumont, 1901.

Vyronis, Speros. *Byzantium and Europe*. New York: Harcourt Brace and World, 1967.

Wallach, Yair. "Jerusalem Between Segregation and Integration: Reading Urban Space Through the Eyes of Justice Gad Frumkin." In *Modernity, Minority, and the Public Sphere: Jews and Christians in the Middle East*, ed. S. R. Goldstein-Sabbah and H. L. Murre-van den Berg, 205–233. Leiden: Brill, 2016.

Weinreich, Peter, Vira Bacova, and Nathalie Rougier, "Basic Primordialism in Ethnic and National Identity." In *Analysing Identity: Cross-culture, Social and Clinical Context*, ed. Peter Weinreich and Wendy Saunderson, 115–171. New York: Routledge, 2002.

Weiss, Philip. "Jewish Ethno-nationalism Is a 'Poison'—Crabapple and Goldman Clobber Zionism in Intellectual Journals." *Mondoweiss*, November 20, 2018.

Weldemichael, Awet Tewelde. *Third World Colonialism and Strategies of Liberation: Eritrea and East Timor Compared*. Cambridge: Cambridge University Press, 2013.

Wolfe, Patrick. "Colonialism and the Elimination of the Native." *Journal of Genocide Research* 8, no. 4 (2006): 387–409.

——. *Settler Colonialism and the Transformation of Anthropology: The Politics and Poetics of an Ethnographic Event*. London: Cassel, 1999.

Yadgar, Yaacov. *Israel's Jewish Identity Crisis: State and Politics in the Middle East.* Cambridge: Cambridge University Press, 2020.

——. *Sovereign Jews: Israel, Zionism, and Judaism.* New York: State University of New York Press, 2017.

Yehoshua, A. B. "Facing the Forests." In *Modern Hebrew Literature,* ed. Robert Alter, 353–392. New Jersey: Behrman House, 1975.

Yizhar, S. "The Prisoner." In *Modern Hebrew Literature,* ed. Robert Alter, 291–310. Millburn, N.J.: Behrman House, 1975.

Yuval, Israel Jacob. *Two Nations in Your Womb: Perceptions of Jews and Christians in Late Antiquity and the Middle Ages.* Berkeley: University of California Press, 2006.

Zeidel, Ronen. "On the Last Jews in Iraq and Iraqi National Identity: A Look at Two Recent Iraqi Novels." *Journal of Modern Jewish Studies* 17, no. 2 (2018): 207–222.

Zertal, Idith. *Israel's Holocaust and the Politics of Nationhood.* Trans. Chaya Galai. Cambridge: Cambridge University Press, 2005.

Zerubavel, Yael. *Collective Memory and the Making of Israeli National Tradition.* Chicago: University of Chicago Press, 1995.

Zreik, Raef. "Palestine, Apartheid, and the Rights Discourse." *Journal of Palestine Studies* 34, no. 1 (2004): 68–80.

——. "When Does a Settler Become a Native? (With Apologies to Mamdani)." *Constellations* 23, no. 3 (2016): 351–364.

CONTRIBUTORS

Hakem Al-Rustom is the Alex Manoogian Professor of Modern Armenian History and assistant professor of history and anthropology at the University of Michigan. His work interrogates ruins of undocumented histories, ethnographic silences, and memory as methods for historical ethnographies in the aftermath of violence. He is the co-editor of *Edward Said: A Legacy of Emancipation and Representation* (with Adel Iskandar, 2010) and his forthcoming book focuses on the ruins of silenced Armenian histories and the politics of indigeneity in Turkey.

Gil Anidjar is a professor in the Department of Religion and in the Department of Middle Eastern, South Asian, and African Studies (MESAAS) at Columbia University. He is the author of a number of books, including *"Our Place in al-Andalus": Kabbalah, Philosophy, Literature in Arab Jewish Letters* (2002), *The Jew, the Arab: A History of the Enemy* (2003), *Blood: A Critique of Christianity* (2014), and *Qu'appelle-t-on destruction? Heidegger, Derrida* (2017).

Bashir Bashir is associate professor in the Department of Sociology, Political Science, and Communication at the Open University of Israel and a senior research fellow at the Van Leer Jerusalem Institute. His primary research interests are nationalism and citizenship studies, multiculturalism, democratic theory, memory, and the politics of reconciliation. He has published in leading journals on these themes. He is the co-editor of *The Politics of Reconciliation in Multicultural Societies* (with Will Kymlicka, 2008) and *The Holocaust and the Nakba* (with Amos Goldberg, 2018).

Moshe Behar is senior lecturer and program director in the Department of Arabic and Middle Eastern Studies at the University of Manchester. His work includes the anthology *Modern Middle Eastern Jewish Thought: Writings on Identity, Politics and Culture, 1893–1958* (2013).

Hillel Cohen, a Jerusalemite, is professor of Palestinian and Zionist history and the chair of the Department of Islam and Middle Eastern Studies at the Hebrew University of Jerusalem. He has published on a wide range of topics relating to the Zionist-Palestinian encounter, Palestinian collaborators and Zionist intelligence agencies, the 1948 refugees, Jerusalem, and more. His most recent book is *1929: Year Zero of the Israeli-Arab Conflict* (2015).

Yuval Evri is a Leverhulme Early Career Fellow at King's College London. His research focuses on the cultural and political history of Palestine at the turn of the twentieth century. The issue of Arab-Jewish thought lies at the heart of his research and teaching interests. His current research explores Arab-Jewish cultural models that emerged in the beginning of twentieth-century Palestine in relation to issues of language, territory, and national identities. Evri was a EUME postdoctoral fellow at the Institute of Advanced Studies in Berlin, a postdoctoral fellow at SOAS–University of London, and a fellow at the Herbert D. Katz Center at the University of Pennsylvania.

Leila Farsakh is associate professor of political science at the University of Massachusetts Boston. Her research interests focus on the political economy of the Israeli-Palestinian conflict and the politics of partition and its alternatives in Israel-Palestine. Among her publications are *Palestinian Labor Migration to Israel: Labour, Land and Occupation* (second edition, 2012) and *Commemorating the Naksa, Evoking the Nakba* (2008). Her forthcoming book, *Rethinking Statehood in Palestine*, is due to be published in 2021.

Amal Ghazal is professor of history and director of the Centre for Comparative Muslim Studies at Simon Fraser University. She specializes in modern Arab intellectual history. Her research has covered a wide range of topics, including religious reform, religious minorities, intellectual networks, anticolonialism, nationalism, and slavery, and a wide geography, from North Africa to East Africa. She has published in leading journals on these issues. She is the author of *Islamic Reform and Arab Nationalism: Expanding the Crescent from the Mediterranean to the Indian Ocean, 1880s–1930s* (2010) and the coeditor of *The Oxford Handbook of Contemporary Middle Eastern and North African History* (2020). She is preparing a manuscript with the title *Minority Status: Performing Difference in Colonial Algeria*. She will be based at the Doha Institute for Graduate Studies in 2020–2022.

Brian Klug is Senior Research Fellow in Philosophy at St. Benet's Hall, University of Oxford; a member of the faculty of philosophy at the University of Oxford; an honorary fellow of the Parkes Institute for the Study of Jewish/Non-Jewish Relations, University of Southampton; and fellow of the College of Arts and Sciences, Saint Xavier University, Chicago. His books include *Being Jewish and Doing Justice: Bringing Argument to Life* (2011) and *Offence: The Jewish Case* (2009). He is the editor of *Words of Fire: Selected Essays of Ahad Ha'am* (2015) and a coeditor of *A Time to Speak Out: Independent Jewish Voices on Israel, Zionism, and Jewish Identity* (2008). His writing has appeared in many journals and periodicals, such as *Ethnic and Racial Studies*, *Ethnicities*, *Foreign Policy*, the *Journal of Jewish Studies*, the *Journal of Palestine Studies*, and *Political Quarterly*.

Maram Masarwi is a lecturer and researcher at Tel-Aviv University and the dean of the Faculty of Education at the Al Qasemi Academic College of Education. Masarwi was a fellow at the Mandel School for Educational Leadership (2005–2007) and she holds a PhD from the Department of Social Work at the Hebrew University. Her doctoral dissertation dealt with "gender differences in bereavement and trauma among Palestinian parents who lost their children in al-Aqsa Intifada." She was a postdoctorate fellow at the Europe in the Middle East–the Middle East in Europe (EUME) Forum of Transregional Studies and the Free University of Berlin. Her research interests are memory and commemoration in the Palestinian society; loss and bereavement in the Palestinian society; and gender and nationalism in the Middle East. She is the author of *The Bereavement of Martyred Palestinian Children: Gender Religion and Nationality* (2019).

Derek Penslar is the William Lee Frost Professor of Jewish History at Harvard University. His research specialties are modern Jewish history in Europe, Israel-Palestine, and North America. Penslar's books include *Shylock's Children: Economics and Jewish Identity in Modern Europe* (2001), *Orientalism and the Jews* (coedited with Ivan Kalmar, 2004), *Israel in History: The Jewish State in Comparative Perspective* (2006), *The Origins of the State of Israel, 1882–1948: A Documentary History* (with Eran Kaplan, 2011), *Jews and the Military: A History* (2013), and *Theodor Herzl: The Charismatic Leader* (2020). He is a fellow of the Royal Society of Canada and the president of the American Academy for Jewish Research.

Jacqueline Rose is internationally known for her writing on feminism, psychoanalysis, literature, and the Israeli-Palestinian conflict. Her books include *Sexuality in the Field of Vision* (1986), *The Haunting of Sylvia Plath* (1991), *Women in Dark Times* (2014), and four books focused on the Middle East: *States of*

Fantasy (1996), *The Question of Zion* (2005), *The Last Resistance* (2007), and *Proust Among the Nations: From Dreyfus to the Middle East* (2012). She is also the author of the novel *Albertine* (2001). Her work has also been collected in *Conversations with Jacqueline Rose* (2010) and *The Jacqueline Rose Reader* (2011). A regular writer for the *London Review of Books*, she wrote and presented the 2002 Channel 4 television documentary *Dangerous Liaison: Israel and the United States*. She is a cofounder of Independent Jewish Voices in the United Kingdom and a fellow of the British Academy. In January 2015, she joined the Birkbeck Institute for the Humanities after previous posts at Queen Mary University of London and Cambridge University.

Ella Shohat is professor of cultural studies at New York University. Since the 1980s, her work has shaped a critical conceptual framework for the study of the idea of "the Arab-Jew" in conjunction with "the question of Palestine." Her books include: *On the Arab-Jew, Palestine, and Other Displacements: Selected Writings* (2017), *Taboo Memories, Diasporic Voices* (2006), *Israeli Cinema: East/West and the Politics of Representation* (1989), *Talking Visions: Multicultural Feminism in a Transnational Age* (1998), *Dangerous Liaisons: Gender, Nation and Postcolonial Perspectives* (coedited with Anne McClintock and Aamir Mufti, 1997), *Between the Middle East and the Americas: The Cultural Politics of Diaspora* (coedited with Evelyn Alsultany, 2013). Her books with Robert Stam include *Unthinking Eurocentrism* (1994), *Flagging Patriotism: Crises of Narcissism and Anti-Americanism* (2007), *Race in Translation: Culture Wars Around the Postcolonial Atlantic* (2012), and *Multiculturalism, Postcoloniality and Transnational Media* (2003). Shohat has also served on the editorial board of *Critique, Interventions,* and *Social Text,* coediting several special issues: "911-A Public Emergency?" (2002); "Palestine in a Transnational Context" (2003); "Corruption in Corporate Culture" (2003) and "Edward Said: A Memorial Issue" (2006). Her publications have been translated into various languages, including Arabic, Hebrew, Turkish, French, Spanish, Portuguese, Italian, Polish, Japanese, and German.

INDEX

Delacroix, Eugene, 96, 100
de-Orientalization, of Jews, 92–93, 104–105, 115–117
"Descent of Jesus, The" (al-Baruni), 75
"Description of a Struggle" (Kafka), 31
designation, of Arab-Jews, 123–124
D'Hulst (count), 127–128
dialogue, 42n3; Arab-Jewish, 13, 25, 33–34, 39; Blanchott on, 25–28, 30, 34, 38, 44n18; German-Jewish, 25–41; James on, 25–26; Kafka on conversations and, 26–28, 30–33, 36, 44n21; logic relating to, 27; Malraux on, 25–26; model example of, 30; pain of, 26; Scholem on, 28–30. See also apocalypse/enmity/dialogue
diaspora, 91, 253
dih ta'limat, 126
Dinur, Ben-Tsion, 186–187
discourses of domination, 178, 179, 194n5
Disengagement Plan, 212
displacement, 127, 144n7; of Arab-Jews, 123–125; of Geniza documents, 128–129
dispossession, 123; of Arab Jews, 6–7, 20n26; of Palestinians, 134
divide and rule imperial policies, 111
Doar Hayom, 156–159
domination: discourses of, 178, 179, 194n5; of Palestinians by Israelis, 179
Dor, Daniel, 208
doubly colonizing enlightenment, 106–109
duality, with dialogue, 27
Dudkevich, David (rabbi), 207

Edge of the Sword, The (Lorch), 185
Edict of Expulsion, 100
Egyptian colonialism, 128
Egyptian Jews, 126, 128–129
Eighteenth Brumaire of Louis Napoleon (Marx), 244
Eliasher, Eliyahu, 167–168
elimination, of Arabs, 133
El martirio de la joven hachuel, ó la heroina hebrea (Romero), 102
Elysée speech, of Macron, 56–57

emancipated Jews, 3, 111–112, 115
Emancipation of the Jews (1791), in France, 100
emblematic embrace: Holocaust as foundational myth, 48, 52–57, 64n18; in Jerusalem, 62–63; New Europe, defining of, 49–52; vicissitudes of Jewish otherness, 58–62. See also Paris, emblematic embrace in
empowerment, disempowerment and, 110
End of Jewish Modernity, The (Traverso), 58
engagement. See Zionism, engagement with Arab question and; specific engagement
Enlightened Europe, 59, 66n40
Enlightened Occident, 100
Enlightenment, 90, 91, 103, 110–113, 127; doubly colonizing, 106–109; post-Enlightenment, 102, 104, 116
Enlightenment modernity, 104
enmity. See apocalypse/enmity/dialogue
Epstein, Yitzhak, 9, 158–159, 161
Escena de Inquisición (Goya), 103
ethnic cleansing, of Jews, 3
ethnic-national identity, 259
ethnic nationalism, 59
ethno-national projects, for self-determination, 2
ethno-sectarian state, in Palestine, 122
EU. See European Union
Eurocentric Jewish history, 126–127, 139
Eurocentric narratives, of bifurcated Oriental reconsidered, 90–93
Eurocentric notions, of citizenship, 1–2
Europe, 48, 63n6; colonialization of, 3, 12, 14, 224; death and rebirth of, 49, 57; modern consciousness of, 139; Old Europe, 49, 50, 52, 57–58, 61; question of Jewish and Muslim "other" of, 10–17. See also New Europe
Europe, question of, 139–143; gray zone, 122–125; Palestinians and Arab-Jews, 133–138; standpoint of defeated, 130–133; two Cairo synagogues, 125–130
European anti-Semitism, 2, 124, 135
European Ashkenazi, 128, 132

RELIGION, CULTURE, AND PUBLIC LIFE

Series Editor: Matthew Engelke